Warning and Disclaimer

This book is designed to provide information about Macromedia Director. Every effort has been made to make this book as complete and as accurate as possible, but no warranty or fitness is implied.

The information is provided on an "as is" basis. The authors and New Riders Publishing shall have neither liability nor responsibility to any person or entity with respect to any loss or damages arising from the information contained in this book or from the use of the disks or programs that may accompany it.

About the Authors

Jihad Battikha is a Computer Graphic Artist working in the Boston area at a rapidly growing multimedia company. His work has been at the forefront of multimedia software design and animation for the last three years. Jihad's experience and skills cover a wide range of disciplines including 3D and 2D animation and interface design and game graphics creation, as well as traditional design and illustration skills. Jihad's work is recognized for its commercial and innovative style and for its wide appeal. Familiar, award-winning titles he's worked on include *Mission Code: Millennium* and *Vote America*, both published by Virtual Entertainment in Needham, MA. To reach Jihad or to view some of his work, visit his web site address at `http://users.aol.com/jbattika`.

Dudley Bryan was born and raised in Cambridge, MA. He was enrolled in a program called METCO in his early years of education, and thereby spent his entire pre-collegiate education in Cohasset, MA. This program provided a means by which inner city children of ethnic families went to school in institutions with little or no ethnic diversity. He spent much of his free time learning about cartooning and computers. During these years, he learned to program in various computer languages, develop the basis of his artistic style and influence, and become involved with video editing and consumer electronics.

Dudley currently works for Virtual Entertainment of Needham and acts as one of their in-house artists and creators in the production of a line of programs for education and family.

Jeff Buell started working with microprocessor-based computer systems in 1976. His interest in graphical user interfaces was sparked by the MacPaint program, which ran on the first Macintosh computer in 1984. While working as a technician developing instructional software at California State University in Fullerton, he used various incarnations of Macromind, now Macromind's Director program, including Videoworks II. One instructional work entitled, "Organic Reaction Mechanisms" was awarded Educom's "Best Natural Science Software" award in 1992. While working as a freelance multimedia developer since 1994, Buell was named to the Multimedia Producer's Magazine's "Top 100 Producers" list for 1995.

Mark Castle and his wife Christine run Castle Productions from a home office in the San Francisco Bay area. They specialize in Lingo programming and project architecture.

Mark worked for Macromedia for five years, leaving in June of 1995 to start Castle Productions. At Macromedia, formerly MacroMind, Mark helped found the Testing department and became a Software Quality Assurance Lead for many products, foremost being Director. He moved from the QA department to help start the Macromedia Consulting Department. Mark was the Macromedia Director Consultant for about a year and then moved to manage Technical Support for Director, Sound, and 3D products for another 10 months.

In addition to their professional lives, Mark and Christine share responsibilities for their two daughters. They are a constant puzzle to their neighbors who wonder what they do for a living.

Bruce Epstein will do anything to avoid doing his own work. He spends a lot of time spouting unverified advice in various multimedia-related fora. He is the proud owner of an original Bell & Howell Apple II computer, and is frightened by the realization that he has been programming for 16 years. Bruce learned nothing in college and has been trying to undo the damage caused by earning a degree in Aeronautical Engineering ever since. He is engaged in a life-long struggle to avoid the temptation to join Mensa. Bruce has never forgiven his parents for making him skip the fifth grade, but will consider doing so if he receives a written apology. He decided to try multimedia programming when it became apparent that no one would fund his desire to wander aimlessly. Bruce spends as much time as possible with his burgeoning family, and in his spare time, runs Zeus Productions, makers of Xtras for Director. His dream is to write a hit song and be the oldest person ever to qualify for the Olympic team, neither of which seem likely. He is in favor of free speech and the right to securely encrypt electronic correspondence. Visit his web site at `http://users.aol.com/ZeusProd` or e-mail `ZeusProd@aol.com`.

Andy Hock graduated from Duke University in 1980. He began his career at Touche-Ross, but resigned a year later to exploit his interest in technology in the home. He started Futurehouse, Inc. in 1981. At Futurehouse, Andy created the first interactive magazine on disk and published the Billboard Top Ten hit, the *Complete Personal Accountant*. Futurehouse was named one of the top 60 Home Software Companies in the early 1980s.

Andy started Lightwaves, Inc. in 1994. The company has developed an expertise in Macromedia, Director, Java, and the Internet. Current clients include Fidelity, DEC, HTL, Union Carbide, Bay Networks, and Mazer Digital, among others. Andy can be reached at `ahock@lightwaves.com`.

Tab Julius is president of Penworks Corporation, a multimedia software development company, and is the publisher of *Lingo User's Journal*, a monthly publication dedicated to Lingo and XObject/Xtra programming. He is author of the book, *Lingo: An Advanced Guide to Director's Scripting Language*, also by New Riders Publishing. In addition to the *Developer's Guide to Lingo*, he has contributed chapters to *More Tricks of the Game Programming Gurus* (1995, Sams Publishing), and *PC Techniques C/C++ Power Tools* (1992, Bantam Books). He has been writing software since 1976 and his commercial credits include the following: Express Publisher v3.0, an award-winning desktop publisher; CD-ROM and Windows versions of many children's educational software games for The Learning Company; and enhanced CDs for bands in the music industry.

Kirk Keller has been developing multimedia projects since 1989. After receiving his M.A. in philosophy at the University of Missouri, he began working in their Digital Media Center as an Advanced Graphics Specialist. During his three years with the University of Missouri, he focused on media development in 3D Modeling, Virtual Environments, and authoring in Macromedia Director.

In addition to his other freelance work, Kirk currently holds a term position with the Missouri Department of Conservation as a computer production specialist for CD-ROM and web development. He can be reached at `kirk_keller@socketis.net`.

Raúl Silva was born and raised in Puerto Rico. He came to Chicago to attend the School of the Art Institute of Chicago where he concentrated in Art and Technology. Raúl is a multimedia programming veteran and has more than 17 years of computer experience. He has worked on a wide range of projects and has specialized in interactive multimedia authoring, overseeing all aspects of title development. Raúl is also an accomplished graphics and interface designer. Most recently, he cofounded AfterShock, a company that develops interactive content for the World Wide Web and creates complete Web solutions. He has also developed custom authoring tools and is a contributing writer for industry-related books and magazines. Raúl is the former Multimedia Coordinator of The Art Institute of Chicago where he worked on interactive multimedia titles and coordinated production efforts with various museum departments. He has won several excellence awards and is recognized as a leading multimedia authority in the city of Chicago and around the world. AfterShock's page can be reached at `http://www.ashock.com`. Raúl's page can be reached at `http://www.tezcat.com/~Raúl`.

Trademark Acknowledgments

All terms mentioned in this book that are known to be trademarks or service marks have been appropriately capitalized. New Riders Publishing cannot attest to the accuracy of this information. Use of a term in this book should not be regarded as affecting the validity of any trademark or service mark.

Dedications

Jihad Battikha

I'd like to dedicate my chapter to my father whose wisdom and guidance has been essential throughout my life and career. Thanks Dad.

Dudley Bryan

I'd like to dedicate this to my friend Oronde Allie. He was one of my best friends and fellow tech-heads, and never stopped trying to learn something new.

Mark Castle

This is dedicated to all the women in my life: mothers, sister, wife, daughters. Without all of you I wouldn't be here. Now get off my back about college.

Bruce Epstein

To my wife Michele and daughter Zoë. They are beacons in my search for all that is important and will always have my adoration and unending love.

Tab Julius

To my family.

Kirk Keller

These chapters are dedicated to anyone who's ever been willing to follow an idea to see where it will go.

Raúl Silva

To my wife Carolyn for her patience, understanding, and belief in me.

Acknowledgments

Jihad Battikha

Acknowledgments must go to all my fellow employees throughout the years from which bits and pieces of powerful knowledge have always flowed. Additional brownie points go to my brother who first got me interested in computers and whose unmatched criticism lead me to push my potential beyond what I thought it could ever be. Also, to my mother who always made sure I ate well even when I moved away from home.

A few companies have met my complete satisfaction over the last few years, which these days is a rare thing. Adobe for their Photoshop, Autodesk for their 3D Studio, and Impulse for their Imagine. My dream, however, is that these three fine products will someday, somehow be integrated into one (with Director thrown in for good measure). Anyone care to take up the challenge?

Dudley Bryan

First, I'd like to thank my managers at Virtual Entertainment for allowing me the flexibility needed to finish my chapters. I'd also like to thank them for allowing me to use some of the artwork I've done for them in many of my figures and examples for Chapters 6, 7, and 8. Thanks go out to the talented programmers and artists I work with as well, for constantly challenging the concepts we work with and helping to find news ideas in everything we do. I'd like to also thank my family and friends for believing in me.

Jeff Buell
Thanks to professor Andy Montana who kept me busy implementing his innovative chemistry instruction visions at CSUF. And thanks to the gang at the Orange County Multimedia User Group for publishing my writing exercises in their newsletter.

Mark Castle
To all my friends who still somehow stay together even though we have to check calendars a month in advance just to have lunch. Cheers and another Castle Beer to all my friends at Macromedia, who have helped me to do the job I would have wanted if it existed when I was back in school. Thanks to the people who have supported me always. It's a blessing and a curse to have family and friends who expect you to live up to your abilities. Mom, I'm not on TV, but I'll bet you cry anyway. Most especially I thank my wife for all the patience and support she always has for me, even after a long day with the kids. Thanks to everyone I ever met.

Bruce Epstein
My eternal appreciation to my wife Michele and daughter Zoë for their patience and sacrifice during this project (even now as they wait for me to write this so that we can leave for vacation) and for always knowing that I would rather spend any given moment with them, even if it is not always possible. My thanks to the staff at New Riders: Steve Weiss for all his time, effort, and e-mails and for taking a chance on letting me write four chapters and for putting up with me in general, Karen Walsh for her patient assistance, Laura Frey for her "less is more" editing and encouraging advice, and Stacey Beheler for her helpful administration.

Andy Hock
First, I'd like to thank my brother Dave, and his wife Judy. Rock steady (well at least limestone steady!) and always there. I'd also like to personally thank Karen Walsh and Stephen Hsu for their copy and technical editing help. Without them, these chapters would never see the light of day. I had no idea how difficult it is to put together a book...especially one with as many authors and different writing styles as this one.

I'd also like to thank my friends who have put up with all the "Sorry, Can't make it...too busy!" phone messages for the past three months. You know who you are!

Tab Julius

I'd like to thank the fine staff at New Riders, the folks at Macromedia, and the readers of *the Lingo User's Journal* (all of whom keep me on my toes).

Kirk Keller

I'd like to thank the following folks:

The folks at Macromedia for creating a great piece of software and for listening to the ideas of their customers; Miles Lightwood, Alex Zavatone, Mark Andrade, and Glenn Picher of Direct-L for letting me use some of their Lingo as examples; the entire Direct-L and ShockeR community for letting me bounce ideas around; Alan Levine of Maricopa's MCLI who took time from his superhuman feat of managing the unofficial Director web site to listen to some of my ideas; the folks at Thoughtport for their network support; the old crew at MU who made things a blast when I was learning Director (Allan Wamsley, Myra Ferguson, Ali Merayyan, Matt Kerner, Aaron Brown, Matt Skipton, Jacquie Sweet, John Toenjes, et. al.); John Kane and Steve Weiss of New Riders for helping me give something back to the Director community; and Karen Walsh, Stacey Beheler and Laura Frey of New Riders for their excellent work and for putting up with me.

Raúl Silva

Thanks to Alex Zavatone from the Macromedia Shockwave Development Team, to Gretchen Macdowall for her help and support, and to Alan Levine for doing so much for the Director developer community.

Contents at a Glance

Director
Power
Solutions

Jihad Battikha

Dudley Bryan

Mark Castle

Bruce Epstein

Tab Julius

Kirk Keller

Raúl Silva

Web Site Authors:

Jeff Buell

Andy Hock

New Riders

New Riders Publishing, Indianapolis, Indiana

Director Power Solutions

By Jihad Battikha, Dudley Bryan, Mark Castle, Bruce Epstein, Tab Julius, Kirk Keller and Raúl Silva

Web site authors: Jeff Buell and Andy Hock

Published by:
New Riders Publishing
201 West 103rd Street
Indianapolis, IN 46290 USA

Printed in the United States of America 1 2 3 4 5 6 7 8 9 0

Library of Congress Cataloging-in-Publication Data

CIP data available upon request

Publisher	Don Fowley
Publishing Manager	David Dwyer
Marketing Manager	Mary Foote
Managing Editor	Carla Hall

Product Development Specialist
Alicia Buckley
Acquisitions Editor
Steve Weiss
Senior Editor
Sarah Kearns
Development Editor
Laura Frey
Project Editor
Karen Walsh
Copy Editors
Keith Cline, Molly Warnes
Technical Editor
Stephen Hsu
Acquisitions Coordinator
Stacey Beheler
Administrative Coordinator
Karen Opal
Cover Designer
Aren Howell
Cover Production
Aren Howell
Book Designer
Anne Jones
Production Manager
Kelly Dobbs
Production Team Supervisor
Laurie Casey
Graphics Image Specialists
Tammy Graham, Dan Harris, Clint Lahnen
Production Analysts
Jason Hand
Erich J. Richter
Production Team
Kim Cofer, Cindy Fields
Tricia Flodder, Janelle Herber, Lori Price
Indexer
Kevin Fulcher

Table of Contents

INTRODUCTION

Macromedia Director has long been at the forefront of multimedia development software packages. Its realm includes the genres of multimedia developers, web masters, graphic designers, game developers, and even web hobbyists. Its use has become so widespread that it is accepted as the standard against which to measure other multimedia development programs. Even with this widespread use, however, Director is still sorely underused.

Director is an extremely powerful program that most users never come close to harnessing. Where do they get the information they need to take this power and utilize it for their projects? Until now, nowhere. Director Power Solutions changes all that. Presented between the covers of this book are solutions and examples that can take you to the next level of expertise with Director.

What This Book Is About

Director Power Solutions presents Director solutions in a real-world setting. Many of the examples and scripts presented are techniques that took the authors months of trial-and-error to develop. Included with these techniques is advice from the expert authors about what they would have done differently, how you can apply these techniques to your projects, and what to watch out for when developing solutions of your own.

This book is about making the most effective use of your time and talents. It runs the gamut of Director applications, including lists, QuickTime, and creating games. What makes this information unique is the fact that it is able to be adapted to your development situation. For example, you not only create a generic script, you *learn the rules* of creating it so you can create your own at any time.

Who This Book Is For

To anyone who has ever said, "There has got to be a better way to do this; I just don't know how," this book is for you.

Director Power Solutions is for anyone who wants to take Director into overdrive. This book doesn't give you an introductory course in Director—it assumes that you have a very comfortable orientation with the program. The authors aim to take you beyond what you have discovered Director can do for you, into the next level. This is where the better way to do something is found—whether it involves lists, Lingo code, animation, controls, or text fields.

What's In This Book

Director Power Solutions covers twenty different aspects of advanced Director usage. The information in these chapters is presented in step-by-step tutorials and accompanying examples. Each chapter is a stand-alone batch of information to use and explore. However, each chapter complements the others to the point that you most benefit from this book by combining techniques and solutions learned from multiple chapters.

Chapter Summaries

Chapter 1, "Using Photoshop to Process 3D Elements in Director," demonstrates integrating a 3D look and feel or adding 3D elements such as buttons to Director movies. It also covers making the integration seamless. The results you get are still not based on real-time feedback, but rather a simulation of it, which in a predefined environment with predefined branching hierarchies is just as good.

Chapter 2, "Understanding Digital Video Within Director," presents a tremendous range of material regarding digital video. It covers advanced concepts such as QuickTime Architecture, QuickTime Frame Rates versus Director Tempos, Data Rate Calculations for Digital Video and Audio, and Compression Techniques and Codecs.

Chapter 3, "Lights, Camera, Action!—Working with Digital Video in Director," analyzes the dozens of digital video cast member and sprite properties in the broader context of digital video playback. It examines each option in the Digital Video Cast Member Properties dialog box and its effect on DV playback in detail. It also explores potential pitfalls when using various options and the subtle differences between digital video on different platforms.

Chapter 4, "Controlling Digital Video via Lingo," explores many real-world applications for controlling digital video via Lingo. This chapter arms you with the knowledge to place a digital video sprite under complete Lingo control, optimize digital video performance while waiting for a video to play, play digital videos at varying speeds in both synchronous and asynchronous modes, and more.

Chapter 5, "Implementing a Saved Game High Score Chart," implements a high score chart and explores various strategies for saving and retrieving user data. You will possess the general knowledge and specific tools to expand your multimedia project's boundaries.

Chapter 6, "Traditional Animation and Director," is intended to help better equip you in creating and managing your animations using Director 5.0. This chapter gives you a starting point that will help you to synthesize the techniques to manage your animations that the computer offers with those that can be picked up traditionally.

Chapter 7, "Palettes and Sound," discusses tricks and tips for palettes and methods for dealing with sound during production. Sound coverage is limited more toward ideas to help work flow and a few of the file formats that might be helpful to use.

Chapter 8, "Quick Work," seeks to reveal a number of special tips and techniques utilizing Director that the author has come across over the years in developing different projects. These tips range from techniques involving Photoshop and DeBabelizer to tips involving just Director itself.

Chapter 9, "Building Generic Handlers in Director," instructs you on how to build handlers that will save time in building future products. Generic handlers help preserve a consistent look and feel to a product. They also maintain a consistency in programming even if more than one developer is involved in the project.

Chapter 10, "Power-Using Text Fields," discusses handlers that are generic enough that they can be used with little or no modification in existing projects you develop. Field cast members can be useful tools that enable rapid prototyping and easy debugging of multimedia applications, use of small databases, application navigation, and quick manipulation of text.

Chapter 11, "Building Multimedia Tools in Director," discusses the necessity of spending time to create development tools for multimedia. Development tools enable increased productivity during the programming and finishing phases of a project. Development tools for clients enable the creation of dynamic multimedia projects that a more sophisticated market will demand in the coming years.

Chapter 12, "Building Shockwave Applications," discusses the new market that Shockwave opens up to the Director developer. The ability to rapidly create rich graphic, audio, and interactive content will go far to ensure a Shockwave developer's success. The key to this rapid Shockwave development is in creating generic Shockwave movies that make extensive use of external parameters, as discussed in this chapter.

Chapter 13, "Automating Demonstrations," creates a demo scheduler. It also shows how this demo scheduler can be altered to fit your development project, how you can easily sort and compile this scheduler, and how you can add to it.

Chapter 14, "The Power of Lists," discusses lists as an efficient way to store and process a group of values. You learn that there are two types of lists: linear and property. You also learn the syntax necessary to create, access, and modify scripts. After going through the examples in this chapter, you should have a good grasp on how to implement this powerful tool into your Director projects.

Chapter 15, "Movies in a Window," teaches you what you need to know to work with Movies in a Window (MIAWs). MIAWs are great for modularizing large Director projects and for providing custom tools, both for authoring and for final projects. This chapter explores possible uses for MIAWs along with the procedure and syntax to implement them.

Chapter 16, "Parent Scripts and Child Objects," talks about what objects, properties, ancestors, and messages are and how to use them. You learn the syntax for objects and learn that objects are made from parent scripts that provide a blueprint for the object. This chapter also presents a real-world example of a movie that uses objects.

Chapter 17, "Using External and Multiple Casts," enables you to create and use multiple or external castLibs in any projects that might require this type of functionality or even in those that may just benefit from using the organization or localization aspects.

On the Web Site

The authors of this book have included working Director files of their solutions and techniques for you to learn from. All these files are located on the New Riders web site at www.mcp.com/newriders. Download these files for use with the text to create the best learning and experimenting environment for yourself. Use the knowledge the authors have imparted and take it one step further by exploring the applications of that knowledge.

The web site also contains three bonus chapters as follows:

"The Nincompoofs: A Multilevel Shockwave Maze Game," teaches how to create mazes in Director. Specifically it shows you how one maze, the Nincompoofs, was created using property lists, the actorList and on stepFrame events, and the whichLine command, among others. It also imparts how these commands can be used to formulate your own maze game.

"Button Scripting," discusses buttons, the most essential parts of a graphic user interface. Various scripting techniques are discussed, in addition to code for more fully functional scripts.

"Creating Complex Controls," travels from a properly functioning button handler to a pretty complex control. It takes a specific example and discusses how altering this example can make it useful in many Director projects you might be working on.

New Riders Publishing

The staff of New Riders Publishing is committed to bringing you the very best in computer reference material. Each New Riders book is the result of months of work by authors and staff who research and refine the information contained within its covers.

As part of this commitment to you, New Riders invites your input. Please let us know if you enjoy this book, if you have trouble with the information and examples presented, or if you have a suggestion for the next edition.

Please note, though: New Riders staff cannot serve as a technical resource for Macromedia Director or for questions about software- or hardware-related problems. Please refer to the documentation that accompanies Director or to the applications' Help systems.

If you have a question or comment about any New Riders book, there are several ways to contact New Riders Publishing. We will respond to as many readers as we can. Your name, address, or phone number will never become part of a mailing list or be used for any purpose other than to help us continue to bring you the best books possible. You can write us at the following address:

> New Riders Publishing
> Attn: Publisher
> 201 W. 103rd Street
> Indianapolis, IN 46290

If you prefer, you can fax New Riders Publishing at 317-817-7448.

You can also send electronic mail to New Riders at the following Internet address:

`ddwyer@newriders.mcp.com`

New Riders Publishing is an imprint of Macmillan Computer Publishing. To obtain a catalog or information or to purchase any Macmillan Computer Publishing book, call 800-428-5331 or visit our Web site at `http://www.mcp.com`.

Thank you for selecting *Director Power Solutions*!

chapter 1

Jihad Battikha

USING PHOTOSHOP TO PROCESS 3D ELEMENTS IN DIRECTOR

This chapter covers the implementation of 3D graphical elements and 3D animated objects whose end purpose is to be used in Director, whether they are related to interface or non-interface uses. The central issue is the seamless integration of these elements on to their backdrops and their uses alongside other, similar elements. The actual 3D creation aspect is far too vast to cover in a single chapter, but regardless of how your project's 3D graphics are created, this chapter covers the steps necessary to ensure that they can be integrated seamlessly into your scene or interface.

A good understanding of 3D terminology and an adequate technical ability to create 3D graphics are required to fully utilize the techniques in this chapter. Almost any current 3D graphics package can be used to re-create the following techniques. It must be noted, however, that 3D Studio MAX (a recent release by Kinetix Software, a division of

Autodesk Software) can simplify the techniques in this chapter quite a bit; the downside is that 3D Studio MAX has a price tag over $3,000 and requires a workstation-class PC. Thus, it may not be a viable alternative for most people who are just looking for an encompassing solution to a single technique among a universe of possible creative needs. If you do not have a capacity for 3D graphics creation, but intend to use a 3D graphics artist as a resource on your product or for your client, you must be able to communicate to him the steps involved to allow yourself a smoother workflow.

The type of 3D discussed here is the prerendered type, not the real-time 3D found in many game engines available for the PC platform. Director cannot as yet create or support the use of real-time 3D graphics. Although the future may hold some promise, real solutions are needed that work today for many types of products and many clients. Essentially, Director simulates real-time 3D feedback in a 2D authoring environment and enables users to keep this back-stage trickery from being apparent to the end user. This scenario is somewhat similar to the movie production ideology in that the viewer never knows how an effect is produced. Any means of getting the job done with a seamless result is desired as long as the procedure is efficient and reusable. For simplicity's sake, this technique is referred to as 2D.

Many Director 5 Xtras (as well as XObjects for Director 4) are available on the market today that add more robust functionality to Director's current available options. A current Xtra from Shell Interactive, 3D Dreams, adds the capability to integrate real time 3D rendering within Director but requires a huge over-head in CPU processing power and is therefore not a viable solution for the consumer marketplace. Some projects, however, can benefit from add-ons like these if the playback platform targeted is capable. Location kiosks that aren't limited to dated hardware, for example, can definitely benefit. For this chapter, it is assumed that the delivery channel is consumer-oriented.

A question that comes up that must be answered is where to use 2D or whether to use it at all. Is it a necessary component of a particular software task that may stand before a multimedia developer or would it be more plausible to utilize a 2D look and feel for the product? How can one differentiate between a legitimate use of the technique and a use of it just for the sake of the technique itself? You cannot rely on 2D saving a bad product, just as a great product does not need 2D. The trick to knowing when to use 2D and when to avoid it is to follow the age-old rule of form follows function. You must always ask yourself the following questions:

- What can I gain by using 3D elements in this project?
- Will 2D support the themes or just get in their way?
- Will it be too costly or time-consuming for this task?
- Is it an adequate or reasonable supposition to assume that the end user will appreciate its use and find it of value to the product or will it simply come across as overuse of an overused style?

Realize that at this point in the industry, 3D is touted as being inherently better than 2D, whether it actually is better for any number of reasons or uses. The distinction must be made early on in product design whether 2D supports or hamper its functionality. The point of this chapter is not to analyze whether you should use 2D, but rather to take the assumption that you have decided to use it and would like its implementation to have a professional look.

You can simulate 2D in any number of ways in Director—even non-linear navigational movement to some degree—depending on the level of complexity you have the time to manage or budget to afford. One of the cooler, if not complex, ways is the use of non-linear video. With proper planning, jumping from point-to-point within a digital movie (such as QuickTime) can be done seamlessly to give the illusion of being immersed inside an environment. Of course, a movie like that needs to be prerendered and cannot be as interactive as even a simulation of a real environment. A person might want to use a 3D look for interface buttons only, or may want to build an entire interface using only 3D created graphics. The latter is more difficult and takes more planning, but it is far from impossible. Using modifications to aspects of this chapter as well as proper planning enables any 3D result that is imaginable within the constraints of Director. Director, even running on a well-equipped PC, does not and probably will not ever come near the performance level of a Nintendo box or Sony Playstation. A multimedia author must keep those limitations in mind and address them when it makes sense:

- Limit the size and number of cast members when it makes sense (the smaller the better).

❧ Try to limit the color range of each singular cast member with proper planning. (A larger range introduces a greater dither amount and more color data, thereby giving Director a difficult time when streaming the graphic from the CD-ROM or hard drive if it is not already loaded into RAM—adding to wait times for the end user.)

❧ Director does not support anti-aliasing edges of graphics (Director 5 now supports anti-aliased text, but as yet still does not support anti-aliased graphics.)

❧ The use of too many layered elements on a given frame adds to preload time without necessarily affecting visual aesthetics in a positive way.

❧ Director may run fine at 30 fps on a developer-level PC even with large graphics files moving across the screen, but one must always remember the limitations of a large audience of end users with limited-capacity PCs. A good limiting number to keep within the range of current consumer platforms is 10–12 fps.

Avoiding the Alias Trap

The way to make a clean-looking integration of 2D elements is to avoid the alias trap. This tends to be the most important, yet misunderstood, aspect of creating Director animations.

Most if not all artists who work in the digital medium should know that a computer display is made up of finite graphical elements called pixels. Drawing a line in a Paint program with aliasing turned off causes that line to be stair-stepped because of the limited number of pixels on the screen. To avoid getting this stair-stepped effect, one must keep aliasing turned on so that smooth edges are maintained and that graphics are more pleasing to the eye (see fig. 1.1). Aliasing basically draws in a range of in-between color pixels that roughly gives a visual smoothness to an otherwise jagged edge. This all works fine if you are using Photoshop or another Paint package for your final artwork. If you intend, however, to have animated graphics or intend to wrap up graphical UI elements in Photoshop for later use in Director, aliasing must be avoided—especially around the perimeter of an animated element.

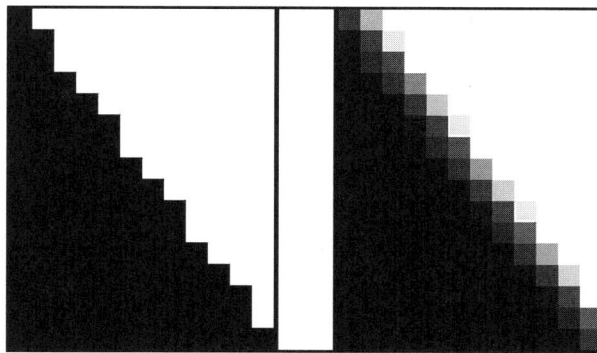

FIGURE 1.1

A visual example of what anti-aliasing does to an edge.

Normal pixels (enlarged greatly)   Same pixels anti-aliased

The biggest mistake that some artists initially make when creating art for a Director product is to create the elements on a white or solid color background in a Paint program and alias the edges to that white background. They fail to realize at that point that after import into Director, those cast member graphics contain a light halo around them.

A Director artist must always maintain a non-aliased perimeter around all the graphics that are imported. Even if a graphic is created and imported on the background that it initially sits on top of on the Director stage, it causes visual glitches if it needs to be moved or animated away from that origin point.

Preparing Your Models and Mapping

When preparing 3D models for an interface, try to maintain beveled edges on buttons and curving edges of all your gadgets, even small and slight ones. Beveled edges help to catch light without glaring the whole surface of the 3D form, and give the sense of solidity. Also, be certain to maintain consistent mapping coordinates on all your objects that can be grouped into a certain type (such as buttons, sliders, or levers). Maintaining consistent texture map resolutions and sizes is additionally important for controlling the harmony of your interface.

Palette Considerations

Whenever coloring your objects with texture maps or even just flat colors, it is important to preserve similar hues and values to your main backdrop and between all the elements grouped on-screen. Also, if you already have a pre-defined palette for your Director project, try to pull colors from that on to your elements before rendering them out. This helps to prevent heavy dithering and alleviates the dizzying task of too many colors from which to choose.

Defining the Background

If you are already working with a final background and are just adding clickable elements that will eventually be layered on top of this graphic in Director, you may be able to save a step from the following techniques. If your 3D graphics software can handle this, render the background as a backdrop in your 3D scene. Make certain to render out your scene in the precise resolution and proportion of your background image. Otherwise, the image is rescaled or tiled to fit the screen size. This approach does not affect your alpha output and saves time in the creation of a large Director animation.

Lighting Considerations

Lighting an interface in 3D is sometimes misunderstood, especially when rendering out many of the interface elements at the same time. For all your interface buttons or parts to be lighted properly and legibly, you must place a light (possibly two) near each of your buttons or parts and then lock that light out from affecting any of the other parts. Most 3D packages have an exclude option for their lights that allows for this type of control. The purpose of this is to maintain a consistent light level among interactive elements of your scene. As long as the lights are not harsh, this should give a nice, even look to your design. If the purpose of your interface is to project a certain mood, you may want to limit this technique and go for a more singular-sourced lighting scenario.

The color(s) of your light(s) also plays a major role in the overall feel of the interface. Avoid complementary colors with your main lights to avoid a color washout on your objects. Use your program's ambient light setting or use small-ranging fill-lights to give one side of your objects a complimentary hue. This pulls some flatter elements in your scene forward.

If your background is predefined, a trick to help choose a light color that won't wash out your scene is to use a heavy Gaussian blur on the background image in Photoshop, and then use the overall hue of that backdrop as your main lighting color. This helps accentuate a subtle, yet effective, bounced-light feel to an interface.

The Alpha Channel—A First Look

Note

So what is an alpha channel anyway? Basically, it's one of the most versatile parts of any graphic image. An image with an alpha channel is one that contains the regular picture data in 24- or 8-bit and contains an extra 8-bit grayscale channel, either created when a 3D renderer generates an image or created by the user in a Paint program. Photoshop is a robust program in that it can handle multiple alpha channels within a single image. Within Photoshop, a person could use an alpha channel for anything from keeping track of selection sets all the way to compositing with transitions over multiple image layers. For purposes here, however, an alpha channel is maintained to allow separating graphics to be imported into Director.

When rendering out images from a 3D renderer like 3D Studio, the user has the option of additionally writing out the file with an alpha channel. The alpha channel maintains all the object opacities and transparencies as a grayscale image for later compositing use. It is important to understand that if the result desired is a completely white-on-black silhouette of the scene objects, no large objects should be looming in the background behind those objects. It would be output as part of the silhouette and not allow for an easy way to separate out the foreground objects.

When you set up your button objects in your 3D editor, do not place any objects behind them. Also, be certain to light them in a way that is neither flat nor too full of contrast; either scenario makes your buttons look strange when composited in your interface. Try to match the lighting and hues with your general interface's look and feel.

When your scene is ready for rendering, be certain to turn on the alpha channel option and then render your file to disk. Please refer to your 3D product's owners manual if you are unsure where this feature toggle is located.

Tutorials: 3D Buttons

Buttons and other navigation clickables on your Director Stage tend to be the most useful type of universal sprite element. They can also be the most difficult to integrate seamlessly especially when they originate as 3D objects. Getting an interface to have a seamless 3D look is not as easy as one may think. The following tutorials will step through the important aspects of this process.

Static 3D Buttons

This exercise goes through a few steps that present a technique for avoiding a graphical halo around non-animated buttons. These steps can also be followed for any graphical element that needs to be layered on top of another on the Director stage.

1. Load a 3D-rendered image (see fig. 1.2) of a button with an alpha channel into Photoshop (preferably Photoshop 3, but 2.5 will do for the following steps).

FIGURE 1.2

A 3D rendered button. Although it isn't readily apparent, an extra image channel, called an alpha channel, has been rendered with this button.

2. If your background was rendered with your scene as a backdrop as mentioned previously, skip this step. If your background was not pre-defined and rendered with your button scene, load your button scene and choose Select, Load from the main menu and then invert the selection by choosing Select, Inverse (see fig. 1.3). Load your backdrop image (see fig. 1.4) and select the entire image area (Ctrl+A on a PC, Command+A on a Mac). Choose Edit, Copy (Ctrl+C, Command+C) and then bring the rendered 3D graphic file back to the front. From the top menu, choose Edit, Paste Into. This should effectively embed your background image behind your rendered objects.

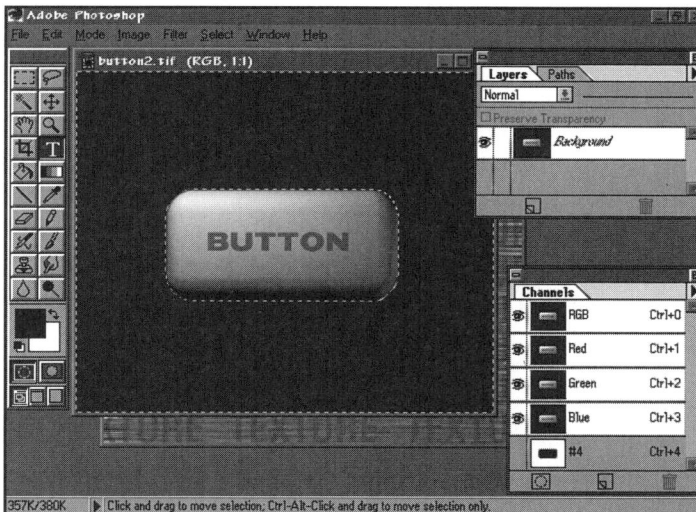

FIGURE 1.3

The alpha channel has been loaded as a selection in Photoshop.

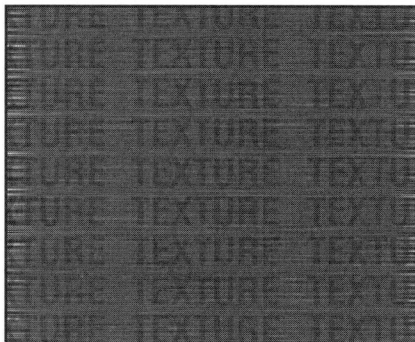

FIGURE 1.4

The background image that will be the backdrop for the 3D button in Director.

3. After your button image is loaded and the background has effectively been merged (from the previous step if necessary), make certain that the channel window is opened in Photoshop and then select the first black-and-white selection channel (usually the only one) from this window. Your image window should now be comprised of the grayscale transparency and opacity levels of your rendered scene, as shown in figure 1.5. This is the alpha channel that was rendered out with your image. If any errors appear in your output or any objects have effectively blocked the silhouette you want, you must rerender the scene. Otherwise, go to the next step.

FIGURE 1.5

The alpha channel is finally seen here. Note that the silhouette creates an anti-aliased edge that matches the perimeter of the button image precisely.

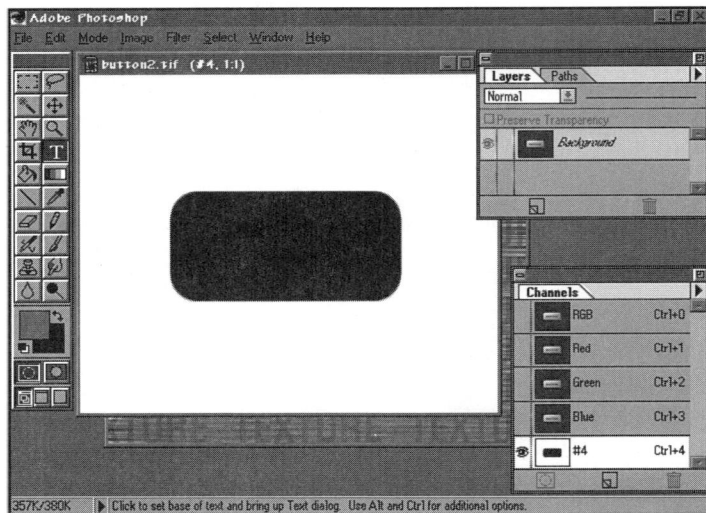

4. Bring up the Brightness/Contrast adjuster in Photoshop by choosing Image, Adjust, Brightness/Contrast from the top menu and drag the contrast slider all the way to the right, as shown in figure 1.6. Your grayscale image should now have a rougher appearance, or more specifically, it should have a pixelated, stair-stepped appearance. Before closing the Brightness/Contrast adjuster, see what happens when you drag the brightness slider back and forth. Your overall silhouette shape should not change drastically, but creates either a tight or loose hole wherever you have a silhouetted object. The distance to the object you want the silhouette to clip is determined by the end purpose and your best judgment. Leave the brightness slider at 0 for now and accept the changes with the contrast slider set at 100.

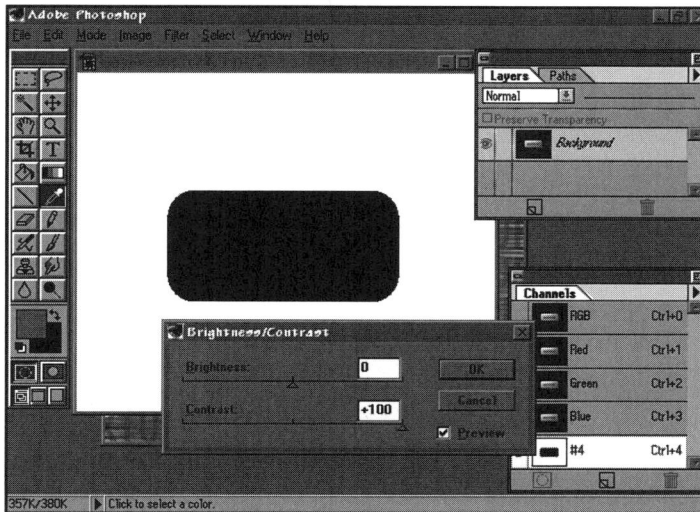

FIGURE 1.6

The Brightness/ Contrast slider is used here to eliminate the anti-aliased effect from the alpha channel.

5. Choose Select, Load from the top menu and click on OK for the defaults. Now choose Select, Inverse.

6. Make certain that your background color in Photoshop is set to pure white. (You can be certain of this by clicking on the tiny, overlapping squares at the bottom-left corner of the color selector on your toolbar.) Now press the Delete key. Your object(s) should now be separated from your backdrops with a clean, non-aliased edge.

7. If you already have an 8-bit (256-color) palette with which you are working, you have the choice to dither within Photoshop before saving your image or having Director dither for you automatically on import. If you don't yet have a palette to reference for your Director movie, or prefer not to use your particular system's palette in Director, dithering in Photoshop is a good idea.

Dithering

Generally, Photoshop does an excellent job dithering images from 24-bit to 8-bit, especially with an adaptive palette set. Unfortunately, sometimes the result is not very aesthetic, especially with predefined palettes. When dealing with a predefined palette, it may be better to use a third-party processing program such as DeBabelizer, or even just dithering on import into Director. Director uses a more

Note

diffuse dithering method than Photoshop and can at times be more forgiving when dithering between ranges. It's worth noting, however, that on import, or even when transforming to a bitmap, Director does not offer the option of dithering to an adaptive palette.

Which program dithers better is really a matter of taste and it usually takes a significant amount of time to strike a decent balance between programs. A nice technique is to take advantage of the best of both worlds by merging the parts of an image that dither better in either product into one unified 8-bit image. This all just depends on how much time is allotted for graphical tweaks such as this.

8. Now import your Photoshop image into Director.

First, import the background to initialize your palette if you have not already done so. Next, import any of the buttons or interface parts that were passed through the previous technique. Position your button(s) or interface part(s) over its respective area. You find that it blends perfectly into the environment without the white fringe or halo effect.

After following this exercise, you may be asking yourself, "Why use a button sprite in Director for an anti-aliased 3D button if it doesn't move? Why not just define a hot spot on the interface where the mouse rollover action occurs?" You find over time that most Lingo programmers prefer using a button sprite for a mouse rollover action rather than defining a mouse region to click on for a few reasons. Even though a sprite channel is conserved by the use of a defined rollover region in Lingo rather than the use of an actual button sprite, a defined hot spot region can only maintain a rectangular aspect, yet a button sprite has the further possibility of being modified with an ink or animated effect if it is later needed for the interface. This conservation of resources may have been a toss-up during the days that Director could handle only 24 simultaneous sprite channels, but in its current incarnation it can maintain up to 48. Besides this, a programmer can also embed a Lingo script into the sprites themselves. That can be a boon for some types of interfaces that require the multiple use of a single button that handles only one task in the entire Director movie.

The Poor Man's Alpha Channel

Some 3D programs cannot output alpha channel data at render time. This is not necessarily a hindrance, but does make it more difficult to composite images for post-processing techniques like the ones in this chapter. It is possible, however, to maintain a similar result by learning a simple technique. This might be called the *poor man's alpha*.

1. If you can't render an alpha channel, render your scene with a black background and make certain that none of your objects in the scene encompasses a palette range near black.

2. When loaded in Photoshop, double-click on the Marquee selection tool in your toolbar to bring up its property window. Uncheck Anti-aliased and set the Tolerance to 64.

3. Now click on any area within your image that is pure black and then choose Select, Similar from the top menu. Make certain that your background color is set to white.

4. Then press the Delete key. You should now have an all-purpose element that can be placed on most medium-range to dark backgrounds.

5. If you have a predefined background, set the Marquee tool's Tolerance setting at 32, and make certain that Anti-aliasing is checked.

6. Load your background image and select the entire image area.

7. Copy the background image into memory, and then bring your rendered image back to the front.

8. Invert the selection and choose Select, Save Selection from the top menu (accept the defaults), and then choose Edit, Paste Into.

9. Bring up the Channels window and select the first grayscale channel in the list (usually the only one in this situation). Now bring up the Brightness/Contrast adjuster and drag the contrast slider all the way to the right.

10. Select the RGB channels to bring them back up, and then choose Select, Load Selection from the top menu.

11. Accept the defaults. Now press Delete, and you have effectively simulated the alpha channel technique outlined earlier.

If your background is not defined or you think that you might want to use an element with other backgrounds that might be light-colored, render the scene with your objects with a 50 percent gray rather than black and follow the same procedure outlined in steps 5–11.

2-State 3D Buttons

Static buttons with the addition of a single select state are referred to as *2-state* buttons. Any apparent or significant visual modification of the button can qualify it as being the second or selection state of that button, but generally only a few types of modifications are widely acceptable as being true selection states. There may be room for argument here, but because the audience for a product must be considered and taken into account, a realization should be made that visuals that relate to actions must make sense for that audience. That considered, most modifications fall under 2 main categories: image-processing or form adjustment. Discussion on these two specific types of 2-state buttons follows.

3D 2-State

Generally, indenting the button model or squashing and resizing it can qualify as a select state for a 3D button. A toggle button can also have two states that are a simulation of a seesaw, meaning one side (whether the top/bottom or left/right) is pushed out while the other side gets pushed. This category of modification is referred to as a *form adjustment*.

Post-Processing 2-State

Color shifts and resizing of buttons in a post-process scenario can give similar results to the aforementioned 3D states, without as much of an impact to production time. Image processing always tends to be easier than form adjustments. Most results achieved with image processing do not, however, yield much of an aesthetic effect compared to making those changes directly to the 3D buttons themselves and rendering those states out.

Some Photoshop effects do, however, yield much better and faster results than their 3D counterparts, such as glows and more consistent drop-shadows.

Generally, the same rules for preprocessing 2-state buttons apply to static buttons as well because their movement, however slight, is always significant. You will render out two sets of similar buttons and repeat the same procedures on both of them.

Make sure your images have been prepared by checking the following:

✻ Palette considerations

✻ Defined background

✻ Lighting considerations

✻ Alpha channel output

If you have created modified 3D states for your buttons, just follow the processing steps outlined earlier for single-state buttons and then import both states into Director. Also, before proceeding with any post-processing techniques for your secondary states such as color-shifts, follow those same steps as well; they are required to avoid any inconsistencies such as size and cropping differences between multiple button sets in an interface.

Rollover 3D Buttons

Rollover 3D buttons contain not only a click or select state, but also a *vicinity* state (as when a mouse cursor moves over the area of the button). This type of button helps to accentuate to the end user which parts of an interface are clickable. Generally, a rollover state is one that changes the button in such a way as to highlight its clickability, yet not actually make it look like it has been clicked on. The following list discusses six possible modifications; the first three represent form adjustments that can be made to the buttons; the last three represent possible post-processing effects.

✻ **Resizing the Button in Place:** This entails either puffing out the size of the button proportionally or stretching the size of the bitmap icon that will be mapped onto the face of the button surface. Modifying the mapping coordinates of a bitmap in place on a button object can sometimes give the appearance of growth without changing the actual visual space that the button takes up.

❀ **Modifying Button's Position in Space:** Shifting the button backward away from the camera is a good technique to use when a quick resize is desired. Shifting the button to the right and down a bit also gives a pushed-in effect. You might want to do both within a 3D editor because sometimes the subtlety of light reflecting off a surface is more believable when the action is performed in a more volumetric fashion than a simple post-effect 2D solution.

❀ **Denting the Button Surface:** Actually pulling in the front surface of an object can give the impression that it is being pushed in, especially when the end user gets it as a feedback to a mouse click. Doing this consistently over an interface gives the illusion that the user interface has an actual depth to it, rather than just being a pretty picture on which to click.

❀ **Glows:** Glows can be done quite easily with Photoshop. Load the selection set for your button and then press Ctrl+C to copy (Command+C on a Mac) the button to the clipboard. Choose Select, Modify, Expand from the top menu and then expand the selection area by a slight amount (2–3 pixels, depending on your taste). Then choose Select, Feather from the top menu and feather the expanded selection a slight amount (again, 2–3 pixels, depending on your taste). Choose the color that you want the glow to be as your foreground color and choose Edit, Fill from the top menu and set the opacity of the fill anywhere from 50 to 100 percent. Then press Ctrl+V to paste (Command+V on a Mac) the original button back in place.

❀ **Color Shifts:** As mentioned previously, a color shift does not yield much of an aesthetic result when done as a post-process effect rather than a geometry modification of a 3D button. It can be done with a decent effect, however, if the color shift is done more naturally than a simple hue or brightness change. Mixing a color or hue shift with a glow is recommended as an alternative.

❀ **Place-Shifting:** Place-shifting means repositioning the button sprite relative to its original position over to the right a few pixels and down a few pixels on the Director stage. This simple maneuver can be done by the artist, but is better left for the programmer to handle in Lingo. The reason for this is that the programmer might need to handle the place-shift in a particular way, such as puppeting the button sprite or calling to a particular rollover routine which also might entail puppeting the button sprite or involve some sort of cast member swap on-the-fly.

An important point to remember is that it is generally easier and better for the programmer when all the multiple states of a button are placed within proximity to each other in the cast window. This way, they can be found and accessed more efficiently and there is less of a chance for error. The general ordering should follow: Idle State, Rollover State, Click State, Animated State. Rollover states could also maintain a looping animation. An animated state of the button could be called up when the button has been clicked. The next section covers the implementation of animated buttons.

Animated 3D Buttons

Animated 3D Buttons are the most difficult type of buttons to implement because they introduce multiple problems. Some problems involve the limitation of the programmer's time to script depending on their necessity to the project. Other problems relate to the logistics of clickable elements that need both a continuos visual presence on the screen and animated variations that originate from the same continuous visual presence. One of the most obvious and immediate problems that is introduced with animated 3D buttons is lighting.

Basically, the only difference when lighting an animated button as opposed to a non-animated or 2-state button is to make certain that the light is not too close to the button when rendering to avoid a glare during a single frame. Also, the position of the light should be adjusted to avoid the same problem.

Another aspect of animated 3D buttons that you have to take into consideration when integrating art into Director is the shadow. Several types of shadows exist that you can implement with the animated button. These include the following:

❋ **Post effect shadows:** These are shadows added to buttons that have been rendered without shadows.

❋ **Sharp shadows:** These are shadows with a sharp edge that imitate the shapes of their respective buttons.

❋ **Soft shadows:** These are shadows with a soft edge that roughly imitate the shapes of their respective buttons.

❖ **Streaked shadows:** These are cast shadows that stretch away from their respective buttons in the opposing direction of the main light source. They can be either sharp or soft.

❖ **Rendered shadows:** These are shadows created at render time in a 3D package. For the following technique outlined to work properly, these types of shadows must be rendered sharp.

The following exercise takes you through the steps to render a shadow. for a stationery animation with a single background use.

Note
All steps from here on will make the assumption that all 3D files have been rendered with an alpha channel and with the background predefined. Refer to the Static button procedures for renderings without alpha channels or those without predefined backgrounds.

1. Cast the light in your scene of button objects or animated interface parts indirectly (based mainly on the overall lighting orientation of your interface). Do not place lights too close to any object because a washout glare may occur on a frame of the animation.

2. Place a singular, pure-white plane at a perpendicular angle to your camera and behind the objects as shown in figure 1.7. Make certain that you have set your lights(s) to cast shadows and have excluded any objects for any particular light (if this feature is available to you in your 3D graphics program). Set the softness or falloff of your shadows to your desired amount.

Note
If your interface has more than one button spaced apart somewhat, it is generally a good idea to make certain that the shadows cast by all the buttons are consistently spaced and sized, unless an aesthetic reason persuades you to do otherwise. Inconsistently shaded, shadowed, and lit buttons tend to be confusing and difficult for an end user to take in, even if the interface is meant to appear as if a single lighting source is used for the whole scene. When lighting your button models, therefore, try to use a directional (or *sun*) light rather than a spot or omni-directional light. If your renderer does not support a directional light, you need to render each button independently, making certain to position your models, camera, and lights consistently for each. A range-based light (such as a spot or omni-directional) tends to drop off gradually over a distance and causes the buttons that are farthest away from them to be darker. This causes problems if the buttons need to be rearranged for user interface modifications. By preparing for this scenario, possible rerender time is saved.

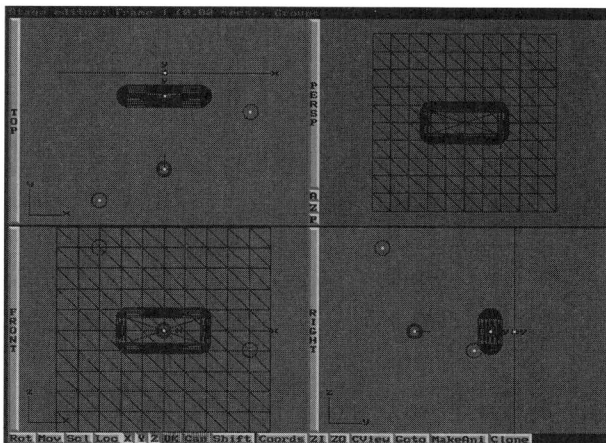

FIGURE 1.7

A view of a 3D Editor, Imagine, showing both the camera and a flat plane perpendicular to the button object to be rendered.

3. Render the animation frames with the white plane backdrop without an alpha channel.

4. Now render a version of the same frames without the white plane backdrop but with an alpha channel.

5. Load the frames (both alpha and non-alpha) into Photoshop.

6. Load the alpha selection in the image with the alpha channel.

7. Float the alpha selection and create a New Layer for the selection as previously demonstrated.

8. Now bring the non-alpha image to the front and select the entire image. Copy it into the clipboard.

9. Bring the alpha image back to the front and select the Layer underneath your button layer. Set the layer type to Multiply and paste the image from the clipboard into this layer. Create a new, empty layer and place it underneath the lowest layer. Now load the background image of your interface and paste it into this final layer. You can modify your Multiply amount on the layer just above the background layer to adjust the darkness of the drop-shadows of the buttons.

Follow the steps outlined for a single background, and continue on if you intend to use the same interface buttons that cast shadows over varying backgrounds. Using the following technique is only necessary if you need to limit the total cast members in your Director movie or want to conserve RAM without necessarily controlling the loading or unloading of particular cast member sprites.

1. Delete the background channel.

2. Select the channel containing the buttons with the drop-shadows and adjust the contrast of the channel to 100 percent.

3. Hide the top layer and make certain that the layer Multiply amount for the layer you're now on is set to 100 percent.

4. Zoom in as tight as you can to a white area of the image and create a 2-by-2 pixel checker pattern by using black and white. Basically, you will have 2 pixels of white and 2 pixels of black offset from each other like a checkerboard.

5. Select this 2-by-2 checker area with the rectangular selection marquee. From the top menu choose Edit, Define Pattern.

6. Fill the selection with white and then deselect it. Bring up the fill dialog (by double-clicking on the fill icon on the Photoshop tool bar) and set the Contents drop-down field to Pattern. Fill the shadow area. It should fill with a tight checkerboard pattern.

7. Now select the button layer.

8. Click on the alpha channel to bring up the black-and-white button silhouette. Set the contrast to 100 percent and the Brightness to –30 percent.

9. Bring back the RGB image by clicking on the RGB channel. Now load the alpha selection you modified by choosing Select, Load Selection from the top menu.

10. Invert the selection and press the Delete key.

11. Now flatten all the layers of this image.

12. Repeat this procedure for all the button animations of this type that you require for your interface.

13. Dither the image down to the palette of your choice or dither on import to Director.

If you have a series of animations for a button that stays at the same general location yet animates in place, you can mass-import into Director. What generally happens at that point is the registrations of the cast member sprites auto-center to the constraints of each of the bitmaps separately. This can cause quite a headache.

1. To check registration after import, click on a single sprite channel block in the Director Score and then select all the buttons that contain a single animation for a single button.

2. Choose Modify, Cast-to-time from the top menu. This streams all the button bitmaps selected in order into the cast as a linear animation. You can scrub back and forth in your animation to check any inconsistencies in positioning and adjust the registration for any offending sprites manually.

3. Registrations should be set naturally by Director automatically, but most times they are not. The reason for this is that Director automatically centers a graphic based on its visual extents and considers any white space around those extents to be non-space on import.

   If your graphics do not import with the registration that you require, then you must hand-set the registration for all of your cast members. The following tip explores a more automated approach to fixing this problem.

4. Now set all the button sprite's channel ink effect in the score to be background transparent.

5. Import the background into the cast and drag it on to a sprite channel underneath the buttons to see the effect of this shadow technique.

Forced Consistent Registration Hack

If you have ever had problems with registration when importing multiple animation images into Director, this workaround resolves the situation. This generally helps those people who prefer to create their animation frames outside of Director. Artists using 3D definitely fall into this category. Although the technique is manually intensive (especially with a large frame count), it is many times less tedious than realigning the registration points of all your cast members one by one.

Tip

1. Load one of the button frames in Photoshop.

2. Place two pixels in opposite corners of the image, away from the general area of the button being animated (one in the top left corner and another in the bottom right, for example, making certain that the invisible bounding box they create is larger than the visual area that the animated button would ever take up). Another variation of this is to simply draw a bounding box roughly around the same area that the pixels would have defined.

3. Use the rectangular selection marquee to select *only* those pixels or, if you chose the drawn bounding box method, use the Marquee tool (set to a tolerance of 0) to select only the line of the box. (You don't need to be exact; just be certain that the selection areas never cut into anywhere the button would animate.)

4. Load all the other button frames.

5. Drag the selection of the two pixels or the drawn bounding box from the first image to all those other frames one at a time. The positioning of the selection is maintained consistently when done this way.

6. Resave all the modified frames.

7. Reimport those frames into Director.

8. Repeat the Cast-to-time animation test. Now your entire animation is registered properly. All that is be left to do is to get rid of those two extra pixels.

9. Use the Eraser tool carefully or fill the bucket set to pure white to remove the unwanted pixels or drawn bounding box from those cast member sprites in the Paint window. If your graphic gets damaged with the Eraser tool by accident, then that particular cast member needs to be reimported.

Warning

Do not modify the registration points at any time after your cast member has been put to the stage. If a registration is messed up by accident, it must be adjusted manually.

The steps that have been outlined so far will work just as well with moving objects as they do with stationary animations. The registration issue becomes moot with the introduction of the tip provided for maintaining registrations for cast members on import.

Tip

Animated 3D Objects

Animated 3D objects are the same as animated buttons, except the lighting consistency and model are not as demanding. Aesthetics issues outweigh intuitiveness of interface in non-interface 3D animated objects. By following the steps in the 3D buttons techniques, you can get a very seamless result. It is the artist's discretion whether to implement shadows, because this is related to the use of the animation. It is recommended, however, to use shadows cast on the backdrop as little as possible unless it makes sense to do so. There is no use in complicating a possibly simple integration of 3D elements to your project.

Preparations and Considerations

The following questions for consideration are just a rehash of the previously mentioned things that will generally affect how easy or difficult it will be to implement an animated or moving object in your Director movie.

* What will your background be?
* Will the lighting change?
* Will you need to reuse the elements elsewhere?

Things to Avoid

As mentioned previously, try to avoid getting fancy with shadows on objects that animate across the screen. This introduces additional time to your development that you might not be able to justify. Besides, the effect might just get lost in the motion. Also, for large motions, try to keep your lights as far from your animated interface objects as possible in your 3D editor, or you may just get undesirable and extreme lighting changes on them that won't quite mesh with the look or feel of your interface.

Tutorial—Interface Layers in Photoshop

The following section outlines some key strategies in Photoshop to allow a smoother workflow in pre-production for a Director interface that will require animated or multi-state objects. Using Photoshop 3.0's Layers capability, an interface can be easily maintained and modified as a project design progresses without the fear of locking oneself into a rigid design.

1. Basically, maintaining a consistent background template for your work is crucial to avoiding surprise difficulties later in a project. After a background has been initialized, start establishing layers with Photoshop for other aspects of the interface. Any interface item that may change or move should be placed on a unique layer. You can group similar state buttons, such as glowing buttons on the same layer to limit the file size and avoid RAM problems. A Layers window from Photoshop 3.0 is shown in figure 1.8. The figure shows an organized way to keep track of interface layers. Similar states or layers are grouped together as much as possible.

FIGURE 1.8

The Layers palette window from Photoshop 3.0.

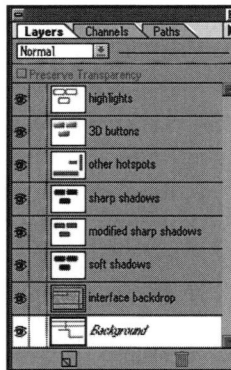

2. The button layers can be dragged and dropped from the previously created non-aliased images in the earlier exercises. Just set your Marquee tool's Tolerance to 0 and uncheck Anti-alias. Then select a white area of the screen (away from any UI elements) of your button graphic. Choose Select, Inverse from the top menu and click on the selection to drag and drop it on to your other image (the background image). While it's still a floating selection on the image that it was dragged to, from the Photoshop Layers menu window, click on the arrow near the top right and choose Make Layer from the list. This turns your floating button selection into its own layer, the clean transparency via the alpha channel technique demonstrated earlier.

If you find that you have multiple buttons at any point that could share the same layer channel, just select one of the button layers and hide every other layer except for the layers you need to merge. From the Photoshop Layers menu window, click on the arrow near the top right and choose Merge Layers from the list.

3. After all your interface layers have been created (including any modification states for the buttons and parts) and positioned in the right place, make a backup file. Start selectively, hiding layer channels that will need to be separated as distinct cast member groupings. Each time a grouping is desired for export, choose Save a copy from the File menu. Choose an image file format that Director can import. The file automatically flattens your layers before saving the file copy. If you have created any alpha channels or masks in the file, to make certain that Don't Include Alpha Channels is checked before saving, or Director may have a problem importing the file—especially if there is more than one. Also make certain that your image resolution is always set to 72 dpi when exporting for Director. After saving, you can now safely continue hiding/unhiding layers from your original Photoshop file for further exports.

   This technique is good if Director is doing the palette dithering, but if you need to dither in Photoshop, see the next step. Otherwise, you can skip that step.

4. After creating all your interface layers, make a backup file. Choose the layers you want to be visible and make certain that all the other layers are hidden. Choose Image, Duplicate from the top menu and make certain to check Merged Layers Only. This creates a duplicate of your current Photoshop graphic. Indexing this new image down to 8-bit automatically flattens it, if it wasn't already flattened. You can now save this image to disk and continue hiding/unhiding layers from your original Photoshop file for further exports.

5. After being imported into Director as cast members, these files may need to be cleaned up from stray near-white pixels that almost always show up around the perimeter of your graphics. Be certain to test your new 2-state buttons within the Score before moving on to the next set. Avoiding mistakes early on can save tremendous development time.

Conclusion

Remember that if your UI tasks are going to be produced by another artist, give the artist this chapter to read to help out when sharing resources and enable a better communication of the results desired.

Hopefully this chapter has demonstrated that integrating a 3D look and feel or adding 3D elements such as buttons to a Director movie is not very difficult. Making that type of ingregration seamless only requires following a few short and simple steps. The results you get are still not based on real-time feedback, but rather a simulation of it, which in a predefined environment with pre-defined branching hierarchies is just as good. Perception is reality, and no-where can it be more apparent in multimedia than a simulation of a real-time event.

chapter 2

Bruce Epstein

UNDERSTANDING DIGITAL VIDEO WITHIN DIRECTOR

Digital video (DV) is at the heart of multimedia. Digital Video formats, especially QuickTime, have been a driving force behind the industry's evolution. Digital Video will continue to be delivered not only via CD-ROM, but also via the Internet and new formats such as DVD (digital video disc). This chapter explores the issues that affect DV playback in general and specifically in Director. This foundation of knowledge will enable you to use DV, regardless of the delivery vehicle or platform.

Although Windows has a larger consumer market share, the majority of DV development is still performed on the Macintosh. The examples focus on QuickTime for Macintosh and QuickTime for Windows, but also apply to formats such as Video for Windows (VfW). Differences between the formats and platforms are noted where appropriate.

This chapter is decidedly QuickTime-centric, for which I make no apologies. I have used QT extensively on both the Macintosh and Windows platforms with great success, and you can too. (Apple recently announced full support for the QuickTime API under Windows, which should result in more Windows-based QT tools).

Technically, *digital video* is not synonymous with QuickTime because there are other formats, most notably *Video for Windows* (VfW). VfW is Microsoft's competing format for DV playback, and it comes with Windows 95 (just as QuickTime comes with every Macintosh computer).

Note

Video for Windows uses Audio Video Interleaved (AVI) files that can be used with Director for Windows, but not on the Macintosh. Using AVI on Windows and QT on the Macintosh requires two separate versions of each file.

QT enables you to use a single QT file on both platforms. Be sure to save your file as Playable on non-Apple Computers. This is called *flattening* or *forking* a movie, but it is properly called *deforking* because it removes the resource fork from the QT file. The resource data is copied to the data fork where it can be recognized by Windows. The *flattened* QT movie can be used on either platform.

Introduction to QuickTime

Everyone has seen a little movie playing on a computer screen and heard the terms *QuickTime* and *QuickTime movie*. What is QuickTime? What is a QuickTime movie? To use QuickTime effectively within Director, you must know that it is more than a digital video format or those little videos playing on your computer screen.

QuickTime is Apple's proprietary standard for the playback of digital media. A QuickTime file or *movie* is a document, just like any text or graphic document in many ways. There is nothing magic about it. It contains audio and video information rather than (or in addition to) the text or graphic information common to other file types.

The magic comes in when QuickTime plays back these files. QuickTime itself is not an application, but rather an Extension (on the Macintosh) and a DLL (under Windows) that enables applications such as MoviePlayer and Director to use QuickTime files.

QuickTime is shipped with Director, but you must license QuickTime from Apple to distribute it with your final application.

Term Limitations—Defining Movies

Apple calls its QuickTime files *movies*. These are the digital video files that you see playing on your computer screen. They look more like a miniature TV picture than a movie, but that's marketing for you.

Many people use the term *QuickTime* to mean *QuickTime for Macintosh* because it first appeared on that platform, but Apple also makes a version for Windows. This chapter uses the abbreviation *QT* to mean *QuickTime* in general, *QTM* for *QuickTime for Macintosh*, and *QTW* for *QuickTime for Windows*. As discussed in later chapters, there can be substantial differences between the platforms. Also note that *QuickTime* can refer to either the QuickTime playback software itself, or to the QuickTime data file. The data files are often referred to as *QT movies*, but someone might simply use the phrase, "I'm playing a QuickTime."

Like many other words, *movie* is used in multiple contexts. Its meaning differs in the phrases, "I'm going to the movies," and, "I'm watching a movie." Likewise, Director and QuickTime both refer to their data files as *movies*, but they are two very different animals. You will soon be able to distinguish the use of the word *movie* in different contexts.

Directorial Debuts—Director Movies Versus Digital Video Movies

Director document files are also called *movies*, but they have nothing directly to do with digital video. A *Director movie* is just a data file containing the assets and Lingo used in Director's cast and score.

Director movies often *contain* QT or AVI movies as cast members that are *imported* into Director's cast window. (Technically, the QT or AVI movies themselves are external to the Director movies, so Director movies actually contain *references* to external DV movies, not the DV movies themselves.)

Note that Director presentations can be *exported* in QT movie format on the Macintosh or AVI format in Windows.

Director can open multiple Director files as subwindows of the main movie; these are called *Movies in a Window* or *MIAWs*. The main Director movie is typically called *the Stage*, or *the main movie* to distinguish it from MIAWs.

A MIAW is just like any other DIR file, except that it is opened as a child of the stage. QT cast members aren't played "in a window"; they are simply sprites on-stage, so do *not* use the phrase *Movie in a Window* to describe your QT sprites.

Director also has a *Digital Video window* that can be used to view your digital video cast members. If you are having trouble with a QT or AVI sprite, make sure that it plays in the Digital Video window first. On the Macintosh, this window can also be used to edit QT cast members. Director is not designed for significant video editing, and you would ordinarily use a separate full-function video editing tool, such as Premiere, to create your videos.

Note

> Terminology is the number one source of miscommunication when discussing digital video and Director. Understanding the terminology helps you to both ask questions effectively and interpret the responses correctly.
>
> Consider this typical problem: "My presentation has three movies, each with four or five movies in it, and the first one doesn't play." When asking for assistance be specific, and indicate the platform and version of QT or VfW that you are using.

QuickTime Waits for No Man—QuickTime's Evolution

When QuickTime movies debuted, they should have been called *flip-books* because they were tiny and jumpy. Today they are typically 320×240 video windows with smooth playback, and should approach VCR quality in the next few years.

MooV Over!—QuickTime and QuickTime VR

QT files should have a .MOV file extension under Windows. Naming your files to comply with Windows conventions, even on the Macintosh, will ease cross-platform development. QT files are also referred to as *MooV files*. *MooV* (case sensitive) is the Macintosh file type code for QT files. QT files are typically played back via MoviePlayer or other QT-capable application such as Director. The creator code for QT movies is typically *TVOD* (case sensitive), which indicates they are MoviePlayer documents.

MoviePlayer comes with the Macintosh System software. MoviePlayer for Windows (either PLAYER.EXE or PLAY32.EXE) is installed by the QTW installer in the Windows directory.

Unfortunately, Apple also used the MooV file type code for *QTVR* (QuickTime Virtual Reality) files. These are not movies in the usual sense, but rather 3D views of rooms or objects the user can manipulate. They are typically played back via QTVRPlayer or via Director using XObjects (both of which come with the QTVR developers kit). Until a QTVR Xtra is released, QTVR files can only be played via the XObjects, not imported into the cast. (Director enables you to import them because it thinks they are standard QT movies, but they won't function properly.)

There are several types of QTVR files: navigable movies, object movies, and panoramic movies (or panoramas). For this reason, standard QT movies are sometimes referred to as linear movies or linear QTs.

QTVR playback is beyond the scope of this chapter, but merits exploration. Refer to Apple's web site at `http://www.apple.com` for more information.

Survival of the Fittest—QuickTime's Open Architecture

The QuickTime format is extremely flexible, and can play back video of varying dimensions, frame rates, and data rates. QuickTime is scaleable, so it can dynamically pixel-double the data before outputting it to the screen. (Refer to the full-screen video example in Chapter 4, "Controlling Digital Video via Lingo.")

As hardware evolves, so does the QuickTime playback software. QT now includes support for MIDI, compressed audio, text tracks, and much more. New versions for both Macintosh and Windows are released frequently and are usually available at `http://www.apple.com`. (Be aware that new versions sometimes introduce bugs, so test heavily before switching to the new version for commercial use.)

QuickTime is designed so that it can be modified to work with almost any video hardware. QuickTime supports both software-only and hardware-assisted playback. New data types and codecs can be added at any time by installing additional components. QuickTime is, therefore, extensible as well as scaleable.

That Synching Feeling—Synchronization

Most people only consider QuickTime a software that plays video, but technically, QuickTime is a specification for synchronizing digital media playback. I assume QuickTime was named as it was because it is a time-based format (it plays back digital media according to a time code). This means that QT does not just display pictures and play sounds, but that it tries to synchronize the pictures and sound.

QuickTime drops video frames to maintain synchronization with the sound. Why doesn't it drop the sound instead? Because your eye is much more forgiving than your ear, due to the greater redundancy in pictures. You can drop out video frames without severely compromising the viewing experience, but discontinuous audio sounds really bad.

Furthermore, audio sounds funny when it is played back at the wrong speed; for example, witness a 78 rpm record played back at 33 rpm. (Note for newbies: A record is an antiquated audio delivery medium most recently made out of vinyl.) QuickTime assures that time-based events occur at a specific rate. Thus a three-minute movie will last three minutes! This was as revolutionary as Fidel Castro when it first debuted, and it is still QuickTime's strongest feature.

Under the Hood—QuickTime File Internals

How does QT read both sound and video data at the same time? It doesn't—it just appears that way! In reality, the data is interleaved, with small chunks of audio and video data being alternated. Generally, video requires more data than audio; the video chunks tend to be larger than the audio chunks of the same time duration. The audio data actually precedes the video data for a given moment in time. Improper interleaving can lead to severe performance and synchronization problems. Taken to an extreme, non-interleaved QT files would play back horribly. You can check a movie's interleaving using MovieAnalyzer, an unsupported tool from Apple that provides various warnings regarding audio/video interleaving errors.

A QT file can also reference other QT files. Suppose that you have raw footage for the video portion of a presentation and you want to experiment with different versions. QT enables you to have your edits file refer to the raw footage in the original QT movie file. Rather than cutting and pasting huge chunks of data, QT creates references in your new file that point to the old file where the data resides. Although this can be useful, it is not supported under Windows and can lead to poor performance, even on the Macintosh.

For your final product, you should resave your edited version in a single file. Most QT editing tools, such as MoviePlayer and Premiere, include the option to Make the movie self-contained, versus "allow external references" or "allow dependencies." Choosing self-contained copies all the data into the new file in the new order so that it can be optimized for playback. Beware that most applications do not save movies as self-contained by default, but enable you to set this option in the Save As... dialog box. Also select the Playable on Non-Apple Computers or a similar option to make the QT file Windows-compatible.

Doing Time—Director Time Versus QuickTime Time

The speed of Director's playback head is controlled by the tempo channel setting, not by a time code. When you set the tempo to 10 frames per second (fps), Director tries to meet that request, but is not guaranteed to do so. Director plays every frame of your animation, regardless of how long it takes. Thus, the accompanying soundtrack may get seriously out of synch with your slide show.

Note that a tempo setting of 10 fps will not *necessarily* cause Director to play the animation at 10 fps. Director will play the animation as fast as it can, which may be *less* than 10 fps, but *no faster than* 10 fps. The tempo setting just prevents your multimedia presentation from running too quickly on higher-end machines. How can you guarantee that Director plays your animation at 10 fps? You can't! You can only pick a tempo that is achievable on the lowest supported computer. This may be only 6 or 8 fps depending on your product and your target platform. You must test and optimize your product to ensure that it works at the desired speed.

I've Been Framed

Contrary to QT, Director is *frame*-based, not *time*-based. Like a dog waiting patiently for its master, Director does not understand the concept of time. When you ask Director to play a 50-frame animation, it may take different lengths of time

Note

on different machines. It may even take different lengths of time on the same machine, depending on what else the machine is doing.

If you need your animation to play at a fixed rate, you can export your Director movie in QuickTime or AVI format. You can then reimport that QuickTime or AVI animation as a cast member back into your Director movie.

QuickTime and VfW are guaranteed, within reasonable limits, to maintain synchronization to an external time code. The frame rate is intrinsic to the DV movie and is completely independent of Director's tempo setting. Thus, the DV movie plays at the same rate regardless of Director's tempo setting.

The speed of a DV movie's playback can only be changed if you

- Modify its intrinsic frame rate in a video editing application
- Change the `movieTime of sprite` property via Lingo
- Change the playback mode in the Digital Video Cast Member Properties dialog box (which is the same as changing the `frameRate of member` property via Lingo)

When Is a Movie Not a Video? — QuickTime Data Types

A QT file can be created by digitizing video from a VCR or video camera, but not all QT files are truly digital videos. Often a QT file is an animation, just like *Snow White and the Seven Dwarves* is considered a movie, albeit a very different one from *Apocalypse Now*. QT animated movies can be created from various software that outputs animations in QT format (including Director) or created from a series of numbered PICT or PICS files with a conversion utility, such as Apple's ConvertToMovie utility.

I referred to QuickTime as a specification for synchronizing digital media playback. This is because QT files can incorporate many data types such as audio, text, and MIDI. Each data type is stored in its own track. QT files can include a text track for sing-alongs, for example. QT files may not include a video track, and can contain multiple tracks of a given data type, such as two audio tracks. QTW will not support multiple audio and video tracks until version 2.5 is released. In Director, you can examine and control the various tracks with new track-related Lingo commands. Consult Director's online Help.

The most common non-video format is audio-only QT files. These QT files contain an audio track but no video tracks. When you open an audio-only QT in

MoviePlayer, the standard controller bar appears without the usual video windows; the controller plays the audio as you would expect.

Audio-only QT files are most notably used in Director when you want to start a sound in the middle of the file, which is not currently possible with AIFF or WAV files (support for this is planned for future versions of Director).

Sizing Up Your Components—Digital Video Performance

Let's examine the factors that affect a digital video's performance and visual quality.

The larger your video window, the better your video will look, right? Wrong! Larger video windows require more data and may force you to compromise on other aspects more important to the user, such as playback performance, color depth, and visual appearance.

Let's take an important moment to discuss the playback platform that you should target. This is probably the most important factor in the eventual quality of your digital video and it affects all successive decisions.

Note

Great Expectations

The appropriate minimum configuration is always a moving target and will be determined by your project's technical and marketing requirements and the current installed hardware base.

Demanding too much performance (Pentiums with 16 MB RAM) reduces your target audience. Demanding too little reduces the quality of your product. The tips below are geared toward what I believe to be the bulk of the current, installed base of multimedia-capable computers. I feel these specifications are more realistic than the 386/33 and 68020 processors often mentioned as minimum playback configurations. (You might use the lower specification for software sold primarily to grade schools, however.)

✤ **PC:** 486/50 MHz or higher, 8 MB RAM (5 MB available), Windows 3.1 or Windows 95 (16 MB RAM and a Pentium processor for Windows 95)

✤ **Macintosh:** 68030 33 MHz, 8 MB RAM (5 MB available) with System 7.x. (16 MB RAM and a PowerPC running System 7.5.x for more demanding applications)

The minimum acceptable CD-ROM drive is double-speed (2x), but may be quad-speed (4x) by the time you read this.

Components Affecting Digital Video Playback

Each component in your system can affect digital video playback. A networked CD-ROM drive, for example, will perform very badly, as will a system with insufficient RAM. The following sections discuss various hardware and software components and their effect on video playback.

Central Intelligence — The CPU

The *CPU* processes digital video from its compressed form into the viewable form. Decompression requires horsepower, and the CPU's attention is divided among multiple tasks. Test early and often on your minimum target CPU under both Macintosh and Windows. Hire a compatibility testing service or test it yourself at a compatibility lab. You can test on friends' or relatives' computers, or even at the local computer store. Consider a formal beta-testing program if you have a client base that can provide you with useful and diverse feedback. Be sure to specify a realistic minimum CPU based on your tests.

RAMming Speed — Memory Requirements and Configuration

Everything on which a computer operates must reside in RAM. If it is not currently in RAM, it must be loaded from disk, which is much slower. If your system is starved for RAM, it may not be able to run QuickTime at all. More likely, however, the system will waste time shuffling data back and forth from RAM to the disk. QuickTime requires about 500 KB of RAM, in addition to that required for each digital video. You can adjust the RAM partition for a Macintosh projector in its Get Info window. You can limit the memory usage under Windows in the General Preferences dialog box. RAM has become very inexpensive, and a RAM upgrade often offers the largest improvement for your dollar.

Minding the Store — Storage Devices

Whether it be a hard drive, floppy disk drive, CD-ROM, network server, or modem connection, some device will be providing the digital video to be played. Two major factors affect performance:

* **Transfer rate:** The *transfer rate* refers to how much data can be transmitted per second from your device, and can vary wildly. A hard drive may

deliver 2 to 10 MB/sec, a CD-ROM 100–900 KB/sec, with floppy disks and networks being somewhat slower (10–100 KB/sec), and 14.4 modems providing only 1–2 KB/sec. Let's put that in perspective. A hard drive is roughly ten times faster than a CD-ROM. A CD-ROM can be ten times faster than a floppy or a network and 100 times faster than a modem.

A video with a transfer rate of 200 KB/sec would run off of a hard drive easily, or even a 2X CD-ROM drive, but could never be run over a modem. It would take about 150 seconds (2 1/2 minutes) just to transfer one second of video via a 14.4 Kbps modem! (Compression schemes that bypass this problem are on their way, however.)

Remember that Director may be loading other assets, such as bitmaps, while playing video. Factor this into your transfer rate requirements, or preferably, avoid loading other assets while playing video.

❖ **Latency:** The latency or seek time is the time it takes from the initial request for data until the data actually becomes available. This is minimal for hard drives, but can be substantial for CD-ROM drives. This is particularly a problem when you read data from two parts of the CD and the playback head needs to keep traveling back and forth. Thus, hitting the CD-ROM in two places at once should be avoided. At least try to keep the two data files close together on the CD-ROM, or preferably, put one of the data files on the hard drive.

Pixels Ahoy—The Video Subsystem

The playback color depth not only affects the user's visual experience, but it also determines the amount of memory Director uses for screen buffers. Both the monitor color depth and the video card seriously impact the performance of digital video, sprite animations, and transitions. Let's examine these components in greater detail.

Plumbing the Depths—Monitor Color Depth

QuickTime is actually optimized to run in 16-bit (thousands of colors) and runs somewhat slower in 8-bit (256 colors). This is especially true of QT movies stored at higher color depths that need to be dithered on-the-fly to 8-bit, such as Cinepak movies. QTVR movies pan much more smoothly in 16-bit color depths.

Because Director is usually doing something in addition to playing digital video, you will probably use Director in 256 colors (8-bit). Although most users' systems support higher color depths, performance suffers. Windows 3.1 provides only 8-bit support for the real-time compositing performed by Director. If you set the monitor to a greater color depth, video is played back at the greater depth, but the bitmaps remain in 256 colors.

Ante Up—Video Cards and VRAM Chips

Video cards can have a tremendous impact on screen performance, especially redraw speeds. The speed and amount of VRAM (video RAM) on the card affects transitions and digital video and determines which resolutions and color depths are possible. Faster video cards allow for larger video windows and sprite animations. Director and QT both support custom features on some video cards that results in optimized playback. Refer to TechNote #3176 from Macromedia that lists the tested and problematic video cards. Refer to the later discussion of the QTW.INI file regarding hardware optimization.

Fore!—The Video Driver

The number one source of QT problems is probably video driver software incompatibilities. Be certain that your users upgrade to the latest drivers, ordinarily available free from the manufacturer. If this doesn't help, use the generic SVGA drivers available from Microsoft at `http:/www.microsoft.com/kb/softlib/mslfiles/SVGA.EXE` and on the Windows 95 CD-ROM. Incompatibilities with boards using Cirrus Logic drivers are common. (About 20 percent of the video boards on the market use Cirrus Logic chips, even if they are not labeled as such.) These boards usually benefit from the generic SVGA driver if upgrading the drivers fails to help.

Projected Maintenance—The Director Projector

Director can create various types of projectors for the Macintosh and Windows. (You'll need a copy of Director for each platform.) You can expect much better performance from native PowerPC and Windows 95 projectors under those operating systems. Standard 680x0 projectors run slowly on PowerPCs because they are run in emulation mode.

Under Windows 95, 16-bit projectors run faster than under Windows 3.1, but 32-bit projectors run even faster. Windows NT requires 32-bit projectors.

Figuring It Out—The Software Configuration

I cannot overstate the extent to which software components can affect digital video playback, and the following components can each play a large role.

Internal Operatives—The Operating System

Expect to see lesser video performance under Windows than you do on the Macintosh. Windows 95 generally gives better video performance than Windows 3.1, assuming sufficient RAM is available. Be sure to test your video playback on all platforms.

Version Aversion—The QuickTime Version

Apple is always coming out with new versions of QTM and QTW, as well as QTVR for Mac and Windows. There are now both 16-bit and 32-bit versions of QTW, and you need to use the one that matches your Director projector, which is also either 16-bit or 32-bit (for D5 only). If running a 16-bit projector under Windows 95, you still need the 16-bit version of QT.

As of this writing, QTVR for Windows is available only in a 16-bit version, but a 32-bit version is expected soon. Until then, you must use 16-bit projectors and 16-bit QTW to use QTVR with Director. The 16-bit and 32-bit versions of QTW can peacefully coexist under Windows. Director automatically uses the appropriate version.

Initial Impressions—The QTW.INI File

Under Windows is a file named QTW.INI that affects QT performance and compatibility dramatically. With it, you can tell QTW to either use only generic commands that ensure maximum compatibility, or hardware-specific tricks that can drastically improve playback with certain video cards. The QTW.INI file is configured automatically by Apple's QTW installer and can be modified via the Windows QuickTime control panel.

Virtuosity—Virtual Memory Configuration

Various memory settings can dramatically affect QT performance. On the Macintosh, these are set in the Memory control panel. Under Windows 95, they are set in the System control panel under Performance\Virtual Memory. Under

Windows 3.1, they are set in the 386 Enhanced control panel under Virtual Memory.

❋ Disable any RAM disks; you generally need the RAM for other things. On the Macintosh, uncheck the RAMDisk option in the Memory control panel.

❋ On the Macintosh, be certain that the 32-bit addressing is on (it is always on for PowerPCs).

❋ The Virtual Memory scheme can also affect performance.

   ❋ Set the Windows 95 System control panel to Let Windows manage my virtual memory settings.

   ❋ Under Windows 3.1, use a permanent swap file, not a temporary one. Experiment with different sizes (I have found that it is best to keep it to 1 or 2 MB or shut it off altogether).

   ❋ On the Macintosh, turn off Virtual Memory and Modern Memory Manager in the Macintosh Memory control panel. (Also disable the Use Temporary Memory option in Director's General Preferences dialog box.)

   ❋ Remember, Director is very RAM-intensive and multimedia applications prefer real RAM over virtual memory. You should quit all other programs before starting your projector.

Let's Do Lunch—Networking

For the most part, networks are not conducive to digital video. Transmission tends to be slow and intermittent, and the CPU must incur substantial extra overhead to manage the network data flow. You may want to disable background networking while using Director by turning off sharing in the Macintosh Sharing Setup control panel. Don't expect video to perform well off a server, and don't try to use a server as a playback machine.

Tip   You can simulate CD-ROM performance by running over a network if local hard drives are too fast to reveal performance problems.

Conflicted?—Software Conflicts

Complicated software systems are bound to lead to occasional conflicts. If you suspect a conflict:

On the Macintosh, try disabling extensions by using the Extensions Manager.

Under Windows 3.1, modify the CONFIG.SYS file to eliminate any unnecessary drivers. Under Windows 95, you can try restarting in Safe Mode. In Safe Mode, Windows 95 uses default settings (VGA monitor, no network, mouse driver, and the minimum device drivers required). You will not have access to CD-ROM drives, printers, or other devices. Consult the Windows 95 Help system for more information.

To start Windows 95 in Safe Mode

1. Restart Windows 95.

2. When you see the message Starting Windows 95, press F8.

3. If you want to start Windows 95 without network support, choose Safe Mode.

4. If you want to start Windows 95 with network support, choose Safe Mode With Network Support.

Coming to Terms with Digital Video Terminology

Digital video contains many attributes, each with its own set of buzzwords. In this section we explore the issues behind the terminology to build a strong working knowledge for optimizing video usage. The following characteristics directly affect the quality and performance of your digital video, and you should understand them in some detail.

Be It Resolved That—Frame Resolution

The size of the QT video window is referred to as its *resolution, dimensions,* or *pixel size.* There are several standard resolutions. You generally see one of the following:

❖ **Full-screen video:** This is played at a 640×480 pixel resolution. It is typically used on very fast machines only or when using hardware-assisted playback because it requires a lot of data and processing power (bandwidth) to fill the screen. You can pixel-double a quarter-screen movie to make it fill the screen, but this is not really the same thing. Note that a full-screen video does not fill a monitor that is larger than 640×480. Because most digital video is played in the foremost screen layer, full-screen video precludes placing, say, interactive controls on the screen.

❋ **Quarter-screen video:** This is played at a 320×240 resolution. All else being equal, a quarter-screen video requires only one-fourth the bandwidth of a 640×480 video. The quarter-screen resolution is most common for CD-ROM titles these days, but larger or smaller videos may be used depending on the target playback machines. This resolution actually looks reasonably good, and you can place the video within a framing graphic to make it look even better.

❋ **240×180 resolution:** This was common before the bandwidth was available for 320×240 movies. A 240×180 video requires roughly half the bandwidth of a 320×240 video and one-seventh the bandwidth of a 640×480 video. Thus, this resolution may be a good compromise for movies that must run on low-end computers or off of single-speed CD-ROM drives.

❋ **QuickTime resolution video:** Sized at 160×120, it is so called because it was once the dominant playback size for QT movies. A 160×120 video requires only one-fourth the bandwidth of a 320×240 video and one-sixteenth the bandwidth of a 640×480 video. This smaller resolution is still common for downloaded videos. Although this resolution is considered too small for CD-ROM titles, it may become the dominant resolution as the Internet begins to support streaming real-time video and more people use personal teleconferencing.

❋ **Other resolutions:** High-end kiosks with dedicated hardware may run video at even larger than 640×480, but you wouldn't see that in a consumer title. I have used videos in letterbox format (320×176 pixel-doubled to 640×352).

You may create your own custom sizes to seamlessly integrate a DV sprite into a bitmapped background. (I used this technique to make it look like a video was playing in the center of a flower.)

You're So Shallow—Monitor Depths

Let's talk about the monitor color depth and how it affects video performance. The *color depth* is a measure of how much storage space is used to encode the pixel color information. All else being equal, the higher the color depth (or bit depth) of a graphic or movie, the greater the throughput and storage requirements.

Because the monitor color depth determines how many bits are used to display each pixel, the term bit depth is often used interchangeably with color depth; however, graphics and video might have a different bit-depth than the current monitor color depth setting. The monitor's bit depth is chosen by the user in the Macintosh Monitors control panel or the Windows 95 Display control panel, or under the Windows 3.1 System Configuration option. Refer to Chapter 4, "Controlling Digital Video via Lingo," for examples on setting the color depth from Lingo.

If the monitor is set to 8-bit color but a bitmap cast member is a 16-bit asset, Director converts the bitmap on-the-fly to match the monitor's color depth. Ordinarily, you create assets that match the preferred monitor's color depth, but a cast library may contain assets of varying bit depth.

Do not confuse either the monitor's or bitmap's bit depth with the concept of 16-bit or 32-bit Windows projectors. These terms have nothing to do with the color depth. They refer to the executable's format and indicate whether the projector is designed for Windows 3.1 (16-bit) or is Windows 95 Native (32-bit).

Note

Oddly enough, a movie played back at a higher monitor color depth does not necessarily perform more slowly than the same video played back at a lower depth. This is because QT is optimized for 16-bit playback and a video plays back best at its intrinsic or natural depth.

Generally, Director sprite animations are slower at higher color depths. This is not always true, however, because Director files also play back best at their natural color depth. A 16-bit Director file (that is, one with 16-bit graphics) will, therefore, play back faster in thousands of colors than in 256 colors. This is because Director doesn't have to convert bit-depths on-the-fly when a movie is played back at its natural depth.

Note that although the color depth of the monitor may vary, a given video's natural bit depth does not change. Thus, a 16-bit video is still a 16-bit video, even when played back on an 8-bit monitor. Likewise, an 8-bit video does not become a 16-bit video when played back on a 16-bit monitor.

The appearance of the video may change, however. A Cinepak movie, stored in 24-bit color, is dithered to 8-bit color on-the-fly through the current palette. The data is transferred at the 24-bit depth, but converted to the 8-bit before display. The following table shows the results of using different color depths with Director.

Color Depth	Bits/Pixel	Bytes/Pixel	Palettized?
monochrome	1	1/8	N/A
4 colors	2	1/4	N/A
16 colors	4	1/2	Limited
256 colors	8	1	Yes
32,768 colors	16	2	No
16.7 million colors	32	4	No

The 16-bit color mode uses only 15 bits for color: 5 each for the Red, Green, and Blue components (the last bit is wasted).

The 32-bit color mode really uses only 24 bits for color: 8 each for the Red, Green, and Blue components (the last 8 bits are available for an alpha channel, although some video cards support true 32-bit color).

Bit Depths in Depth

Let's examine each of the possible color depths and their usage in Director.

* **Monochrome (1-bit):** This monitor mode is rarely if ever used. Even a video using black and white for effect ordinarily uses a 256-shade grayscale instead. You may use numerous one-bit graphics when creating Shockwave files because they occupy very little space.

* **4 colors (2-bit):** It is a two-bit mode. Enough said.

* **16 colors (4-bit):** Not to be confused with 16-bit color (thousands), this color depth is used primarily for Shockwave animations due to the lower bandwidth requirements. This is a palettized mode (see the later section, "The Artist's Palette"), but the only 16-color palette enabled under Windows is the standard EGA palette.

* **256 colors (8-bit):** Using 256 colors provides a good balance between performance and quality. This is the standard color depth du jour for multimedia for several reasons:

  * Most Mac and Windows computers support it as a minimum.

  * Windows 3.1 does not fully support higher color depths for real-time compositing (which is what Director needs), and it never will.

- Because you can choose your 256 colors from a range of 16.7 million colors, it often approaches the quality of higher color depths, but is more efficient.
- Cinepak movies can be dithered on-the-fly into 8-bit color.

When you use 8-bit graphics, a palette must be in effect. If you don't create a custom palette, you can use the System palette that comes with Director. It is easiest if your entire project uses one custom palette, but switching palettes is possible. Refer to the discussion of palettes in sections, "The Artist's Palette" and "Palettes for Blockheads" later in this chapter, as well as Chapters 3, "Lights, Camera, Action—Working with Digital Video in Director," and 4, "Controlling Digital Video via Lingo."

- **Thousands of colors (16-bit):** This color depth enables up to 32,768 simultaneous colors to de displayed. This is a non-palettized mode, which means you can mix and match any number of 16-bit graphics and they will continue to look fine. In fact, applying a palette should have no effect, and palette fades won't work in this mode. Because QT is optimized for 16-bit playback, it actually performs faster at this color depth, but Director sprite animations are slower at these higher depths.

  I often gear my projects to run in 256 colors, but allow users to choose 16-bit color if they prefer to see enhanced video quality. I would not use this depth for consumer titles just yet, but it is appropriate for kiosks or other dedicated hardware, or projects geared toward a high-end market.

- **Millions of colors (32-bit):** This color depth, sometimes called true color, is a non-palettized mode providing 16.7 million possible colors, but is sometimes indistinguishable from 16-bit color. Until Director makes use of the 8-bit alpha channel inherent in 32-bit videos, I would avoid this color depth because it severely degrades performance on most systems. I currently recommend its use only for something that requires perfect color matching involving the Pantone color wheel, for example.

Note that at 8-bit color depth, a 640×480 bitmap requires 300 KB of RAM. For a 640×480 stage size, Director allocates 600 KB in total—300 KB for the stage's graphic buffer and an equal amount for the off-screen compositing buffer. At 32-bit color depth, Director must allocate a whopping 2.4 MB just for the stage and off-screen buffer.

The Artist's Palette

The 8-bit (256 colors) mode is a palettized mode. This means that the full color information is not actually stored for each pixel. Instead, an 8-bit code is stored, and used as an index to look up the actual color in a table. (This is why palettes are also called color-lookup-tables, or CLUTS). The index ranges from 0 to 255, and is used to indicate which of the 256 colors to choose from the palette.

The palette itself contains 256 separate 32-bit entries or colors. Think of it as an artist's palette with room for only 256 colors of paint. Imagine that Director is painting by numbers and picks the color for a pixel based on its number, or pixel value. A pixel value of ten, for example, would signify that the pixel should be drawn using the tenth color in the palette. The palette is stored only once, but is used to look up the correct color for each pixel, so that an 8-bit index is mapped to a 32-bit color. This reduces the storage space required for an 8-bit graphic compared to a 32-bit graphic by a factor of four. Because there are only 256 entries in the palette, you must select the particular 256 32-bit colors you want to use out of the millions of possible 32-bit colors.

For 16-bit and 32-bit images, the full color information is stored for each pixel and a palette is not used. This gives a greater selection of colors at the expense of storage space. Each pixel in a 32-bit graphic can be a different 32-bit color because full color information is stored for each pixel. Similarly, each pixel in 16-bit graphic can be a different 16-bit color. Note that a 16-bit graphic can contain any number of 16-bit colors (32000+ possibilities), whereas an 8-bit graphic can contain your favorite 256 32-bit colors out of 16.7 million possibilities. With the right custom palette, you can have an 8-bit image with more subtle tones than a 16-bit image because there are 32-bit color entries in an 8-bit palette that are not available with only 16-bits of color information. Custom palettes can be created in many applications, such as DeBabelizer or Photoshop.

Note that only one palette can be in effect at any one time. You cannot mix 8-bit graphics when different palettes are on the screen without psychedelic results (or remapping to a common palette). This is because the pixels say, "Make me the color to which number 169 is mapped," and if it is not the expected palette, the colors will be meaningless.

Palettes for Blockheads

When a video appears blocky, it is often due to having an insufficient range of color tones in the palette. Thus, if your video has faces in it, there should be enough fleshtones to sufficiently show the smoother gradations of skin colors. Likewise, you should have a range of blue tones in your palette for sky and water, and a range of green tones for grass and trees.

Refer to the section on QT and palettes in Chapter 4, "Controlling Digital Video via Lingo" to ensure that the correct palette is instantiated when playing a QT movie.

What's My Data Rate?

The amount of data per second contained in a video is known as its data rate or bandwidth, although bandwidth is often used to describe something's capability to handle data. The data rate is a crucial factor in digital video performance.

The appropriate data rate is primarily dependent on what your minimum target playback platform will support. The data rate is fixed when you create your final video with your favorite digital video editing software, such as Premiere, MovieShop, or Movie Cleaner Pro, and becomes intrinsic to the digital video file. This is the data rate with which Director and your hardware must keep pace. If not, QuickTime will drop video frames.

Several items affect a video's data rate, and below we discuss the tradeoffs involved. The movie's resolution and color depth define the data requirements for a single frame of video.

bytes in one frame = (width × height × color depth)/8

(We divide by 8 because color depths are expressed in bits, but we are calculating the number of bytes needed.)

For example, a 320×240-by-8-bit frame requires

(320×240× 8-bit)/8 = 76,800 bytes or 75 KB

(Divide by 1,024 to convert from bytes to KB.)

Frame Here to Eternity—The Frame Rate

Naturally, a digital video file contains many such frames. How many frames per second (fps) are needed for the appearance of smooth motion? It depends on how much the video changes from one frame to the next.

Cinematic (35 mm) movies typically run at 24 fps, but if you sit up close and the scene pans rapidly, you notice that the picture is blurred and jerky. Broadcast TV runs at 60 fields per second, but it is interlaced. Only every other scan line is sent in each field (half an interlaced frame) so the entire picture is transmitted only 30 (actually 29.97) times per second.

When QuickTime debuted, movies were about 3 fps, but 12 or 15 fps is now common. At 12 to 15 fps, most video is acceptable, although perceivably jumpier than broadcast TV. At 20 to 24 fps the distinction is small unless there is a lot of motion in the video. At 30 fps, it would be comparable to broadcast TV (assuming you are using 32-bit color).

Finding the appropriate frame rate is a delicate balancing act that depends on the nature of your video and the target playback platform. You should have noticed that higher resolutions, color depths, and frame rates all increase the required data rate. Whereas you may desire 15 fps, this might require a lower resolution to fit your video into the allowable bandwidth (see the previous discussion of hardware transfer rates).

Your frame rate will probably be between 10 and 15 fps. The frame rate is fixed when you create your video with your favorite digital video editing software, such as Premiere, MovieShop, or Movie Cleaner Pro. The frame rate becomes intrinsic to the movie, and QuickTime tries to play back your video at this rate. You should experiment with various settings before creating your final digital video files.

In reality, this process is somewhat iterative. Make your educated guess about the consumer installed base, and then you choose a resolution and frame rate. Then test your video from a CD-ROM and go back to the drawing board until you get satisfactory results.

The Lazy Man's Guide to Frame Rates

I'm going to try to save you a lot of the guesswork; my experience has shown a 320×240×12 fps video to be a good compromise for CD-ROM playback. Assume that you have decided on this spec, and take a look at the required bandwidth at a 16-bit color depth:

320×240×12 fps×16-bit/8 = 1,843,200 = 1.76 MB/sec

Yikes, that is about ten times what a double-speed CD-ROM can handle!

In reality, the video would probably be compressed; this is explored in the next section.

Codecs to the Rescue

You may have heard such terms such as Cinepak, Indeo, and Codec. Uncompressed digital video contains a boatload of graphic information—too much for a CD-ROM's bandwidth. Luckily, someone came up with the clever idea of compression, a concept as old as spoken language.

A compressor needs to reduce the amount of data transmitted while still delivering the desired information. Compressed information needs to be interpreted, naturally, by a decompressor. The two work in tandem, giving rise to the term Codec, short for COmpression–DECompression. Cinepak from Radius, and Indeo from Intel and two popular video codecs.

In all cases, the compressor scrunches the data down and the decompressor unscrunches the data to recover the original information.

Codecs are optimized for different tasks and therefore have different characteristics, such as:

* What type of data they work best with
* How long they take to compress data
* The degree of compression they achieve
* Whether the codec will compress to a target data rate
* How much processing power and time they take to decompress data
* What bit depths and resolutions at which they operate

Cinepak

Cinepak is by far the most popular codec, and it is appropriate for digital video source material. Cinepak's biggest advantage is that it enables you to set a target data rate, and automatically adjusts the quality to achieve it. Thus, if you request a 200 KB/sec video, you generally get what you asked for. Most other codecs only enable you to specify the desired quality settings, and yield a data stream of unspecified bandwidth. If the bandwidth is too high, you need to repeat the process with lower quality settings.

Animation Compression

The Animation codec is better suited to hand-drawn or computer-generated cartoons with a high degree of consistency and repetition.

For more information on codecs and lots of other great stuff, refer to Charles Wiltgen's QT FAQ (`http://www.QuickTimeFAQ.org`). Charles is Apple's QuickTime Technologies Evangelist, and a frequent contributor to the QT developer's mailing list.

Codecs Are Us

Digital video codecs must rapidly decompress the data at run-time to be useful for real-time video playback. An asymmetric codec takes longer to compress the data than to decompress it. Asymmetric codecs ordinarily decompress faster than symmetric codecs because more time has been taken to compress the data efficiently. Although compression can be a tedious process during development, short decompression time is much more important to the final product.

A general purpose compression utility such as Aladdin's StuffIt can be usedV,o compress video for downloading or placing on a floppy disk. A file compressed with StuffIt needs to be decompressed in advance, however, because StuffIt is not designed to decompress video in real time.

Macromedia's Shockwave may offer compression of real-time video streams by the time you read this.

Generally you don't buy or use codecs directly. Codecs are typically licensed by a hardware or software vendor and included as part of their product. Movie Cleaner Pro, for example, performs compression with a variety of codecs, including Cinepak. QTM and QTW both include the Cinepak codec.

You may encounter some proprietary codecs that must be licensed for distribution. Analyze their strengths and weaknesses carefully, and solicit the opinions of other developers before paying for a proprietary playback scheme.

> If you have a lot of video to digitize and compress, consider dedicating a PowerPC or other fast CPU for this task during production. *Tip*

Data Rates (and Storage Requirements) Revisited

We saw that the required data transfer rate for uncompressed video can be calculated as:

(width× height× bit-depth)/(8× fps) / 1,024 = KB/sec

If you multiply this rate by the duration of your video in seconds, you will find that video requires a lot of disk storage.

A 320×240 video, for example, with 16-bit color at 12 fps that lasts one minute requires:

320×240× 16-bit/8×12 fps / 1024 * 60 = 108,000 KB = 105.4 MB/min.

Wow, a minute of uncompressed video can take over 100 MB of disk storage!

The storage requirements for compressed video are harder to predict, but easier to calculate than those for uncompressed video. By definition, if you Cinepak (used as a verb) your video to 200 KB/sec, it requires 200 KB of storage per second of screen time.

Thus, for a minute of video:

200 KB/sec×60 sec = 11.7 MB/min.

This implies a compression ratio of 9.2 to 1, which is typical for Cinepak. If you are not satisfied with the quality of the compressed video at that rate, you must alter the settings to allow for a higher data rate.

Note that if you request a peak data rate of no more than 200 KB/sec, your average data rate may be more like 180 KB/sec and, therefore, your storage and throughput requirements are lower. Some applications report the average data rate and some report the peak data rate, so be aware of the possible discrepancy.

The Audacity!

Don't forget to include the audio bandwidth in addition to the video bandwidth in your data rate calculation.

Audio bandwidth can be calculated as:

(sample rate× bit-depth× number of channels)/8

Thus, 11.025 KHz 8-bit monaural sounds require

(11.025×8× 1)/8 = 11.025 KB/sec.

CD-quality (44.1 KHz, 16-bit stereo) sound requires

(44.1×16×2)/8 = 176.4 KB/sec

The Lazy Man's Guide to Data Rates

In most situations, the data transfer rate of the device providing the video is the limiting factor, be it a CD-ROM, network connection, Internet connection, or even a hard drive. Note that the recommended transfer rate is substantially below the ideal transfer rate. For CD-ROM playback, use the following guidelines:

CD-ROM Speed	Ideal Transfer Rate	Recommended Rate
Single (1x)	150 KB/sec	90–100 KB/sec
Double (2x)	300 KB/sec	180–200 KB/sec
Quad (4x)	600 KB/sec	400–500 KB/sec
Six-spin (6x)	900 KB/sec	600–750 KB/sec

Pushing Pixels Past Video Bottlenecks

In some cases, the video subsystem is the limiting factor in digital video performance, as is the case with PCs with slow video cards or laptops. Secondary monitors on Macs attached to a NuBus video card also perform more slowly than the on-board video.

A codec that does not compress well, or uncompressed video, can require too many pixels to redraw each frame, resulting in a high pixel rate (pushing too many pixels). A 320×240×30 fps uncompressed video stream requires 2.2 Megapixels to be drawn to the screen per second. Even if your hard drive can provide data that fast, the video subsystem won't keep up. Reduce the data rate, which is directly proportional to the pixel rate, to solve the problem.

It's Geek to Me—Compression Settings

There are many technical aspects of compression, but it can be divided into two broad categories.

* **Lossless compression:** No data is lost in the compress/decompression process. This is required for things like electronic banking or text documents in which the copy must be identical to the original.

* **Lossy compression:** Not all of the original information is retained. This generally applies to analog phenomena such as video and audio. If the copy is pretty close to the original, you get the general idea because little or no relevant information is lost.

Most codecs can perform either lossless or lossy compression, as controlled by the quality settings. If you set the quality to maximum, most codecs perform lossless compression. Lower quality settings may result in lossy compression. Some programs use quality settings ranging from 0 to 1024, others use values from 0 to 100, and some just have a slider that goes from Low Quality to Best Quality.

Most codecs enable you to specify the quality parameters, but will output the video at an unspecified data rate. Cinepak enables you to either enforce the quality limits or automatically adjust the quality to achieve your target data rate.

Time Is on My Side—Temporal Compression

Because video changes very little from frame to frame, codecs can eliminate the redundant information in successive frames. Suppose that you take a video of yourself waving in front of your house. Assuming there are no tornadoes, the house is in the same place in every frame, and the codec can take advantage of this temporal similarity. Thus, temporal compression refers to compression from one moment in time to the next. The less your video changes from frame to frame, the better a candidate it is for temporal compression.

GIGO

The phrase Garbage In, Garbage Out was never more true than when applied to digital video compression. You never get great looking video with a reasonable data rate if the source material is poor. If you do not have the option of re-shooting

Tip

video, you need to specify a faster minimum CD-ROM speed, or reduce the resolution, frame rate, or quality of your final product.

Try to shoot video against stationary backgrounds, and keep the subjects as stationary as possible. This does not mean they have to be lifeless—it just means that they should move their faces more than their arms or body.

It is crucial when using cartoon or computer-generated animations that you use the original graphics, not a video tape of the graphics. Taking a video of an animation introduces horrible variations that prevent you from being able to use Animation compression and look bad using Cinepak as well.

Spatial Compression

Suppose that you are standing in front of a solid blue wall. The codec could exploit the fact that the whole wall is the same blue color to reduce the required data. Spatial compression refers to compression within a single frame. The more similar different sections of a single picture are, the better a candidate that picture is for spatial compression.

To Key or Not to Key—What Is a Keyframe?

Temporal compression gives rise to keyframes and difference frames. A keyframe retains all the video information; a difference frame includes only the differences between the current and previous frames.

As a scene changes, the differences eventually accumulate to the point that it becomes counterproductive to use difference frames, and another keyframe needs to be inserted. Thus, keyframes retain quality and difference frames improve performance (to a point).

QT cannot draw a difference frame without first accessing the previous keyframe. Periodic keyframes, therefore, improve random access within a QT file.

Like other digital video attributes, the keyframe interval is specified in your video editing software. The appropriate keyframe setting depends entirely on the nature of the video. In cartoon animation, where the scene may change very little (a character's mouth moves but nothing else), you may set your keyframe interval to 200 frames or more.

Try using about one keyframe per second for video. For 12 fps video you would use a keyframe interval of every twelfth frame. You might need more frequent keyframes for video with fast-moving action. The appropriate setting depends heavily on the subject matter and how much it moves.

All codecs enable you to set the keyframe interval. Cinepak even generates natural keyframes when the scene changes drastically.

Generally, larger intervals between keyframes lead to lower quality and a lower data rate, and more frequent keyframes lead to higher quality and a higher data rate. This is because keyframes tend to require much more data than difference frames.

Conclusion

This chapter has presented a tremendous range of material regarding digital video. We have covered everything from the basic terminology to advanced concepts such as

* The QuickTime Architecture
* QuickTime Frame Rates versus Director Tempos
* Hardware Components Affecting Digital Video
* Software Components Affecting Digital Video
* Data Rate Calculations for Digital Video and Audio
* How Palettes Function
* Selecting the Minimum Playback Platform
* Determining the Specifications for Your Digital Video
* Compression Techniques and Codecs

This chapter has focused on concepts that are universal to digital video, regardless of whether or not you are using Director. The next two chapters examine the specific uses of digital video in Director.

chapter 3

Bruce Epstein

LIGHTS, CAMERA, ACTION!— WORKING WITH DIGITAL VIDEO IN DIRECTOR

Digital video is a rich and engaging medium. As bandwidth increases, digital video will dominate the Internet as it now dominates the CD-ROM market. In Chapter 2 we explored the technical issues that impact digital video (DV) creation and playback. This chapter explores the use of digital video in Director. It examines the digital video cast member and sprite properties that are accessible via Lingo and Director's GUI and control of digital video via Lingo. It covers the properties set in the Digital Video Cast Member Properties dialog box and the corresponding Lingo commands. Then it explores the digital video sprite properties that can only be set via Lingo.

Going well beyond the material covered in the Director manuals, each command is covered in depth to help you optimize digital video playback. Along the way we discuss the interplay between Director and digital video so you understand how they interact and why. For each property or command, we analyze the related issues and caveats on both the Macintosh and Windows platforms. After completing this chapter, you will be prepared to control every detail of digital video playback, which is covered in depth in the next chapter.

Importing a Digital Video Cast Member

The first thing you need to work with digital video (DV) in Director is a digital video file. Once you have created your digital video file in your favorite video editing tool, use `File...Import` to import it into Director's cast. Digital video cast members, such as QuickTime (QT) movies and AVI files, are always *externally linked*; the cast member points to an external file, rather than the file being imported into Director. On the Macintosh, QT files are recognized by the Finder by their file type code (MooV). Under Windows, QT files must have the .MOV extension and Video For Windows (VfW) files must have the .AVI extension to be imported properly.

Note

QTVR cast members cannot be imported into the cast like standard linear QT movies can. Macromedia has announced a QTVR Sprite Xtra that may be released by the time you read this. The Xtra will enable QTVR files to be imported into the cast like any other standard asset. Until then, QTVR movies can only be accessed via an XObject, available in the QTVR developers kit from Apple.

Curtain Call—The Digital Video Cast Member Properties Dialog Box

This section explores the properties that control a DV cast member's appearance and playback rate in Director. You can control DV movies by setting various properties in the Digital Video Cast Member Properties dialog box (see fig. 3.1).

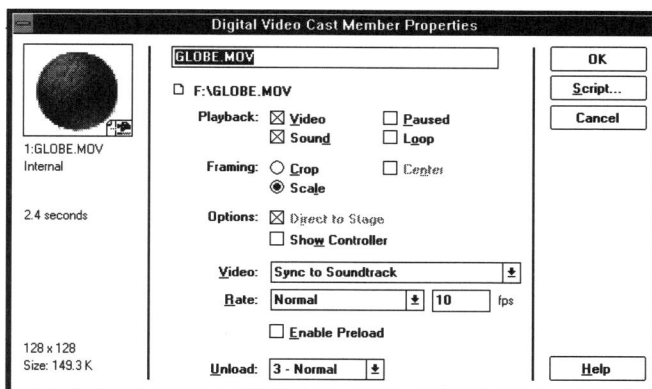

FIGURE 3.1

Director's Digital Video Cast Member Properties dialog box.

This section examines each option in the dialog box in depth. See table 3.1 for the Lingo equivalents of the dialog box settings.

Dismissed! — Dialog Editing and Dismissal Options

The various options in the Digital Video Cast Member Properties dialog box can be modified in the usual manner. The Undo menu command affects only the cast member name and the numeric (fps) entry fields. It will not undo changes to the linked fileName, radio buttons, check boxes, or pop-up menu options.

Three buttons enable you to dismiss the dialog box.

* **OK:** This option accepts the changes you have made and permanently modifies the cast member properties.

* **Cancel:** This option aborts the changes you have made and reverts the properties back to the way they were before you edited them. Unfortunately, this option does not affect the linked file name, which will remain changed even if you select Cancel.

* **Script:** This option accepts the changes you have made and permanently modifies the cast member properties before opening up the cast member Script window. You cannot Cancel or Undo your changes.

Static Information

The following static information about the digital video is shown on the left side of the dialog box:

✣ **Thumbnail:** This graphic represents the first frame of the video to help you identify the external file asset. Beneath the thumbnail, the file name and the name of the cast library that cast member occupies are listed.

✣ **Duration:** The duration of the external DV file is listed in seconds. Note that the duration of member Lingo property is measured in ticks (1/60th of a second), not seconds.

✣ **Dimensions:** The width and height of the cast member in pixels are listed as nnn × nnn.

✣ **Size:** The Size listed in the dialog box is wrong and is not related to the external file size. The size is also different under various versions of Director. The size of a QT file that was actually 360 KB, for example, is indicated as 385 bytes on the Macintosh, 0 bytes under Windows 3.1, and 208 KB under Windows 95. Similar tests with other files reveal seemingly random results. On the Macintosh, this may be the size of the QT header information that is physically imported into the Director file, but the reported size is clearly wrong under Windows. The following Tip includes a Lingo routine to determine the actual external file size.

Tip

Sizing Up Digital Video

The size of member Lingo property does not correctly return the size of externally linked assets. To obtain the actual size of a QT movie or AVI file on disk, you can use the FileIO XObject or Xtra. Here is an example using the FileIO XObject:

```
on getExternalFileSize extMember

  -- Returns the file size of an external asset, such as a QT movie, in KB

  -- This assumes that the FileIO XObject is open

  set fileObj = FileIO (mNew, "read" , the fileName of member extMember)

  if objectP(fileObj) then
    -- Get the file's length
    set fileSize = fileObj (mGetLength)
    fileObj (mDispose)
    -- convert to KB
    set fileSize = integer(fileSize / 1024.0)
    return fileSize
```

```
      else
      -- Error code
        return -1
      end if

  end getExternalFileSize
```

Cast Member Name

The cast member name can be used to refer to a cast member without concern for its position in the cast. This field defaults to the name of the imported DV file (without the directory path). When you change the linked DV file (see "Linked File Name"), this cast member name does *not* change. Avoid duplicate cast member names because Director will use the lowest numbered matching cast member when accessing cast members by name via Lingo.

Linked File Name

This field indicates the path to the linked DV file to which the cast member points. Click on the name (not the document icon next to it) to change the link.

Be aware that if you relink the cast member to point to a different external file and later select Cancel in the Digital Video Cast Member Properties dialog box, the change is *not* canceled. The *new* file will be linked in.

If you replace the external DV file, you should relink it so that Director can re-read the DV file's header. This header contains information such as the DV dimensions, duration, frame rate, and number of tracks. It is used to access the external file when the DV is played.

The `fileName of member` property can be set at runtime to dynamically switch DV movies, but this can cause several problems. If all your DV movies are known in advance, you are better off importing each one into a separate cast member. You can use `the memberNum of sprite` property to swap them on to the stage dynamically.

Limit the length of the path name to avoid problems locating the file. Director 4.0.4's ReadMe file states: Director does not support links to files whose path name is longer than 255 characters on the Macintosh and 64 characters on Windows.

Director automatically adjusts the path name to conform to the platform on which the projector is running. It uses either *drivename:folder1:folder2:filename* on the Macintosh or *D:\folder1\folder2\filename.ext* under Windows.

To ensure compatibility across all platforms and versions of Windows, use file names that conform to the DOS *eight dot three* standard (up to eight characters followed by a three letter extension) such as MYVIDEO1.MOV. Avoid file names containing spaces, backslashes, colons, hyphens, or other non-alphanumeric characters (underscores are acceptable). CD-ROM burning software sometimes requires that file names conform to the *ISO 9660 standard*. Hyphens are acceptable in DOS names but may be converted to underscores unless you select the Allow DOS filenames option in your CD-ROM burning software.

Directory names should be eight characters or less and should not contain spaces or other special characters. QT files should have a MOV extension and VfW files should have an AVI extension.

Tip

When a Director file is protected or included in a projector, Director freezes the fileName links. If the file is subsequently moved you encounter the dreaded Where Is...? dialog box.

Avoid this by linking to DV files in the same folder as your Director file before protecting the DIR file. If the DV files are in a different folder, ensure that the relative path from the Projector to the files is the same as it will be in the final Projector. That is, set up your hard drive in the same fashion as the eventual CD-ROM before protecting your Director files.

Playback Options

The playback options control whether the audio and video portion of a DV movie play, whether it starts playing automatically, and whether it loops when done.

Video

The Video check box indicates whether Director should play the video tracks(s) of the DV movie. If unchecked, the video is not visible, but the audio track still plays. Uncheck this option to improve performance for audio-only DV files.

When you change the video of member Lingo property, Director also resets the movieTime of sprite property to zero (0), which restarts the movie at the beginning.

Sound

The Sound check box indicates whether Director should play the audio tracks(s) of the DV movie. If unchecked, the audio is not audible, but the video track still plays. Uncheck this option to improve performance for DV movies without audio tracks.

Setting the sound of member Lingo property to FALSE initializes the volume of sprite property to zero. Changing the volume of sprite via Lingo or the controller overrides the sound of member setting. To disable an audio track, use the setTrackEnabled command.

Paused

The Paused check box indicates whether the DV movie plays immediately when it appears on stage. Select this option when you *don't* want a DV to start playing immediately. This enables you to set a DV sprite's attributes while it is off-stage, before bringing it on-stage in a subsequent frame. See Chapter 4, "Controlling Digital Video via Lingo."

If Paused is checked, you need to either start the DV sprite by setting its movieRate of sprite property to TRUE (1), or provide the user with a video controller. If you check the Show Controller option (not available for AVI files), the QT movie is automatically paused at the start because Director assumes that the user will control the movie. The next chapter shows you how to implement a custom controller for both QT and AVI files.

> **PausedAtStart not Paused**
>
> The Paused check box (or the pausedAtStart of member property) indicates whether the DV movie should be paused when it *first* appears. To check if a video is currently paused, use
>
> ```
> if the movieRate of sprite n = 0 then put "Digital Video is paused"
> ```

Tip

Loop

This check box indicates whether the movie should repeat from the beginning after it has completed. When unchecked, the movie stops at the end of the file. If loop is unchecked, the `movieRate` automatically returns to zero (0) when a QT movie ends, but not for AVI movies. Refer to the next chapter for more information regarding the control of AVI playback.

You can't use the tempo channel to wait for a looping video to finish. If you want to loop your video, set the `loop of member` property to TRUE and wait in the frame using `go to the frame`. When creating a looping video, make certain that the beginning and end of your video combine seamlessly to provide the illusion of a continuous loop. Use visual fade-ins and fade-outs if necessary.

Framing Options

A digital video *sprite* is created when a digital video *cast member* is placed on stage (or in the score). The framing options determine the appearance of the cast member within the sprite's rectangle on the stage.

* **Crop:** This option prevents the DV cast member's pixels from being scaled inside the sprite's rectangle. Instead, the image is cropped if the sprite box is smaller than the cast member's dimensions and left at normal size of the sprite box is larger.

* **Center:** This option determines whether the video is centered or aligned in the upper left corner when it is cropped. You should inspect `the crop of member` Lingo property before relying on the value reported by `the center of member` property.

* **Scale:** This option causes the cast member to be stretched to match the sprite's dimensions. DV sprites perform better if you only stretch sprites in 100 percent increments. (That is, you can double the size of a DV sprite to 200 percent, but it performs poorly if you increase it by, say, 66 percent.)

Stage Display Options

Director ordinarily composites sprites in an off-screen buffer before displaying them on the stage. This intermediate step allows Director to layer the sprites as indicated by the channel numbers in the Score and add ink effects to the sprites as well. When an `updateStage` is performed, the entire screen refreshes at the same time, rather than one sprite at a time.

Digital video playback is processor-intensive and there is not always sufficient time to enable Director to perform compositing of DV sprites. In this case, the digital video software, either QuickTime or Video for Windows, can send the video directly to the Stage, bypassing Director's off-screen compositing step.

The following options determine whether the DV playback bypasses Director's compositing buffer and whether the QT controller is visible.

Direct to Stage

This check box determines whether the video is played directly to the Stage or whether it is first passed through Director's compositing buffer. Changing this property at runtime confuses Director and leads to screen artifacts.

The Direct to Stage option may be set for QT movies on the Macintosh, but is always active for QT movies on Windows. This option may also be set for AVI files under Windows (AVI files are not supported on the Macintosh).

In all cases, it is highly recommended that you play all videos Direct to Stage for improved performance. When using QT movies, if playing the video non-Direct to Stage on the Macintosh, any sprite ink effects are lost under QT for Windows.

Go Directly to Stage, Do Not Pass Go

When Direct to Stage is active, the video sprite plays in front of all other sprites, even ones in higher channels. (It is similar to the trails effect.) Director is not aware of what QT or VfW draws to the stage, so you must force Director to refresh the sprite area after the video completes. Several techniques enable you to accomplish this:

❈ Use a cover sprite that forces Director to redraw a screen region.

❈ Use a fast chunky transition over the entire stage to redraw it.

❈ Make the DV sprite temporarily invisible with Lingo to force a refresh.

❈ In earlier versions, if you moved a QT sprite offstage, QT would refresh the vacated area. This no longer works, so use one of the techniques above.

Note

Show Controller

This check box determines whether the standard QT controller is shown, enabling the user to control the video playback. This option can only be chosen when the video is played Direct to Stage. When this option is checked, the movie is automatically paused at the start and will not play until started via the controller or the movieRate of sprite property. Changing this property at runtime confuses Director and leads to screen artifacts.

The controller is not available for AVI files and the controller of member Lingo property always returns FALSE for Video for Windows (AVI) cast members. The next chapter shows you how to implement a custom controller for both QT and AVI files.

The controller does not include a sound volume control if the QT file does not contain at least one audio track.

If the QT file contains an audio track, even if the sound of member property is FALSE, the controller contains a sound volume control, enabling the user to modify the volume of sprite setting.

Tip

You're in Control

If activated, the controller always appears below the QT sprite on-stage. When placing your QT movie in a graphic frame, be certain to leave room for the controller. The standard QT controller is 16 pixels high on the Macintosh and 19 pixels high under Windows (another reason to use a custom controller).

Beware! The controller's height is reflected in the Sprite Properties dialog box and in the bottom of sprite Lingo property, but not in the height of sprite and height of member Lingo properties.

The controller appears in the foremost video layer, as does the entire video when played Direct to Stage.

The controller itself is drawn using the colors from positions 1, 7, 248, and 256 of the Windows palette. If you are using a custom palette under Windows, make the first and last ten colors the same as those in the Windows System palette to avoid conflicts.

Video Playback Controls

Both QuickTime and Video for Windows are designed to maintain synchronization between the audio and video tracks of a digital video file. In the most common usage, the DV software drops video frames to maintain synchronization if necessary. Director enables you to control the exact method of playback, including whether to drop frames in an attempt to synchronize to the soundtrack or to display every frame without regard to synchronization.

The intrinsic frame rate of a digital video file is specified when it is created in your particular digital video editing software. Director enables you to control whether the intrinsic frame rate is used or not with the options that follow:

Video

The Video option controls the playback synchronization mode of the DV movie.

❊   **Sync to Soundtrack:** This option plays the DV file in the customary time-based mode, and QT or VfW drops video frames to maintain audio and timecode synchronization.

❊   **Play Every Frame (No Sound):** This mode plays the DV file as if it were a straight animation, and QT or VfW does *not* drop frames to maintain synchronization. This mode disables the audio track(s) and is appropriate only for, say, visual transitions in which you want to see every frame of the animation. Performance in this mode is slower than in the standard mode.

Revealing the Frame Rate's Secrets

The `frameRate of member` property does *not* indicate the DV movie's intrinsic frameRate; it indicates the mode in which Director plays back the video. See table 3.1 to interpret the `frameRate of member` property.

Director does not reflect changes to the frameRate at runtime, so set it before playing your video.

If you copy and paste a DV cast member, Director always resets the `frameRate of member` Lingo property to zero (0), which plays the video in Sync to Soundtrack mode. Director also resets the Frames Per Second field to the DV movie's intrinsic frame rate.

Use the Duplicate command to duplicate the DV cast member instead, because it does not suffer from the same problem.

Tip

Finders Keepers: Finding a DV Movie's Intrinsic FrameRate

You *can* trick Director into yielding the intrinsic frame rate of a DV movie by setting its frameRate to an invalid value. This causes the frameRate to reset to the intrinsic rate. The following Lingo uses this trick to return a DV cast member's intrinsic frame rate:

```
on getFrameRate dvMember

  set oldSetting = the frameRate of member dvMember

  -- Set an invalid frame rate to force it to release its secret frameRate
  -- We use -3, because -1 and -2 have special meanings.
  set the frameRate of member dvMember = -3

  -- The frameRate will not be set to -3, but rather to the DV's natural¬
FrameRate.
  set intrinsicFrameRate = the frameRate  of member dvMember

  -- Restore the previous frameRate
  set the frameRate of member dvMember = oldSetting

  return intrinsicFrameRate
end getFrameRate
```

Rate

The Rate options are active only when the Play Every Frame (No Sound) mode has been chosen. In this case, the Rate options determine how fast Director attempts to play the video, but video frames are not dropped if the rate cannot be achieved. The actual rate might be slower.

❖ **Normal:** This option plays every frame of the DV movie no faster than its intrinsic frame rate.

❖ **Maximum:** This option plays every frame of the DV movie as fast as it can. (In Director 4, this option was named Play as fast as possible.)

✤ **Fixed:** This option plays every frame of the DV movie at the rate specified in the adjacent Frames Per Second field.

✤ **Frames Per Second:** This option specifies the frames per second rate for Fixed playback of the DV movie. The default value is the DV movie's intrinsic frame rate, which is defined when the video is created in your DV editing software.

Memory and Loading Options

The Enable Preload and Unload options control how the DV cast members are loaded and unloaded from memory. A fair amount of confusion has surrounded the loading and unloading of assets in Director for some time. Director ordinarily unloads cast members only to make room for others that are needed. In this case, Director unloads cast members at its discretion based on the amount of RAM needed, the purge priority of cast members in RAM, their size, and the last time they were used.

Director always tries to keep the cast members that are needed in the current frame (both puppets and sprites in the Score) in RAM. If there is insufficient RAM for the required cast members, Director drops out the sound and may drop out large background cast members from the lower channels. Use the traceLoad command to watch the loading and unloading of cast members in the Message window.

Enable Preload

The Enable Preload option determines whether a DV movie's data can be preloaded into RAM before playing the movie. The amount of memory used for the preloading of digital video is controlled by the preLoadRAM system property.

In theory, there is no need to preload digital video because it is streamed from your CD-ROM or other device at an acceptably low rate. If this is not the case and sufficient RAM is available, you can preload the digital video. Keep in mind that this may cause a long delay while the video is preloaded, but that the video plays smoothly once loaded into RAM.

This is of practical use only for very small videos in which you want to play every frame, such as a simulated visual transition that has been constructed in Premiere.

Unload

The Unload option is largely irrelevant because DV data is purged immediately after playback. Note that cast members in the current frame are not purged regardless of their purge priority. The Unload option has four possible settings:

❖ **Normal:** Director purges Normal cast members at its discretion to make room for new cast members. This is the default for all cast members.

❖ **Next:** Director purges cast members set to Next only *after* all Normal cast members have been unloaded. Cast members set to Next are not purged *first* as is erroneously described in the Lingo Dictionary and online Help under purgePriority.

❖ **Last:** Director purges cast member set to Last only after all other cast members—except ones tagged Never—have been unloaded. This setting is advisable only for small cast members that are needed frequently.

❖ **Never:** Director does not unload cast members set to Never. Note that such cast members are not necessarily loaded, but if they are, they are not be unloaded. No good reason exists to use this setting, and it should be avoided. In a low memory situation, Director might need to unload even those cast members used throughout a project. If you set too many cast members to Never, Director may lock up or cause the machine to crash. Use the Last setting for vital cast members instead.

Lingo Equivalents to the Digital Video Cast Member Properties Dialog Box

All the properties that are editable in the Digital Video Cast Member Properties dialog box are settable via Lingo. Table 3.1 indicates the Lingo equivalent for each of the options in the dialog box.

TABLE 3.1

LINGO EQUIVALENTS TO THE DIGITAL VIDEO CAST MEMBER PROPERTY DIALOG BOX

Cast Member	Info Option Lingo Equivalent	See Also
Cast Member Name	the name of member	the castLibNum of member
File Name	the fileName of member (includes path)	the name of member
Video	the video of member	the sound of member
Sound	the sound of member	the volume of sprite, the soundLevel, the soundEnabled
Paused	the pausedAtStart of member	the controller of member
Loop	the loop of member	the movieTime of sprite
Crop	the crop of member = TRUE	the center of member
Scale	the crop of member = FALSE	the center of member
Center	the center of member	the crop of member
Direct to Stage	the directToStage of member	the ink of member, the controller of member
Controller	the controller of member	the directToStage of member, the pausedAtStart of member
Sync to Soundtrack	the frameRate of member = 0	the movieRate of sprite
Play Every Frame (no sound)	no synchronization	(refer to the following entries)
Normal	the frameRate of member = −1	the movieRate of sprite
Maximum	the frameRate of member = −2	the movieRate of sprite
Fixed	the frameRate of member = n (n > 1, specified in fps field)	fps field in dialog box
Enable Preload	the preLoad of member	the preLoadRAM, unLoad, unLoadCast, the loaded of member, preLoad, preLoadCast, the ramNeeded, the traceLoad, preLoad, preLoadCast

continues

Table 3.1, *Continued*

Lingo Equivalents to the Digital Video Cast Member Property Dialog Box		
Cast Member	*Info Option Lingo Equivalent*	*See Also*
Normal	the purgePriority of member = 3	
Next	the purgePriority of member = 2	
Last	the purgePriority of member = 1	
Never	the purgePriority of member = 0	
Dimensions	the width, height and rect of member	the width, height and rect of sprite
Duration	the duration of member/60.0	the movieTime of member
Size	See Tip for finding DV's true external file size	the size of member, the duration of member
FrameRate	See Tip for finding DV's true intrinsic frameRate	the frameRate of member, the movieRate of sprite

Digital Video-Related Lingo Commands

There are dozens of Lingo commands that pertain to digital video issues. The majority are digital video cast member properties and sprite properties, some of which are general properties that apply to various data types, and some of which are specific to digital video assets. Some digital video properties can only be tested, and others can also be set. Additional Lingo commands provide information about the system rather than about an individual digital video cast member. The following section explores these system-wide digital video properties.

Digital Video System-Wide Properties

The following properties pertain to the playback environment, rather than a specific digital video cast member. They can be all be tested, but only the `digitalVideoTimeScale` can be set.

* **the `digitalVideoTimeScale`:** This system property determines the time units that Director uses to measure time for digital video cast members. It defaults to 60 (1/60th of a second) on the Macintosh and under Windows, and can be tested and set.

❋ **the `quickTimePresent`:** This system property indicates whether QuickTime is installed. It can be tested but not set. Most Macintosh computers will have QuickTime installed, although it might not be the latest version. In Director for Windows 5, the 32-bit version of QTW is required when running the 32-bit version of Director or a 32-bit projector. The `quickTimePresent` is only TRUE if the appropriate version is installed. Likewise, when running the 16-bit version of Director or a 16-bit projector under Windows 3.1 or Windows 95, the 16-bit version of QTW is required.

> You can launch your QT installer if the user does not have QuickTime installed by using the following code:
>
> ```
> on checkForQT
>    if not (the quickTimePresent) then
>       alert "You need to install QuickTime to use this product"
>       -- Put the name of your installer here:
>     open "QTINSTAL.EXE"
>       quit
>    end if
> end checkForQT
> ```

Tip

❋ **the `videoForWindowsPresent`:** This system property indicates whether Video for Windows is installed. It can be tested but not set. It always returns FALSE on the Macintosh. Video for Windows is installed as part of Windows 95 and with Director 5.

Digital Video Cast Member and Sprite Properties

In an earlier section we examined the DV cast member properties that can be set via the Digital Video Cast Member Properties dialog box. This section provides a complete listing of all the digital video cast member and sprite properties, including ones that are not specific to digital video assets. The following list is in alphabetical order.

Properties that pertain exclusively to digital video cast members or sprites are indicated by an asterisk (*). Two asterisks (**) indicate that the property is set via the Digital Video Cast Member Properties dialog box. Properties that pertain to other types of cast members and sprites are discussed in specific regard to DV issues. Review this list carefully, even if you are familiar with these properties.

* **the backColor of sprite:** This property specifies the background color of a sprite. It defaults to 0 (white) and can be tested and set. It is only relevant if you are using the DV non-Direct to Stage with the background transparent ink effect (applicable only to QT movies on the Macintosh or AVI files on Windows). Refer to the ink of sprite and directToStage of member properties.

* the bottom of sprite: This property indicates the location of the bottom edge of the DV sprite relative to the top of the stage. This property can be tested but not set. Change the value via the loc of sprite or rect of sprite properties instead. This value does include the height of the standard QT controller if the controller of member property is set (not available for AVI sprites). The height of the standard controller is an additional 16 pixels on the Macintosh and 19 pixels under Windows. Refer to the loc of sprite, rect of sprite, controller of member, top of sprite and height of sprite properties.

* **the cast of member:** This property indicates the castLib number and member index associated with a cast member. The cast of member n is equivalent to member n. This property can be tested but not set. Refer to the memberNum of member, cast of sprite, and castNum of sprite properties.

* **the cast of sprite:** This property indicates the castLib number and member index of the cast member associated with a sprite. This property has been replaced by the member of sprite property in Director 5. This property can be tested and set. Refer to the memberNum of member, cast of member, castNum of sprite, and member of sprite properties.

* **the castLibNum of member:** This property returns the number of the cast library in which the cast member exists. This property can be tested but not set. Refer to the member of sprite, memberNum of sprite, and castLibNum of sprite properties.

* **the castLibNum of sprite:** This property returns the number of the cast library in which a sprite's cast member exists. This property can be tested but not set. This may be useful for asset management now that Director 5 supports multiple casts. The first internal cast is always castLibNum 1 (one). Refer to the member of sprite, memberNum of sprite, and castLibNum of sprite properties.

* **the castNum of sprite:** This property returns a *unique* number identifying the cast member of the sprite in question. It is equal to

(the castLibNum) × 131072+the memberNum

It is *not* equivalent to the `memberNum` of sprite property in Director 5. The memberNum of sprite returns the offset of a member *within* a cast library, which is not unique, whereas the castLibNum includes the offset from the beginning of the first cast library. This property can be tested and set. Refer to the `memberNum of sprite`, `member of sprite`, and `cast of sprite` properties.

☀ **the `castType of member`:** This property indicates the asset type of the cast member and returns #digitalVideo for QT and AVI cast members. This property can be tested but not set. Use the following to determine a sprite's type:

```
the castType of member (the member of sprite x)
```

Refer to the type of member property.

☀ **the `center of member`**:** This property controls whether the center or upper-left portion of a movie is visible when it is cropped. It can be tested and set. Refer to the discussion of Framing Options in the DV Cast Member Properties dialog box and the `crop of member` property.

☀ **the `controller of member`**:** This property determines whether the standard QT controller is visible. This property can be tested and set, but setting it at runtime is not advised. The height of the standard controller is an additional 16 pixels on the Macintosh and 19 pixels under Windows. This height is *not* reflected in the `height of sprite` and `height of member` Lingo properties, but it *is* reflected in the Sprite Properties dialog box and in the bottom of sprite property. Refer also to the `directToStage` and `pausedAtStart of member` properties.

☀ **the `crop of member`**:** This property determines whether a DV cast member is scaled or cropped when it is displayed as a sprite smaller than the DV movie's original dimensions. This property can be tested and set. Refer to the discussion of Framing Options in the DV Cast Member Properties dialog box and `the center of member` property.

☀ **the `digitalVideoType of member`*:** This property specifies the cast member's digital video type and returns either #quickTime or #videoForWindows. This property can be tested, but not set. Testing this property for a non-digital video member results in a syntax error, so always test `if the type of member = #digitalVideo` first. Refer to the `type of member` property.

* **the directToStage of member**:** This property determines whether the video is played through Director's compositing buffer or directly to the stage, bypassing Director. This results in much better performance and causes the sprite to behave as if the trails of sprite property is set. This property can be tested and set, but setting it at runtime is not advised. Refer to the discussion of Stage Display Options in the DV Cast Member Properties dialog box and also to the controller of member property.

* **the duration of member*:** This property specifies the length of the DV movie in ticks (60ths of a second). To convert to seconds, divide by 60. This property can be tested, but not set. If the movieTime of sprite x = the duration of member y, the movie has reached its end.

* **the fileName of member**:** This property specifies the external file to which this DV movie is linked. This property can be tested and set. Refer to the earlier discussion of this property for important details regarding file-naming conventions.

* **the foreColor of sprite:** This property defaults to 255 (black) and is not generally useful to change, but it can be tested and set.

* **the frameRate of member**:** This property specifies the playback mode, not the actual frameRate of the DV cast member. This property can be tested and set. Refer to the earlier discussion of this property for complete details on the available modes and also to the movieRate of sprite property. The next chapter also provides examples of using this property.

* **the height of member:** This property specifies the height of the original DV cast member and can be tested but not set. The height of the DV movie should always be an integer multiple of four (4) for optimal performance. This value does *not* include the height of the standard QT controller even if the controller of member property is set (not available for AVI sprites). The height of the standard controller is an additional 16 pixels on the Macintosh and 19 pixels under Windows. Refer to the controller of member, top of sprite, height of sprite, bottom of member, and width of member properties.

* **the height of sprite:** The height of the sprite on-stage should always be an integer multiple of the cast member's height for optimal performance. This property can be tested, but not set directly. Set the loc of sprite or rect of sprite instead. This value does *not* include the height of the standard QT controller, even if the controller of member property is set

(not available for AVI sprites). The height of the standard controller is an additional 16 pixels on the Macintosh and 19 pixels under Windows. The sprite's height, as indicated in the Sprite Properties dialog box *does* include the height of the controller, if any. Refer to `the controller of member`, `rect of sprite`, `loc of sprite`, `top of sprite`, `height of sprite`, `bottom of member`, and `width of member` properties.

✱ **the `ink of sprite`:** This property can be set to background transparent to enable the background graphic to show through a DV sprite. This setting is ignored when a cast member is played Direct to Stage, in which case the ink is treated as copy. With QT sprite on the Macintosh and AVI sprites under Windows, this can be used for non-Direct to Stage sprites. Under Windows, QT is always played Direct to Stage and this setting is ignored. Refer to `the directToStage of member` and `backColor of sprite` properties.

✱ **the `left of sprite`:** This property indicates the location of the left edge of the DV sprite relative to the stage. This value should always be an integer multiple of four (4) for optimal performance. This property can be tested, but not set directly. Set the loc of sprite or rect of sprite property instead. Refer to `the top of sprite`, `width of sprite`, `height of sprite`, `loc of sprite`, `bottom of sprite`, and `right of sprite` properties.

✱ **the `loaded of member`:** This property indicates whether the cast member is currently loaded in RAM and is mostly meaningless for DV cast members; the DV header may be loaded, but the video and audio data are always streamed from disk. It can be tested and set indirectly using the `preLoad` or `unLoad` command. Refer to the `preLoadRAM` and the `purgePriority of member` properties.

✱ **the `loc of sprite`:** This property indicates the coordinates of registration point of the DV sprite on-stage. This property can be tested and set. To move a DV sprite off-stage, first puppet the sprite and then set its location to some location off-screen, such as

```
set the loc of sprite x = point (-1000, -1000)
```

Refer to `the regPoint of member`, `locH of sprite`, and `the locV of sprite` properties.

✱ **the `locH of sprite`:** This property indicates the horizontal coordinate of the registration point of the DV sprite on-stage. This property can be tested and set. The regPoint is always located at the midpoint of left of sprite and right of sprite properties. Refer to the regPoint of member, loc of sprite, and locV of sprite properties.

☆   **the locV of sprite:** This property indicates the vertical coordinate of the registration point of the DV sprite on stage. This property can be tested and set. The regPoint is always the located at midpoint of top of sprite and bottom of sprite properties. Refer to the regPoint of member, loc of sprite and locH of sprite properties.

☆   **the loop of member**:** This property specifies whether the movie repeats from the beginning after it reaches the end. This property can be tested and set. Refer to the discussion of the DV Cast Member Properties dialog box's Loop option and also to the duration of member property.

☆   **the media of member:** This property is intended to allow you to copy data from one cast member to another. This property can be tested, but not set. The property is 0 (zero) for all linked assets—including QT movies and AVI files—and cannot be used to copy linked cast members.

☆   **the member of sprite:** This property specifies the sprite's cast member index as well as its castLibNum. This property can be tested and set. This is the preferred syntax to replace the cast of sprite property used in earlier versions of Director. Use this property rather than the memberNum of sprite property when swapping new DV movies into your digital video sprites. Refer to the memberNum of member, memberNum of sprite, cast of sprite, castLibNum of member, and castLibNum of sprite properties.

☆   **member n:** This Lingo keyword is used in other expressions and specifies the cast member's index as well as its castLibNum. This can be used to uniquely identify a cast member regardless of the cast library in which it resides. Refer to the memberNum of sprite, cast of sprite, castNum of sprite, castLibNum of member, and castLibNum of sprite properties.

☆   **the memberNum of member:** This property specifies the offset of a cast member within a cast library. This property can be tested but not set. This does *not* uniquely identify a cast member because any cast member at the same offset within a different cast library has the same memberNum value. The member keyword should be used instead to uniquely identify a cast member. Refer also to the memberNum of sprite, member of sprite, the castLibNum of member, and the castLibNum of sprite properties.

- **the memberNum of sprite:** This property specifies the offset of the cast member associated with the sprite, but *not* its castLibNum. This property can be tested and set. This does *not* uniquely identify a cast member because the value is relative to the beginning of the cast member's cast library, and any cast member at the same offset within a different cast library has the same memberNum value. The member of sprite property should be used instead to uniquely identify a sprite's cast member. Refer to the memberNum of member, member of sprite, castLibNum of member, and castLibNum of sprite properties.

- **the memberType of member:** Although this property is documented in the Lingo Dictionary, using it causes a syntax error. Refer to the type of member and castType of member properties instead.

- **the modified of member:** This property indicates whether a cast member has been edited since the file was last saved and is set to TRUE if you edited a DV cast member. Ordinarily, you edit your DV assets in a separate video editing tool, such as Premiere, but it is possible to edit QT movies in the Digital Video window on the Macintosh. If you manually set this property to TRUE, which you ordinarily would not do, Director attempts to resave your external DV cast member.

- **the movieRate of sprite*:** This property specifies the playback speed of the DV, *relative to the DV file's intrinsic frame rate*. It can be tested and set. Setting the movieRate of sprite equal to 0 (zero) stops the movie; 1 (one) indicates normal speed; 2 (two) indicates double speed, and so on. The audio continues to play even if the movieRate is faster or slower than normal, or even backward. Refer to the movieTime of sprite, duration of member, and frameRate of member properties. Refer also to Chapter 4 which contains extensive examples of this property's usage.

- **the movieTime of sprite*:** This property specifies the current location within the movie in ticks (60ths of a second). It can be tested and set. To convert to seconds, divide by 60. By comparing the movieTime to the duration of member property, you can determine if the movie has reached the end. Refer to the movieRate of sprite and duration of member properties. Refer also to Chapter 4, which contains extensive examples of this property's usage.

- **the name of member**:** This property refers to the cast member name that can be used to refer to the cast member, regardless of its position in the cast. It can be tested and set. It defaults to the name of the linked DV file, excluding the path specification.

❋ **the number of member:** This property is useful for finding the number of a cast member, given its name.

❋ **the pausedAtStart of member**:** This property determines whether to play the movie immediately when it first appears in the Score. It can be tested and set. This is equivalent to initializing the movieRate of member property to zero. To start the movie playing, set the movieRate of sprite property to 1. Refer to the discussion of the Paused option earlier in this chapter as well as the movieRate of sprite property.

❋ **the preLoad of member**:** This property specifies whether Director can preload DV movie data into RAM. It can be tested and set. Setting this property tends to give faster startup and performance until the preloaded data runs out, at which point a hitch in the playback may be noticeable. The amount of memory used to preload the DV data is limited by the preLoadRAM system property. Refer to preLoad, preLoadMember, the purgePriority of member, and the preLoadRAM.

❋ **the puppet of sprite:** This property determines whether the sprite is controlled via the Score or Lingo. This property can be tested and set. Set the property to TRUE (1) to control the sprite via Lingo and set it to FALSE to return control to the Score. Use the updateStage command to force changes to take effect. The property can be used in conjunction with the rect of sprite property to dynamically resize a DV sprite, as demonstrated in the next chapter. Refer to the rect of sprite, width of sprite, and height of sprite properties.

❋ **the purgePriority of member**:** This property specifies when Director may purge this cast member. It can be tested and set to one of four values (0 to 3). It is meaningless for most DV cast members because, although the header may remain loaded, the video and audio data are always immediately purged after being played. Refer to the detailed discussion of the memory loading earlier in the chapter.

❋ **the rect of sprite:** This property specifies the sprite area of a DV sprite. It can be tested and set, but the sprite must be puppeted for changes to take effect. The next chapter demonstrates how to use this property to dynamically resize a DV sprite. Refer to the puppet of sprite, width of sprite, and height of sprite properties.

❋ **the regPoint of member:** This property is supposed to indicate the offset of the cast member's registration point relative to its upper left corner. It can be tested but not set for DV cast members (it can be set for bitmap cast members). The regPoint of a DV cast member is always erroneously reported as point (0,0), but is actually located at the center of the cast member. To find the true regPoint use

```
set QTregPoint = point ((the width of member x)/2, (the height of
    member x / 2)).
```

✲ the right of sprite: This property indicates the location of the right edge of the DV sprite relative to the left of the Stage. This property can be tested, but not set directly. Set the loc of sprite or rect of sprite property instead. Refer to the left of sprite and width of sprite properties.

✲ the scale of member**: If a DV cast member is scaleable, it is resized on-stage if it is a different size than the DV sprite. Otherwise the DV cast member is cropped. Although there is a Scale option in the Digital Video Cast Member Properties dialog box, there is no Lingo property of the same name. If the crop of member property is FALSE (0) then the DV cast member is scaled when it appears on-stage. The crop of member property can be tested and set. Refer to the crop of member property.

✲ setTrackEnabled*: This function turns individual DV data tracks within the DV file on or off. It is most useful for DV movies with multiple sound or text tracks that you want to change at runtime. This is convenient for localization. Refer to the trackCount of member, trackType of member, trackCount of sprite, and trackType of sprite properties and the trackEnabled function.

✲ the size of member: This property is supposed to reflect the size of the cast member, but it returns meaningless (and different) values on the Macintosh, Windows 3.1, and Windows 95. The value returned by Lingo does not match the size of the external data file and does not even match the size shown in the DV Cast Member Properties dialog box. Refer to the Tip at the beginning of this chapter that demonstrates a way to retrieve the actual file size.

✲ the sound of member**: This property specifies whether the DV file's audio tracks are audible. This property can be tested and set. It may be TRUE even though the DV file does not contain any audio tracks. Refer to the trackCount of member and trackType of member properties to determine if a DV file contains audio tracks. Refer also to the video of member and volume of sprite properties, the setTrackEnabled command and the trackEnabled function.

❋ **the startTime of sprite*:** When a digital video movie is played, the startTime property determines where playback begins and is measured in ticks. This property can be tested and set, and defaults to 0 (zero). Refer to the Director 5.0.1 ReadMe file for more information because this property was omitted from the Director 5 documentation. Refer also to the duration of member, stopTime of sprite and movieTime of sprite properties and the examples in the following chapter.

❋ **the stopTime of sprite*:** When a digital video movie is played, the stopTime property determines where playback ends and is measured in ticks. This property can be tested and set, and defaults to the duration of the cast member associated with the sprite. Refer to the Director 5.0.1 ReadMe file because this property was omitted from the Director 5 documentation. Refer also to the duration of member, startTime of sprite and movieTime of sprite properties and the examples in the following chapter.

❋ **the stretch of sprite*:** This property indicates whether a sprite is stretchable and can be tested and set. It is generally not useful to set it for a DV sprite, unless you will be changing the sprite's size on-the-fly. To scale a DV sprite, set its crop of member property to FALSE. Refer to the crop of member and rect of sprite properties.

❋ **the timeScale of member*:** This property specifies the time unit on which the digital video's frames are based. QuickTime's digital video timeScale is typically 600 (1/600th of a second). This property can be tested, but not set. For Video for Windows, the timeScale is 60 (1/60th of a second).

❋ **the top of sprite:** This property indicates the location of the top edge of the DV sprite relative to the top of the stage and should be an integer multiple of four (4) for optimal performance. It can be tested but not set. Use the loc of sprite or locV of sprite commands to change the sprite's location. See the loc of sprite, locV of sprite, left of sprite, the width of sprite, the height of sprite, and the bottom of sprite properties.

❋ **the trackCount of sprite or member*:** This property indicates the number of tracks in the DV sprite or cast member. This property can be tested but not set. A standard DV file might contain two tracks—a single audio track and a single video track. Refer to the trackType of member, trackType of sprite, and trackText of sprite properties and the trackEnabled function.

❋ **trackEnabled(sprite n, trackNum)***: This function indicates whether the specified track of the specified sprite is enabled. If not enabled, the track does not play. This attribute can be tested, but not set with the trackEnabled function. Use the setTrackEnabled command to enable and disable individual tracks. QuickTime for Windows version 2.1.2 and earlier only support one audio track and one video track and do not support text tracks, so the value reported may not be reliable in some cases. Refer to the trackCount of sprite, trackCount of member, and trackType of sprite properties and the setTrackEnabled function.

❋ **trackNextKeyTime(sprite n, trackNum)***: This function indicates the time of the next key frame that follows the current time for the specified track and sprite. This property can be tested, but not set. It can be used to find the next key frame in a video track, but does not appear reliable in the most recent version of Director (5.0.1). Refer to the movieTime of sprite and duration of member properties and the trackPreviousKeyTime function.

❋ **trackNextSampleTime(sprite n, trackNum)***: This function indicates the time of the next sample frame that follows the current time for the specified track and sprite. This property can be tested, but not set. It can be used to find the next audio sample in an audio track, but does not appear reliable in the most recent version of Director (5.0.1). Refer to the movieTime of sprite and duration of member properties and the trackPreviousSampleTime function.

❋ **trackPreviousKeyTime(sprite n, trackNum)***: This function indicates the time of the previous key frame that precedes the current time for the specified track and sprite. This property can be tested, but not set. It can be used to find the previous key frame in a video track, but does not appear reliable in the most recent version of Director (5.0.1). Refer to the movieTime of sprite and duration of member properties, and the trackNextKeyTime function.

❋ **trackPreviousSampleTime(sprite n, trackNum)***: This function indicates the time of the previous sample frame that precedes the current time for the specified track and sprite. This property can be tested, but not set. It can be used to find the previous audio sample in an audio track, but does not appear reliable in the most recent version of Director (5.0.1). Refer to the movieTime of sprite and duration of member properties and the trackNextSampleTime function.

❋ **trackStartTime(sprite or member n)*:** This property indicates the starting time of the specified track within the DV file associated with the specified sprite or cast member. This is ordinarily zero (0) for tracks that start at the beginning of the DV file. It can be tested but not set. It is *not* analogous to the startTime of sprite property that is used to cue a certain segment of the DV file. Refer to the startTime of sprite, stopTime of sprite, and duration of member properties and the trackStopTime function.

❋ **trackStopTime(sprite or member n)*:** This property indicates the stopping time of the specified track within the DV file associated with the specified sprite or cast member. This is ordinarily equal to the duration of the DV file for tracks that last until the end of the DV file. It can be tested but not set. It is *not* analogous to the stopTime of sprite property that is used to cue a certain segment of the DV file. The trackStopTime (member *member*) property operates incorrectly in both the alphabetical and categorical Lingo menus. If you use these menus to insert the command into your Lingo code, the keyword member is omitted, leading to a syntax error unless you add the keyword manually. Refer to the stopTime of sprite, startTime of sprite, trackStartTime of sprite, and duration of member properties, and the trackStartTime function.

❋ **trackText(sprite n, trackNum)*:** This function returns the text of the specified track of the specified sprite and can be tested, but not set. For non-Text tracks, it returns <Void>. Note that there is no trackText of member function. Refer to the trackType of sprite and trackType of member properties.

❋ **trackType (sprite or member n, trackNum)*:** This function returns the type of the specified track of the specified sprite or member. It can be tested, but not set. Possible values are #video, #sound, #text and #music. This function returns <Void> if the specified track number is greater than the track count. Refer to the trackCount of sprite or member property.

❋ **the trails of sprite:** Playing a DV movie Direct to Stage creates *trails*, in effect, but this property can be tested and set separately. Refer to the discussion of the Direct to Stage option which includes hints for erasing trails left by a DV sprite.

❋ **the type of member:** This property indicates the cast member's asset type. It can be tested, but not set. It returns #digitalVideo for QT and AVI cast members. Use the following to determine a sprite's type:

```
the type of member (the member of sprite x)
```

rather than the type of sprite property. Refer to the digitalVideoType of member property.

❋ **the type of sprite:** This returns the integer 16 for digital video cast members and some other types too. Thus, it is fairly unreliable. It can be tested, but not set. Use the type of member or the castType of member property instead.

❋ **the video of member**:** This property specifies whether the DV file's video track is enabled. It can be tested and set. It may be TRUE even though the DV file does not contain any video tracks. Refer to the trackCount of member and trackType of member properties to determine is a DV file contains video tracks. Refer also to the sound of member and volume of sprite properties, the setTrackEnabled command, and the trackEnabled function.

❋ **the visible of sprite:** This property specifies whether the DV sprite is visible on-stage. This can be used to eliminate the trails left by DV sprites played Direct to Stage. Refer to the earlier discussion regarding cleaning up Director artifacts.

❋ **the volume of sprite*:** This property specifies the volume of the DV sprite. It can be tested and set. Useful values range from 0 to 255, but it can be set louder as well. Note that the volume of sound property does not affect DV sprites, but the soundLevel does. The Lingo Dictionary entry under "digitalVideo" refers the user to the volume of member property. No such property exists. Use the volume of sprite property instead. Refer to the soundLevel property.

❋ **the width of member:** This property specifies the horizontal dimension of the DV cast member. The width of the DV movie should always be an integer multiple of four (4) for optimal performance. Refer to the height of member and width of sprite properties.

❋ **the width of sprite:** This property specifies the horizontal dimension of the DV sprite. This property can be tested, but not set directly. Set the loc of sprite or rect of sprite property instead. The width of the sprite on stage should always be an integer multiple of the cast member's width for optimal performance. Refer to the height of sprite and width of member properties.

Relevant Sound-Related Lingo Commands

The Macintosh possesses multiple sound channels, so you can play QuickTime sound tracks simultaneously with other non-QuickTime audio files or sound cast members. Windows has only one sound channel, but Director's Macromix DLL mixes digital sounds to simulate multichannel audio.

Unfortunately, QuickTime for Windows and Video for Windows seize the sound channel, so that Director cannot play AIFF, WAV, or cast member sounds while a DV file with an audio track is playing. Likewise, Macromix seizes the sound channel when it plays a sound, so DV audio will not be heard. Use these commands to kill any sounds that Director is currently playing and enable DV audio to be played:

```
puppetSound 0
sound close 1
sound close 2
```

Conclusion

This chapter has analyzed the dozens of digital video cast member and sprite properties in the broader context of digital video playback. We have examined each option in the Digital Video Cast Member Properties dialog box and its effect on DV playback in detail. We have explored potential pitfalls when using various options and the subtle differences between digital video on different platforms. This chapter has included numerous notes on Director's deficiencies and quirks and how to overcome them. You now have a solid understanding of the technical aspects of digital video and the Director commands for digital video control. Chapter 4 covers specific Lingo examples that implement the most commonly requested functionality for controlling digital video.

chapter 4

Bruce Epstein

CONTROLLING DIGITAL VIDEO VIA LINGO

In Chapter 3, Lingo commands that can be used to analyze and manipulate virtually any aspect of digital video playback were examined. This chapter explores some real-life scenarios for controlling digital video via Lingo.

This discussion applies to the most common digital video formats: QuickTime for Macintosh (QTM), QuickTime for Windows (QTW) and Video for Windows (VFW). Subtle differences are noted where appropriate. The exact performance of each type of digital video can vary with the version of Director and the version of QTM, QTW, or VFW in use. Although these examples are a strong foundation and can often be used verbatim, be certain to test your individual configuration carefully. Note that VFW uses movies in AVI format whereas QTM and QTW use movies in MOV format.

Digital video (DV) playback is just like using a tape recorder or VCR. You have rewind, fast forward, stop, and play controls. The most important Lingo commands for controlling DV sprites are the `movieTime of sprite` and the `movieRate of sprite` properties.

The `movieTime` specifies the current point in the DV sprite (similar to the tape counter on a VCR) and is measured in ticks (60ths of a second). It ranges from 0 to the length of the DV cast member, as specified by the `duration of member` property. The `movieRate` specifies the playback speed of the DV sprite in question, which can be positive (play forward), negative (play backward), or zero (stopped).

Digital Video Sprite and Member Properties

In addition to the standard properties that pertain to all types of media, Director supports numerous properties specific to digital video cast members and sprites. These properties are covered in detail in Chapter 3, "Lights, Camera, Action!—Working with Digital Video in Director." Let's examine how these properties are tested and set via Lingo.

Differentiating Between Sprite and Member Properties

Don't confuse digital video `sprite` properties with `member` properties. `member` properties are generally set in the Digital Video Cast Member Properties dialog box, and apply to all sprite instances of a cast member in the Score. Director generally does not like to change these member properties at runtime, although there are Lingo commands to do so.

Changing the `directToStage of member` property at runtime, for example, will confuse Director and leave various artifacts on the screen. Thus, don't expect to have the same DV movie play Direct to Stage in one part of the Score and non-Direct to Stage elsewhere. If need be, create two different cast members that link to the same external DV file, but with different member properties. The `directToStage` property is used for illustrative purposes, and applies only to QT movies on the Macintosh and VFW (AVI) movies under Windows. Changing the `directToStage` property at runtime does not effect QTW sprites under Windows.

On the other hand, sprite properties are intended to be set at runtime and can be different for each sprite instance of a particular cast member. Digital video-specific sprite properties behave somewhat differently from generic sprite properties. You need not puppet a DV sprite to set its `movieRate`, `movieTime`, `volume`, and `visible` properties. Do not puppet the sprite unless you have other reasons for doing so.

For illustrative purposes, `sprite` x or `member` y are used in the following code examples. In your Lingo, you would either substitute in the sprite channel or member number, or set some value for x or y, perhaps as a parameter to a generalized function.

Thus, if the Lingo is presented as the following

```
set the directToStage of member y = TRUE
```

you would actually need to substitute some valid value or variable for y, such as

```
set the directToStage of member "MyVideo" = TRUE
```

or

```
set whichCastmember = "MyVideo"
```

```
set the directToStage of member whichCastmember = TRUE
```

A `put` statement or `alert` statement demonstrates the results of an `if` clause, as in

```
if (the movieRate of sprite x = TRUE) then put "The movie is ¬
playing"
```

Use this for debugging when necessary, and remove these statements prior to completing your project.

Note

Avoiding Digital Video Sprite Errors

You may encounter the dreaded `Not a digital video sprite` error when trying to set a DV sprite property. *Sprite properties can only be set in the frame in which the sprite appears.* That is, to set a DV sprite's `movieTime` property, the playback head must be in the same frame as the DV sprite.

To set the `movieTime`, `movieRate`, and `volume` sprite properties before the DV sprite appears on the stage, you can place the sprite off-stage or make the sprite invisible before going to the frame. (In this case, you also should set the `pausedAtStart of member` property to TRUE to prevent the DV from playing while it is off-stage.)

Tip

> To prevent syntax errors, you can also check the type of a sprite using
>
> ```
> if the castType of member (the member of sprite x) = ¬
> #digitalVideo then
>
>     -- Okay to set digitalVideo sprite properties
>
>     set the volume of sprite x = 255
>
> end if
> ```
>
> If you still encounter `Not a digital video sprite` errors, check that you are referencing the correct sprite channel. If specifying the sprite channel with a constant, make certain the sprite is in the proper channel. If using a variable, check its value in the Debugger, Watcher, or Message window.

The Basics: Start, Stop, Rewind, Fast-Forward

You may want to allow the user to control the playback of digital video within your application via a DV controller. For QT movies, you can enable the standard QT controller via the Controller check box in the Digital Video Cast Member Properties dialog box. The standard controller is not available for VFW (AVI) files. You may provide a custom controller if

❉   The standard controller doesn't look good in your custom palette

❉   You prefer different artwork for your controller buttons

❉   You want to add or remove features from the set provided by the standard controller

❉   You want to provide a controller for VFW (AVI) files

You can use these basic components to a simple DV controller with Lingo. Refer to the sample movie showing the full implementation.

Playing a DV Sprite at Normal Speed

On the most basic level, you can control a DV movie by specifying its playback rate via the `movieRate of sprite` property. You must set the `movieRate` to play a

DV sprite that is set to pausedAtStart or has its controller enabled, both of which prevent it from playing when the sprite is first placed on-stage. The following will start the movie playing at normal speed:

```
set the movieRate of sprite x = 1
```

Stopping a Digital Video Movie

You can stop a DV sprite from playing by setting its movieRate to zero. The following will stop the movie:

```
set the movieRate of sprite x = 0
```

When you stop the movie, the movieTime of sprite property remains set to the point where the movie was stopped. You can implement a pause and resume feature by toggling the movieRate on and off, as follows:

```
set the movieRate of sprite x = not (the movieRate of sprite x)
```

Recueing a Digital Video Movie

Whenever you start a DV movie, it always begins playing at the position specified by its movieTime property. Thus, by adjusting the movieTime, you can control which portion of the DV movie is played. The beginning of a DV movie corresponds to a movieTime of zero. The following will rewind the DV movie:

```
set the movieTime of sprite x = 0
```

Note that this resets the DV movie instantly to the beginning, so it is really recueing the movie, not rewinding it. The next section, "Rewinding a Digital Video Movie," explains simulating a rewind.

Rewinding a Digital Video Movie

By setting the movieRate to a value other than zero or one, you can create simple special effects. Set the movieRate to a negative number to play the DV movie backward. The more negative the movieRate, the faster the movie plays backward. Negative numbers between 0 and –1 result in slow-motion backward playback. Numbers less than –1 result in fast, backward playback. As you play the movie faster, QT or VFW will ordinarily drop video frames to achieve the specified playback rate. If you set too fast a rate, the video may jump abruptly.

The movieRate can be an integer value, such as –2, or a decimal value such as –1.5. The following plays the movie backward at twice the normal speed:

```
set the movieRate of sprite x = -2
```

Note that Director will also play the audio portion of the DV movie backward. You may want to shut off the DV audio by using

```
set the volume of sprite x = 0
```

Restore the volume using

```
set the volume of sprite x = 255
```

Fast-Forwarding a Digital Video Movie

By setting the movieRate to a value greater than one, you can fast-forward the movie. The higher the movieRate, the faster the movie plays. Rates between 0 and 1 result in slow playback. Numbers greater than 1 result in fast playback. As you play the movie faster, QT or VFW will ordinarily drop video frames to achieve the specified playback rate. If you set too fast a rate, the video may jump abruptly. The movieRate can be an integer value, such as 2, or a decimal value such as 1.5. The following plays the movie forward at twice the normal speed:

```
set the movieRate of sprite x = 2
```

Note that Director will also play the audio portion at a faster rate than normal.

Jumping to the End of a Digital Video Movie

You may need to jump to the end of a DV movie. The duration of member property reflects the length of a DV cast member and is measured in ticks (60ths of a second). By setting the movieTime of sprite to the duration of member, the DV movie is fast-forwarded instantly to the end. Note that the movieTime is a sprite property, whereas the duration is a member property. Use the member of sprite property to determine the cast member associated with a sprite.

```
set the movieTimeof sprite x = the duration of member (the member of¬
    sprite x
```

Use the `member of sprite` property rather than the `memberNum of sprite` property when using multiple casts to ensure that the cast member is uniquely identified, including its `castLibNum`.

Note

Beyond the Basics: Deeper into the movieRate and the movieTime

Now that we have explored basic Lingo control of DV sprites, we can use the `movieRate` and `movieTime` properties to implement more sophisticated features.

Restarting a Digital Video Movie

It is often desirable to restart a DV movie, or you may give the user the option of restarting a DV movie. This is accomplished by using the following script. Note that the movie is paused before changing the `movieTime` to prevent the visual *hitch* that occurs if you set the `movieTime` while the movie is playing.

```
on restartVideo dvSpriteNum
  -- Stop the video
  set the movieRate of sprite dvSpriteNum = 0
  -- Reset the video to the beginning
  set the movieTime of sprite dvSpriteNum = 0
  -- Start the video playing again
  set the movieRate of sprite dvSpriteNum = 1
  end restartVideo
```

Take Pause and Get Unhitched

A common error is to rewind the movie, often in an initialization routine, even though it was not paused. This makes the DV movie appear as though it has trouble starting smoothly.

You cannot stop a DV movie using `set the movieRate of sprite x = 0` until the sprite is actually placed on-stage. (Remember it is a `sprite` property, not a `member` property.) By that time, it is too late because the movie starts playing immediately when on-stage. A few frames will play and any rewinding will be noticeable.

Tip

When controlling such a DV sprite, you must set the `pausedAtStart of member y` = TRUE (or check the Paused option in the DV Cast Member Property dialog box). This ensures that the movie does not start playing before you instruct it to do so.

Implementing a movieTime Scrub Controller

Earlier, we implemented the basic features of a custom DV controller. This section covers the hardest part of such a controller—the slider that controls the `movieTime`. Note that the following scripts update the video frame while the slider is being dragged, and update the slider position as the DV movie plays. Refer to the sample movie for a complete implementation.

The following global variables are used in the example, and assumed to be initialized elsewhere:

* `gSliderSprite` is the sprite along which the shuttle slides

* `gShuttleSprite` is the shuttle sprite itself, which is presumed to be puppeted and constrained (using `the constraint of sprite` property) to the `gSliderSprite`

* `gVideoLength` is the duration of the DV cast member (refer to later examples for calculating the duration of a DV movie)

* `gVideoSprite` is the DV sprite number

* `updateShuttlePosition` is the handler that moves the shuttle as the video is played. It is placed in a Director movie script and is called repeatedly from a frame script as follows:

```
on exitFrame

  updateShuttlePosition()

  go the frame

end
-- This handler repositions the shuttle based
-- on the video's movieTime property
on updateShuttlePosition
    global gSliderSprite, gShuttleSprite, gVideoLength, gVideoSprite
  -- Get offset of shuttle along slider
  set percent = float (the movieTime of sprite gVideoSprite)/¬
```

```
gVideoLength
  set hOffset = percent * (the width of sprite gSliderSprite)

  -- Position the shuttle sprite
  -- This assumes it is already a puppet
  set the locH of sprite gShuttleSprite = the left of sprite¬
gSliderSprite + hOffset
end updateShuttlePosition
```

The following mouseDown handler should be placed in a sprite or cast script attached to the shuttle sprite.

```
-- Drag the shuttle around.  Note that it is a mouseDown handler
-- not a mouseUp handler.
-- The shuttle is assumed to be constrained by the slider bar
-- and assumed to be puppeted
on mouseDown
  global gVideoSprite
  -- Stop the DV from playing during the "scrub" action
  set oldRate = the movieRate of sprite gVideoSprite
  set the movieRate of sprite gVideoSprite = 0
  repeat while the mouseDown
    set the locH of sprite (the clickOn) = the mouseH
    updateStage
    -- This updates the video position. See following example script
    determineMovieTimeFromShuttle()
  end repeat

  -- Start the movie playing again
  set the movieRate of sprite gVideoSprite = oldRate
end mouseDown
```

The determineMovieTimeFromShuttle handler is used to change the viewable frame of the video. It is called from the mouseDown script attached to the shuttle.

```
-- Change the movie time based on the shuttle position
on determineMovieTimeFromShuttle
  global gSliderSprite, gShuttleSprite, gVideoLength, gVideoSprite

  -- Get offset of shuttle along slider
  set hOffset = the locH of sprite gShuttleSprite - the left of sprite¬
gSliderSprite
```

```
-- Determine the position of the shuttle
-- as a percentage of its slider range
set percent = float (hOffset) / (the width of sprite gSliderSprite)

-- Set the movieTime to the time indicated by the shuttle
set the movieTime of sprite gVideoSprite = (gVideoLength * percent)
end determineMovieTimeFromShuttle
```

Altering the DV Movie's Playback Rate

Two digital video properties are vying to control the playback rate of DV sprites: the frameRate of member and the movieRate of sprite properties.

Synchronous Video Playback

A DV movie is usually played back at its natural rate, which corresponds to a frameRate setting of 0. This is ordinarily set via the Video: Sync to Soundtrack setting in the DV Cast Member Property dialog box. The movieTime of sprite property is used to start and stop the video and even play it backward.

In this mode video playback is synchronized to a timecode, and QT or VFW drops frames to achieve the requested frame rate. If the natural frame rate of the movie is 10 fps and the frameRate of member property is set to 0, setting the movieRate to 1 plays the movie at 10 fps. Setting the movieRate to 2 plays the movie at 20 fps, and so on. The following table summarizes the common settings for playing a DV sprite at different rates. Note that in all cases the frameRate of member should be 0, and the movieRate set per the following table.

To Play DV at This Rate	Set the movieRate of Sprite x = n
stopped	$n = 0$
normal speed	$n = 1$
reverse normal speed	$n = 1$
fast forward	$n > 1$, such as 2
fast reverse	$n < -1$, such as -2
slow motion forward	$0 < n < 1$, such as 0.5
slow motion reverse	$-1 < n < 0$, such as -0.5

Asynchronous Video Playback

On some occasions, you will need to play back every frame of a DV movie without regard to the time code. This is most common when the DV is an animation or visual transition that you want to complete without dropping any frames. This is ordinarily set via the Video: Play Every Frame (no sound) setting in the DV Cast Member Property dialog box, but can also be set prior to runtime via Lingo. The frameRate or member property should not be altered at runtime. The movieTime of sprite property is still used to start and stop the video as described previously.

In this mode QT or VFW will not drop frames and synchronization is not guaranteed. The following table summarizes the possible settings for the frameRate property and their affect on playback speed. Set the movieRate to 1 to play the video, and set the movieRate to 0 to pause the video.

Dialog Box Setting	*The frameRate of member Equivalent*
normal speed	$n = -1$
maximum speed	$n = -2$
fixed speed	$1 < n < 255$, such as 15 fps

The frameRate of member property does not seem to reliably affect DV sprites already placed into the Score. Set the frameRate before starting your Director movie and not at runtime.

To play your movie backward at a fixed asynchronous rate, set the frameRate to a positive integer and set the movieRate to -1.

> Ordinarily it is a bad idea to play a DV movie backward. The video and audio data are interleaved in a way that is optimized for forward playback.
>
> Furthermore, the DV codec compresses the data for forward decompression. (The keyframes precede the difference frames in time.) Although you can use set the movieRate of sprite x = -1 to play a movie backward, it will not perform nearly as well as the same movie playing forward.

Tip

This is tolerable in some situations (no one expects a video running backward to look perfect). You may, however, need perfect backward playback when using a DV movie with no obvious time arrow, such as an animation of a sliding door.

In such a case, create a second version of the digital video in reverse, compressed and interleaved for backward playback. You can accomplish this in most digital video editing software programs. You will need twice the storage space for the forward and backward versions, but the performance difference will be noticeable.

Waiting for Digital Video Movies

Several ways exist for waiting for a DV movie to play inside Director. The following examples explore each method's strengths and weaknesses.

Tweening a DV Sprite in the Score

Tweening out DV sprites in the Score often requires a large number of frames, which is cumbersome and pointless. It may be viable for very small videos, but remember the Score's tempo is not guaranteed. The number of frames required to accommodate the entire video is, therefore, indeterminate.

This method by itself is rarely viable, but it is often used in combination with other methods. For example, a DV sprite may be tweened out over three frames. The first frame is used to perform initialization, the second frame is used to wait for the video to play, and the third frame is used for cleanup.

Waiting via the Tempo Channel

The Tempo channel's "Wait for End of Digital Video in Channel x" option causes the playback head to wait until the end of the DV movie is reached. Director waits for the `movieTime of sprite` property to equal the `duration of member` property, not just for the movie to stop playing. This method is useful if the user is required to sit through the entire length of the DV movie. Unfortunately, it is not very flexible.

The Tempo channel's "Wait" command is ignored if `QuickTime` controller is visible. Even if the QT cast member is set to `Loop`, if its controller is active, the Tempo channel waits for the movie to play only once through.

The Tempo channel setting is similar to a tight repeat loop (optimized for performance) and can interfere with interactivity. As a rule, the Tempo channel settings work best with linear presentations with minimal interactivity.

Lingo enables you to optimize playback of your DV movie while maintaining complete control over interactivity. Let's examine some Lingo alternatives to the Tempo channel.

Determining Whether a Digital Video Movie Is Playing

The `movieRate` property is non-zero when a QT sprite is playing, and zero when a QT sprite is stopped. Unfortunately, the `movieRate` is not set to zero for VFW sprites, even when the end of the AVI file is reached. You can check whether a DV sprite is currently playing, as follows. Refer to the next example for details of the `endOfVideo` handler.

```
on isPlaying dvSpriteNum
    if (the movieRate of sprite dvSpriteNum) then
        if (the digitalVideoType of sprite dvSpriteNum = #quickTime) then
            -- The QT movie is playing (either forward or backward)
            return TRUE
        -- Otherwise we need more info for VFW sprites
        else if endOfVideoReached(dvSpriteNum) then
            return TRUE
        else
            return FALSE
        end if
    else
        -- The movie is stopped
        return FALSE
    end if
end isPlaying
```

Hot-Shot Style

You may notice that in the preceding section, I did not explicitly compare the `movieRate` to some value, as is typical in an `if` clause. When you omit the comparison, Lingo checks whether the expression evaluates to any non-zero number.

Tip

The statement

```
if (x) then put "x is not zero"
```

is equivalent to

```
if (x <> 0) then put "x is not zero"
```

If you use this technique, you will look unintelligent to those who don't understand it, but really cool to the hard-core hipsters.

Be careful regarding your comparison. If you only want to check whether an expression is positive, do not use this technique; it will evaluate to TRUE for any non-zero number, including negative numbers. The isPlaying handler returns TRUE if the DV movie is playing, regardless of whether it is playing forward (positive movieRate) or backward (negative movieRate).

Waiting for a Digital Video Movie to End

The isPlaying handler relies on the fact that the movieRate of sprite property is set to zero automatically when a QuickTime movie ends.

The movieRate property is not set to zero when a Video For Windows (AVI) movie ends. Therefore, you must check the duration of member property against the movieTime of sprite property for AVI sprites.

This is also useful for determining whether the end of a QT movie has been reached, as opposed to the movie simply being paused.

```
on endOfVideoReached dvSpriteNum
  set movieLength = the duration of member (the member of sprite¬
dvSpriteNum)
  if the movieTime of sprite dvSpriteNum < movieLength
    return FALSE
  else
    return TRUE
  end if
end endOfVideoReached
```

In a real project, you would record the video's duration once in a global variable, rather than repeatedly calculating it each time you check whether the end of the video has been reached.

The following sections assume you are using QuickTime sprites and rely on the fact that the movieRate property is set to zero when a QT movie ends. This is not true for VFW sprites and results in an infinite loop when using AVI files. See the preceding isPlaying and endofVideoReached handlers to determine whether the end of an AVI file has been reached.

Note

Waiting in a Repeat

In this example, a tight repeat loop is used to wait for the video in an exitFrame handler of a frame script. The repeat loop retains control as long as the movieRate property remains non-zero. Note that the updateStage command redraws the screen repeatedly within the repeat loop.

```
on exitFrame
  -- Check if the movieRate is non-zero
  repeat while the movieRate of sprite x
    updateStage
  end repeat
end exitFrame
```

This example waits as long as the QT movie is playing. When the QT movie reaches the end and stops playing, Director exits the loop. Unfortunately, this method disables all interactivity while in the repeat loop. This is only acceptable if the user must sit through the entire QT movie.

If you are waiting in a repeat loop, do not forget the updateStage command. Without it, your video appears to be paused.

Tip

Looping in a Frame

In this example, instead of entering a tight repeat loop, the playback head is allowed to loop repeatedly in the Score. This enables Director to process events while waiting for the video to complete. The updateStage is performed implicitly as the playback head loops.

```
on exitFrame
   if the movieRate of sprite x then
      go the frame
   end if
end exitFrame
```

This method allows Director to poll for events during each loop, thereby enabling interactivity; Director incurs a lot of overhead when it loops in the Score, repeatedly checking for mouse, key, idle, and other system events.

Tip

Overhead, Over Dale

At a Tempo setting of 10 fps or more, Director spends all its free time looping and checking for system events. If you increase the frame rate, Director just spends more time calling the various event handler routines. Thus, increased frame rates can lead to decreased DV playback performance.

If you make the tempo too slow, say 1 fps, Director does not poll `for` events often enough. Button response will be slow and Director may spend an inordinate amount of time in the `idle` handler. Avoid idle handlers while playing videos, therefore, and use a tempo of 3 fps to improve responsiveness.

Never loop in the first or last frame of a movie because those special frames incur substantial overhead penalties.

Handling Events Efficiently During Digital Video Playback

In this example, we attempt to process events efficiently while optimizing DV performance. We loop in a tight, efficient `repeat` loop most of the time. If the mouse is clicked, Lingo exits the `repeat` loop. If the QT movie is still playing, Lingo loops in the frame. If not, the playback head advances. In either case, Director processes pending events, such as mouse clicks. This yields the best of both worlds—efficient event handling and optimal QT performance.

Because we don't want Director to devote all its time to looping in the frame, set the tempo to 3 fps in the Tempo channel preceding the frame in which you are waiting for the DV movie to play. Don't use the `puppetTempo` command because it is ignored when Director loops backward in the Score, as when looping in a frame.

```
on exitFrame
  -- Wait while the movie plays
  repeat while the movieRate of sprite x
    -- Process mouse and key events
    if the mouseDown then exit repeat
    if the keyPressed then exit repeat
    updateStage
  end repeat
  -- Keep looping if the movie is still playing
  if the movieRate of sprite x then
    go the frame
  end if
end exitFrame
```

This method works exceedingly well for most QT playback. It may not be acceptable if other sprites are animating while the video plays. Experiment to find a tempo that animates the sprites at an acceptable pace without causing Director to spend all its time processing events.

Additional methods of waiting for QT movies in various scenarios follow.

Stopping the Digital Video on MouseDown

This routine waits for the video to play, but will stop the video if the user clicks the mouse button. This is useful for allowing the user to interrupt video playback.

```
on exitFrame
  repeat while the movieRate of sprite x
    if the mouseDown then
      -- Include this line if you want the video to stop
      -- playing when the user clicks
      set the movieRate of sprite x = 0
      exit repeat
    end if
    updateStage
  end repeat
end exitFrame
```

Waiting for User to Exit the Digital Video

The previous examples assume that you want to continue along in the Score after the QT movie stops. The QT movie may stop before it reaches the end if the user has control over the playback. You may prefer to wait indefinitely until the user explicitly chooses to exit.

This script will loop forever while handling mouse clicks. Provide a button that jumps elsewhere in the Score to give the user a way to exit the DV playback.

```
on exitFrame
   -- Loop forever
   repeat while TRUE
      -- Exit the loop to process the mouse event
      if the mouseDown then exit repeat
      updateStage
   end repeat
   go the frame
end exitFrame
```

Movie Intervals and Durations

Following are some sample Lingo scripts dealing with DV movie time intervals. Use these utilities to set and test various time-related DV properties.

Determining a Digital Video's Length

Check the duration of member property to determine the duration of a video. The duration is measured in ticks (60ths of a second). This example converts a DV movie's length to seconds.

```
on videoLengthInSeconds dvSpriteNum
   set dvSize = the duration of member (the member of sprite dvSpriteNum)
   return (dvSize / 60.0)
end videoLengthInSeconds
```

Jumping to a Digital Video Cue Point

You may need to jump to a particular location in a DV file to synchronize certain events or allow the user to cue different portions of the video. When storing a series of JPEG images in a DV file, you can view each JPEG image by setting the appropriate movieTime, for example:

```
set the movieTime of sprite x = desiredTime
```

To Set to This Time	Set the movieTime of sprite x to
beginning	0
end	the duration of member y
n ticks from the beginning	n
n ticks from the end	(the duration of member y) − n
current time	the movieTime of sprite x
current time + n seconds	(the movieTime of sprite x) + n × 60
current time −n seconds	(the movieTime of sprite x) − n × 60
n seconds into the DV	n × 60
midpoint of DV0	.5 × (the duration of member y)

Playing a Segment of a Digital Video Movie

You may need to play a particular segment of a DV movie. This example plays a video segment from the specified entry point through the specified exit point. Put the playSegment handler in a movie script and call it from the frame in which the DV sprite exists. It can be called from a mouseDown handler in a sprite script, or from a frame script, as follows:

```
on exitFrame
    -- Play the video in sprite 1 from 1000 to 15000 ticks
    playSegment (1, 1000, 1500)
end exitFrame
on playSegment dvSpriteNum, entryPoint, exitPoint
  -- Pause the video
  set the movieRate of sprite dvSpriteNum = 0
  -- Start the video at the specified entry point
  set the movieTime of sprite dvSpriteNum = entryPoint
  -- Restart the video
  set the movieRate of sprite dvSpriteNum = 1
```

```
-- Wait for the video to reach the exit point
repeat while the movieTime of sprite dvSpriteNum < exitPoint
  updateStage
end repeat
-- Stop the video again
set the movieRate of sprite dvSpriteNum = 0
end playSegment
```

Note

> The `startTime of sprite` and the `stopTime of sprite` properties don't always work predictably, and the same functionality can be simulated reliably with the preceding `playSegment()` handler. If you choose to use them, refer to the Director 5.0.1 ReadMe file that documents the proper syntax. (They were omitted from the Director 5.0 documentation, but are still valid.) Consult the same ReadMe file regarding the erroneous example on pages 108-109 of *Learning Lingo*, in which you should substitute `startTime` for `trackStartTime` and `stopTime` for `trackStopTime`.

Synchronizing Animations to a DV Movie

You may want to synchronize an animation to a video or the soundtrack of an audio-only DV file. Assume that you want to synchronize the soundtrack to a series of eight graphics for which markers are set in the Score. The following example waits for a certain point in a DV movie before advancing to the next marker. You can initialize the slide show in your `startMovie()` handler.

```
on startMovie
  global gSlideNum , gTimeList
  -- Offset Time in ticks for each slide to be dismissed
  set gTimeList = [500, 1000, 1400, 2100, 2400, 2900, 3500, 4000]
  set gSlideNum = 1
end startMovie
```

Use the following frame script throughout the frames that comprise the slide show.

```
on exitFrame
  global gSlideNum , gTimeList
  -- wait for the movie to reach the next time limit
  if the movieTime of sprite x < getAt (gTimeList, gSlideNum ) then
    -- We're still waiting
    go the frame
```

```
    else
      -- Go to the next slide
      set gSlideNum = gSlideNum + 1
      go next
    end if
end exitFrame
```

We demonstrated this technique using a DV sprite, but you can do the same thing using an AIFF or WAV file by starting a timer when you start the sound. The only advantage of an audio-only DV is that you can stop and restart the audio at any point, not just the beginning. Standard audio files can be imported directly into the cast so that they need not be streamed from the disk on-the-fly. Note that AIFF files are cross-platform, but they must have an .AIF extension under Windows. WAV files are Windows-only and must have a .WAV extension.

Tip

Digital Video Interactions with Director

Playing digital video inside Director is more complicated than playing it in standalone applications such as MoviePlayer or MediaPlayer. We have already seen how to optimize DV performance inside Director. Let's explore some of the interactions between digital video and Director and how to ensure seamless cooperation between the two.

Digital Video and Cursors

The cursor often flickers when it is over a DV sprite. While there is no way to prevent this, you can hide the cursor while it is over the QT sprite using

```
set the cursor of sprite x = 200
```

You will not be able to see the mouse while it is over the QT, but at least it won't flicker.

Be certain to restore the cursor using

```
set the cursor of sprite x = 0
```

You may choose to hide the cursor entirely, especially if playing an uninterruptible full-screen video. Hide the cursor using

```
cursor 200
```

Restore the cursor when the video ends using

```
cursor 0
```

Some XObjects, such as QTVR, set the cursor without Director's knowledge. You must fool Director into resetting the cursor by changing it to a dummy value and then back to the desired setting. This example changes the cursor to a watch (Macintosh) or hourglass (Windows) and then back to a pointing arrow:

```
cursor 4
cursor -1
```

Digital Video and Transitions

Digital video playback and Director transitions both make heavy demands on the processor and video subsytem. Because a playing DV sprite is constantly changing, any transition will include the DV sprite's bounding box in its changing area. Windows PCs perform transitions slowly while a DV movie is playing. This is because the DV movie is changing even as each subframe of the transition occurs. Always stop the DV movie from playing before performing a transition. Never loop in any frame with a transition, but especially not one with a DV sprite.

Digital Video and Palettes

It is common to use custom 8-bit palettes in Director to achieve good image quality while maintaining adequate performance. Whereas Director supports higher bit depths on the Macintosh and under Windows 95, under Windows 3.1 Director supports only 8-bit graphics. Because only one palette can be active at any given time, you must employ a palette that encompasses the colors used in both your bitmaps and your digital video. (An application such as DeBabelizer can be used to create optimal custom palettes). To ensure the proper appearance of custom palettes using DV and Director, follow the guidelines set forth in the following sections.

Importing and Setting a QT Palette

You cannot directly import a DV movie's custom palette—it will be ignored and might even confuse Director. Instead, create a dummy PICT or BMP with your custom DV palette embedded in the file. Import that bitmap into your cast with the monitor set to 8-bit color depth, and choose to import the palette when prompted. Then place that palette in the Score where you want it to take effect. The DV movie will use Director's current custom palette. Refer to the caveats following.

PuppetPalette

The `puppetPalette` command does not work as advertised. Specifically, it is canceled whenever you loop in the frame or go backward in the Score. Thus, it is not a satisfactory way to instantiate a palette for DV. Instead, set the custom palette in the Score's Palette channel. You should generally play your DV movies Direct to Stage. Be aware that custom palettes are often ignored by DV movies that are not played Direct to Stage.

Incorrect QuickTime Palette on Macintosh

When QuickTime was originally designed, Apple did not expect users to change the palette for the QT movie on-the-fly. Thus, the first time a QT movie is played in Director, the QuickTime software stores Director's current custom palette for future use. Normally, subsequent palette changes in Director are ignored by QuickTime. The FixPalette XObject remedies the problem, which occurs only on the Macintosh. Simply instantiate the XObject and make a call to its `mPatchIt` method. You would call the following `FixQTpalette` handler from the frame script of the frame in which the new palette is located. A QT sprite need not be present in the frame from which `FixQTpalette` is called, but a custom palette *must* be set in that frame in the Score.

The FixPalette XObject is available in the Macromedia forum on CompuServe (Go Macromedia) and America Online (keyword: Macromedia), and from Macromedia's web site (www.macromedia.com).

```
on FixQTpalette
  -- Required on the Macintosh only
  if the machineType < 256 then
    -- Open the FixPalette Xlib
    openXlib (the pathName & "FixPalette.Xobj")
```

```
     -- Instantiate the FixPalette XObject
     set gFixPalObj = FixPalette(mNew, the stageLeft, the stageTop, the¬
 stageRight, the stageBottom)
     -- Make sure it worked
     if not objectP(gFixPalObj) then
       put "could not instantiate gFixPalObj"
     else
       -- Perform the patch
       gFixPalObj(mPatchIt)
       -- Dispose of the XOobject instance
       gFixPalObj(mDispose)
     end if
      -- Close the Xlib
     closeXlib (the pathname & "FixPalette.Xobj")
   end if
 end FixQTpalette
```

In reality, you would not repeatedly open and close the XObject every time you needed to call mPatchIt (which you must do every time the QT palette changes). Refer to the QT controller movie for a real-world version of these scripts.

Incorrect Palettes Under Windows

Director and the Windows OS have competing desires to instantiate their own palettes. If you use a custom palette that is significantly different from the Windows palette, this can cause undesired colors to appear.

Director's palette overrides the Windows palette when Director is launched. If any Windows system dialog box is posted, however, Windows will reassert its palette. System dialog boxes include alert boxes created with Lingo's alert command, any Where Is...? dialog box that Director may post if it can't find a file, and any File Browser dialog box brought up via FileIO.

Ironically, Windows does not reassert its palette until after it posts the dialog box. Therefore, the Windows dialog box itself will appear in Director's custom palette. To ensure that the Windows dialog box appears correctly, the first and last 10 entries in your custom palette should match those in the Windows System palette provided with Director. A Windows system dialog box will not only reassert the Windows palette, but also freeze out Director from reasserting its palette.

Three possible solutions are

❋ Avoid Windows system dialog boxes. Create custom dialog boxes with MIAWs if necessary.

❋ Use `go to movie` *x* to jump to another Director movie. This temporarily alleviates the problem, at least until another system dialog box is posted.

❋ Use `go frame (the frame) of movie (the movie)` to restart the current movie. Be aware that this reruns the `startMovie` handler in the current movie.

> If you initialize your project in your `startMovie` handler and want to prevent it from being repeatedly reinitialized, use a global variable to ensure that it is only done once.
>
> ```
> on startMovie
>
>   global gBeenDone
>
>   -- If we have not already been initialized, do it now
>
>   if not (gBeenDone) then
>
>     -- Set the flag to indicate we've performed initialization
>
>     set gBeenDone = TRUE
>
> -- perform other initialization here
>
>   end if
>
> end startMovie
> ```

Tip

Modify the DIRECTOR.INI file setting as follows:

```
[Palette]
Animation = 0
```

Modifying the DIRECTOR.INI file (in the same folder as Director for Windows) prevents the problems during development. Be certain to rename the DIRECTOR.INI file to match your projector name for distribution.

Thus, if your projector is named "MYDEMO.EXE", rename DIRECTOR.INI to "MYDEMO.INI" and place it in the same folder as your projector.

The only drawback to this workaround is that it substantially slows Director's palette fades. If you do not use palette fades, it is an excellent solution.

More Digital Video-Related Scripts

Several useful DV-related scripts are sprinkled throughout the previous two chapters. Be certain to explore them in addition to the following examples.

Ensuring Optimal Performance on 4-Byte Boundaries

Generally, the stage size does not change throughout the application. If you use non-standard dimensions for your DV movies, for performance reasons, the width and height should be divisible by four. In addition, all DV sprites should be placed at an offset that is a 4-pixel multiple.

The Director stage is always on a 16-pixel boundary, so you can calculate the offset relative to the stage's left edge, and it will still be valid relative to the monitor's left edge.

To ensure that the size of your DV cast member is divisible by four use

```
if (the width  of member y) mod 4 <> 0 then alert "Bad Width"
if (the height of member y) mod 4 <> 0 then alert "Bad Height"
```

To ensure that the size of your DV sprite is divisible by four use

```
if (the width  of sprite x) mod 4 <> 0 then alert "Bad Width"
if (the height of sprite x) mod 4 <> 0 then alert "Bad Height"
```

To ensure that the left edge of your DV sprite is on a 4-pixel boundary use

```
if (the left of sprite x) mod 4 <> 0 then alert "Bad Alignment"
```

Setting the Monitor's Color Depth

QuickTime is actually optimized for 16-bit playback. However, your Director presentation will run slower and require more memory at higher color depths. The monitor's color depth can be tested and set on the Macintosh, but only tested under Windows. This example checks the monitor depth and sets it to 256 colors on the Macintosh.

```
on setDepth
   global gOldDepth
   -- Save the old color depth
   set gOldDepth = the colorDepth
   if the colorDepth <> 8 then
```

```
      -- This will be ignored under Windows
      set the colorDepth = 8
      if the colorDepth <> 8 then
          alert "Please set your monitor to 256 colors"
      end if
    end if
end setDepth
```

It is polite to restore the previous color depth, which you can do as follows:

```
on stopMovie
    global gOldDepth
    -- Restore the old color depth
    set the colorDepth = gOldDepth
end stopMovie
```

> Under Windows, specify the required color depth in the documentation and the ReadMe file, and warn the user if the color depth is incorrect.
>
> Microsoft has released a utility called QuickRes that will change the Windows 95 monitor color depth on-the-fly. You can obtain the utility at `http://www.microsoft.com/ windows/software/powertoy.htm`

Tip

Note that some Macintosh video cards may support color depths of 8 and 32 bits, but not 16 bits. Be certain to check the color depth again after you set it to see if the operation succeeded, as in the following example.

```
-- On the Mac, try to change the color depth
if the colorDepth < 16 and the machineType < 256 then
  set the colorDepth = 16
 -- Didn't succeed
  if the colorDepth < 16 then
      -- Try 32-bit
set the colorDepth = 32
  end if
end if
if the colorDepth < 16 then
alert "You really need thousands or millions of colors to appreciate my¬
work"
end if
```

The Semi-Holy Grail: Full-Screen Video

Everyone wants full-screen video. If your hardware can support it, no intrinsic limitation prevents QT or VFW from playing 640×480 video. In reality, the current hardware and software do not support the necessary bandwidth, so you have to resort to pixel-doubling. Luckily, QT and VFW are scalable, so they can efficiently double the size of a video on-the-fly without significant performance degradation. It tends to look a little blocky, but is surprisingly acceptable, especially from a few feet away.

Ensuring Even-Multiple Scaling

When stretching DV sprites, you should always scale them in 100 percent increments for optimal performance. Thus, it is fine to double the size of a DV movie, but don't multiply it by a factor of, say, 180 percent. You can even cut a DV member in half (so a scale factor of 50 percent is fine), but people usually want bigger video, not smaller video.

To ensure that sprites are the correct size relative to the original DV cast member, use

```
if (the width of sprite x) mod (the width of member (the member of¬
sprite x)) <> 0 then alert "Improper Width Scaling"
if (the height of sprite x) mod (the height of member (the member of¬
sprite x)) <> 0 then alert "Improper Height Scaling"
```

Pixel-Doubling

Pixel-Doubling is probably one of the easiest, yet most impressive techniques. Three ways to blow up a quarter-screen (320×240) video to full-screen (640×480) are

❀ Pixel-doubling a QT movie outside Director

❀ Stretching the DV sprite on-stage

❀ Stretching a DV sprite via Lingo

Pixel-Doubling a QT Movie Outside Director

You can create a QT movie that has been pixel-doubled before importing it into Director. On the Macintosh, you can use the MoviePlayer application, which is free from Apple, to save your QT movie in a pixel-doubled format.

1. Open the QT movie in MoviePlayer.

2. Under the Movie menu, choose Double Size.

3. Resave the movie.

> When porting to Windows, use "Save As..." and check the Make movie self-contained and Playable on non-Apple computers options to make the movie Windows-compatible. Most Macintosh QT applications can save QT files in a Windows-compatible format, and have similarly named options for achieving the same results.

Tip

The QT movie is now permanently pixel-doubled and there is no need to change its size from within Director. Just import the QT movie into Director's cast, place it on-stage, and you are ready to go. Although MoviePlayer for Windows enables you to temporarily pixel-double a QT movie, you can't save it in this format. Once saved on the Macintosh, however, a QT movie will remain pixel-doubled under Windows. Windows 95's Multimedia control panel also enables you play videos full-screen, but they cannot be saved in this format.

Stretching the DV Sprite On-Stage

As a rule, you should never stretch bitmap sprites on-stage because it destroys performance, but DV sprites are another story. Because both QT and VFW can efficiently pixel-double a DV sprite on-the-fly, you can stretch any DV sprite by a factor of two, using the following method:

1. Place the sprite on the stage

2. Open the Modify menu and choose Sprite, Properties

3. Hit the Restore button to return the sprite to its original size

4. Check the Maintain Proportions check box

5. Type in a 200 percent scale factor and click OK

6. Reposition the sprite on-stage as necessary, setting the left and top offsets to zero pixels

Stretching a DV Sprite via Lingo

You can stretch a DV sprite on-the-fly via the following Lingo. You can call this handler from a sprite, cast, or frame script in the frame in which the DV sprite exists.

```
on stretchIt dvSpriteNum
  puppetSprite dvSpriteNum, TRUE
  set the stretch of sprite dvSpriteNum = TRUE
  set the rect of sprite dvSpriteNum = rect (0, 0, 640, 480)
  updateStage
end
```

Be certain to unpuppet the sprite when the video ends or you will not be able to see anything else on-stage.

For all of the preceding methods, remember to use dimensions and alignment that are both multiples of four pixels.

Conclusion

This chapter explored many real-world applications for controlling digital video via Lingo. This chapter has armed you with the knowledge to

❋ Differentiate between the digital video sprite and member properties and how to use them

❋ Place a digital video sprite under complete Lingo control

❋ Create a custom digital video controller, complete with start, stop, re-wind, fast-forward, slow motion, and a scrub shuttle to control the video time position

❋ Determine whether a movie is playing

❋ Optimize digital video performance while waiting for a video to play

❋ Play digital videos at varying speeds in both synchronous and asynchronous modes

❋ Cue a digital video segment for playback

❋ Synchronize a digital video or audio track to a Director slide-show style presentation

❋ Mitigate digital video conflicts with Director cursors and transitions

✴ Manage digital video with custom palettes inside Director and avoid palette conflicts

✴ Play digital video in full-screen mode

This chapter and the two that preceded it have poured massive knowledge about digital video and Director into your unsuspecting brain. These lessons will serve you well in all your future multimedia pursuits.

5

Bruce Epstein

Implementing a Saved Game and a High Score Chart

Many multimedia applications require you to save information from a user's session. It might be as simple as the user's name, rank, and serial number, or as complex as the state of a murder mystery investigation. The user might enter information directly, such as the answers to a quiz, or your program might generate data in response to the user's actions, such as an inventory list in an adventure game.

An application that enables the user to create something or achieve a hard-earned level of success should enable him to save and restore his work or status. The lack of a Save Game Feature (SGF) is a glaring deficiency in many Director applications. To make your application worth using, you should probably implement an SGF. This reminds users that you value and respect their intelligence and creativity. Nothing is more satisfying that saving a tangible yardstick of personal progress. Young users especially love to show off their accomplishments to others.

SGFs even enhance applications in which the user does not want to save his work. The data might be necessary for a teacher or supervisor, as in the case of a quiz or training material. Your program could be customized for repeat users, perhaps by greeting them by name. You can implement a High Score Chart (HSC) for competitive games. Finally, data can be recorded to facilitate market research or usability analysis on behalf of the product publisher or developer.

Implementing a Save Game Feature

An SGF can be implemented in several ways depending on your application. Factors include whether there are multiple users, user-interface issues, save and load times, data security, and where data is to be stored.

> *Tip*
>
> Many programmers attempt to save the state of a projector using Lingo's `saveMovie` and `save castLib` commands. This is ill advised, however, because these commands do not work from a projector, are slow and wasteful, and can lead to an enlarged Director file. These commands are intended for utilities written during development and not for runtime applications. Use the techniques discussed here, which save and retrieve data using small external text files, to implement an SGF.

Assume that you want to create a High Score Chart for your incredibly great video game called *The Monkey's Uncle*. You'll record the high scores in a file so that they are saved on disk. Let's start with the basics and add features as we progress.

These examples use the FileIO XObject (Macintosh) and DLL (Windows) that ship with both Director 4 and 5. Macromedia now also distributes FileIO Xtras that have nearly identical functionality. The FileIO operations are encapsulated within simple handlers that you can modify to use the FileIO Xtras if you prefer. The terms *FileIO XObject* and *FileIO* refer to the Macintosh XObject and Windows DLL versions collectively, and *FileIO Xtra* refers to the new Macintosh and Windows FileIO Xtras. Before using the examples, make certain that the appropriate FileIO XObject, DLL, or Xtra is open.

> *Tip*
>
> The 16-bit FileIO DLL is not fully compatible with Windows 95 and NT, and the FileIO Xtras that originally shipped with Director 5.0 were beta versions. If you are using the FileIO Xtras, you should obtain the latest version (currently 1.0.1) from Macromedia's web site. Refer to the FileIO ReadMe file for complete information.

> You can check the version of the FileIO Xtra using the following:
>
> ```
> put version (Xtra "FileIO")
> -- "FileIO 1.0.1 May 31 1996"
> ```

Saving Data to a File

Assume there is data in a field cast member and you want to save it to a file. Refer to the examples under "Constructing the Saved Game Data" and "Retrieving Data from a File" for ways to construct and retrieve the data.

> The examples in this chapter assume that only one file is open at a time, and that the file object is stored in a global variable (gFileObj) for simplicity and clarity. If your project requires multiple simultaneous files, you can use a list of file objects or several global variables. In this case, you would need to modify the example routines to accept the file object as a parameter. (This is demonstrated by the bufferedWrite and bufferedRead handlers later in the chapter.)
>
> *Note*

These steps demonstrate the component subroutines used to create, write to, and close the sample data file. They are followed by an example routine that uses these subroutines to save the high scores.

1. First, create the file. For now, assume that the programmer specifies the file's name and location.

   The createFile routine attempts to create the specified file and returns TRUE if successful. The createDataFile routine may be called as follows:

   ```
   set success = createDataFile (the pathname & "hiScore.txt")

   on createDataFile dataFilePath
     global gFileObj

     -- Dispose of previous file handle, if any
     if objectP(gFileObj) then
       gFileObj (mDispose)
     end if

     -- Open the specified file for write access
     set gFileObj = fileIO (mNew, "write", dataFilePath)

     -- Check if the file was successfully created
     if objectP(gFileObj) then
   ```

```
      return TRUE
   else
      alert "Error creating file" && dataFilePath && "error code:" &&¬
gFileObj
      return FALSE
   end if
end createDataFile
```

2. Next, write the data to the file. This routine assumes that the file has been previously opened with createDataFile.

   This routine accepts the userData to be written as a parameter and returns the status code as returned by FileIO.

   The writeFile routine may be called as follows:

```
set success = writeToFile ("this is some data")

on writeToFile userData
   global gFileObj

   if not objectP(gFileObj) then
      alert ("Can't write to file, because it isn't open" && gFileObj)
      exit
   end if

   set statusCode = gFileObj  (mWriteString,  userData)

   return (statusCode )
end writeToFile
```

3. Close the file and dispose of the file object.

```
on closeDataFile
   global gFileObj

   if objectP(gFileObj) then
      gFileObj (mDispose)
   end if

end closeDataFile
```

4. Lastly, create the high-level routine that saves the high scores to the file. This assumes that the high score data already exists in a field cast member called "High Scores". This routine would ordinarily be called whenever the user achieves a new high score to save the data to disk. Refer to

the `saveHiScoreData` routine in step 2 of the "Constructing the Saved Game Data" example, which calls the `saveHiScores` routine.

The `saveHiScores` routine may be called as follows:

```
saveHiScores (the text of field "High Scores")

on saveHiScores userData
  set success = createDataFile (the pathname & "hiScore.txt")

  if success then
    -- NOTE: Error trapping, such as for disk full errors,
    -- is left as an exercise to the reader.
    set success = writeToFile (userData)
    closeDataFile()
  else
    alert "Unable to save high scores"
  end if

end saveHiScores
```

Retrieving Data from a File

Here is an example of how to read the information back into Director at runtime. It assumes that the FileIO XObject library is still open and builds on the previous example.

1. First, open an existing data file. This example still assumes that only one file is open at a time, and that the programmer specifies the file's name and location.

    This routine tries to open the specified file and returns TRUE if successful.

    The `openDataFile` routine may be called as follows:

```
set success = openDataFile (the pathname & "hiScore.txt")

on openDataFile dataFilePath
  global gFileObj

  -- Dispose of previous file handle, if any
  closeDataFile()

  -- Open the specified file for read access
  set gFileObj = fileIO (mNew, "read", dataFilePath)
```

```
-- Check if the file was successfully opened
if objectP(gFileObj) then
  return TRUE
else
  alert "Error opening file" && dataFilePath && "error code:" &&¬
gFileObj
  return FALSE
end if
end openDataFile
```

2. Next. read the data from the file. This routine assumes that the file has been previously opened with openDataFile.

The readFromFile routine returns the contents of the file, and may be called as follows:

```
set userData = readFromFile()

on readFromFile
  global gFileObj

  if not objectP(gFileObj) then
    alert ("Can't read from file, it isn't open" && gFileObj)
    exit
  end if

  set fileData = gFileObj  (mReadFile)

  return (fileData )
end readFromFile
```

Note

When a function, such as readFromFile, returns data, the parentheses following its name are required! They indicate that Director should assign the variable userData to the value returned by the function. Without the parentheses, Director interprets readFromFile as an unassigned variable, which causes a syntax error.

3. Lastly, create the high level routine that reads the high scores from the file. This assumes that the high score data exists in a file called "hiScore.txt" in the same folder as the projector. It reads the data into an existing field cast member called "High Scores".

```
on retrieveHiScores
  set success = openDataFile (the pathname & "hiScore.txt")

  if success then
     set hiScoreData = readFromFile ()
     put hiScoreData into field "High Scores"
     closeDataFile()
  else
     alert "Unable to retrieve high scores"
  end if

end retrieveHiScores
```

Constructing the Saved Game Data

Now that you have seen how to save and retrieve data to and from a file, let's examine ways to create the data in the first place.

In the previous example, it was assumed that the high score information was already in a field cast member. Imagine that it contains a list of user names and high scores, such as Hillary 690.

Bill	550
Elizabeth	500
Bob	400

> In reality, this formatted table would have to be constructed from the raw data, but a formatted table is not convenient for manipulating the data. The data would be stored in a coded format to make it easier to interpret when it is retrieved (see the following example).
>
> Avoid aggravation by storing data in a form that is easy to manipulate programmatically. Then, format the data as necessary for display purposes.

Tip

Assume that the previous high scores are already stored in a list, and the user has just finished playing *The Monkey's Uncle*. These steps will add the user's name to our high score chart:

1. First, check whether this user is worthy of immortality on the high score chart. This routine assumes that the list of high scores is stored in the global list *highScores*, and that you are storing the top ten scores. See the next example for routines that actually create these lists.

The checkHiScore routine checks if a score makes the top ten list. It returns a number (1 through 10) if it rates, or zero (0) if it does not. This determines where the user's name is inserted into the high score chart using the recordHiScore routine in step 4 of this example.

```
on checkHiScore newScore
  global highScores -- the list of high scores

  -- It is assumed that the scores are
  -- already in the list in descending order
  -- (i.e. [100, 90, 80, 70, 60, 50, 40, 30, 20, 10])
  -- Is the score higher than any on the list?
  repeat with x = 1 to count (highScores)
    if newScore > getAt (highScores, x) then
      exit repeat
    end if
  end repeat

  -- Stick it in the list if it is high enough
  if x <= 10 then
    addAt (highScores, x, newScore)
    if count (highScores) > 10 then
      deleteAt (highScores, 11)
    end if
    return x
  else
    return FALSE
  end if

end checkHiScore
```

2. Next, format the list of high scores and the associated names for writing out to a data file. The data is stored so that retrieval and interpretation are simple, in the form

```
userName, userScore <CR>
```

in which userName can be any string, and userScore is an integer. We separate the two data items on each line using a comma to enable us to parse them using the "item...of" chunk expression. The lines of data are separated by carriage returns, so that each line can be retrieved using the "line...of" chunk expression.

```
on saveHiScoreData
  global highScores -- the list of high scores
```

```
global highNames  -- the list of high score names

set tempText = EMPTY

-- Create the formatted text
-- Use up to the top ten, if they exist
repeat with x = 1 to min (10, count (highScores))
  put string(getAt(highNames, x)) & "," & ¬
      string(getAt(highScores, x)) & ¬
       RETURN after tempText
end repeat

-- Eliminate the trailing RETURN
delete the last char of tempText

saveHiScores (tempText)

-- Note: This routine is defined below
updateHiScoreChart ()
end saveHiScoreData
```

Garbage Collection

This example assumes that the user names do not contain commas. In a real application, you would have to prevent the user from entering troublesome characters.

This illustrates a crucial difference between *user-specified* data and *programmer-specified* data. User-specified data can be unpredictable. If you need to interpret the user data, you should try to ensure consistent data entry. Avoid free-form fields when possible, by providing check boxes or picklists, such as for state postal abbreviations.

Note

3. Now, convert the high scores and user names into the top ten list in the format shown previously. This routine puts the resulting text table into the field "High Scores".

```
on updateHiScoreChart
  global highScores -- the list of high scores
  global highNames  -- the list of high score names

  set tempText = EMPTY

  repeat with x = 1 to count (highScores)
```

```
      -- This does not make nice columns, that is up to you
      put string (x) & "." && getAt(highNames, x) & ¬
              TAB & TAB & string(getAt(highScores, x)) & ¬
              RETURN after tempText
  end repeat
 put tempText into field "High Scores"
end updateHiScoreChart
```

4. Lastly, create the high-level routine to save the user's high score to a file. This routine checks if the user's score made the top ten list, and then calls saveHiScoreData to format and save the data. It assumes that the current user's score is stored in the global userScore. The task of asking the user to enter his name is left as an exercise to the reader.

```
on recordHiScore
  global userScore -- current user's score
  global highNames -- the list of high score names

  set newHi = checkHiScore (userScore)

  if (newHi > 0) then
    -- Letting the user type in her name
    -- is left as an exercise to the reader
    set userName = the text of field "UserName"
    alert "You are number" && newHi && "on the all time list"
    addAt (highNames, newHi, userName)
    saveHiScoreData()
  else
    alert "Sorry, you didn't make our hall of fame"
  end if
end recordHiScore
```

Parsing the Retrieved Data

This section demonstrates how to retrieve the data from the file and re-create the high score chart. You know exactly how to interpret the data because you specified its format in the first place!

1. Create the routine to parse the data and re-create the data structures. This routine accepts the userData as read from the file, and extracts the user name and high score for each entry.

```
on parseHiScoreData userData
  global highScores -- the list of high scores
```

```
global highNames  -- the list of high score names

-- Make sure that the itemDelimiter is a comma
-- Otherwise, we can't extract the items as expected
set oldDelimiter = the itemDelimiter
set the itemDelimiter = ","

-- Reset the lists
set highNames  = []
set highScores = []

set numLines = the number of lines in (userData)
repeat with x = 1 to min (10, numLines )
    setAt (highNames,  x, string (item 1 of line x of userData))
      -- Convert the user score back into an integer
    setAt (highScores, x, value  (item 2 of line x of userData))
end repeat

-- Restore the old itemDelimiter
set the itemDelimiter = oldDelimiter
end parseHiScoreData
```

Stringy Data and Common Commas

Data read from a file is always returned as a string. Convert the high scores to integers, using `value()`, before stuffing them back into the highScores list.

Each line of the data file is in comma-delimited format and contains the user's name score separated by a comma. You can easily parse the data because item 1 is the user name and item 2 is the score. The user name can contain spaces, or any punctuation, other than a comma or a carriage return.

Tip

2. The updated version of the `retrieveHiScores` routine now parses the data file and updates the high score chart for the user.

You might ordinarily call `retrieveHiScores` in your `startMovie` handler, and omit the alert message if no high score file is found.

```
on retrieveHiScores
  set success = openDataFile (the pathname & "hiScore.txt")
  if success then
    set hiScoreData = readFromFile ()
    -- This line is now commented out
    -- put hiScoreData into field "High Scores"
```

```
   -- These lines are new
   parseHiScoreData(hiScoreData)
   updateHiScoreChart()

   closeDataFile()
 else
   -- This line is for debugging purposes
   alert "Unable to retrieve high scores"
 end if

end retrieveHiScores
```

Using Alternative File Names and File Paths

The prior examples transparently (without the user's knowledge) save and retrieve a hard-coded file name from the same folder as the projector. This is fine when only one small file name is required. Of course, if the projector is on a CD-ROM, files cannot be written to the same folder.

Therefore, you'll often write files to the user's hard drive. If you don't allow the user to specify a location, write your data files to the Macintosh Preferences folder, or to a subdirectory off the Windows directory.

If there are multiple users, or a single user can store multiple games, you should allow the user to choose the file name or the folder in which to save his work.

You might allow the user to choose the file name, but not the folder, to make certain that all data files are stored in a known location. The major drawback of using this technique is that users might not know where to find their data. In this case, make certain when the user is asked to retrieve a file, that the file browser shows the correct folder. If you are storing multifile data sets for each user, you might allow the user to choose a folder but not a file name. This may require that you ask the user to locate their data when the application is restarted, or you could include a login feature which remembers the data location for each user.

Lastly, you might allow the user to specify both the file name and folder location for his stored data, as shown in the next example.

User-Specified Saved Game File

The example demonstrates how to bring up a file browser dialog box to allow the user to select the location for his saved data. This technique is appropriate only when the user controls the saving and retrieving of the game state. It would not be appropriate for data that should remain hidden from the user.

To allow the user to specify the file to be created and then determine the file name chosen, use the following code:

```
-- Bring up the file browser
set gFileObj = fileIO (mNew, "?write", "suggest.txt")

-- Check if user selected Cancel, or chose a file
if objectP(gFileObj) then
   -- Record the user's file choice
   set userFilePath = gFileObj (mFileName)
else
   if gFileObj = -43 then
      put "The user selected Cancel"
   else
      put "Other Error occurred" && fileIO (mError, gFileObj)
   end if
end if
```

The question mark (?) instructs FileIO to bring up the standard file browser dialog box (see fig. 5.1). Note that when using the FileIO XObject if the user selects Cancel, error code –43 (File not found) is returned. Your Lingo should trap for this possibility and other error codes (refer to the documentation for the FileIO XObject).

FIGURE 5.1

The Write File Browser
dialog box.

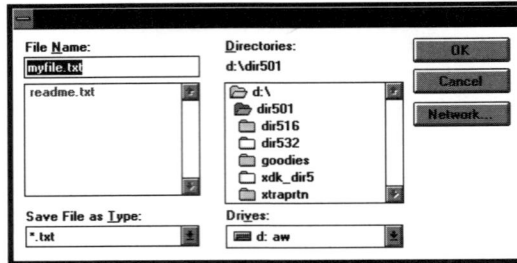

The browser will show the current folder, with a default file name of
suggest.txt. The user can change the folder or the file name before selecting
OK.

> **Tip** The FileIO Xtra can be used to achieve the same results as the FileIO XObject,
> but the procedure is quite different. Here is the previous example rewritten using
> the FileIO Xtra.

```
global gFileXtraObj

  -- Create an instance of the Xtra
  set gFileXtraObj = new (Xtra "FileIO")

  if not objectP(gFileXtraObj) then
    alert "Could not instantiate Xtra"
    exit
  end if

  -- Set the filter mask to let the user choose
  -- between showing all files or only *.TXT files
 -- on the PC, or TEXT files on the Mac
  if the machineType = 256 then
    setFilterMask (gFileXtraObj, "All Files,*.*,Text Files,*.TXT")
  else
    setFilterMask (gFileXtraObj, "TEXT")
  end if

  -- Bring up the file browser, specifying the Title and default file
name
  set userFilePath = displaySave (gFileXtraObj, "Dialog Title",¬
"suggest.txt")
```

```
   if userFilePath = EMPTY then
     put "The user selected Cancel"
else
     put "Attempting to Create File" && userFilePath
     -- Create the file, and open it for write access
     createFile (gFileXtraObj, userFilePath)

     set resultCode = status (gFileXtraObj)
     -- The displaySave() method does not directly inform Lingo
     -- whether a user is replacing an existing file.
     -- The workaround is to attempt to create the file using
     -- createFile() and check the error code for
     -- a "File Already Exists" error (-122)

     if resultCode = 0 then

       put "Successful file creation"

     else if resultCode = -122 then
       -- If the user attempted to overwrite an existing
       -- file error code -122 is returned.
       -- You must decide how to handle this situation
       -- You may wish to ignore the error
       -- Writing data to the file will overwrite existing data
       put "The user decided to overwrite an existing file"

     else
       put "Other Error occurred" && error (gFileXtraObj, status¬
(gFileXtraObj))
       exit
     end if

     -- Open the file with Read/Write Access
     openFile (gFileXtraObj, userFilePath, 0)
     put "Attempt to OpenFile - Status" && status (gFileXtraObj)

   end if
```

I prefer the Xobject's simpler syntax over the convoluted methodology used by the FileIO Xtra, unless one needs native 32-bit support under Windows 95 and NT.

User-Specified Game to Retrieve

If the user is allowed to specify a file to save, you should allow him to specify a file to retrieve as well.

When using the FileIO XObject's read mode, the third parameter specifies the actual file path to the file you want to open. When using ?read mode, however, this parameter indicates the type of file to be shown in the dialog box (see fig. 5.2).

On the Macintosh, this is the case-sensitive four-character file Type code associated with every Macintosh file. (Use ResEdit to view a file's Type.)

Under Windows, this is the three character case-insensitive extension, such as txt (omit the period when specifying the extension).

To allow the user to select from existing TEXT files on the Macintosh, use the following code:

```
set gFileObj = fileIO (mNew, "?read", "TEXT")
```

The FileIO Xtra uses a combination of the new, setFilterMask, displayOpen and openFile methods to perform the same operation. Refer to the previous tip and the FileIO Xtra ReadMe file regarding proper use of the Xtra.

FIGURE 5.2

The Macintosh Read File Browser dialog box.

The Macintosh file browser shows the TEXT files in the current folder. The user cannot type a file name as he can on the PC (see fig. 5.3), but he can select from the displayed files in the list and browse the folder tree.

To allow the user to select from existing ".txt" files under Windows, use the following code:

```
set gFileObj = fileIO (mNew, "?read", "txt")
```

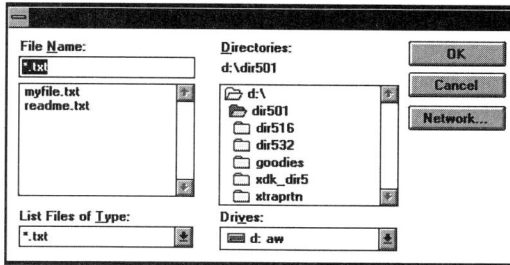

FIGURE 5.3

The Windows Read File Browser dialog box.

The Windows file browser will show the ".txt" files in the current directory. The user can select from the displayed files, browse the directory tree or type a file name.

It Takes All Types

You may want to display files of all types in the Browser dialog box.

To show all available files on the Macintosh using the FileIO XObject, use

```
set gFileObj = fileIO (mNew, "?read", "")
```

To show all available files under Windows using the FileIO DLL, use

```
set gFileObj = fileIO (mNew, "?read", "*")
```

To show all available files on the Macintosh using the FileIO Xtra, set the filter mask before calling displayOpen or displaySave:

```
setFilterMask(fileInstance, "")
```

Similarly, when using the FileIO Xtra under Windows, use

```
setFilterMask(fileInstance, "All Files,*.*")
```

> **The Paths Less Traveled: The System or Windows Path**
>
> Use the FileIO Xtra's new getOSDirectory method to locate the Macintosh System Folder or the Windows Directory, as follows:
>
> ```
> put getOSDirectory()
> -- Macintosh
> -- "HD:System Folder:"
> --or
> -- Windows
> -- "C:\WINDOWS"
> ```

Tip

Note that the FileIO Xtra ReadMe file mistakenly refers to this method as "getCSdir". You do not need to create an instance to use this method, but don't forget the parentheses! Note that the returned value includes a trailing colon (:) on the Macintosh; under Windows it does not include a trailing backslash, in contrast to the pathName. Use the following code to create a path to a file in the Windows directory:

```
set winFilePath = getOSDirectory() & "\" & winFileName
```

The Default Folder

Neither the FileIO XObject nor the FileIO Xtra allows you to specify a default folder in which to begin browsing for files. Ordinarily, the file browser will begin at the last folder used.

The `mSetDefaultPath` method in MovieUtilities.XObj (Macintosh) or MOVUTILS.DLL (Windows) will set the default path for the file browser. (These XObjects were distributed free of charge by Macromedia with Director 4). Use this method before bringing up a file dialog box. Note that the XObject's default folder setting may be overridden by a setting in the General Controls control panel on the Macintosh.

Selecting a Folder

You may want to allow the user to select a folder, without requiring him to specify a file name. This is useful when the user is picking a destination for his data, but you are controlling the individual file name(s). Unfortunately, the FileIO XObject and Xtra do not allow the user to specify a folder alone. Refer to the Xtras section of Macromedia's web site for third party utilities.

Saving and Retrieving Different Data Types

Use FileIO to store all sorts of data, such as global variables and lists. You can store and retrieve the frame number and movie name to indicate where the user last left off in a linear animation, for example.

Remember, all data is written out as a string—a series of ASCII characters. To retrieve data of various types, use Lingo's type conversion routines.

The following table indicates the functions used to convert the string values read from a file into each possible data type.

To Restore Data Type	Use This Function
integer	integer (stringItem) or value (stringItem)
float	float (stringItem) or value (stringItem)
string	(no conversion needed)
symbol	value ("#" and stringItem)
<void>	value ("<Void>")
list	value(stringItem) (don't use "list()")
objects	N/A (see FileIO Limitations)

How Do You Know What Type of Data You Are Restoring?

If you know the exact format of the data that is written out, then you know exactly how to interpret it when it is retrieved. You could, therefore, hard-code the type conversions for each piece of data as it is parsed from the file.

If the data to be written varies, you need to include codes to indicate the data type. When writing out integers, for example, use type code 1; for strings use type code 2; for lists use type code 3. When retrieving the data, read the type code first to know how to convert that particular datum.

Use this technique if the data file is read into a variable named myData that contains the following

```
1
123
2
45.6
3
[1,2,3]
4
foo

parsedata (myData)
-- "Item 1 is an integer: 123"
-- "Item 2 is a float: 45.6000"
-- "Item 3 is a list: [1, 2, 3]"
-- "Item 4 (foo) is of unknown type: 4"
```

```
on parseData fileData
  set numLines = the number of lines in fileData

  repeat with x = 1 to numLines
    set typeCode  = line x   of fileData
    set thisDatum = line x+1 of fileData
    set itemNum = (x/2) + 1
    case (typeCode) of:
      "1": set myInt = integer(thisDatum)
        put "Item" && itemNum && "is an integer:" && myInt

      "2": set myFloat = float(thisDatum)
        put "Item" && itemNum && "is a float:" && myFloat

      "3": set myList = value(thisDatum)
        put "Item" && itemNum && "is a list:" && myList

      otherwise:
        put "Item" && itemNum && "(" & thisDatum & ") is of unknown¬
type:" && typeCode
    end case

    set x = x + 1
  end repeat

end parseData
```

FileIO Limitations

Although FileIO is quite flexible, it does have practical limitations to its use. The following items describe some issues of which you should be aware, and hints to avoid trouble.

Speed

Text parsing and type conversions in Lingo can be slow, especially when converting strings to lists or vice-versa. For a large data file, the overall time delay can be significant (it could take several minutes to perform thousands of type conversions). The key is to optimize the operations that are performed repeatedly. If performance becomes an issue, try the following:

❧ Save and retrieve only the data that is required to recreate a particular state.

❧ Parse the data from a variable, which is much faster than parsing data stored in a file or field.

❧ Limit the amount of text. Director accesses the early lines of a field faster than later lines. For any given line, access is also faster if the field contains less text. You can increase performance by deleting the lines you have already parsed. Make a copy of the data first if necessary.

❧ Use XObjects or Xtras, which are written in C, and perform much faster than Lingo. Several third-party Xtras are available for database access and text manipulation. Refer to the Xtras section of Macromedia's web site for more information.

File Size

On the PC, each file read/write operation is limited to 64 KB of data, and any excess data will be lost unless you buffer it yourself. Write the data in smaller chunks, if necessary, using the following code:

```
on bufferedWrite fileObj, dataToWrite
  -- This assumes that fileObj is the instance handle for
  -- a file opened in write mode
  set temp = dataToWrite
  set limit = 64 * 1024
  repeat while length (temp) > limit then
    fileObj (mWriteString, char 1 to limit of temp)
    delete char 1 to limit of temp
  end repeat
  fileObj (mWriteString, temp)
end bufferedWrite
```

You can use FileIO's mGetLength method to check the length of a file. Although text fields are limited to 32 KB, variables can hold considerably more data. If necessary, read the data in chunks, and accumulate it in a variable, using the following code:

```
on bufferedRead fileObj
  -- This assumes that fileObj is the instance handle for
  -- a file opened in read mode
```

```
set temp = EMPTY
set limit = 64 * 1024

repeat while fileObj (mGetLength) - fileObj (mGetPosition) > limit¬
then
  -- put "reading"
  put fileObj (mReadLine) after temp
end repeat
put fileObj (mReadFile) after temp

return temp


end bufferedRead
```

Type Conversions

Your data file can be structured in a variety of ways. You may separate items by spaces or commas, or place each item on its own line. This section demonstrates the syntax for retrieving various data types from a file. The particulars of your situation will depend on your needs and the file structure you choose.

❖ **Integers:** `set myInt = integer (gFileObj(mReadWord))`

This conversion may be slow. Refer to the earlier tips for increasing performance.

❖ **Floating Point Numbers:** `set myFloat = float (gFileObj(mReadWord))`

This conversion may also be slow. Refer to the earlier tips for increasing performance.

❖ **Strings:** There is no need to perform type conversion for strings, but parsing a large string can be slow. Read the entire string in a variable, not a field, and parse it in memory, as described earlier.

Remember that an EMPTY string is written out as *nothing*, not even a space. Separate data with commas or line breaks to avoid confusion.

Separating strings with commas allows a string to contain spaces and still maintain its integrity. Beware of strings containing commas that will confuse Lingo's `"the item…of"` chunk expression.

One solution is to write each string on its own separate line.

Line Breaks

On the Macintosh, line breaks are written as <CR> (ASCII 13). On the PC, they are written as <CR><LF> (ASCII 13 and 10). Although FileIO will handle this transparently, you have to add a <CR> using the Lingo constant RETURN wherever you want a line break, such as in the following:

```
gFileObj (mWriteString, "Text with a CR at the end" & RETURN)
```

Omit the RETURN following the last line of data to avoid adding a blank line to the end of your file.

The trailing RETURN character is included by mReadLine. Remove it by deleting the last character of the line, or using the "line 1 of…" chunk expression, which removes the trailing RETURN.

```
set thisLine = gFileObj (mReadLine)
delete the last char of thisLine
set textWithoutReturn = thisLine
-- or
set thisLine = gFileObj (mReadLine)
set textWithoutReturn = line 1 of thisLine
```

When you view a text file in a PC word processor, non-printing characters may appear as solid black boxes and the lines may not wrap.

Symbols

If you save symbols to a file, they will be stripped of the pound character (#) and saved as strings. There is no Lingo function to re-create a symbol from a string, but you can use the following:

```
set mySymbolicValue = value ("#" & symbolString)
```

<Void Values>

When you write out a <Void> value, it is written out as an empty string. When you retrieve it, you might not know to interpret it as a <Void> value. You can write out void integers and floating point numbers as zero ("0"), void strings as the EMPTY string (""), void lists as "[]" and void property lists as "[:]". If you store them in this manner, when you read them back in, they will contain valid values. So long as your code does not rely on them being <Void>, this method works well. Refer to the *voidP* Lingo function in the Lingo Dictionary or on-line Help. There is no Lingo function to re-create a <Void> value, but you can do so using the following:

```
set myVoidValue = value ("<void>")
```

Alternatively, you can declare a global, but never assign it a value (so that it is implicitly void) and then use it to assign other variables. For convenience, I name this dummy variable *void*, but you can use any name you like. For example

```
global void
set myVoidValue = void
```

Lists

Retrieving entire lists is an easy way to restore large amounts of data from a file. To re-create a list from a string, use the value() function, such as

```
set myList = value (stringHoldingList)
```

or

```
set myList = value (gFileObj (mReadLine))
```

This works for both linear lists and property lists, but can be slow for large lists. Remember that the 64 KB transfer limit prevents you from retrieving very large lists in one piece. You must either shorten the list or break it into smaller pieces for storage and retrieval.

You cannot use the value function to re-create lists that contain <Void> values or lists containing empty sublists.

The following examples will not work. They cause myList to contain <Void>.

```
set myString = "[1, <void>, 3]"
-- or
set myString = "[[1,2,3], [:]]"
set myList = value (myString)
```

Don't forget to re-sort lists that were sorted prior to being stored. Remember to use the following code when duplicating a list

```
set list2 = duplicate (list1)
```

or

```
set list2 = value(string(list1))
```

Objects

Because objects refer to memory locations, you cannot save and retrieve objects to or from a file. If you save an object, which is actually a memory address, it is meaningless when you reread it later. Thus, you cannot save child objects or XObject instances to a file. Instead, you must reallocate them at runtime.

If need be, you can store the properties of various child objects in a file. Later, you could re-birth the objects, and reassign their properties. Even though the child objects themselves have been reallocated to a different part of RAM, the net effect is the same. For example

```
set myObj = new (script "Parent Script")
set the myCustomProperty of myObj = integer (gFileObj (mReadWord))
```

Viewing Your Data Files

You can view your text files by opening them in a word processor. On the Macintosh, a file can be opened with TeachText after setting its Type and Creator to "TEXT", and "ttxt" respectively. For example

```
set gFileObj (mSetFinderInfo, "TEXT", "ttxt")
```

Note that the Type and Creator codes are case–sensitive.

On the PC, you can create a file with an extension such as ".WRI", ".DOC", or ".TXT" as these are usually associated with a word processor under Windows. (Refer to the WIN.INI file that defines these associations.)

Double-Clicking to Start a Projector or Reload Saved Game

On the Macintosh, by setting the Type and Creator codes of both your data file and your Projector, you can cause your Projector to be launched automatically when a document is double-clicked on. Invent a Creator code and use it for both your Projector and your documents. They are automatically associated with each other by the Finder. Be certain to pick a Creator code that does not already exist. (Refer to Apple's procedures for reserving Type and Creator codes on their web site.)

On the PC, you would also need to modify the WIN.INI file to associate a particular file extension with your projector.

While this will launch your Projector on either platform, the Projector won't know which file to open. If there is only one possible text file, you could check for its existence and open it automatically. If there is more than one possibility, you could write the name of the last saved file to a known place and reload it from there. Unfortunately, a general solution is not currently available.

Protecting Your Data Files

In some cases, you will not want to give the user unlimited access to the data files. You have several choices, none of which are foolproof.

❋ Encrypt the data so that it is meaningless to the casual observer. This requires that you decrypt the data when you retrieve it. You can use an encryption Xtra, or write your own in Lingo. Simple encryption will dissuade the casual observer, but not the hard core hacker, and Lingo encryption may be slow for large amounts of text.

❋ Hide the data files by modifying their properties with an XObject or Xtra. Again, this will only dissuade the casual observer, as "hidden" files are easily seen with a variety of tools on both the Macintosh and PC.

❋ Place the files in a *drop-box*, a directory where the user has write privileges, but not read privileges. This is appropriate for student test results that are only to be read by the teacher. Obviously, this precludes the user from re-reading those files at a later date.

> **Shameless Plug**
>
> Several companies, including mine—Zeus Productions, market Xtras that add this type of functionality to Director. Refer to the Xtras section on Macromedia's web site, and the advertisements in the back of the book.

Note

Concocting File Versions

When you allow a user to retrieve a file, you must ensure that the file selected by the user is in fact a proper data file. On the Macintosh, when using the FileIO Xobject, you can limit the dialog box to show files of a certain type in `"?read"` mode. The FileIO Xtra uses the *setFilterMask* method to limit the viewable files.

On the PC, you can force a file have a certain extension by simply replacing any user-specified extension with the preferred one.

On either platform, you can implement a file version check—add a line of header information at the top of every file that includes your application's name and version number. When creating a file, you should write the header; when opening a file, you should verify the header. This has the advantage of being a robust cross-platform solution that also enables you to do version checking in case you update your application in the future. For example

```
-- This global is declared external to any handler,
-- so that it is accessible to all routines.
global gVersion
on startMovie
   set gVersion "The Monkey's Uncle, Version 1.0"
end


on writeVersion fileObj
  fileObj (mWriteString, gVersion)
end


on readVersion fileObj
  set versionString = fileObj (mReadLine)
  if versionString <> gVersion) then
    alert "File has wrong version information:" && versionString
  end if
end
```

Conclusion

We have covered a lot of territory in this chapter. We implemented a high score chart, and explored various strategies for saving and retrieving user data. You are now equipped with the knowledge to allow the user to:

- Save the game state between sessions
- Pick the file and folder name for storing data
- Achieve immorality on your game's top ten list

Additionally you have learned to:

- Record user preferences and option settings
- Record quiz Data
- Convert data back to its original data type
- Buffer data to surmount the PC FileIO transfer limit
- Speed up data parsing and retrieval
- Determine the user's System or Windows folder
- Perform file I/O under Windows 95 and NT using the new 32-bit Xtra
- Protect your files from prying eyes
- Add a version header to your data file

You now possess the general knowledge and specific tools to expand your multimedia project's boundaries. Enjoy the journey, and good luck in all your multimedia pursuits.

chapter 6

Dudley Bryan

TRADITIONAL ANIMATION AND DIRECTOR

Director 5 has many tools by which users can create dramatic characters for their animations. Originally called VideoWorks, Macromedia Director started off as a tool for animation, and in its latest release provides several new features geared toward enabling an animator to move through production more naturally.

Traditionally, concepts like pencil tests, in-betweening, and onion skinning represented crucial steps in the creation of a quality exhibition. In Director 5, creators can easily bring these concepts into their development process, but creators must also be aware of the potential problems and pitfalls inherent in working with the computer.

This chapter demonstrates one way of moving through the creation process of an animated scene using Director. This technique will benefit anyone who wants to include animated characters in a product. The look achieved with this technique resembles that seen in many popular commercial entertainment products on the market today.

Having a basic idea of an effective process can save a significant amount of time during development; conversely, many hours can be lost if an effective plan is not followed from the start. Throughout this chapter, you will learn tips, tricks, and techniques for speeding up the animating process.

Starting Up: Before the Pixel

Before the first pixel is drawn on the screen, groundwork that sets the stage for everything that comes after needs to be established. A crucial step in organizing a successful animation project is the completion of concept sketches and storyboards. Without these, the project deadlines can spin out of control as major elements change based on decisions made after detailed work has commenced. Guarantees that changes will not crop up cannot be made; eliminating unnecessary complications early on, therefore, is always a smart decision.

Note

> Although the methods described in this chapter demonstrate a way to create effective animations using Director, these methods are by no means the *only* way. Experimenting with new and different techniques for managing tasks will reap time-saving rewards, and can improve the final product's quality.

As a recommended course of action, determine in advance which characters need to be in the scene, what they will do, and which parts of the screen they will occupy (if applicable). Although an obvious step, remember that good planning saves time and heartache later on when deadlines approach and time becomes scarce.

The light table is a friend to all animators and artists. Light tables range from the size of a desk to small boxes slightly larger than a sheet of typing paper. Light tables can be found in most art stores, and if need be, can even be constructed make-shift using a transparent surface to draw on and any light source that can shine from underneath it.

Tip

The light table can be used to create multilayered sketches of a proposed scene. Start with a sketch of the background. Multiple artists working on different elements of the same scene can use these initial sketches as a visual agreement. Whether painted or rendered in 3D, the artist responsible for the background can use the sketch as a template to create the final artwork. Meanwhile, the artist(s) working on the foreground characters can work with reasonable assurance of how the final environment will look by referencing the sketch through the light table. The artist simply places the sketch on top of the light table, and placing a clean sheet of paper over *that*, begins to create using the light table to see through everything beneath. As a side note, this sketch can be made by hand or generated on the computer and printed out for reference.

After creation of the background sketch, the light table can be used to test sketches of the characters as they will appear in the scene. By using the light table to see through the coupled pages, the character artist should work out a selection of poses and key frames of animation as detailed in the storyboards.

If the artist prefers to work entirely inside the computer, the effect of the light table can be easily duplicated using onion skinning in Director 5. First, the background sketch needs to either be scanned in and imported, or if created in a 3D or 2D graphics program outside Director, simply imported. By creating a new cast member and setting the background to the background sketch (and Showing Background), you can freely draw the characters while referencing a facsimile of the scene in which they will appear. These onion skin-related commands are all accessible through the Onion Skin toolbar under the View menu.

Note

The term *key frame* should not be confused with the *frames* that are the basis of much of Director's operations. As used here, the term *key frames* refers to the specific or *key* images (cast members) that compose an outline of a character's sequence of motion. Similar to digital video, the key frames in animations represent complete frames between which interpreted frames are created. This term exists outside of Director and is potentially confusing because Director has modified the meaning of many traditional terms to better relate its process of development to the real world.

When the character artist finishes these drawings, they can be scanned and imported into Director.

Sketches drawn in this way are valuable because they can be quickly combined with their backdrops (along with quick coloring) to show a representation of the final scene for review by everyone involved. Initial artwork done this way can also help the resident Lingo programmer construct a working model of the project as it's being created. The sketches would be used as substitutions for the real artwork until it is finally created.

Animation Tips

To keep this chapter simple, an assumption will be made that the artist will be using a single palette to create the animation. Although projects are by no means limited to one palette, the potential for multiple palettes has a larger scope than this chapter seeks to cover.

Frames Per Second and Your Target Platform

Keep in mind the limitations of your target platform when creating your animation. Due to the amount of memory the target system has, you might want to design your animations to use between six and ten frames per second. You need to decide this at the beginning so that the project has an air of consistency. Be mindful that although 30 frames per second looks beautiful when running on a machine that can handle it, this proves a tall order for many average PCs. Director not only needs to load all these cast members into memory, but it needs to be capable of putting them on the screen just as quickly (a feat also dependent on the speed of the computer's video card). If you are targeting a system on a high-end computer (a Pentium or Power Macintosh system with more than 16 MB of RAM), this will not pose much of a problem. If you are trying to play consistently over a wide range of machine configurations, however, limiting your frame rate is crucial.

Size and Frame Number Considerations

The amount of viewing area your animations fill during continuous playback is important. If your lowest target system is a 486 33 MHz machine, you should not get too carried away when it comes to using a large number (or size) of unique cast members. The term *unique cast members* refers to the idea that in Director (and traditional animation), appropriate images can be reused. As many users of Director know, this provides computers with a strong advantage; it enables Director to animate with objects already loaded into memory. The final system performance improves each time this effect is utilized. Although every key frame of a character is a unique cast member, when the animation is complete, the character animation is composed of more unique cast members than key frames. Key frames are a basic shorthand of how a character will move, but completing the range of motion requires a larger number of unique cast members of which the key frames are a subset. Figure 6.1 shows the relationship between key frames and unique cast members.

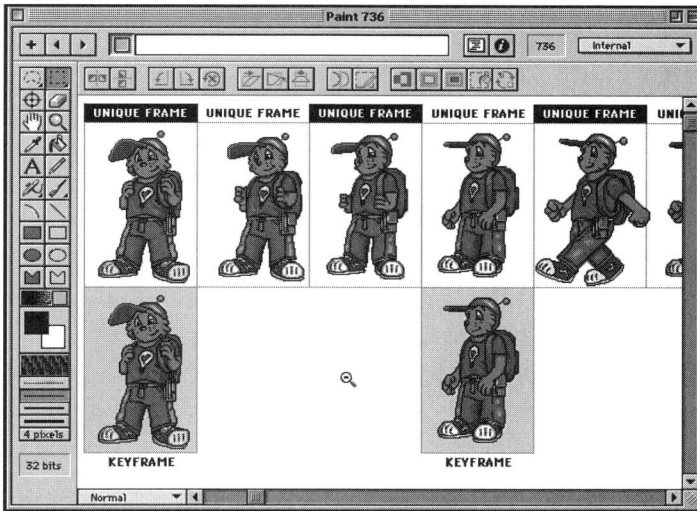

FIGURE 6.1

The relationship between key frames and unique cast members.

Smaller Parts Make for a Faster Whole

Some developers design their animations in such a way that setting the frame rate of playback as high as possible poses no problem. They use the fewest possible unique cast members to perform a scene. The result is an animation both functional and quick, even though it is a departure from the way traditional animation is perceived. By using multiple cast members to compose one figure, they can recycle a small number of unique cast members—a great advantage. Instead of just one cast member, an artist can build a character with a number of cast members. Such building can range from separating the head, top, and lower half of the body to breaking down the character into eyes, mouths, arms, chest, and legs.

This effect can, however, backfire. Even though this technique can keep the memory usage low, using too many cast members changing on-screen at the same time can be slower for Director because it must control more elements. To enjoy the best of both worlds, divide the character into objects such as head, right arm, left arm, torso, and legs. If the character wears a dress, the bottom half could be divided further into dress, left shoe, and right shoe. All this depends on what you want to have the character do (keeping things simple is always preferred).

Using the key frame scans made from the previously discussed sketches, the character artist can proceed in translating the cartoons to the computer.

The Style of Your Line

Artists can translate or create traditionally animated artwork on the computer in many ways. Some artists use anti-aliased lines (see the first character in fig. 6.2). This method is the hardest to work with because artwork is difficult to change after it has been created. Also, much cleanup is involved because the image needs to blend properly when placed on a background in Director. Usually it can be scanned in grayscale from line art, and then colored frame by frame using programs like Photoshop. If done correctly, this results in a drawing that looks smooth and that has barely visible pixels. Anti-aliasing enables images to use varying line widths and retain many details of a character's expression by simulating a higher image resolution.

Alternatively, an artist may choose not to use anti-aliasing, and instead use a varying outline with a hard-pixel edge (see the middle character in fig. 6.2). This generally produces mixed results and can sometimes look a little clunky if too little attention is paid to the line work. Many artists these days have discovered the nice little trick of creating animations with a one-pixel thin line (see the character on the right in fig. 6.2). Everyone has a preference, but the one-pixel line seems to always look the cleanest. *One-pixel line* refers to the idea that the outline of the character is drawn using a line that at no time is thicker than one pixel. An award-winning Living Book titled *GranMa & Me* uses this technique. *Freddi Fish*, by Humungous Entertainment, also uses the one-pixel rule to create a basic yet compelling style. This look can be created using almost any art program. My personal favorite is Director's own Paint window. You'll learn that being familiar with the Paint window tools helps a lot.

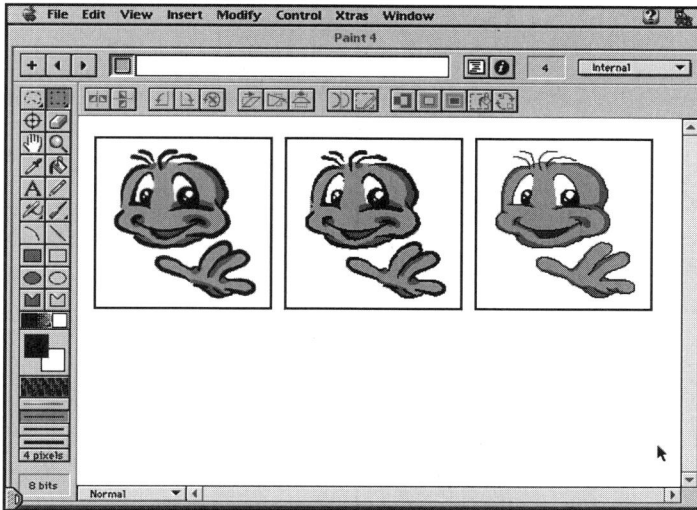

FIGURE 6.2

The effect of using different line types for an animation.

One of the most useful items in Director's Paint window is the Brush tool. Set to one pixel, this tool has the utility of a precision instrument when editing your artwork. However, because the Brush tool creates non-contiguous lines if you move too quickly, you might be more comfortable using the Pencil tool instead. The Pencil tool is also handy because it auto-erases any pixel that is already the color with which you are editing. The color the pixel changes to when auto-erasing is the background color you've set in the tool strip. Even given this, I prefer using the Brush tool and the Eyedropper together. I need to work slowly enough to get a contiguous line, but I find that not having the bulky pencil icon following me around makes it much easier to see what I'm doing. If I lose my place (which is easy when using one pixel with which to paint), I simply press and hold the D key, and the Eyedropper lets me know where my prodigal pointer has gone. Periodically pressing the D key and clicking to quickly change your paint color by sampling colors from the screen speeds your editing, especially when editing with multiple colors.

Tip

The single pixel technique is also the easiest to clean up if characters need to be resized for any reason; any fudged pixels can easily be straightened out by taking away the extra pixels click by click.

From Scans to the Screen with Director 5

After determining the key frames you need for a given scene, you are ready to work. The following is one method of translating scanned sketches into final characters in Director 5.

Bringing in Your Scans

1. After scanning the images into an image editing application, adjust the brightness and contrast so that there is a stark difference between the line drawing and its background (the background should be pure white and not light gray). If possible, check the dots per inch (dpi) of the image. If it is not 72 dpi, then adjust it. (Note: scan the background image first into an area as close as possible to 640×480 pixels [or the height and width of your stage]. Make certain that the characters are scanned in the same way as the background so that they match up again later on.)

Tip

All images should be set to 72 dpi if you want them to retain the pixel for pixel relationship of how it appears in Photoshop versus how it appears in Director. Director assumes that all the graphics you import appear at the resolution of the screen, and it interprets screen resolution as 72 dpi. If an image's dpi is higher than 72, the image appears smaller when imported into Director. If an image is lower than 72 dpi, it appears larger when imported into Director. As a result, a common problem developers run into is having Director state that it is out of memory when importing an image. This may mean that the dpi of the image is incorrectly set. Dpi settings accidentally set into multiple decimal places sometimes produce error messages. Checking the dpi can save you a headache.

2. Import the scans of the background sketch and the character sketches into Director. (Note: At this time, you can dither the images to the palette you will be using.)

3. Make certain that the background has been scanned in at the full size of the stage, and that the image is 72 dpi.

4. Make certain that your original sketches are set up properly. Looking at them in the cast window, confirm that the arrangement is sequential and that the images were not imported out of order.

Tip

When manipulating the order of your cast members, you need to always keep in mind the way in which Director's cast window works. Selecting a cast member and dragging it to any position *before* its current position in the cast window shifts forward those cast members it jumps. Dragging a cast member or group of cast members to any position *after* the original cast member's position adds blank cast members to the cast window in the spaces jumped (the number of blank spaces equals the number of cast you are moving). This effect can be used to open up needed space between your key frames.

Blank spaces can be dragged or dropped in the cast to insert blank cast members. When moving a block of cast members by dragging, the insertion point is based on the position of the mouse cursor, not the position of the selected block. Always remember that if you only want to rearrange cast members (and not add unnecessary spaces), move them backward; never drag them forward in the cast window.

When you're finished moving cast members, squelch any unused blank holes between cast members. Extinguishing them can be accomplished under Director 5 by choosing the Sort option from the Modify menu after selecting all your cast members. Selecting the Empty at End option forces the blank spaces to the end of the order. Alternatively, from the Cast menu, choose Sort Cast Members By Order in Cast under Director 4.04. This is more or less good housekeeping à la Director.

5. If the key frames of the character motion were all scanned into one image, you need to break these up into separate cast members. After separating, make certain that when moving from one to the other in the Paint window, their relationship to each other is adequate. In the Paint window, you can flip easily from cast member to cast member using the forward and backward arrows on the keyboard. If flipping them one after the other causes them to jump erratically, try adjusting the registration points. The registration points not only adjust how the cast members appear on-stage, but in the Paint window, they have a direct effect on how the cast member positions relate to each other. You could try using the Marquee tool to reposition misaligned cast, but you might not get the results you want. Only by manually setting the registration point can you be sure that Director is altering the relationships of the sprites the way you want.

Note

Beginning with Director 5.0, the Paint window automatically centers the view of all the cast members according to the registration point as you move from cast member to cast member. In previous versions, the position of the sprite in the window and the registration point were two different attributes that could potentially confuse the authoring process. Because onion skinning didn't exist in previous versions, the feature this most affected was the Reveal ink feature. This ink enables you to paint on one cast member using pixels from the preceding cast member (essentially, a rub-through effect). Previously, to properly align images, the developer only needed to shift the previous cast member using the Hand tool. Because all cast members are only viewed and related by the registration points in Director 5, lining up cast members for all relational procedures requires adjusting this point, and not the image itself.

Be careful. Although moving cast members using the Marquee tool may seem like a solution, it may also cause Director to reset the registration point to the center of the cast member. It's best to go right to the source of the problem from the beginning.

6. Set up Director to enable you to use your sketches as reference for creating the final (single-pixel outline) cast members.

7. Open your first sketch in the Paint window.

8. Choose Onion Skin from the View menu. Onion Skin is a new feature of Director 5.

9. On the Onion Skin toolbar that appears, click on the Onion Skin button, and set both toolbar value fields to zero (see fig. 6.3).

10. Click on the Set background button to set the current sketch as reference image number one.

11. Click on the Track background button and set the Show Background button on.

12. Click on the Add button from the Paint window to create new cast members.

FIGURE 6.3

The use of Onion Skin to get results.

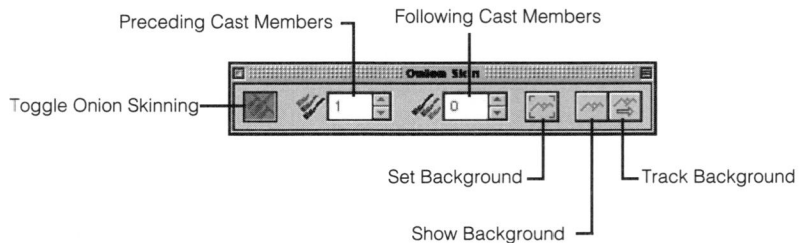

Preceding Cast Members — Following Cast Members

Toggle Onion Skinning —

Set Background — Track Background

Show Background —

You should now see the first sketch of your series in light tones behind your blank slate. Begin designing your final art on top of this. As you create new cast members, your reference changes and follows you.

13. After your key frames have been redesigned as single-pixel cartoons, you can turn off background/track-background and concentrate on creating any additional in-between frames by hand. (Note: Leave Onion Skinning on).

14. Use the cast window to select and delete your reference frames.

15. Add the necessary spaces between your new key frames by dragging the key frame cast members forward in the Cast window. Alternatively, you can drag blank cast members between the key cast members. Assume that you have three cast members that represent three key frames in your character's motion. In this example, you add one new cast member between one and two, and between two and three.

16. Open the Paint window by double-clicking on the first member of this series. Even though in step 15 you added an empty cast member between the first and second casts, Director does not recognize this yet as an image on which to work. Clicking on the Add button enables you to edit the next free cast member in the Cast window.

17. Use the Onion Skin toolbar to increase the Preceding Cast member field to 1. You should now see your first key frame image in light gray. Use Onion Skinning to create all the necessary tweening steps in animating your character. Keep an eye on the amount of free spaces in the cast window between your key frame images. Add and subtract them as necessary.

The preceding method of animation is best used for scenes in which the character appears small in relation to the entire stage, and the character's body is so lively that separating it into pieces would not conserve a significant amount of memory. You can also use it to work on scanned pieces of characters and not necessarily whole figures.

Colorizing the Animation

After all your frames are complete, you can color your characters using the fill bucket. Although this is a fast and easy way to assign color, there is also an easy way to enhance the depth of your characters using the Brush tool in conjunction with it. The animated cast members at this point are simply black-and-white line drawings (single pixel line drawings).

1. Work on the first key cast member to establish the color scheme of your character using the current palette. By color scheme, I mean you should ask yourself, "What colors are used to create this character and establish its mood? Does the character use dull grays and blues (mean, sad), or does it wear a bright red shirt and yellow pants (happy)?" For every color you pick to appear in the character, determine at least one shade color for each regular color you pick that will enable you to give the character depth. The *shade color* is simply a moderately darker version of the normal color (it can also be referred to as a kind of "half-bright"—an old term for those Amiga fans out there).

Note

You can easily spot a workable shade color using the Blend ink from the bottom of the Paint window. Use the filled Rectangle tool to draw a sample of the normal color on the screen (set the rectangle to no frame). Select the color black from your palette and select the Blend ink. Draw another square over half of the square you drew originally (Note: Make certain that Preferences in the Paint window has Blend Percentage tuned anywhere from 40–50 percent. Experiment to find out what settings get the best results). The Preference window can be reached by choosing File, Preferences, Paint from the menu. Set as described, Blend should make the color about half as bright as the original color. You now have a shaded version of your color. Figure 6.4 shows an example of what a shade color might look like. Alternately (for more colorful choices), you could choose to pick out or even create these colors manually, but it could turn into a lengthy proposition. The good thing about using Blend is that you can use it to instantly find any number of valid intermediate colors from the palette. Intermediate colors refer to the colors that fall between any two colors in your drawing. This can be done by clicking on one of the colors and simply drawing on the other. You can use it to soften edges or anti-alias a cartoon by hand. It is a more precise solution than using the Smooth ink.

FIGURE 6.4

Example of shade color and coloring options.

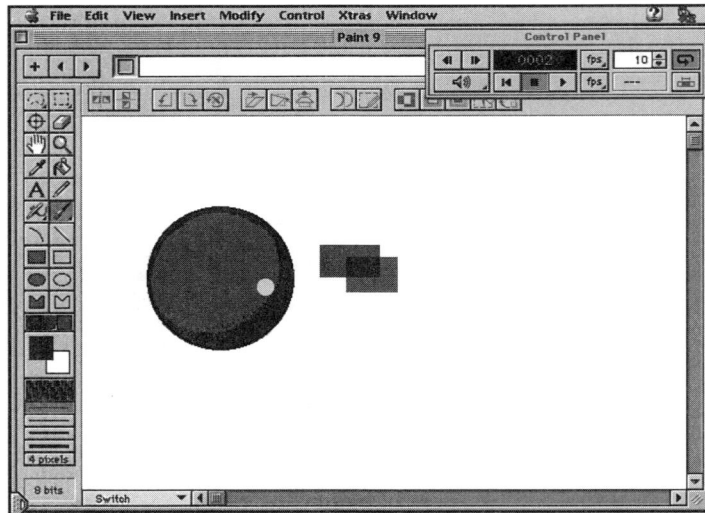

2. Suppose you have a ball and you want it to be red. Determine the shade color for red in your palette.

3. Set the foreground color as the shade color of the ball. Change the destination color (in the gradient area of your tools) to the regular color (red in this case).

4. Fill the ball with the shade color using the Paint bucket (you can use the Eyedropper to choose the color from the screen).

5. Pick the Brush tool and select an appropriately sized brush, and also select the switch ink with which to paint.

6. Drawing the ball adds your highlight. Again, pick a bigger brush to cover more ground.

You can use this procedure methodically to add two or more levels of shading. Best of all, it is relatively quick to apply, and can be done in the presence of other colors already added to the character.

Finishing Touches

Other finishing touches that could be added to characters include things like shadows and idle states. Both are separate cast members that are combined with the character on stage to produce certain effects. Shadows can be added and easily be made to appear translucent on the ground.

Adding Shadows

Adding shadows to your characters can be a nice effect at certain times. Generally not something to be used a lot, shadows is an effect that can imply a mood or a light source. You could do this by setting a black shadow to 50 percent transparency on the stage, but this might not be the fastest or most reliable route to go. Some machines could have problems with blending the sprite repeatedly if the processor is not very quick. The following steps describe the easy (and relatively processor-friendly) way to create one type of shadow effect. It should be noted that this effect can also be used to simulate shining light as well (see fig. 6.5).

1. Design all the necessary shadow positions for your characters in solid black blobs. (These blobs are to be amorphous shapes that define the area of the shadow of each character. They should all be created in the Paint window.) You can also convert them to one bit cast members after finalizing their shapes.

2. Place all of the solid black blobs on the stage and apply the background transparent score ink effect.

3. After all the animation work has been done, all the shadows can be filled with a 50 percent gray pattern. Background transparent enables the

ground underneath to show through, and the effect is moderately convincing even at 640×480 (see fig. 6.6). The effect isn't meant to be as clean as a real shadow, but can serve almost as effectively. The exception to this is that the shadow begins to look strange when placed on top of another pattern or a heavily dithered backdrop. Also, it should be noted that as with any sprite/ink effect, you probably don't want to use too many because it begins to bog down the performance of the animation. Whenever possible, you can combine the shadow with the figure itself to conserve Director's resources.

FIGURE 6.5

The use of background transparent for shadows and lights.

Creating Animated Idle States

Idle states enable characters to show some degree of life even when nothing is happening on the Stage (the computer is possibly waiting for user input). Character breathing is generally one form of idle state. Nothing is happening in the scene, but as in normal life, things breathe. This is especially helpful with kids, who might not notice the act in and of itself, but will notice that without it the scene seems that much more boring.

To avoid having the character look unnaturally stiff, you can have it blink. Blinking is the easiest of effects to add, and in its simplest form is composed of one extra cast member that shows the character's eyes closed. This is popped on and off periodically.

When designing blinks of more than one frame, it's best to use more frames to close the eyes than to open them. The ratio is probably around three to one:

* Eyes fully open
* Slightly open
* Slightly closed
* Fully closed
* Slightly open
* Fully open

Use whatever seems most natural.

FIGURE 6.6

The use of background transparent for shadows.

Fixing Your Registration Points

It's important to note that in a perfect world, artists working in Director always want the registration points of a cast member in the center of the character. It's bad luck, and if spacing is critical, it's best handled from the Score, and not by off-setting registration points. Generally, leave any registration point adjustments to the Lingo-programmer (or the last person or task to work on the project, even if it's yourself).

I have often run into problems where cast members interact with each other, and the registration point in a few of them gets altered. Throughout the Score, the cast members experience an offset. It's easy to mistake it for a Score problem and overlook the fact that it's happened wherever that cast member appeared. When working on complicated movies, it's best not to introduce potential anomalies until the last phases, if at all. To take a good step when finalizing graphics, go through every graphic cast member with the Paint window and double-click on the Registration tool to recenter it. If anything changes in the movie, correct it in the Score. You'll be a happier person because of it.

Conclusion

This chapter was intended to help better equip you in creating and managing your animations using Director 5.0. Far more could be said about animation in general that could easily be applied to Director's work environment. It wouldn't hurt to check out the abundant resources available at your local library or bookstore on animation techniques and process. Hopefully this chapter gave you a starting point that will help you to synthesize the techniques the computer offers with those that can be picked up traditionally.

chapter 7

Dudley Bryan

PALETTES AND SOUND

Palettes and sound are two very important elements of multi-media. Although as development issues go they are quite different, when they are handled they can either make or break your project. This chapter discusses tricks and tips for palettes and methods for dealing with sound during production. Sound coverage will be limited toward ideas to help work flow and a few of the file formats that might be helpful to use.

This chapter is written from the point of view of the art side of multimedia development.

Palettes

Since the dawn of multimedia, one of a developer's greatest assets was a wide range of colors with which to illustrate his or her particular brand of interaction. On earlier computers, developers were limited to 3 colors, 4 colors, 16 colors, and even 32 colors. As 256 color computers became more common, the emerging world of multimedia embraced it. In that genesis, certain techniques and tricks were discovered and used to enhance the experience of the end user. Effects such as fade to black, multiple palettes, palette cycling, and palette transitions were implemented to create avante-garde special effects. Many of these creations left other developers at a loss as to how certain effects had been achieved.

These days, many of these options are in the standard tool set of the multi-media developer and are by no means revolutionary. Interestingly enough, the long road leading to this point provided not only a foundation of knowledge on which to build, but a window through which to view the expanded possibilities of the computers of the present. These possibilities were made apparent by examples of what had been accomplished with the limitations of computers past.

Oftentimes to conserve memory, developers still use graphics that are one bit-plane deep—made up of two colors: black and white. Many even use graphics with 16 colors instead of the full range of 256 (considered the standard for multimedia) to reduce loading time or the amount of hard disk space the final production will occupy. Macromedia Director chimes in with a full battery of tools and flexibility to implement these techniques. Becoming more familiar with them will bring your projects that much closer to the forefront of dazzling and effective multimedia.

Sounds

As an artist, I admittedly do not have much of a background in sound production. Day-in and day-out I do, however, deal with the various types of media that eventually combine with my own. In the previous section, I gave a preface to my dealings with palettes as they enhance the visual effects of a production. Another important aspect that I can't overlook is how I deal with adding sound and how it affects my work flow. Much like in the graphics world, sound exists in certain resolutions or "depths" of quality. Much like 24-bit is a pinnacle of quality level for graphics, 16-bit 44 KHz stereo is an extremely high level of sound quality (CD quality). I'll touch briefly on generally accepted multimedia standards for sound and a couple of formats and tips that might make work easier.

Palette Basics

The majority of developers today work in 8-bit or 256 colors when creating their presentations. Both the Macintosh and Windows operating systems have different considerations when working in this color depth.

Windows and Macintosh—Kinks and Considerations

Outside of Director, there are noteworthy differences between what the MacOS expects of its palettes and what the Microsoft Windows 3.1.1 and Windows 95 looks for in their palettes. When you load a Macintosh 256 color image, you notice that in the palette, the first color is always white; the last color in the palette is always black. Macromedia Director was a product originally created on the Macintosh operating system. Because of this, Director expects this formatting out of all image palettes loaded into it. On a Windows machine, Director makes the same demands as on the Macintosh. Although you might not run into this problem when creating your work, it is chief among the reasons why certain palettes will not load into Director. If the first color is not white, Director does not load the palette from the image. Additionally, this fact becomes important to note as DeBabelizer's built-in Windows palette presets will not work correctly with Director. The following are some other kinks and considerations to keep in mind when working with palettes in Director:

❖ **Cross Platform Needs—First Ten and Last Ten:** Many developers stick to the idea of reserving the first ten and last ten colors of the palette for the Windows system colors. Reports are that this not only preserves the correct colors for system-related dialogs, icons, and windows, but that it also marginally improves the performance of animation playback.

❖ **The Invalid Palette:** Generally when Director tells you that your machine has an invalid palette, it means that that palette is not formatted in an acceptable way. This could mean that the image has not been what

DeBabelizer calls "Macintized." As stated earlier, white must be the first color in the palette in order to load in Director.

❖ **Creating 8-Bit Graphics in a 16-Bit Color Development Environment:** If you are operating in a 24/32-bit video mode while using Director, newly created cast members are automatically 24/32-bits as well.

❖ **Fade to Black:** Fade to black is one of the cleaner methods of handling changes between palettes.

Transitions Between Two Different Palettes

If you think a palette-to-palette transition is necessary, you could use a method to ensure that it looks as good as possible. Most palette-to-palette transitions look strange because the colors in either palette represent such stark brightness and color differences when compared to each other. These differences make the change from one to the other fairly distinct. To reduce the distinction, focus attention on establishing some commonality between the two palettes. One good way of accomplishing this is to sort the palettes of both images by their brightness. As images and palettes transition into each other, the most noticeable change that could be made is a light color changing to a dark color. If in both palettes, light colors change to light and dark colors do likewise, the overall effect is much smoother. The following is one way to quickly smooth a palette transition.

1. In the Cast window, locate the two palettes to transition.

2. Select and duplicate them in the cast.

3. In the Palette window, go to each of the duplicated palettes and click on the Sort button.

4. When asked what to sort by, click on Brightness.

Figure 7.1

The Sort Colors dialog box with the Sort By Brightness option being invoked.

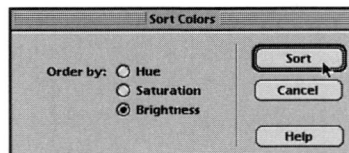

5. Using the Cast window, select all the cast members that belong to one palette. From the menu, select Modify, Transform Bitmap to change them from the old palette to the sorted version of that respective palette. Do not select Dither; instead, choose Remap Pixels.

6. Repeat the Transform Bitmap procedure on the remaining cast members belonging to any other sorted palettes.

After this, make certain that the original palettes involved are deleted; they should no longer be referenced by any of the remaining cast members. You might want to keep them around in case you change your mind, but it's up to you.

Dos and Don'ts

The following is a general list of some important dos and don'ts when handling palettes in Director. Although dos and don'ts could potentially go on forever, these are some basic guidelines that you may encounter more often than not when developing your project. The format of this section will cover what to do, and then state why not to do the opposite.

❖ Check all palette effects on as many target playback systems as possible. This refers to any system that can accurately represent those that will show your final product. Preferably these should be machines that cover a good cross-section of the various units for which your projector was designed.

On the Windows side, exotic palette effects may have problems with certain video cards. As with many of Director's special effects, check this out before relying heavily on something that might not be best suited for the level of compatibility you need.

❖ Check associations between cast members and palettes after moving them by means of copying the Score to another movie. This can be done by getting cast member properties on these cast members. Getting cast member properties returns palette confirmation information on multiple cast members provided they all have the same palette. If the Properties window does *not* show the associated palette of the cast members selected, one or more of the selected cast members is using a different palette (or one or more of the selected cast members is not a bitmap cast).

FIGURE 7.2

The Cast Member Properties window.

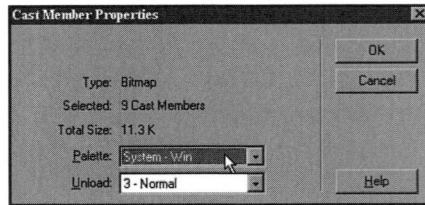

In previous versions of Director, this procedure sometimes caused images to forget the palette with which they were associated. With the computer set to a bit depth of 256 colors, this is not as bad of a problem; the screen forces all cast to a last set palette regardless of the image's individual association. Generally you will see if there is any type of palette conflict (shown by bizarre or miscolored sprites). If the user's machine is set at thousands of colors or higher, each cast on the screen will appear in whatever palette to which it is assigned, even if that palette is "wrong." The palette to which the orphaned image will default is the current system palette. The image with the lost palette will appear with the wrong colors. Performing a quick check never hurts.

❧ Use the naming convention for movies that contain multiple palettes. Try naming palettes to match the primary image that goes with it. If a certain background is named "LivingRoom," for example, the palette could simply be called "LivingRoom.pal."

Non-descriptive names on palettes such as "Palette 1" begin to impede development if a palette for a particular image needs to be referenced or retrieved quickly.

❧ Most importantly, don't go palette crazy. Try using methods of combining common colors from different images into super palettes that can be used for several images (unless the images are far too different). *Super palettes* is the general name widely used when referring to palettes solely created to unite a number of images under one palette (instead of several). The most common colors from all the images are tallied up and sorted into a new palette, and all the images are dithered to it. Super palettes can be made in DeBabelizer—in fact, they are one of DeBabelizer's specialties and the procedure for creating them is well explained in the manual.

In Director 4, a maximum custom palette limit of around 54 existed. Director 5 has no such limitations, but this by no means is a free license. Always use as few palettes as necessary to get the job done. It reduces the possibility of grievous complications if things need to be changed.

Working in 16-Bit Mode with 8-Bit Images

In Director, images can be anywhere from 1 (two colors) bit-plane to 32 bit-planes in color depth (trillions of colors). All new images created in the Paint window are initially given the same bit depth as that to which the computer is currently set. Unfortunately, this makes it difficult to create new images of different bit depths quickly. If your computer's video was set to a color depth of 24-bit, for example, and you wanted to create a series of 8-bit characters, you would be out of luck. You set it like this because your backdrop for the stage was a 24-bit image that you did not want to convert to 8-bit yet (and it looked horrible when viewed in an 8-bit video mode). Or, maybe you switch regularly between Photoshop and Director and hate to endure the rigors of resolution switching (which always makes your computer seem to lurch in agony). You might feel you either had to resort to working in 8-bit, to converting your cast back to 8-bit afterwards, or something else equally awkward. The following is a method you can use to work on creating 8-bit series without resorting to any uncomfortable alternatives.

1. With the environment computer in 16-, 24-, or 32-bit mode, set up a fairly small and generic new image in the cast as a starter graphic.

2. Transform this 16-, 24-, or 32-bit image to an 8-bit cast member with the palette you desire. (In the Paint window, the bottom box on the Paint toolbar can be double-clicked to bring up the Transform Bitmap dialog box.) (See fig. 7.3.)

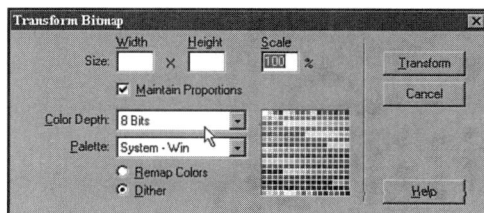

FIGURE 7.3

The Transform Bitmap dialog box.

3. Duplicate this image as many times as necessary throughout the cast by using the Cast window, Cut, and Paste.

4. Now, you can move quickly from one of these preset 8-bit cast members to another when creating new graphics. All these graphics behave as

placeholders that are in time written over, but initially are used to maintain the correct resolution of *new* cast while you create.

Working with 24-Bit Backdrops

Often when animating a large project, the artist working on the background might not be the same artist who is working on the character animation. One way of dealing with this issue is to have the artists agree on a subset of colors that will be the final palette. This subset consists of 32 or more colors that the character animator needs to work on. This leaves the final "fee" palette with 236 colors.

Cycle Animation—An Exercise

In the section, "Palettes," the advantage of color cycling was touched on. The effect described here is one of the more basic techniques traditionally used. The effect is the simulation of movement when nothing is really happening.

1. Make certain that you are in 8-bit; palette cycling does not work in screen modes of higher color depth.

2. Create a custom palette. Do this by opening Director's Palette window (make certain that the System palette is selected), double-clicking on a color, and selecting OK from the Palette dialog box that comes up. Director will ask you the name of the new palette you've created. Name it Cycler.

3. In the Palette window, select color 16. (To find what color number you have clicked on, look in the box in the lower-left corner of the Palette window to the right of the tools.)

4. Go to the Edit menu, and choose Copy (or use Ctrl+C Ctrl+V on the PC and Command+C Command+V on the Mac). Move to color register 23 and Paste the color.

5. Select color register 16 again. Drag the mouse to select the range of colors between 16 and 23 as well. Select the In-between button from the top of the window (or, press Command+B on the Mac or Ctrl+B on the PC). All the colors should be the same now.

6. Repeat this procedure for the colors in register 24 through 31. You now have *two* ranges that use only two different colors.

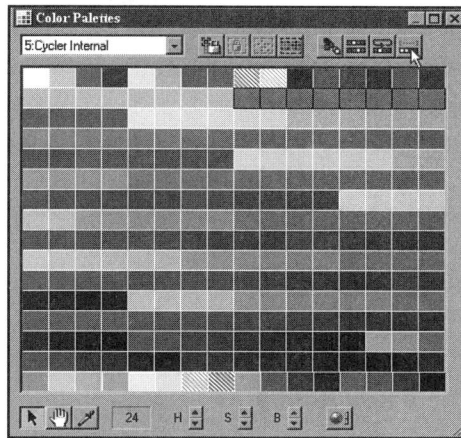

FIGURE 7.4

The Color Palettes window with the two new ranges.

7. Go into the Paint window and select the Filled Square tool. Make a black rectangle on the screen.

8. Click on the Cast Member Properties button from the top of the window and set the palette of the cast member to Cycler.

9. In the Paint window, transform the cast by double-clicking on the resolution box in the lower-left corner of the toolbar. This square must be 640 pixels wide and 80 pixels high.

10. Return to the Paint window and click on the center of the gradient color chip. A pop-up menu appears. At the bottom, select Gradient Settings. You are in the Gradient Settings window.

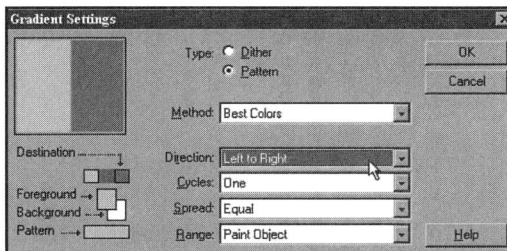

FIGURE 7.5

The Gradient Settings dialog box.

11. Use the Destination chip to specify that you want to gradate from the color you had seen as number 16 to the color you saw as number 31. This range should encompass both register sets of the two different colors.

12. Select Pattern as the Type and choose Adjacent Colors as the Method.

13. Choose Left to Right for a duration.

14. Click on OK and go to the Paint window. Select the Paint Bucket from the toolbar and choose Gradient as the ink (from the bottom of the window).

15. Fill in the rectangle and it should appear to turn into two colors.

FIGURE 7.6

The Paint window being used to create a filled rectangle with two adjacent colors gradated without dithering.

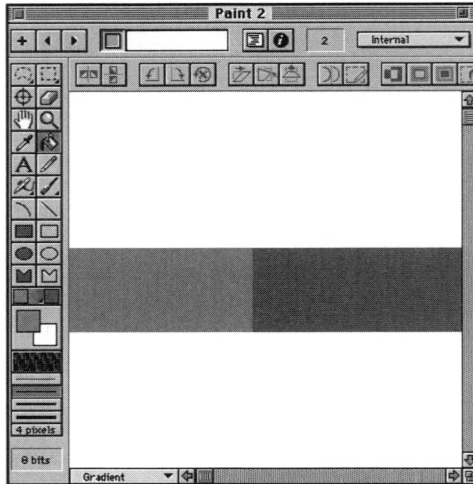

16. Place the cast member on the bottom of the stage and set the palette of the frame to Cycler. Also, while in the Palette dialog box, set the cycle rate to 10 fps. Be certain to select the range of colors to cycle as well.

17. Upon playing the movie, a sidewalk should appear to be moving across the bottom of the screen.

Many variations can be made of this effect. You can use it for the sensor on a robot or computer control panel, or use a more sophisticated scheme to make clouds float across the sky. Your imagination can enhance the rudimentary concept presented here.

Sound Basics

For most developers, the use of digital audio begins and ends with importing and playing a sound at some point during an animation. This section is meant to address sound from the point of view of the animator. Much more could be said about sound than you will find here, but for the animator, this section serves to provide a certain level of insight into what can be a mysterious topic.

Director 5's handling of external cast really comes in handy when dealing with large projects involving numerous sounds. The capability to hold all sounds as an external file separate from the whole is wonderful because the media does not need to be "stuck" in one movie, or shared cast. It can be used like a common resource whose changes in data or quality can carry quick global impact to the entire project.

Note

Windows and Macintosh—Kinks and Considerations

When it comes to the universal sound format, the uncompressed AIF file seems to garner, for the most part, the most respect on both platforms. Both platforms import it into the cast, and both platforms can stream these samples off the hard drive during playback of the movie. Streaming audio is one way of handling the playback of extra long sound files in low memory conditions.

Generally speaking, the most adequate audio format to work in is 8-bit 22 KHz mono. Although the audio can still be brought down an additional degree of quality, it is believed that 11 KHz is fairly poor and only does justice to speech. Keeping the sound at a minimum of 22 KB gives it enough range to breathe and carry with it a reasonable level of fullness. Often, programs like SoundEdit 16 II perform what is called *dithering*. This process serves to enhance the sound quality and mask the fact that the quality level has been lowered as much as it has. This technique mirrors the dithering techniques prevalent in the graphics world.

File Formats

When beginning production, it is always helpful to review different options that different digital media provide when looking at the project goals. Sorting through or at least touching on issues regarding file formats during early production is a valuable habit; often, changing formats causes unforeseen difficulties (especially at the last minute). The following list discusses the most common file formats in detail.

❖ **AIF:** AIF is a standard on the Macintosh and on the PC. Director can stream this audio format on both platforms. (*Streaming* means that the projector loads and plays bits of the audio at a time.) Because of that, AIF is the format of choice for dual-platform development. AIF is also easily interchangeable with QuickTime on the Macintosh. If necessary, AIF files can be easily converted to QuickTime audio movies by dropping them on to the Movieplayer.

❈ **QuickTime—Midi/Digital Audio:** QuickTime midi and digital audio is an effective tool in controlling certain aspects of audio. QuickTime enables more control than ordinary audio; it is a time-based architecture that enables the user to reference data in non-linear ways. QuickTime users can, for example, have one file that contains many different audio samples, and call to different portions of the QuickTime audio to play a specific segment. Also, with the addition of midi to the QuickTime architecture, Lingo programmers can have their music take up less memory and can also play both audio and midi at the same time. You can play a QuickTime converted midi file at the same time as a character on-screen is speaking (with the speech playing through the Score), for example. As a warning however, although QuickTime midi and Director's digital audio can play at the same time, QuickTime digital audio and Director's digital audio cannot play at the same time on the Windows platform. Director itself can play up to two tracks of audio.

❈ **WAV:** This Windows-based standard is a flexible method of handling audio on the PC. My experience has generally focused on the more cross-platform standards like the above mentioned, but this format provides widespread and much appreciated usability on the PC. In the Windows environment, I've noted that WAV audio is very well integrated as part of the operating system and has a high number of editing and manipulation tools available that save to it. If your project is not going to be cross-platform, this format is more than suited to providing the best in performance and reliability.

Exporting Sounds from Director

After sounds have been imported in Director, you cannot get the sounds back out without using the external editor functionality on the Mac. In most cases, setting up the default sound editor (on the Macintosh) enables the user to double-click on the sound and have that sound open in the user's sound editor of choice. In this situation, "saving" the sound automatically updates it in the cast (and not simply a file). Macromedia plans to support this type of hot linking between its suite of multimedia programs more and more in the future. Alternatively, on either platform, sound files can be copied out and pasted back in from an external sound editor. As a note, be sure that any imported sound files are fairly small because larger files should be linked to avoid high memory requirements to play correctly.

On the Macintosh, a more universal option is to export the animation frames that the sound plays across as a QuickTime movie. You might think that doing this outputs all the sounds that play in the movie as one long audio track, but in truth, the export is deceptively more sophisticated.

A QuickTime movie supports multiple channels of each of the media types it supports; it can not only contain several video tracks playing on top of one another or one after the other, but it can utilize several audio tracks as well. When a QuickTime movie is exported, Director creates a separate audio track for each sample of audio that plays in the movie. This proves a great benefit because applications like Movie Player can be used to extract or separate these audio bits from the movie and can save them as AIF format, at which point the sounds can again be edited as individual samples. Movie Player is currently available only for the Macintosh, although Apple has already begun making steps to make editing QuickTime movies just as easy no matter which platform is used.

The following is the basic procedure used in extracting sounds by using the QuickTime export option:

1. Play through all the *sounds* you will be exporting at least one time. It is possible that Director will overlook the sample if it does not have it loaded into memory before export. This could be seen as bug *or* feature.

2. In the Score, select ten more frames than necessary to listen to the samples in entirety. Make certain that the frames selected in the Score allow enough time for the entire audio to play.

3. Choose Export from the File menu, and select the option Selected Frames from the options presented.

4. Set the Format to QuickTime Movie and click on the Options button.

5. Depending on exactly what you are trying to accomplish, the following might not be appropriate for your situation. If you are trying to obtain only the digital audio information, make certain that the Frame Rate is set to Tempo Settings; Compressor can be set to None. Set the video to be as small as possible because it is basically unnecessary (try a size of 160×120). Keep the necessary audio channels turned on. Proceed with the export.

6. After the movie has been created, load the movie into Movie Player 2.0 or a later version on the Macintosh.

7. After the movie is loaded, click on Extract tracks.

8. Movie Player shows a list of the separate movie tracks. Each sound file shows as an individual track.

9. Extract the desired track. Getting information on the movie enables you to see where the actual sound starts. This further enables you to delete the additional empty space. This should not be necessary because the actual length of the track matches the digital audio exactly, so experiment.

10. From the File menu, choose Export.

11. Choose Sound to AIF as the output format in the Export dialog box. Clicking on the Options button enables you to specify the level of sound quality you want to save.

Tip

To ensure compatibility with the Windows environment, make certain that the sample rate is set at 11.025 or 22.050 KHz. Sounds do not play correctly (or at all) if the rate is not correct.

Sound Tips for Animation

The following are a couple of tips to help users deal with sound. Both are fairly straightforward and can save time.

Estimating Frame Numbers

When creating an animation for a particular character, a time comes when the character needs to be synchronized with his or her speech audio. This can be a process marked by arbitrary guesswork, but a lot of the uncertainty can be alleviated by following this simple technique. If you know the frame per second rate at which your animation will run, multiply this times the duration (in seconds) of the accompanying audio. If you are designing your animation to operate at 10 frames per second, for example, and the character's speech audio will last for 20 seconds, you know you need 200 frames of character animation. If designing the character animation at 8 frames, and there are 30 seconds of speech, you know that you need to animate 240 frames. After you drop in some sample animation and the audio, you can check to see how well the estimate matches your actual performance. For large areas of digital audio, this method really helps in cutting out a lot of the grunt work because you can set up containers of frames in which to work. You can concentrate more on animating for a longer period without constantly creating more frames after finishing each sequence.

Coloring the Score at Ten-Frame Intervals

In the Score, try colorizing segments of cells at intervals of 10 frames. For example, color 10 frames yellow, the next 10 blue, the next red, and so on. As a quick reference when animating, this helps to indicate how many frames you are moving across. This proves especially helpful when quickly assessing the length of frames on to which you are placing the audio. It helps you not to lose track of where you are in the Score in relationship to the rest of a given section. It can be thought of as an even more subtle marker system.

Using Markers

Setting up markers in Director is often a nice way of keeping track of particular areas in a Director movie. When dealing with a large number of digital sounds synchronized with animation, sometimes the markers achieve another helpful purpose. Consider naming markers after the sound file that plays during the section of animation the marker is set in front of. As a time saver, you can also keep a printed chart that details what dialog or sound effect goes with a particular sound file. These charts enable you to quickly navigate your movie by its marker more easily than by using markers to mark arbitrary events.

Conclusion

A cautionary note must be made that the cutting edge of multimedia development is sometimes trumped by what is referred to as the bleeding edge. I usually think of the bleeding edge as anything that is not necessary—that which, for whatever reason, is causing your projects undue problems. Always be prepared for the ugly truths that lie behind things that tickle your fancy. (They are usually issues of compatibility across multiple system configurations.) Even though Director is a wonderful tool director, it has its share of problems; sometimes "keeping it simple silly" is the best trick in the book.

chapter 8

Dudley Bryan

QUICK WORK

This chapter seeks to reveal a number of special tips and techniques utilizing

Director that I have come across over the years in developing different projects.

I have attempted to make this chapter as clear as possible. These tips range

from techniques involving Photoshop and DeBabelizer, to tips involving just

Director itself. The interests are wide ranging and cover many aspects of

creating artwork and visual effects in the development environment. If you

have ever had one of those moments when you say to yourself, "There has to

be a better way," or if you have found a far easier way to do the same task

after hours of wasted time, it's worth giving this chapter a look.

Procedure 1: Handling Layers in Photoshop and Director

Photoshop 3's layers provide a rich selection of options that enable the creation of different versions of the same artwork in one file. Although advantageous, these layers are also some of the most torturous aspects of using Photoshop 3 because exporting these layered images has never truly been a one-step process. One way of getting around this shortcoming is to use a tool that Macromedia itself distributes with Director. It is the charming and invaluable FKEY, known as screen clip. FKEYs represent a method developed long ago for the Macintosh by which developers could add custom-made built-in commands to the operating system. Much like the standard FKEY for screen capture (Command+Shift+3), the screen clip defaults during installation to Command+Shift+6 unless you change it to a different number. (My general preference is Command+Shift+4; this sets it up to be right next to the other capture FKEY.)

Note

Using screen clip is a simple and natural way of grabbing images from your screen to use in your projects on the Macintosh. You should make a few quick notes, however:

- Screen clip captures in whatever resolution you have that screen set to. If you are in 24-bit, you will get 24-bit data put into your clipboard. If in 8-bit, you will have 8-bit data put into your clipboard. This is most important, as grabbing palette information often comes in handy (in an application that actively switches the palette of the screen).

- Screen clip grabs exactly what you are seeing on the screen. Note that screen clipping a zoomed in image captures data effectively double the size desired. Obviously, dithering falls under this warning also. If working in 256 color on a 16-, 24-, or 32-bit image in Photoshop, do not use screen clip. You'll end up with dithering that most likely does not do your image justice. Either switch to a higher bit-plane mode, or skip this tip entirely.

- Other screen capture utilities exist for the Macintosh and Windows-based computers that give the user a wider range of choices when capturing screen data. Test them to see which are best for you.

❋   On the Windows platform, one nice built-in method of screen capture involves pressing the Print Screen key on the keyboard. This copies the entire screen to the clipboard, from which point it can be brought into Director and cropped.

After installing the FKEY, you're ready to go. Assume that you have just finished creating an elaborate series of custom titles in Photoshop, for example. Many of the custom titles might be on separate, hidden and unhidden layers because they share similar information. Ordinarily, this presents an unfortunate snag in development as each individual combination requires that you: save a separate flattened version of the image and then import it into director, duplicate the merged image, and copy it into Director; or that you flatten the image and copy the data manually (hoping that you can undo or revert the layered information afterward). The best way that I've found (at least when it involves selective sections of the composition and not the image as a whole), of bringing a layered composite into Director is to use screen clip. Pressing this FKEY turns your mouse pointer into a crosshair (or marquee tool). With this, you can select a square region of the graphic that will be copied immediately into memory (see fig. 8.1). From here, switching back to Director is a snap, at which point you just paste the graphic into the Score.

Another spin on this tip is to create a template layer in Photoshop. This layer's only purpose is to show you the exact area in the image that needs to be clipped to memory. To do this, create a marquee one pixel wider than necessary and perform a stroke on it with whatever color shows up best on top of your image. Now, screen clipping will be quicker to perform because the exact area(s) of the clip is already outlined. Make certain to clip inside your square region to avoid grabbing the outline around the image you copy into Director.

To further showcase the speed of this method, I'll present a short example of how this can be used. In this example, the project being worked on features a title at the top of the screen that changes at different times in the program. Although the title changes, the background does not. The Photoshop image consists of five layers, as shown in figure 8.2.

FIGURE 8.1

*The screen clip
FKEY in action
using a template
layer in Photoshop.*

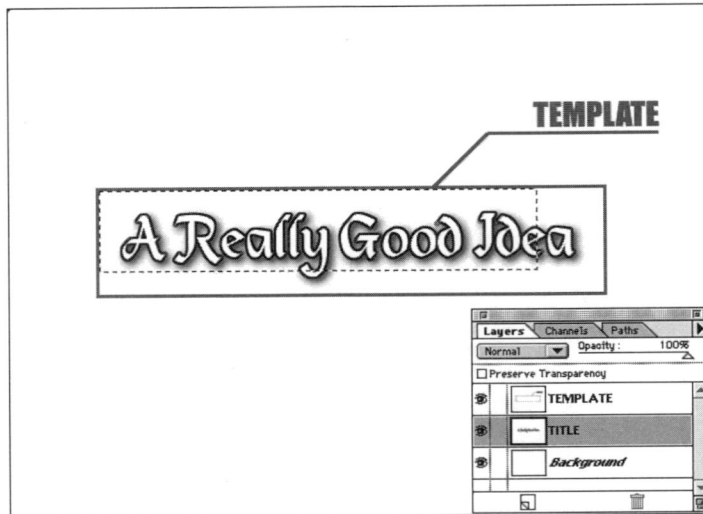

1. The title 1: "Steve's Quick Tips"

2. The drop shadow for title 1

3. The title 2: "Lisa's Awesome Advice"

4. The drop shadow for title 2

5. The background image for the screen itself

FIGURE 8.2

*An overview shot
of the project.*

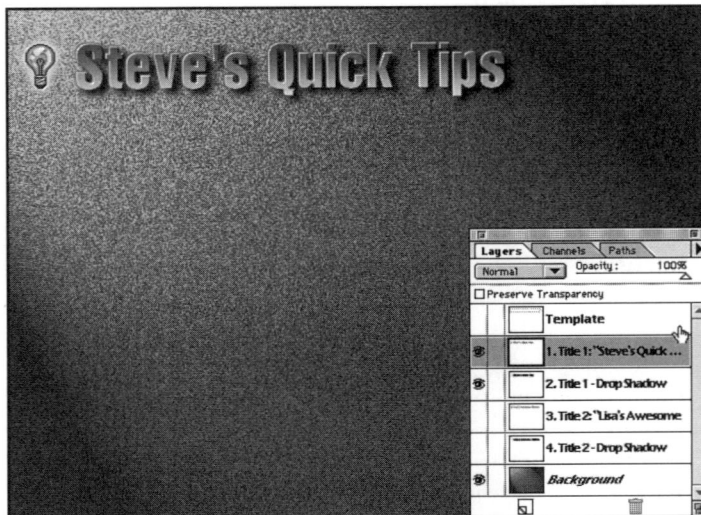

The assumption is made that Director is already loaded. The backdrop image used should also already be in Director because only a section of it needs to be updated. Steve's title is in the same screen location as Lisa's, but because they are different headings for the same screen, layers separated them.

1. Create an additional template layer that consists of an unfilled rectangle around the area of the title. (Remember: Make it one pixel wider than the area to be clipped, and make certain that the rectangle covers the combined area of both titles.)

2. Enable layers 1, 2, and 5 for Steve.

3. Make certain that the area of the title is not being obscured by a window (screen clip will grab this too). Now, invoke the FKEY and create a marquee just inside the area identified by the template rectangle (see fig. 8.3). The area is captured to the clipboard. (In Windows you can simply press the Print Screen key to perform a full screen image capture to the clipboard.)

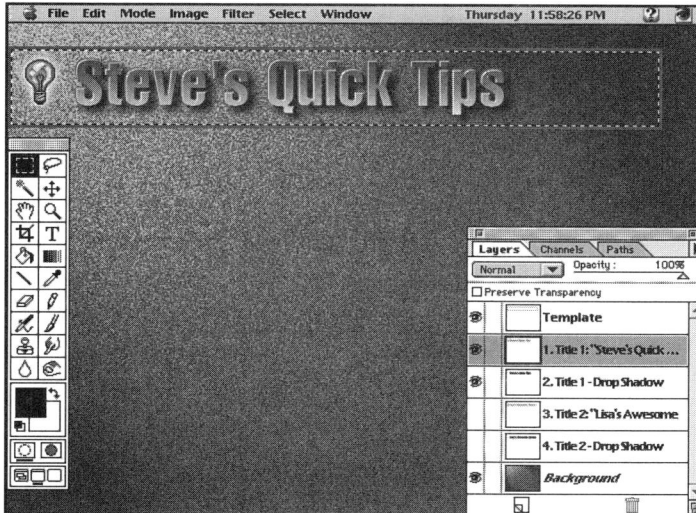

FIGURE **8.3**

Steve's layers being used and the selection of the area inside.

4. Switch over to Director and paste the image into the cast.

5. Switching back over to Photoshop, turn off Steve's layers and turn on Lisa's layers (3, 4, and 5). Once more, using the template as reference, screen clip the area of Lisa's title. (Again, use the Print Screen key on the PC.)

6. Switch over to Director and paste them into a blank space in the cast window. On the PC, you need to crop the image according to the visible template of the title.

7. For the most part, you're done! The new cast you created should be the same size and enable you to switch between titles as they appear on the stage.

This is a real timesaver when you have many titles that need to be handled this way. The only thing you lose is the option of having your image dithered in Photoshop. Xtras are coming out, however, that will enable you to perform high-quality dithering in Director. I personally feel, however, that Director's built-in dithering is fine for most *basic* tasks.

Procedure 2: Transform Bitmaps

Transforming bitmaps (a handy feature provided in Director) has multiple uses. Like many tools, though, it has its share of pitfalls, too. Many people familiar with Photoshop know the difference between resizing an index mode graphic and a graphic resized in RGB mode. For the most part, resizing a graphic in RGB mode gives you the option of employing more complex pixel interpolation. Sophisticated pixel interpolation enables your image data to look as close to its original resolution as possible through anti-aliasing. Using index mode in Photoshop automatically rules out this option because Photoshop doesn't anti-alias by using colors from a custom palette. On the other hand, Director enables you to choose the form of pixel interpolation that best suits your needs, regardless of the palette or color depth of the image.

Though not as clearly apparent as one would like, Transform bitmaps enables access to both methods of resizing through the Remap Pixels and Dithering options. Remap Pixels, aside from being used to reassign the color usage of one image with the closest mapping color of another image, also enables the user to resize images without anti-aliasing the image. This proves very useful when resizing simple images of line drawings, or text in certain situations. Some drawing styles require no anti-aliasing (to avoid complicating the drawing, or making the data too blurry). The one-pixel thin lines on a cartoon character provide an example of this (see fig. 8.4).

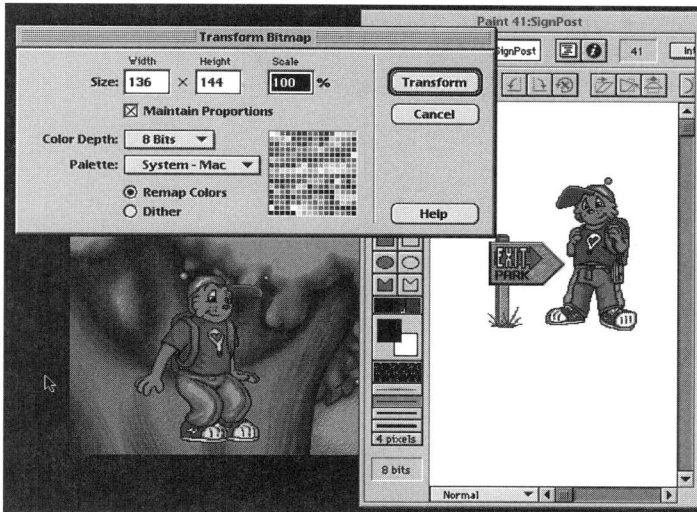

FIGURE 8.4

Transform Bitmap dialog box in front of the Paint window showing a character that should not be "Blurred." Remap colors is used instead of Dither.

In this case, set the Transform Bitmaps dialog box to remap pixels.

On the other hand, if you want to have your image smoothed after resizing, remember to set the dialog box to dithered. This is not, however, the only note to remember. Many obvious problems that crop up exist because non-rectangular cast members anti-alias to the background color when resized (by default, this color is white). This creates a problem when the cast member appears on-stage with an ink-like matte or background transparency; a whitish fringe appears to be around the bitmap. Obviously that's a problem.

An initial solution might be to painstakingly remove all the white, pixel by pixel, cast member by cast member, meticulously editing the altered images. By looking at the problem a little closer, a better and more efficient solution presents itself.

One method to avoid the white fringe effect (taking into account the effect desired) requires that the surrounding area in each of the cast members be filled by a color that best enables it to subsequently blend into its final background. In many cases, that color can be black or neutral gray.

1. Go to each cast member to be resized and draw an unfilled rectangle over it in the same color as that will surround the image. This color is based on whatever you feel will help the image blend on stage once it has been anti-aliased to it. (See fig. 8.5.)

FIGURE **8.5**

The unfilled squares being drawn.

2. Next, go back to each cast member and fill the empty space of the rectangle to finish it off.

3. After the cast has been resized, the second half of the operation can begin where this color is refilled with white to restore its irregular shape again. (See fig. 8.6.)

4. Some tweaking may still be desired, but for the most part, the plague of the white fringe has been averted.

FIGURE **8.6**

The image returned to its irregular shape using the fill bucket.

Procedure 3: Importing RTF Files

One of the nicer features Director 5 provides is the capability to import RTF files. As many people know, RTF stands for Rich Text Format. RTF represents a computer text-based standard that enables multiple fonts, text layout, and other typographical features to be understood universally under one file format. This is a very welcome addition. It saves developers from having to perform all their text formatting solely in Director (and gives them the option of using a real word processor). As a general note, some color-capable word processors like Microsoft Word even enable you to save color information with your RTF file.

How It Works and When It Doesn't

Aside from the basic understanding of RTF, a few other things are useful to note about Director and RTF files. These things might be avoided forever, or they may pop up the first time you use it, but regardless they are valuable tips to note.

Formatting Before Importing

First, according to the manual, Director creates new cast members every time it encounters a page break in the RTF file. Apparently a bug made it through Macromedia's testing and might form a bothersome stumbling block for you. If your RTF file contains two page breaks in a row (a simple mistake when pasting close page breaks into a document), Director will report that it is out of memory, and refuse to load the rest of your data. This oversight is not so harsh when you have less than a page of text. When your RTF document is multiple pages in length, however, you might spend a lot of wasted time thinking that your document was too big (not just formatted incorrectly). An additional anomaly is that Director has problems with text set to double spaced rather than single spaced. Best advice: Keep formatting like this simple, and change it only after importing.

Placement on the Stage

Another point of confusion might stem from the way Director is structured. This requires a little patience with Director's interface. Assume that your RTF data (imported as multiple casts) is now inside Director, for example, and you are looking to apply further formatting to them. First, select the area of the Score in which you want the cast members to appear. Select all the new text cast members in the cast window and choose Cast To Time from the Modify menu. The cast members are immediately thrown on to the stage over a series of frames. Because the cast members might not be the exact same number of lines, you note that they do not share a common *top*. Your first instinct might be to select all the cast members in the score and get sprite properties on them. Thinking that the sprites will all realign their *top* coordinates, you name a new top location for all the sprites in the dialog box. Looking at the Score, you realize that this was not the case. Your sprites have all moved in relation to each other. The simple solution to this dilemma is to use Director 5's new align tool under the Modify menu. What you are probably looking to have happen can be done by selecting the stubborn sprites in the Score, and choosing to align the tops and the lefts as shown in the Align window. This will now enable you to change the top and left coordinates of the windows at the same time, (without surprise). Figure 8.7 shows the final results of the Align tool.

FIGURE 8.7

The properly aligned RTF text fields as corrected by the Alignment toolbar.

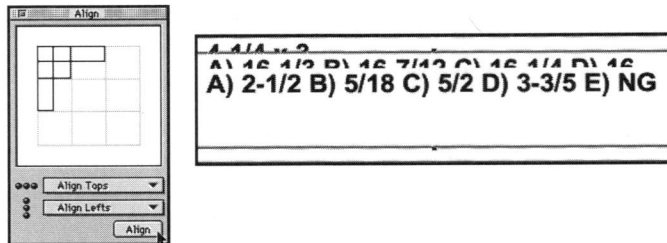

The final thing to note about changing your sprite attributes is that global changes to your sprites cannot be made while the Score is active. Much like using Cast To Time requires that the Cast window be active, the Font option under the Modify command has the stipulation that the Score *not* be the active window. Although you might use the Score to pick out your cast, make certain that you click once on them on the Stage before applying your changes or the Font menu will be ghosted. My guess about this is that Macromedia did not want users making the incorrect assumption that font characteristics were animatable or frame specific. Certain commands in Director have this way about them. Noting which ones they are could save you a lot of time (by not making incorrect assumptions).

Procedure 4: Easy Palette Effects and Tricks

One of the coolest aspects of Director is its handling of multiple palettes. Using Director's palette channel, you can swing effortlessly from stop to stop in the great palette jungle that is multimedia. Each image you create can have its own customized palette; more importantly, different palettes can be applied to the same 8-bit image to achieve different results. One problem that could arise during all these changes is that certain common cast members might appear over several different backgrounds that in turn use several different palettes (navigational buttons, for example). In such a situation, if a completely different palette is used, the cast members would obviously appear to be discolored when placed on the backdrop using the different palette. This is also the case with cartoon-based multimedia. You might have certain cartoon characters that appear throughout the production, even though each background uses its own palette in order to look as true to its original colors as possible. This situation can be handled three ways:

❋ Give it up! Dither everything to the Windows system palette and you'll have no worries.

❋ Create a super palette that combines the best colors of all your backdrops, and dither and remap everything to that.

❋ Create optimized palettes for each background and incorporate a common sub-palette among them.

The last option is the only one not normally discussed, so the following describes how to accomplish it. This example uses DeBabelizer, which is not currently available on the Windows platform.

1. In Director (or by other means), create a sub-palette of the colors you want to use for your foreground elements or cartoon characters. Assume for this example that you are using 32 colors. We'll refer to them as the character colors. Save an image with these colors at the top (and black for everything else). Realize that using 32 colors now gives you only 222 left (2 colors reserved for white and black). Note that if you plan to make a Windows' *friendly* palette (see Chapter 7, "Palettes and Sound"), you need to reserve the first 10 and last 10 for the Windows system, and make the appropriate adjustments (this leaves only 201 custom colors for backgrounds).

2. Take your character colors image into DeBabelizer, and from the Palette menu choose Palette, Save. Call it character palette.

3. Load in the 24-bit version of your background, and from the Palette menu choose Reduce Colors. Set it to 222.

4. From the Palette menu choose Rearrange, and click on No Arrange First (to clear out auto-arranging that DeBabelizer might already have in memory). Make certain that the Both option is on. (See fig. 8.8.)

FIGURE 8.8

The Rearrange dialog box with the Both option selected and the No Arrange option clicked.

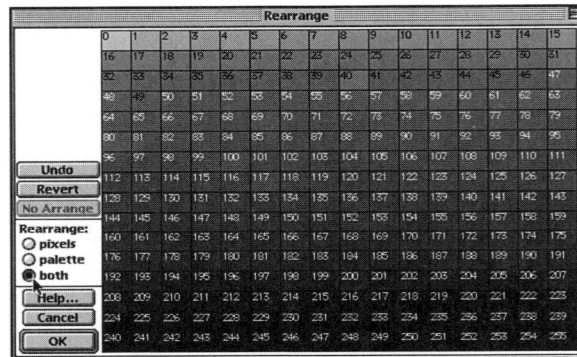

5. Select and drag the last 32 black registers to the top, and click on OK (see fig. 8.9).

6. After this, make another trip to the Palette menu and choose Merge Colors.

7. In the From section, set it to Character palette. Type 32, and set the Start at to 0. In the To section, select the current palette. Make certain that it starts to add the colors in at register 0 as well.

8. Click on Final, and make certain that the palette you are creating looks correct. The 32 character colors should be on top, and the new custom colors should be on the bottom. Click on OK. (See fig. 8.10.)

9. You have now created the palette for this image, and any buttons or characters using the top 32 colors will look okay on this screen. Save and import the picture, and its palette, into Director. (To further make use of

the full palette, you might also want to Save the palette in DeBabelizer, reload the 24 bit image, and redither it. You then make use of any of the extra 32 character colors that appeared in the image).

10. Perform this procedure for every screen you use that has a custom palette to be used in the movie.

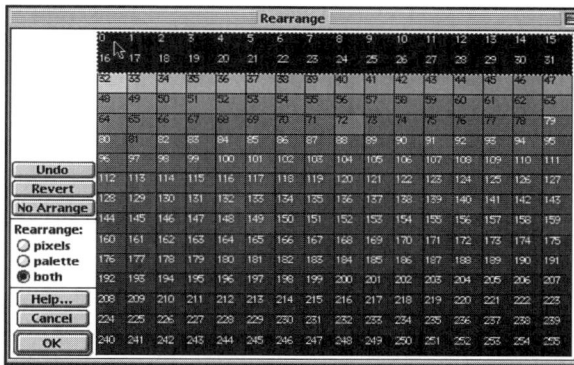

FIGURE 8.9

The Rearrange dialog box after the 32 colors have been selected and moved to the top of the palette.

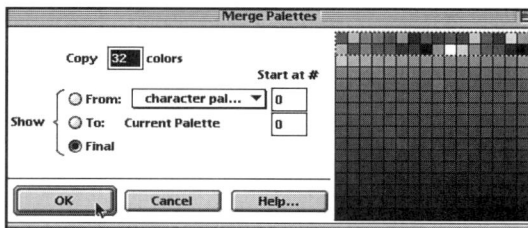

FIGURE 8.10

The Merge Palettes dialog box with all the options discussed in the procedure being set.

After all this is finished, you can feel free to move your characters to any of the backgrounds without concern. The only real question is whether or not this works effectively on your target machine (some Windows video cards reportedly have problems with palette effects).

Using this technique offers a nice bonus in that the entire background can be faded out by making a palette transition that goes from the background palette to the character palette (which has black in place of the custom colors).

A number of effects can be achieved from this. First, a nice idea is to use this effect to move the characters to another environment. Fade the background to black, have the character keep walking, and fade in the new background after making the swap. You can also, in essence, have the lights go out by making the custom colors darken; the character colors can be muted to all bluish tones (to simulate darkness and night, such as in a cave). Regardless, different takes on this technique can provide a wealth of exciting effects.

Procedure 5: Optimizing Playback After Resizing a Bitmap

When it comes to resizing bitmapped cast members in real time, Director is not very quick. This is a big no-no in the performance department. It generates a noticeable hit to the speed of the animation (especially on Windows). Playing back a number of separate bitmaps is much more speedy.

A method of solving this is to resize the image in Director, and subsequently export the sprite being resized as a collection of separate images. Import these back into Director and clean them up.

Procedure 6: General Tips

The following assorted tips are listed in the hope that they might provide some useful measure of insight into some new and old areas of Director. Many of them might seem obvious to some people, but could help spark a few new ideas for others.

Use External Casts Dynamically

A great thing about external casts is that they can be brought in and out on-the-fly. They can be used to exchange palettes and drawing updates among artists working in Director, and can be used to organize (and thereby streamline) the way you work. If you have not done this yet, try creating separate casts for media elements that exceed 15 members. Generally, sound files and graphics can be separated into their own casts. Further division can be made as necessary. The only thing to worry about with external cast, as opposed to internal, is that the cast members are not moved around when more than one movie is referencing it. This confuses the movie and produces unwanted problems. For instance, if you move a particular cast member in one movie, Director automatically updates the Score references of that movie. Unfortunately, the Scores of any other movies referencing this cast are not updated. As a result, the movie(s) that wasn't updated tries to look at the moved cast members as though they were in their original positions. Needless to say, these problems can become very complicated to fix.

Save Often Under Different File Versions

This is a sure-fire way to avoid going insane. Director is generally quite stable. For unknown reasons, however, and without warning, sometimes a file being saved over and over again becomes corrupt. When this happens, for the most part, it's all over. Even if you manage to pry the file back open, most (if not all) of the graphics are hopelessly mangled and torn apart. In cases like this, it's comforting to have at least some version of the artwork still intact. Scripts and Score information might still be useable, but it's questionable whether the movie itself should be trusted. Best advice: salvage what can be salvaged, and create an entirely new movie. It is my belief that saving and compacting helps prevent this problem. Macromedia released an update that solves much of this problem for Director 5, but always walk the safest route whenever possible.

Drag and Drop till You Drop

Everybody's work style is different, and not everyone can adapt his or her style to every new shortcut that comes around. Of all the time-savers to come around, however, drag-and-drop methodology is definitely on the top of the list. Many people still aren't used to it, and resist it with all their might. Investing a little work time to master it, however, could easily save you mounds of accumulated time over a day. Some of the best demonstrations of this have been implemented in Director 5.

In Director 4, Macromedia gave their users a taste of what was in store by enabling elements of the Score to be dragged around. Holding down the Option key (on the Mac) or the Alt key (on the PC) enabled you to duplicate Score information being dragged. Not holding down the modifier key would just move the information to another section of the Score. This drag-and-drop functionality could be disabled at any time by holding down the spacebar. Realizing that this feature might take a little getting used to, Macromedia even allowed No drag and drop to be the default, and the spacebar to be used to activate it.

This feature and others like it still live on in Director 5. Better than that, it's been joined by a number of additional drag-and-drop cousins. The following section lists many (if not all) of the drag-and-drop features I've found especially useful.

General Director Tips

Note that in all of Director's media content windows (Paint, Text, Field, and Video), a little gray box appears in the upper left-hand corner next to the name of the current cast. This is called the Place button. Getting used to using this button enables you go straight from creating information to dragging it into the Score, or on to the stage. Another, even faster, method is to press Command+Shift+L (on the Mac) or Ctrl+Shift+L (on the PC). This does not enable you to choose the placement, but it is a swift way of getting any worked on cast member on to the Stage and centered, especially when the Stage is hiding under mounds of windows.

Score Window

All of that mentioned earlier about Director 4's Score still exists in Director 5 as well. This includes the capability to create film loops by dragging Score cells into the Cast window. Also, dragging a number of cast members from the cast window into the score generally lumps them into one frame; holding down the Option key on the Mac or the Alt key on the PC, however, enables the cast members to appear one after the other extending out as many frames as needed.

Cast Window

Director 4 enabled cast members to be dragged around and moved anywhere the user wanted. Copying sprites required a trip to the menu; now, duplicate sprites can be created by just dragging the cast member while holding down Alt (PC) or Option (Mac). The most charming new thing about the cast window is that media can be dragged in from outside of the program quite easily. This includes aliases or shortcuts of those files (which are treated exactly like the files themselves). This is nice because you can use your normal OS (Windows or MacOS desktop) to locate all your data, and dump aliases of these files into folders marked for a particular project. Even if these files are scattered for other purposes around your system, they can be referenced through aliases when dragging them into the cast window.

Another great new aspect of the Cast is having multiple casts. In the upper left-hand corner of the cast window is the Cast Selector. This pull-down menu enables you to choose which cast to work on. Holding the Option/Alt key down while selecting a different cast opens a new window instead of changing the current one. Even better, for long casts, you can open multiple instances of the same cast window by holding down the modifier key and selecting the same cast from the Cast Selector.

You can *also* open an external cast on-the-fly by either double clicking it from the Desktop, or dragging in onto the Director application (this lets you open the cast without linking). You can link on-the-fly by dragging from the Desktop into the Cast window.

As a cautionary note, always use drag and drop when moving cast members, and not Cut and Paste. Cut and Paste will ruin the references you have to these items in the Score. Fixing this can be remedied by using the Exchange Castmembers function under the Edit menu (Command+E on the Mac and Ctrl+E on the PC).

Procedure 7: Highlighting Regions of Your Movie for Tutorial Purposes

A simple trick (that can be used in a number of ways) stems from the need to highlight a particular region of the screen. The technique is specific to wanting to highlight a region, in effect, by dimming the rest of the Stage. Obviously, if you were overly concerned with having a full complement of image-editing options open, this task would be done by using a dedicated image editing program such as Photoshop, Painter, or Xres. Accomplishing the task through the use of Director's ink effects and blend controls, however, has a few benefits.

Assume that the user has a particular portion of the Stage that needs to be highlighted, for example. Assume further that the user is being prompted to notice something happening in the corner of the screen (for example, a help screen that describes certain aspects of a product's navigation). Your screen size measures 640×480, and you are in 256 color mode (although as with any recipe, this technique can fit many different configurations). Also assume that the highlight shape you are looking to use is an oval, and that you currently have your movie loaded and cued to the screen on which you want the highlight to appear.

1. Open the Paint window and create a new cast member. Draw a small black square. Its color should be neutral gray (equal percentage of white and black).

2. Use the Transform Bitmaps function to resize the object to the size of your screen. (This is a quick way to get a simple screen-sized graphic.)

3. Drag this cast member into the Score, centering it over the underlying screen. Note: This cast member should be highest in the sprite order to appear over everything).

4. Set the sprite's ink to darkest, and set the Blend amount to 50%. On completion, your stage should look darkened.

5. Return to the Paint window and draw a white square in the general region where you want to have your highlight on the main stage.

6. Look on the Stage and examine how well it worked (see fig. 8.11). The area in which the white square was drawn should now be see-through, and the black area should be translucent (due to the sprite ink). As necessary, adjust your square in the Paint window by using the filled Rectangle tool (and gray and white).

FIGURE 8.11

The Stage at the beginning of the procedure.

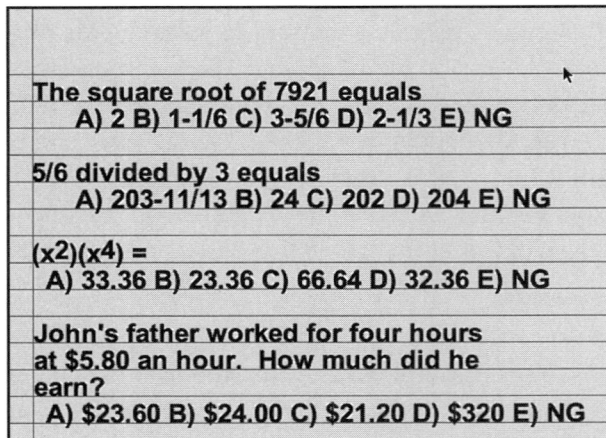

The square root of 7921 equals
   A) 2 B) 1-1/6 C) 3-5/6 D) 2-1/3 E) NG

5/6 divided by 3 equals
   A) 203-11/13 B) 24 C) 202 D) 204 E) NG

$(x^2)(x^4) =$
   A) 33.36 B) 23.36 C) 66.64 D) 32.36 E) NG

John's father worked for four hours at $5.80 an hour. How much did he earn?
   A) $23.60 B) $24.00 C) $21.20 D) $320 E) NG

7. Double-click on the Gradient tool and create a range that gradates from white to the gray you used (with white being in the middle). Set gradient direction to Shape Burst.

8. Using the white square to reference the area in which to create the oval, draw your oval. Make sure to draw an oval large enough to completely cover the square. (Alternatively, you might just fill in the square with the Paint Bucket and rely on memory or trial and error for correct placement.)

9. You should now have a gradient of white to gray inside an oval (the center being white).

10. Fill inside the oval with a gradated shape burst. It should appear now as a burst of white. (Invert the gradient direction if it is the opposite.)

11. Look on the stage. The area now appears to have a soft-edged shadow over it, as shown in figure 8.12.

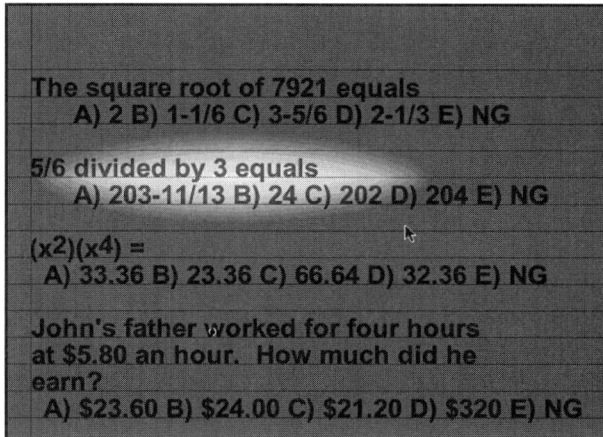

FIGURE 8.12

The soft-edged final appearance using the technique.

The square root of 7921 equals
   A) 2 B) 1-1/6 C) 3-5/6 D) 2-1/3 E) NG

5/6 divided by 3 equals
   A) 203-11/13 B) 24 C) 202 D) 204 E) NG

$(x^2)(x^4) =$
   A) 33.36 B) 23.36 C) 66.64 D) 32.36 E) NG

John's father worked for four hours at $5.80 an hour. How much did he earn?
   A) $23.60 B) $24.00 C) $21.20 D) $320 E) NG

Generally, the fuzzy edge has a nicer overall effect than a coarse sharp pixel edge. You can vary this entire look depending on your needs by creating screen-wide horizontal and vertical blends, or extra wide spotlights that are dissolved in.

Nice aspects of this technique include the following:

❖ The technique is not hard coded; changes can be made on-the-fly because everything you need is in Director. If an external editor is used, it requires the author to keep leaving Director to re-edit the image. This is most important because changing any element of the screen requires another trip outside Director.

✤ Using this technique, the highlight region needs only be specified once, and the elements underneath it can be altered numerous times.

✤ Although performance is definitely an issue, this technique can also be utilized in creating a dynamic spotlight that moves around the screen. Essentially, a number of images can be referenced according to criteria (like mouse position) to simulate a spotlight in the darkness lighting up pieces of a scene.

Conclusion

In the final analysis, the continual struggle to create dazzling multimedia is basically a neverending battle for truth, knowledge, and the path of least resistance. Truth embodies the desire to find answers and solutions that truly work and that don't lead us to dead-end problems that necessitate completely reworking large sections of our product. This involves not only issues about having a clear development direction, but constantly knowing that the strongest weapon is knowledge. It can never be stressed enough that the greatest resource for any authoring platform lies in those developers that labored before you. Draw upon those resources constantly, as no one should have to reinvent the wheel. In this electronic age we live in, the capability to link up with developers around the nation and the world has never been greater. Online services such as CompuServe and America Online provide helpful and informative forums through which to post questions to Macromedia and fellow developers (and get them answered fairly quickly).

The Internet is also an invaluable source of information because multiple Director sites and forums of information are instantly available to you through search engines and well-managed hyperlinks from related sites. The Internet also provides an invaluable connection for people to talk one-on-one with each other through e-mail. Because response is not only convenient and quick for the person responding, e-mail is likely one of the easiest and most response-assured ways of communicating today.

Concerning the path of least resistance, realize that all three of the points brought up at the beginning of this section flow together. Truth follows knowledge, and the path of least resistance is that path followed by keeping the most informed. Because the world is changing so quickly, and new technologies, tricks, and techniques are being constantly created, it can be said that the greatest obstacle for the developer today is not necessarily lacking the latest greatest miracle tool, but lacking the knowledge to effectively utilize it.

chapter 9

Kirk Keller

Building Generic Handlers in Director

Most advanced developers know the basics of Director research: trade ideas on the Direct-L list server; rummage through the archives at Maricopa's and Macromedia's web sites; read the manuals. When asked to contribute to this book, I wanted to deliver to the advanced developer something that, to my knowledge, has not been covered in any single resource—a philosophy of coding in Director (or, actually, coding in general).

This philosophy can be summed up in one basic, but very important, idea: Every project you produce should give you tools that continue to work for you.

Although Marxism is supposed to be dead, Karl Marx did hit on one important revelation about the products of human labor. When we produce something, the labor that goes into it does not just disappear. It remains there. When you spend a day building a program that calculates days of the week, for example, that program continues to work the next day—even while you are engaged in some new programming task. In a very real sense, multimedia projects become additional "employees." They go on to work for the clients who pay us to create them.

The Director developer needs to adopt a mindset of constantly considering how the script he is writing for one situation can be used in the future.

What will be discussed in this chapter and the next three are methods by which actual code or tools immediately can be used in projects, with no time-consuming "tweaking" of scripts.

These chapters presuppose a basic understanding of the Director environment and of Lingo scripting. They focus on how to most effectively use scripting to save time and produce products that require less troubleshooting.

This chapter will do the following:

- Discuss the nature and importance of generic handlers
- Discuss the basics of building a generic handler
- Discuss how to find useful algorithms for handlers
- Examine useful generic handlers

Understanding the Importance of Generic Handlers

One of the first ways most Director developers begin to get their code to work for them is by creating generic handlers.

A *generic handler* is a handler that can be used in a Director environment without modification of its code. The creation of this type of handler might require more time than a specific handler. Forethought must go into how to build a handler so that its usefulness extends beyond the present application.

The time invested pays for itself, however, when one considers the advantages of a generic handler.

The four main advantages of using generic handlers are that they easily enable the following:

* Eliminating duplicate code

* Building a code library for future projects

* Creating new functions in Lingo

* Coordinating efforts of programming teams

Eliminating Duplicate Coding in a Project

An example from personal experience best demonstrates the need to eliminate duplicate Lingo in a project.

When creating the *Pictures of the Year* CD-ROM for the UMC School of Journalism, over twenty movies contained multiple spots where background music could be faded out while a QuickTime audio of a contest judge or photojournalist began.

During the final testing of the product, it became clear that I had not accounted for the fact that some IBM machines might not support multichannel sound. The sound routine as it was written proved unstable on this type of machine. Because every spot in every movie that dealt with sound used the same handler located in a shared cast, the task of troubleshooting this problem was limited to redesigning the one handler rather than keeping track of over 60 instances of the handler.

Early identification of duplicated code and the reduction of this code to one handler in a cast member available to all movies used in the project pays for itself in the long run.

It is not unusual in a project to feel that you do not have the extra time to track down duplicated code and replace it with generic handlers. If that code proves to be defective during the final phase of the project, however, you have not saved any time—especially because you, at that point, might not remember every place where you used similar defective code in a project.

Building a Code Library

Building handlers to house often-used code in a project is helpful. Building generic handlers that can be used from project to project, however, is invaluable. The Director developer should view every handler created as the creation of an additional hired hand. Taking the additional time to develop a code library enables Director developers to approach a project knowing that he already has sophisticated code completed for the project and time to create additional code that will, in turn, be used in future projects.

Allowing Additional Lingo Functions

To aid in the design of scripts, handlers can be designed so that they can be called as functions. In this sense, they look and function in much the same way as existing Lingo functions and commands. Although a Lingo command does not exist that can return the average of three numbers, a handler can be designed to be called as an averaging function.

Creating generic handlers and using them in this manner enables the Director developer to easily create a library of additional Lingo functions while keeping the overall scripting uncluttered and easy to debug.

Coordinating Developers' Efforts

Generic handlers enable increased productivity in development projects involving multiple parties. By using handlers as additional Lingo functions, other developers within a project team can easily understand and use these new functions. The use of a common set of handlers by a development team ensures that the incorporation of Director movies into a final product goes smoothly. Furthermore, because the complex coding is contained within a generic handler, the use of generic handlers enables sophisticated scripting tasks to be delegated to employees who might still be getting up to speed on scripting in Director.

Building Generic Handlers

Building generic handlers is not a step-by-step process. By looking at generic handlers and understanding the general features of a generic handler, however, Director developers learn how to build their own.

Generic handlers can easily be built if the developer keeps the following in mind:

* Whenever possible, replace the use of global variables with parameters.

* Make no references to particular cast members.

* Replace important fixed values with parameters the user can set.

* Eliminate functions that presuppose conditions that might not exist in other movies.

* Embed alert messages or error codes in the handler to alert the user of errors in calling the handler as well as identifying the handler with the problem.

* Use comments or alert messages in the handler to document the use and nature of the handler.

* Create setup conditions in the handler that enable the user to easily implement the handler.

Following these rules ensures that the handler constructed is generic enough to enable you to easily import it into any project and use it immediately.

To understand the importance of each of these general points, consider the creation of a generic handler that averages three numbers.

This kind of handler is probably first created by developers because they have three particular values to be averaged. You might have a program with three variables, one, two, and three. The program needs the average of these variables to be placed in a variable called average (see listing 9.1).

When originally created, this code might not even exist in a separate handler. In this example, however, it does.

Listing 9.1—The Original Handler for Getting the Average of Three Numbers

```
on average
  global one, two, three, average
  set average = (one + two + three)/3
end
```
The average handler explicitly deals with all the variables in our program.

Using Parameters

The problem with our average handler is that if we use it in future projects, it only works with the global variables named in it.

References to particular cast members, important values, or particular conditions in the Score such as puppetsprite channels should be done with parameters whenever possible. This enables the programmer to tailor the handler to a particular project without the need to rewrite the handler or even understand the code within the handler.

The first step in making the average handler generic is to eliminate the use of global variables and replace them with parameters. If the handler referred to particular cast members, you would also change this reference to a variable set by a parameter.

The revised handler is shown in listing 9.2. All global variables have been eliminated. Now values are passed to the handler by parameters. The calculated average is then returned to the main program with the return Lingo command. The main program uses the returned value by using the result Lingo command.

Listing 9.2—The average Handler with No Global Variables

```
on average firstno, secondno, thirdno, avg
  set avg = (firstno + secondno + thirdno)/3
  return avg
end
```

Eliminating global variables in the generic handler enables it to be used in programs where the values you want to average are not in variables called one, two, and three. Because the handler does not use global variables, you don't have to worry about this handler changing pre-existing global variable values when you add it to another movie.

Counting Parameters

Some generic handlers might have their function depend not only on the parameters that are passed to it, but the number of parameters as well.

The average handler works for three numbers. If a program calls for the average of more than three numbers, however, the handler is useless. The average handler would be better if it could take any number of values to average. This can be done by using the paramCount function and replacing hardcoded values with variables (see listing 9.3).

Listing 9.3—The average Handler Using paramCount and No Hardcoded Values on Average

```
repeat with a = 1 to the paramCount
  set b = b + param(a)
end repeat
return  b/the paramCount
end
```

The handler in Listing 9.3 does not need a parameter listing at the top of the script to identify particular parameters passed to it because it deals with all passed parameters in the same manner. The param function is used to keep track of which parameters have been added to the sum to be averaged. The paramCount function determines the number of parameters passed to the handler. The paramCount replaces the hardcoded value of 3 previously used to get the average of three numbers. With this hardcoded value replaced with a variable, the handler can be used to average any series of numbers.

To briefly digress from our average handler example, the paramCount function can also be used to create optional parameters. A handler may have a final parameter that can toggle on or off the trails property of a sprite. The handler could use the paramCount function to determine whether this additional parameter has been passed to the handler.

Using the voidP Function to Check Parameters

Another method that can be used to determine which parameters have been passed to a handler is the voidP function. This function returns a FALSE value if the parameter it checks has not been initialized. Suppose you created a handler that scaled cast members. An optional parameter could be added that would save the cast member to another location before the scaling procedure. The handler would look something like this:

```
on ChangeCast castmember,savelocation
    if voidP(savelocation) then
        duplicate member castmember, savelocation
    end if
    set the height of member castmember to 10
end
```

If no parameter for a save location is passed to the handler, the handler scales the cast member without making a backup beforehand.

In addition to the voidP function, other functions such as the integerP, stringP, floatP, objectP, listP, or symbolP functions can be used to ensure that the parameter that has been passed to the handler is the correct type.

The average handler, for example, can use the floatP and integerP functions to alert the programmer if he sends the handler anything other than numbers to average.

Care should be taken in the use of these property functions, however. Because of the way Director handles lists and objects, for example, listP and objectP functions return TRUE for either lists or objects. The listP function also returns a TRUE value if the item it is checking is a rect or point.

Although they are not foolproof, these additional property functions can reduce the chance of misuse of a generic handler.

Embedding Alerts in a Handler

If several programmers work in your development environment, it is useful to embed alerts inside generic handlers to explain misuse of the handler. This enables programmers who might not be completely familiar with the generic handler to determine quickly the problem with the call to the handler.

In listing 9.4 the average handler uses the floatP and integerP functions to make sure the parameters it has are numbers. If the parameter is a number, then it's averaged as it was before. If the parameter is neither a floating point number nor an integer, however, the alert command is used to tell the user there is a problem and what parameter has caused the problem (see fig. 9.1). The alert also states what handler has the problem. To prevent the code that called the handler from crashing, the average handler returns a value of 0 if the handler is misused.

Listing 9.4—The average Handler with an alert Added

```
on average
  repeat with a = 1 to the paramCount
    if not (integerP(param(a)) or floatP(param(a)) then
        alert "AVERAGE handler error: Parameter"&&a&&"is not a number.¬
    Operation aborted."
        return 0
    else
        set b = b + param(a)
    end if
  end repeat
  return  b/the paramCount
end
```

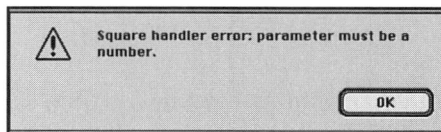

FIGURE 9.1

Embedded handler alerts enable the user to determine the problem in a handler call.

If the handler is particularly complex, the alert might go into more detail concerning the order and nature of the parameters being passed. Although a programmer could easily open the movie script containing the handler and examine the parameters, embedding this information in an alert saves time because it can be accessed by making an incorrect call to the handler from the Director message window.

Creating New Lingo Functions with Handlers

Most Director developers are aware of how handlers can return values via the return command. This value can then be placed into a variable with the result command. The following is an example of this type of exchange:

```
on startmovie
  random_frame
  put the result into showframe
  go to showframe
end
on random_frame
set frm = getAt(["one","two","three"],random(3))
  return frm
end
```

The scripting required to pass values can be shortened by treating handlers as additional functions in Lingo. The same function in this set of Lingo script can be accomplished with the following change to the `startmovie` handler:

```
on startmovie
   go to random frame()
end
on random_frame
set frm = getAt(["one","two","three"],random(3))
   return frm
end
```

The generic `average` handler can also be treated as a Lingo function. To print the average of 14 and 6 to Director's message window, one can simply use the following command:

```
put AVERAGE (14,6)
```

At this point, you've created a generic `average` handler. This handler can be placed in any movie or cast library and can easily be used as an additional Lingo function. Developers need only know how to call the `average` function.

Finding Useful Resources for Creating Generic Handlers

Director developers have a number of resources at their disposal when it comes to finding information necessary for creating a particular handler. These include the following:

* Algorithm sources and books
* Algorithms written in other programming languages
* Internet Sources such as Direct-L, ShockeR, and Maricopa

Algorithm Sources and Books

Geometric and algebraic algorithms can be found in introductory textbooks or mathematical handbooks. It is typically a small matter to convert these algorithms into Lingo script. Use of these algorithms enables the Director developer to incorporate a wide range of features into a multimedia project.

Another source of algorithms are technical books devoted to computer algorithms. One such book is *Computer Graphics: Principles and Practice*, by James Foley (ISBN 0-201-1211-7). It covers basic algorithms in graphics complete with pseudocode that the avid Director developer can convert to Lingo script.

Converting from Other Languages

After you find a useful algorithm, you still need to put it into a program form for use in a Lingo script. This task, however, might already be done for you. Many useful algorithms have already been created for other programming languages such as Java or Basic that can be converted to Lingo script with little trouble. In fact, many of these books were published in the mid 80s and can be found in your local library. The `calendar` handler listed later in this chapter, for example, was converted from a Basic routine written in 1985.

When looking for algorithms in Basic or some other language, try to find resources that do not cater to a particular platform. This reduces the possibility that the routine depends on some type of hardware-specific commands (for example, peeks and pokes).

With Basic programs, the following rules can help make the transition to Lingo easier:

* Convert data strings into lists

* Convert data `read` statements into `GetAt` commands

* Convert `print` statements into `put` commands

* Convert routines using `goto line` number commands to `if...then...` statements

* Convert `gosub` routines into additional handlers

Using Direct-L, ShockeR, and Maricopa

The best resources for Director handlers are the Direct-L list server and the Director web site hosted by the Maricopa County Community College District. Both contain handlers that other developers have found quite useful. With little effort, these handlers can be modified to become generic handlers.

The traffic on Direct-L can become quite high at times (around 100 to 200 messages per day). If you do not think you want that much e-mail, you can subscribe to the list server in digest mode. This sends you a daily compilation of the activity on Direct-L in one message. Another option is to go to the Maricopa web site and do a search of the Direct-L archives or search the archives via e-mail.

Alan Levine, who helps manage the Maricopa site, has also created a Tips & Scripts area on Maricopa. This area contains a compilation of handlers, general scripts, and programming techniques in Director.

Both resources contain a large number of Lingo handlers. In fact, while doing research for this chapter, I even found a few examples that duplicated what I thought were unique solutions of my own.

Note

Handler Resources on the Net

Several resources on the Internet can be used to find examples of handlers. The best are the Direct-L and Shockwave listservs and the Maricopa web site.

To subscribe to Direct-L, send e-mail to `listserv@uafsysb.uark.edu`. In the body of the e-mail message, send the following:

```
SUBSCRIBE DIRECT-L your name
```

This subscribes you to the list.

More information on how to use the Direct-L listserv can be found at

`http://www.earn.net/lug/notice.html`

Maricopa also has a search form for Direct-L located at

`http://www.mcli.dist.maricopa.edu/director/digest/index.html`

You can also read recent Macromedia Director messages sorted by date (courtesy of Verity, Inc.) at

`http://www.mccmedia.com/direct-l/`

To receive a daily compilation of Direct-L posts as one e-mail message, receive posts as separate messages, or temporarily stop receiving e-mail, send the following respective e-mail messages to `listserv@uafsysb.uark.edu`

```
set direct-l DIGEST
set direct-l MAIL
set direct-l NOMAIL
```

To subscribe to the Shockwave (or ShockeR) listserv, send e-mail to `list-manager@lists.webcontent.co.uk`. In the body of the e-mail message, send the following:

SUBSCRIBE shockwave your name

Send problems with the Shockwave listserv to owner@lists.webcontent.co.uk.

Maricopa's Director web is located at

http://www.mcli.dist.maricopa.edu/director/

Looking at Useful Generic Handlers

Creating handlers that are generic is a skill that must be developed. Sometimes the best way to learn this type of skill is to look at examples. The following handlers are examples of algorithms, Basic programs, and handlers that have been modified to create generic handlers.

Converting from Basic—calendar

I created the calendar handler for a project that needed to list a monthly calendar in one of its screens.

A search at AltaVista for "basic perpetual calendar" brought up a Basic program that created a perpetual calendar. (The original Basic listing can be found on the web site.) After minor modifications such as converting data strings into lists and goto statements into conditionals, the calendar handler was completed (see listing 9.5).

Listing 9.5—The calendar Handler Converted from a Basic Program

```
on calendar M,Y
  -- ----------------------------------------------------------------
  -- The basic program for this routine appeared in Astronomical
  --    Computing, Sky & Telescope in July of 1985.
  --
  -- It was converted to Director Lingo by Kirk Keller March, 1996
  --    M = (month: 2 digit number)    Y = (year: 4 digit number)
  -- Puts resulting calendar into text field "calendar"
  -- For the text to align properly, you should use a non-proportional
  --    font such as courier
  -- ----------------------------------------------------------------
  set d=["  1","  2","  3","  4","  5","  6","  7","  8","  9"," 10","
    11"," 12"," 13"," 14"," 15"," 16"," 17"," 18"," 19"," 20"," 21","
    22"," 23"," 24"," 25"," 26"," 27"," 28"," 29"," 30"," 31"]
```

```
set e=[31, 28, 31, 30, 31, 30, 31, 31, 30, 31, 30, 31]
set c=[]
if Y<100 then set Y=Y+1900
set J=367*Y-integer(7*(Y+integer((M+9)/12))/4)+integer(275*M/9)+1721031
set K=0
IF M<=2 THEN set K=-1
set J=J-integer(3*(integer((Y+K)/100)+1)/4)
-- Now we find out how many days the month has
set K= getAt(E, M)
-- Is the month Feb?  If so, then we check for leap year
IF M=2 THEN
  set W=integer(Y-100*integer(Y/100))
  set X=integer(Y-4*integer(Y/4))
  set Z=integer(Y-400*integer(float(Y)/400.0))
  if X=0 then
    if W<>0 and Z<>0 then
      set K=29
    end if
  end if
end if
set X=J-7*integer(J/7)
repeat with I = 1 to 42
  addAt C, I, "   "
end repeat
repeat with I = 1 to K
  setAt C, (I+X), getat(D,I)
end repeat
-- Now print out the calendar
put " SU MO TU WE TH FR SA" into line 1 of field "calendar"
repeat with I = 1 to 6
  set J = 7*I
  put getat(C,J-6)& getat(C,J-5)&getat(C,J-4)&getat(C,J-3)&¬
getat(C,J-2)&getat(C,J-1)&getat(C,J) into line I+1 of field "calendar"
  end repeat
end
```

This handler requires the following parameters:

♣   **M:** A numerical value of the month of the year being calculated

♣   **Y:** A two or four digit numerical value of the year being calculated

If you compare this handler with the original Basic program, you notice that the "data" statements in the Basic program that listed months and days of the week have been converted to lists. read commands have been replaced with

GetAt Lingo commands. Decision branches that refer to line numbers have been replaced with If...Then Lingo commands.

The calendar handler does not follow all the rules for a good generic handler. The handler presupposes that a field cast member called "calendar" exists. The aesthetics of the handler also presuppose that a nonproportional font is being used in the "calendar" field cast member.

The calendar handler can accept two digit years (for example, 96 or 97). Inputting a four digit value ensures proper functioning after the year 1999. Another point about this handler is that it correctly calculates that the month of February in the year 2000 will only have 28 days even though the year 2000 is a leap year. (This is a feature that, for some reason, is lacking on many commercial calendar programs.)

To highlight particular days in the field cast member displaying the calendar, the hilite_calendar handler can be used.

Listing 9.6—The hilite_calendar Handler for Use with the calendar Handler

```
on hilite—calendar hday
  -- ------------------------------------------------------------
  -- This routine is designed to work with the calendar handler
  --    written by Kirk Keller, but it can be used to highlight any
  --    text field (with basic modifications)
  -- Written by Kirk Keller (c) March 1996
  -- It uses text field "calendar"
  --    hday = (number of day to be highlighted)
  -- ------------------------------------------------------------
  set L = the number of lines in field "calendar"
  -- start checking the lines, skipping the first line for days of week
  repeat with I = 2 to L
    set W = the number of words in line I of field "calendar"
    repeat with J = 1 to W
      if word J of line I of field "calendar" = hday then
        -- nothing
        set the textstyle of word J of line I of field "calendar" = ¬
      "outline"
        set the textstyle of word J of line I of field "calendar" = ¬
      "condense"
      else
```

```
            -- nothing
         end if
      end repeat
   end repeat
end
```

This handler requires the following parameters:

nhday—A numerical value of the day to be highlighted

This handler also presupposes the existence of a "calendar" field cast member. It searches each word in the field cast member for a match to the day to be highlighted. When found, it changes the font style of that word to be outlined. To preserve the layout of the calendar, the font of the highlighted date is also condensed.

Because the font style of individual words is being altered by this handler, highlighted dates are not preserved if the field cast member is saved as text or if some other types of modifications are made to the field cast member.

Creating Additional Lingo Functions—Arrays

The following array handlers are a good example of how generic handlers can be used to create additional Lingo functions.

One feature that Director currently lacks is arrays. Arrays can be useful data structures for storing spatial data. If one were to build a children's memory card game, for example, in which the Director movie displayed a 4×4 grid of cards, an array could be used to easily store and retrieve information about each of the cards.

Although Director does not have arrays, it does have lists. These lists can store almost any type of information available in the Director programming environment—including other lists. This lists feature enables you to build a set of Lingo functions that use lists to create arrays.

Consider the following 3×3 array:

4	10	13
6	15	7
8	55	3

Assume the point of origin is at the bottom left corner. Typically this array is read so that the position second over on the x axis and third up on the y axis contains the value 10. Each position on the array is reached by referring to both an x and y value.

One could also consider the x axis, however, to contain a column of numbers. The first x position, viewed this way, would contain the column 8, 6, 4. Viewed this way, it's clear that this array can be read as a list of x positions with each x position containing another list containing the column at that position. This results in a list in which each element in the list is yet another list. This forms the basis for the GetArray and SetArray handlers that we can use as new Lingo functions (see listing 9.7).

Listing 9.7—The AddArray Handler for Adding Values to an Array and the GetArray Handler for Retrieving Values from an Array

```
-- Each element in the major list is a list
-- of all y elements for the x
on AddArray x,y,value,array
  if count(array) >= x then
    set ytemp = getAt(array,x)
  else
    set ytemp = []
  end if
  setAt ytemp, y, value
  setAt array,x,ytemp

end
on GetArray x,y,array
  set ytemp = []
  set ytemp = getAt(array, x)
  set value = getAt(ytemp,y)
  return value
end
```

By using the return and result commands, one can get a value from a global array MapValues by using the following commands:

```
-- GetArray 2,2, MapValues
-- put the result
```

These two lines print the value for cell 2,2 in the MapValues array in the Director Message window. By using the GetArray handler as a function, however, these commands can be reduced to one line:

```
-- put GetArray(2,2, MapValues)
```

This creates a handler that looks and functions the same as standard Lingo commands such as GetAt() or SetAt(). These can be given to a development team along with a description of their function. The development team does not even have to understand the basics of the code within the handler—a definite advantage if part of your team is still getting up to speed in Director scripting.

Building a Generic Button Handler

Scripts to control the actions of buttons are usually contained within Cast scripts or Score scripts. By building a generic handler that is called from the Cast or Score, however, a sophisticated set of button and slider actions can be developed that can be immediately implemented in a project. This approach also ensures consistency of slider and button behavior in a project being created or revised.

A general button handler that moves when depressed is the following button handler (shown in listing 9.8).

Listing 9.8—A Generic button Handler

```
on button
  if the number of member "clickdown" > 0 then
    puppetsound "clickdown"
  end if
  set the locH of sprite (the clickon) = the locH of sprite (the clickon)¬
    + 3
  set the locV of sprite (the clickon) = the locV of sprite (the clickon)¬
    + 3
  updatestage
  repeat while the mousedown
    -- nothing
  end repeat
  if the number of member "clickup" > 0 then
    puppetsound "clickup"
```

```
   end if
   set the locH of sprite (the clickon) = the locH of sprite (the clickon)¬
      - 3
   set the locV of sprite (the clickon) = the locV of sprite (the clickon)¬
      - 3
   updatestage
end
```

The `button` handler does not need to create puppetsprites because the depressed location of the button is frozen while the mouse is down. The handler automatically determines which sprite is supposed to be depressed. The handler also determines whether `"clickup"` and `"clickdown"` audio cast members exist. If so, the handler plays them at the appropriate moments. To use this handler with a particular button, the script in listing 9.9 is added to the cast member or the Score.

Listing 9.9—The mousedown Handler Required to Call the button Handler

```
on mousedown
   button
   -- whatever commands the button is to
   -- execute would be placed here.
end mousedown
```

Using Algorithms for Graphics: Moving in a Circle

Director's scripting language easily enables the movement of sprites in a horizontal or vertical position. Other movements such as circular motion are more difficult to create.

After a series of discussions on Direct-L, Matt Anderson, Mark Andrade, and Glenn Picher wrote these two handlers for circular motion. Both of these handlers provide a good example of how generic handlers can enable Director developers to quickly and easily incorporate complex physical effects into their movies without spending costly programming time re-creating the algorithms needed for such effects.

Mark Andrade's `CirclePath` handler rotates a sprite 360 degrees about a point of rotation with a radius of 50 pixels (see listing 9.10).

Listing 9.10—Mark Andrade's CirclePath Handler

```
on CirclePath   -- Mark Andrade
  put the locH of sprite 1 into cx
  put the locV of sprite 1 into cv
  set radius = 50
  repeat with angle = 1 to 360
    set the locH of sprite 1 to cx+cos(angle*3.14/180)*radius
    set the locV of sprite 1 to cv+sin(angle*3.14/180)*radius
    updatestage
  end repeat
end CirclePath
```

The handler uses simple trigonometric calculations to determine the horizontal and vertical position of the sprite for each step through the 360 degrees of rotation.

By using the rules for creating generic handlers, you can modify Mark's handler to produce the generic handler in listing 9.11.

Listing 9.11—The CirclePath Handler Made into a Generic Handler

```
-- Mark Andrade's CirclePath handler (generic version)
on CirclePath circlemember, radius,startangle,endangle
  if the paramCount = 0 then
    alert "CirclePath handler: This handler requires these
      parameters"&RETURN&"Number of sprite to be moved, radius of move-
      ment, starting angle, ending angle"
    return
  end if
  put the locH of sprite circlemember into cx
  put the locV of sprite circlemember into cv
  repeat with angle = startangle to endangle
    set the locH of sprite circlemember to cx+cos(angle*3.14/180)*radius
    set the locV of sprite circlemember to cv+sin(angle*3.14/180)*radius
    updatestage
  end repeat
end CirclePath
```

The radius of the circular movement, the sprite that is moved, and the beginning and ending points of movement have changed from hardcoded values inside the handler to parameters that can be passed. An `alert` feature has been added that returns a description of the parameters if none are passed to the handler.

Glenn Picher, one of the Direct-L veterans, wrote the very clever `mouseDown` handler in listing 9.12 that enables you to click on a sprite and pick it up, moving it along a circular path.

Listing 9.12—Glenn Picher's Circular Path Routine

```
on mouseDown  --Glenn Picher
  repeat while the stillDown
    put the mouseH into mx
    put the mouseV into my
    put mx - 320 into xAtMouse
    put my - 240 into yAtMouse
    if xAtMouse <> 0 then
      --there's a valid "triangle" to figure out the angle using ¬
      arctangent
      put atan(float(abs(yAtMouse))/float(abs(xAtMouse))) into ¬
      angleAtMouse
      if angleAtMouse = 0 then
        --it's a horizontal line
        set yAtCircle to 0
        set xAtCircle to 100 * (xAtMouse/abs(xAtMouse)) --set proper ¬
      direction
      else
        --it's a true triangle
        set yAtCircle to sin(angleAtMouse) * 100.0 *  ¬
      (yAtMouse/abs(yAtMouse))
        set xAtCircle to cos(angleAtMouse) * 100.0 * ¬
      (xAtMouse/abs(xAtMouse))
      end if
    else
      --it's a vertical line
      put 0 into xAtCircle
      if yAtMouse <> 0 then
        set yAtCircle to 100 * (yAtMouse/abs(yAtMouse))
      else
        --brute force to avoid divide by zero error
        put 100 into yAtCircle
      end if
```

```
        end if
        set the loch of sprite (the clickOn) to 320 + xAtCircle
        set the locv of sprite (the clickOn) to 240 + yAtCircle
        updatestage
    end repeat
end
```

The entire movement routine is executed while the mouse is pressed. The location of the mouse relative to a point of rotation (320,240 in this example) is calculated. Based on the relative position of the mouse, one of three trigonometric calculations are performed with a fourth error-trapping calculation added to prevent division by zero. The position of the sprite is then moved to this new calculated location and displayed using the updatestage command.

Glenn's circular motion routine is an excellent tool for any developer to have in his or her development library. Following the rules for making a handler generic, you can modify Glenn's routine to produce a handler that is more generic in nature, as shown in listing 9.13.

Listing 9.13—Glenn Picher's Circular Movement Routine Made into a Generic Handler

```
-- This movie handler moves a sprite in a circular path while
-- the mouse is down. It requires x & y points of rotation.
-- This handler is a modification of Glenn Picher's original
-- handler listed on Direct-L in 1995.
on DragInCircle orgx,orgy
    -- orgx & orgy are the center of rotation points

    -- rd is the radius of the rotational path
    -- this is calculated here
    -- r2=x2 +y2
    set rd = sqrt((the loch of sprite (the clickOn) - orgx)*(the loch of ¬
        sprite (the clickOn) - orgx)+(the locv of sprite (the clickOn) ¬
        -orgy)*(the locv of sprite (the clickOn) - orgy))

--  set rd = abs(the loch of sprite (the clickOn) - orgx)

    repeat while the stillDown
        put the mouseH into mx
        put the mouseV into my
        put mx - orgx into xAtMouse
```

```
      put my - orgy into yAtMouse
      if xAtMouse <> 0 then
        --there's a valid "triangle" to figure out the angle using ¬
        arctangent
        put atan(float(abs(yAtMouse))/float(abs(xAtMouse))) into ¬
        angleAtMouse
        if angleAtMouse = 0 then
          --it's a horizontal line
          set yAtCircle to 0
          set xAtCircle to rd * (xAtMouse/abs(xAtMouse)) --set proper
      direction
        else
          --it's a true triangle
          set yAtCircle to sin(angleAtMouse) * float(rd) * ¬
      (yAtMouse/abs(yAtMouse))
          set xAtCircle to cos(angleAtMouse) * float(rd) * ¬
      (xAtMouse/abs(xAtMouse))
        end if
      else
        --it's a vertical line
        put 0 into xAtCircle
        if yAtMouse <> 0 then
          set yAtCircle to rd * (yAtMouse/abs(yAtMouse))
        else
          --brute force to avoid divide by zero error
          put rd into yAtCircle
        end if
      end if

      set the loch of sprite (the clickOn) to orgx + xAtCircle
      set the locv of sprite (the clickOn) to orgy + yAtCircle
      updatestage
    end repeat
  end
```

The DragInCircle handler requires the following parameters:

❊ **orgx:** The horizontal point of rotation for the sprite

❊ **orgy:** The vertical point of rotation for the sprite

Several things have been done to make this routine into a generic handler.

The routine has been placed in its own handler. Now it can be accessed by any cast member and not just the one that has the original mouseDown handler.

A number of hardcoded values have been changed to variables set by parameters. Instead of the point of rotation being fixed in the handler, this handler enables the user to set the point of rotation by passing parameters to the handler.

The handler has a feature added to it that makes it easier for users to implement in program. The routine in its original form made it difficult to place the initial position of the sprite to be moved. The DragInCircle handler uses the Pythagorean Theorem to calculate the distance from point of rotation to the registration point of the sprite to be moved. To use this routine, the user positions the sprite on the stage and puts the following script into the mouseDown handler for the sprite:

```
on mouseDown
   -- Drag around point 240,320
   DragInCircle 240,320
end mouseDown
```

Conclusion

Taking the time to build generic handlers saves time in building future products. Generic handlers help preserve a consistent look and feel to a product. They also maintain a consistency in programming even if more than one developer is involved in the project.

Numerous resources are available for the construction of generic handlers. One resource of ready-made generic handlers is *Plug-N-Play Lingo*, by Gretchen Macdowall, New Riders Publishing, scheduled for release in January, 1997.

The fact that these handlers can be used immediately in any future project enables the Director developer to spend time building handlers capable of complex graphics or of filling a gap in existing Lingo functions or commands.

10

Kirk Keller

POWER-USING TEXT FIELDS

Multimedia developers who use Director talk about the use of lists for tracking variables and navigation points. Although lists are useful, they do have some drawbacks.

When rapidly prototyping or debugging, sometimes it is difficult to view the values of a list. The debugging options new to Director 5 make this task somewhat easier, but it can sometimes still be slow.

Some multimedia applications require that the user be able to view the values of a list and select particular values. This requires the additional step of placing list values into a text field and sometimes placing the string in the text field back into the list.

The use of text fields themselves as an alternative to Director's list function avoids these drawbacks. When using text fields to hold values, changing a value is as simple as editing a text field. At any time during the programming and debugging stage, you (the programmer) can trace changes in variables because these are literally changes in the text field.

Of course, this use of text fields should not be seen as a replacement for all uses of Director's variables and lists (or database Xtras such as FileFlex). Programs that use text fields to hold values run more slowly than programs that use lists or variables. When dealing with Director applications that do extensive data and text manipulation, however, the use of text fields offers a quick, easy solution without significant speed loss.

This chapter begins with a discussion of the differences between text fields and other types of text in Director such as bitmapped text images and Director's new Rich Text Format. Examples are then provided of how text fields can be used effectively for data, text, and Lingo manipulation. This chapter is split into the following sections:

- ✤ Understanding the difference between field cast members, text cast members, and bitmapped text

- ✤ Searching and retrieving text from field cast members

- ✤ Executing data from field cast members

- ✤ Moving between Lingo scripts and field cast members

- ✤ Altering fonts in field cast members

Understanding the Difference Between Field Cast Members, Text Cast Members, and Bitmapped Text

Most experienced Director users understand the difference between cast members that are bitmapped text and those that are traditionally considered text. Bitmapped text is just a bitmapped image of what was at one time text information. When text becomes bitmapped, it contains none of the text information (such as words or sentences) that it did as text. Now it is just a graphic image. Bitmapped text cannot be used for any of the techniques discussed in this chapter.

With the release of Director 5, developers have two types of text items. These are field cast members that were available in earlier versions of Director and text cast members (or rich text) that is new in Director 5. Director documentation now refers to this new type of cast member as "text." Until you understand the difference between these two types of text, however, I'll continue to refer to the text available in text cast members as "rich text."

The rich text used in text cast members offers a number of features that are not found in text fields:

* Rich text enables paragraph formatting and definable tabs in the text cast member.

* Rich text can be anti-aliased for a smooth, clean appearance.

* Rich text does not require its font information to be installed on its host machine.

* Rich text can animate more quickly.

* You can import Rich Text Format (RTF) files into text cast members and preserve the format of these files.

Text cast members have the following serious drawback, however:

* Text cast members cannot be edited outside the Director authoring environment and, thus, cannot be edited when a Director application is running.

The reason for this is simple. Text cast members actually become bitmapped images when the Director movie is running. As bitmapped images, they are able to retain the look you want from text that appears in multimedia applications. They can be anti-aliased. They do not require font information on the host computer, so they look the same on any machine. They can also quickly animate.

The downside, of course, is that although they can be edited in the Director authoring environment, they cannot be used to keep text information such as words because this information is lost when the multimedia application is made into a finished product. The information is lost because the text cast members are no longer really text in the finished product, but are actually pictures of text. The Director application can no more read the text in these pictures or bitmapped images than a word processor can read the text in an imported graphic image.

Because of this behavior of text cast members, the techniques discussed in this chapter only work with field cast members. It is important to remember the difference between text cast members and field cast members.

Searching and Retrieving Text from Field Cast Members

The following example demonstrates how fields can be useful for holding values and data. Perhaps it is a little oversimplified, but it serves as a launch point to discuss basic principles.

A local company wants you to build a multimedia application that lists its salespeople, their area of specialization, and their area of coverage. They do have a map of the sales areas, but they do not yet have a complete list of the salespeople, their area of specialization, or what areas they serve. "We'll get that information to you soon," they say. By using fields as data fields, you can develop the interface without the data.

Using Words and Items in Text Searches

You can work with the company to ensure that the list they ultimately give you is in the following form:

Person's name, area of specialization, sales area

On the web site, you'll find a Director movie called SALES.DIR. Open SALES.DIR in Director to see how to use this data. A sample data field called "salesperson data" contains the following two lines:

```
Kirk Keller,Director development,1
Fred Wilkes,Kirkware development,2
```

These lines serve as sample data for development purposes. Each line of this field has three items. These are separated by a comma as the item delimiter. The first item is the name of the salesperson, the second item is the salesperson's area of specialization, and the third item is the area of coverage.

> The comma is the default character used to separate (or delimit) items in a field. Sometimes, however, you might want to change this. This is especially true if your items themselves contain commas (for example, "Inkfill, inc.").
>
> The character used by Director to delimit items can be read and set by the `itemdelimiter` Lingo command.
>
> To set the character that separates items to a colon, use the following command in your `startmovie` handler:
>
> `set the itemdelimiter = ":"`
>
> Remember, however, that this remains the delimiter for all text fields in the Director application until you set a new delimiter.

Director enables you to search field cast members by character, word, item, or line. Because you are dealing with data in which each part of a record contained more than one word (for example, first and last name in salespersons' names), you must use items separated (or delimited) by commas as well as words.

Three buttons enable the user to search by salesperson's name, areas of specialization, and areas of coverage. If the user searches by name, a list of names appears in the "choices" field cast member. Likewise, if a user searches by specialization or area, a list of specializations and areas appears in the "choices" field cast member. If the user clicks on one of these results, that result displays in the "search item" field cast member, and a match from the database displays in the "results" field cast member.

FIGURE **10.1**

*The SALES.DIR
movie main screen.*

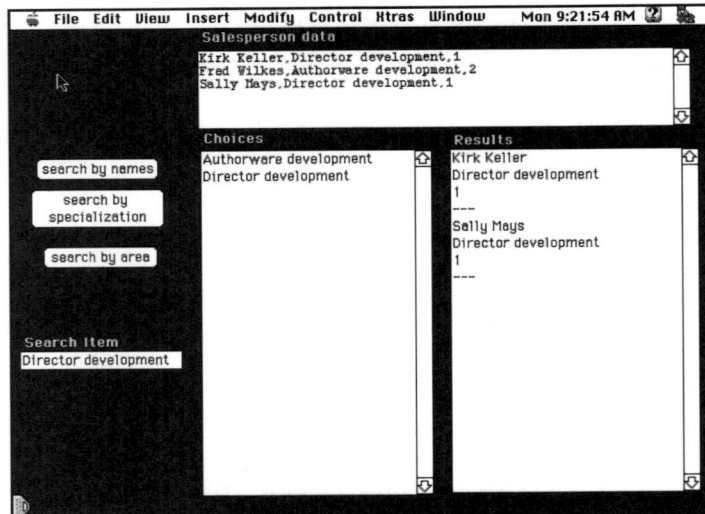

Using the GETLIST Handler

Searching requires the application to list all items by listing name, specialization, or area in the "choices" field cast member. This is done by using the GETLIST handler. All handlers for this movie are kept in the "movie" Lingo cast member.

The GETLIST handler looks like that in listing 10.1.

Listing 10.1—The GETLIST Handler

```
on GETLIST searchfield,wordno,itemno,destinationfield
  repeat with a = 1 to (the number of lines in field searchfield)
    -- if wordno is zero, then that means we pull the whole item
    if wordno = 0 then
      put item itemno of line a of field searchfield into line a of¬
      field destinationfield
    else
      put word wordno of item itemno of line a of field searchfield¬
      into line a of field destinationfield
    end if
  end repeat
end
```

Now, examine each line of this handler.

The handler accepts the following parameters:

* **searchfield:** the field cast member being searched
* **wordno:** the number of the word being searched
* **itemno:** the number of the item being searched
* **destinationfield:** the field cast member in which you want the resulting list displayed

For now you just want to do searches of whole items, so you can ignore the wordno parameter. To get the handler to ignore the wordno parameter, enter a zero value for it. To get a list of all the names in the "saleperson data" field (item 1) and place the resulting list in the "choices" field, call the GETLIST handler and pass it these parameters:

```
GETLIST "salesperson data",0,1,"choices"
```

To list all last names of the salespeople, call GETLIST in this way:

```
GETLIST "salesperson data",2,1,"choices"
```

The first line of the handler begins a loop that goes through all the lines of the text field being searched. If you have passed a 0 value for wordno, it knows you want to list the entire item and not just particular words in that item. Depending on the value of wordno, the handler places either a word from an item or the entire item in a line of the field cast member that displays the resulting list.

With this generic handler, searching by name, specialization, or area is simple. In the cast script for the "search by specialization" button, put this Lingo:

```
on mousedown
  GETLIST "salesperson data",0,2,"choices"
end
```

Using the GETLINE Handler

If you click on the "get names" button, the GETLIST handler lists the names of the salespeople in the "choices" field. The user can now click on a particular name in the "choices" field and get the rest of the information about the particular salesperson. This requires writing a handler that can find out which line of the "salesperson data" has information that matches the item on which the user has clicked. Do this with the GETLINE handler.

The GETLINE handler enables you to find a line that matches a particular word, item, or string within a line. For what you are doing here, you are interested only in finding a line with an item that matches what the user clicked on in the "choices" field. Because of this, you need only to examine the first line and last nine lines of the handler in the example in listing 10.2.

Listing 10.2—The GETLINE Handler

```
on GETLINE searchfield,wordno,itemno,thingtomatch
  set templist = []
  -- search for item match
  if wordno = 0 and itemno <> 0 then
    repeat with a = 1 to (the number of lines in field searchfield)
      if item itemno of line a of field searchfield = thingtomatch then
        append templist, a
      end if
    end repeat
    -- search for word match
  else if wordno <> 0 then
    repeat with a = 1 to (the number of lines in field searchfield)
      if word wordno of item itemno of line a of field searchfield = ¬
      thingtomatch then
      append templist, a
      end if
    end repeat
  else
    -- search for line match
    repeat with a = 1 to (the number of lines in field searchfield)
      if line a of field searchfield contains thingtomatch then
        append templist, a
      end if
    end repeat
  end if
  return templist
end
```

The GETLINE handler accepts the following parameters:

- ☀ **searchfield:** This is the field cast member being searched
- ☀ **wordno:** This is the number of the word being searched
- ☀ **itemno:** This is the number of the item being searched
- ☀ **thingtomatch:** This is the word or item you are attempting to match

The GETLINE sets up a temporary list that keeps the number of the lines that fit the match criteria. This list returns when the handler completely goes through the field cast member being searched.

To find out which lines of the field cast member "salesperson data" contain "Fred Wilkes" as the first item, call the GETLINE handler with the following parameters:

```
GETLINE "salesperson data",0,1,"Fred Wilkes"
```

To find lines that contain "Fred Wilkes" anywhere on the line, call the GETLINE handler with the following parameters:

```
GETLINE "salesperson data",0,0,"Fred Wilkes"
```

With the GETLINE handler understood, look at the cast script of the "choices" field shown in listing 10.3.

Listing 10.3—The Script for the "choices" Field

```
on mousedown
  if the mouseline = -1 then exitput line (the mouseline) of field¬
  "choices" into field "search item"
  put "" into field "results"
  GETLINE "salesperson data",0,0,(the text of field "search item")
  set MATCHLINE = []
  put the result into MATCHLINE
  set b = 1
  repeat with c = 1 to count(MATCHLINE)
    repeat with a = 1 to (the number of items in line¬
    getAt (MATCHLINE, c) of field "salesperson data")
      put item a of line getAt(MATCHLINE, c) of field "salesperson¬
      data" into line b of field "results"
      set b = b + 1
```

```
      end repeat
      put "---" into line b of field "results"
      set b = b + 1
   end repeat
end
```

The cast script is a mousedown handler so that it executes when the user clicks on the "choices" field. The first line checks to make certain that the user has not clicked on the scroll bar. The second line puts the line the user has selected in the "search item" field cast member. This field cast member acts as a global variable for the program.

The handler now clears the "results" field to prepare it for new results. The GETLINE handler is called and told to search the "salesperson data" field cast member for the lines that contain a match to the text found in the "search item" field cast member. The number of the lines that contain the match are returned from the GETLINE handler and placed in the MATCHLINE list. The mousedown handler now finds out the number of items in those matching lines of data and places each item on a separate line in the "results" field cast member. This is done for each element in the MATCHLINE list with three dashes separating each matching line of data.

One problem arises with the search engine at this point: the engine assumes that each line has a unique item. This means that the database cannot contain two salespeople who have a specialization in Director development, for example. If this occurs, the GETLIST handler lists "Director development" twice.

To see the problem with this, add the following line to the "salesperson data" field cast member:

```
Sally Mays,Director development,1
```

Searching by name still works with no problem. Searching by specialization, however, now gives us two lines with "Director development" in them. The results are also not in alphabetical order. You can fix this by using the SORTLIST handler.

Using the SORTLIST Handler

The SORTLIST handler takes the information from a field cast member, sorts it alphabetically, and removes duplicate listings. The SORTLIST handler Lingo is as follows in listing 10.4.

Listing 10.4—The SORTLIST Handler

```
on SORTLIST searchfield
  -- create temporary list
  set templist = []
  -- put the items into a list for sorting
  repeat with a = 1 to (the number of lines in field searchfield)

    add templist, (line a of field searchfield)
end repeat
  -- sort the list
  sort templist
  -- put the items back in the field
  put "" into field searchfield
  put getAt(templist, 1) into line 1 of field searchfield
  set b = 2
  repeat with a = 2 to count(templist)
    if getAt(templist,a) <> getAt(templist,a-1) then
      put getAt(templist,a) into line b of field searchfield
      set b = b + 1
    end if
  end repeat
end
```

The SORTLIST handler accepts the following parameter:

❋ **searchfield:** This is the field cast member that is being sorted

This handler puts the lines of the field cast member into a temporary list and uses Director's sort command to sort that list. The elements of the list are then placed back into the field cast member. After the first element is placed, all succeeding elements are checked for duplication before being added to the field cast member.

The SORTLIST handler would be called from the various search buttons. If you look in the cast scripts of the search buttons in this example, you see that the handler call is there, ready to be uncommented. Enable this line of each search button handler and run the problem again. Now the text in the "results" field cast member looks better.

You now have a fully functional simple database. The advantages of this approach are many. One is that you can rapidly prototype a multimedia application even if your customer is not yet certain of the exact nature of its data. Suppose the company decides to add a phone number to the data. You can add a new item separated by a comma; a particular line would look like this:

```
Fred Wilkes,Kirkware development,2,555-3452
```

To enable a search by phone number, you add a button that calls the GETLIST handler as follows:

```
on mousedown
   GETLIST "salesperson data",0,4,"choices"
end
```

Adding information to the database becomes as simple as copying and pasting the text into the field cast member from a word processor or using Director's fileio Xtra to bring an ASCII file into the field cast member.

Performing Multileveled Searches

In the salesperson database, the "search item" field cast member is used as a variable that the GETLINE handler uses. The "choices" field cast member is also used as a list that is generated on-the-fly while the application is being used. Field cast members can be used in this manner to create complex multilevel searches. Field cast members can also be used to store search rules. An example of this appears later in this chapter with the REPORT.DIR movie.

Executing Data from Field Cast Members

The salesperson example demonstrated how field cast members can be used to create a database. Field cast members can also hold possible Lingo commands to be executed by the Director application. One use for this is in building navigation tools for multimedia applications.

The NAVIGATE.DIR and MAP.DIR movies are examples of a navigation tool that I programmed for the CD-ROM project, *Pictures of the Year '96*, produced by the University of Missouri School of Journalism. Both of these movies can be found on the web site .

The *Pictures of the Year '96* project was on a tight schedule, and the exact location of some areas of the project was still being decided during the programming phase of the project. This meant that while at one phase of production two items of interest might exist in the same Director movie, by the end of the production phase, they might exist in two different movies (or not exist at all). What was needed was a navigation tool that would always be in working order, but that would enable quick and easy changes to the frame and movie the Director application would go to when navigating to a particular item of interest.

ote

> This approach of using field cast members to hold information for navigation was of great use due to the number of movies used in the *Pictures of the Year '96* project (41 total by the end of the project). It also provided, however, an unexpected benefit during last-minute debugging. During the pressing of the hybrid CD-ROM, it was found that all the Director movies would need to have their names modified so that Director would not confuse the movies with file directories that had similar names (for example, NPY.DIR and the NPY directory). The construction of the navigation tool enabled us to complete the needed navigation changes in minutes instead of hours.

The actual navigation movie is the MAP.DIR movie. It is called from the NAVIGATE.DIR movie as a MIAW (Movie in a Window). The MAP.DIR movie is generic enough that minor changes to its graphics and two text fields enable you to use it as a navigation tool.

When the MAP.DIR movie is called from the NAVIGATE.DIR movie, it presents the user with a navigation map. This map lists all areas of interest in the project and highlights the current location of the user with a red outline. If the user clicks on a new area of interest, the MAP.DIR movie tells the main movie to go to that frame/movie.

The MAP.DIR movie uses the SCREEN global variable. This variable contains the name of the current area being shown by NAVIGATE.DIR. For simplicity's sake, this area name is also the name of the marker placed at the beginning of this area in the NAVIGATE.DIR movie. The three possible areas of interest in the NAVIGATE.DIR movie are sales, services, and history. This information, along with the name of the movie that called it (obtained by the moviename function) gives the MAP.DIR movie the basic information it needs to navigate. At this point, we'll concern ourselves with only the MAP.DIR movie.

Navigation is determined by two field cast members: "location" and "movies". The "location" field cast member is used to highlight where the user currently is on the navigation map. The "movies" field cast member is used to navigate to the item the user selects from the navigation map.

The "location" field cast member lists every possible location from which the user might be calling the navigation map. The layout of the text is as follows:

Navigate	Sales	7
Navigate	Services	8
Navigate	History	9

Each line contains three words. The first word is the name of a movie at which the user might be located. The second word is the name of an area or marker in the movie. The third line is the number of the sprite that can highlight this particular location on the navigational map. By examining this field cast member, you can see that the red box that would highlight "services" is located in sprite channel 8 of the map movie. Because all the locations in this example are located in the NAVIGATE.DIR movie, the first word in the "location" field cast member is redundant. If this navigational map referred to more than one movie, however, this word would be necessary.

The highlight of the current location is done in the MARK_LOCATION handler (see listing 10.5).

Listing 10.5—The MARK_LOCATION Handler

```
on MARK_LOCATION
  global SCREEN
  tell the stage to set MNAME = the moviename
  -- slice off the .dir or .dxr extension with this handler
  SLICE_EXTENSION mname
  put the result into mname
```

```
repeat with a = 1 to (the number of lines in field "location")¬
  -- we check against the text cast which has the names of the movies¬
  and the
  -- appropriate sprite numbers associated with them.
  if MNAME = word 1 of line a of field "location" then
    if SCREEN = word 2 of line a of field "location" then
      set the ink of sprite value(word 3 of line a of field¬
      "location") = 36
      exit repeat
    end if
  end if
end repeat
updatestage
end
```

The handler gets the name of the movie that called it from the moviename Lingo
function. After removing the .DIR extension, it looks for a match between this
name and the first word of each line in the "location" text field. If it finds a
match, the handler then checks the second word of the line to see if it matches
the value in the SCREEN variable. If it finds a match, it then looks at the third
word of that line to determine which sprite it needs to make visible (via an ink
effect) on the navigational map.

Using the do Command

When the user clicks on an area, the movie calls one button script.

Listing 10.6—The mousedown Handler for the MAP.DIR Movie

```
on mousedown
  repeat with a = 2 to 4
    if rollover(a) then
      do line a of field "MOVIES"
      updatestage
      exit repeat
    end if
  end repeat
  tell the stage to close window "MAP"
end
```

This `mousedown` handler first checks to see which sprite has been clicked on. These sprites are in channels 2–4. The `"MOVIES"` field cast member contains possible movie commands in lines 2–4. If the user clicks on sprite 3 (that is over the `'services'` icon), this handler uses the `do` command to execute the third line of the `"MOVIES"` field cast member. In this case, the handler essentially issues the following Lingo command:

```
tell the stage to go to frame "services" of movie "Navigate"
```

If, during the production process, the location of `"services"` changes, all that is needed to correct the navigational map is to change this line of text and the line of text in the `"location"` field cast member that determines when the user is at the `"services"` location.

Creating Templates for do Commands

Field cast members not only can hold text data to be executed with the `do` command, but can also hold rules or templates for the execution of this command. One example of this use of field cast members is the movie REPORT.DIR. This movie can be found on the web site.

The REPORT.DIR takes a text document that has been read into the "data" field cast member and parses the text according to a set of rules. The parsed text is then converted into an HTML document and placed in the "output" field cast member.

The heart of this application is the `"rules"` field cast member. This cast member contains rules about how the application is to parse keywords and the body of text associated with them see listing 10.7.

Listing 10.7—The Text in the "rules" Field Cast Member

```
"</dir>"&RETURN&"<hr>"&RETURN&"<center><h2><ANAME="&QUOTE&¬
    HEADER&QUOTE&">"&HEADER&"</A></h2></center>"&RETURN&"<hr>"&RETURN
"</DIR>"&RETURN&"<p>"&RETURN&"<B>"&HEADER&"<¬
    /B>"&RETURN&"<p>"&RETURN&"<DIR>"&RETURN
"<B>"&HEADER&"</B>"&RETURN&"<p>"&RETURN&"<DIR>"&RETURN
"<LI><B>"&HEADER&"</B>"&BODY&RETURN&"<P>"&RETURN
"<hr>"&RETURN&"<center><h2><A NAME="&QUOTE&HEADER&QUOTE&">"¬
    "&HEADER&"</A></h2></center>"&RETURN&"<hr>"&RETURN
```

In the report document, for example, is a recurring header called STORES. This header comes at the end of one directory list in the HTML document (identified by a </DIR> command) and the beginning of another. The HTML document needs to have this header in bold and separated by paragraph markers (identified by the <p> command). Thus, the HTML code for the area around this header will be the following:

```
</DIR>
<p>
<B>STORES</B>
<p>
<DIR>
```

The reader familiar with HTML notices that the <p> command is not paired with a </p> command. This is a common practice in HTML because a </p> command is usually treated by web browsers as functionally equivalent to a new <p> command. The rest of this exercise presumes a general knowledge of HTML code.

If you look at line two of the "rules" field cast member (refer to listing 10.7), you see that it contains the following string:

```
"</DIR>"&RETURN&"<p>"&RETURN&"<B>"&HEADER&"¬
</B>"&RETURN&"<p>"&RETURN&"<DIR>"&RETURN
```

This is the HTML code listed earlier with carriage returns (the RETURN command) included. You should notice two things about this rule.

One is that instead of the word STORE in this rule we have HEADER. This is because headers other than the STORE header in the report need to be parsed in this manner. The VENDING MACHINE header also requires this type of markup.

The other is that this line of text, with its RETURN commands and HEADER variable, is actually written as if it were a Lingo command. This rule will be executed as a Lingo command by the do command in the RUN_DATA handler.

The RUN_DATA handler does the actual work of parsing the report. It looks at each line of the report and sees if that line begins with a header listed in the "areas" field cast member.

If the handler finds a match between a line of the report and this area list (shown in listing 10.8), it will then do the rule associated with that area header. The rule number is the first item on the area line. The rule for the STORES header, for example, is 2.

Listing 10.8—The Data in the "Areas" Field Cast Member

```
5,CENTRAL REGION
3,WAREHOUSES
2,STORES
4,Big River:
4,New Haven:
2,VENDING MACHINES
4,Maramec Spring:
1,NORTH CENTRAL REGION
2,VENDING MACHINES
```

FIGURE 10.2

The main screen of the REPORT.DIR movie.

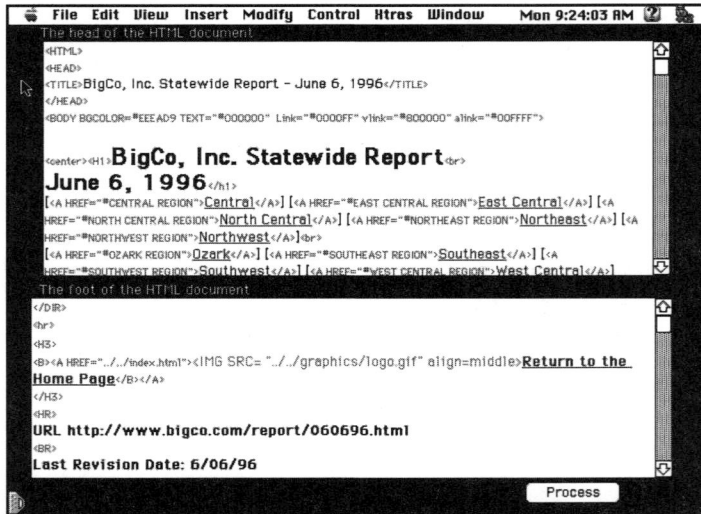

To finish the complete format of the HTML document, the REPORT.DIR movie also enables the user to edit dates and file names in the head and foot portion of the final HMTL document.

This is the RUN_DATA handler.

Listing 10.9—The RUN_DATA Handler

```
on RUN_DATA
   set AREALINES = the number of lines in field "areas"
   set DATALINES = the number of lines in field "data"
   set LL = DATALINES

   put "" into field "output"
   set BODY =""

   -- Now put in the footer info
   put field "file foot" into field "output"

   repeat with L = AREALINES down to 1

      -- set up a flag for a match
      set FLAG = 0

      -- Loop until we find a match.
      -- Since we're using a comma as the delimiter, we allow
      -- for commas occurring in the text line we're looking at by allowing
      -- the match areas to have up to 4 commas in them
      repeat while LL > 0
         if line LL of field "data" contains (item 2 to 6 of line L of¬
         field "areas") then
            -- We split any following data out of the line which
            -- has the area marker that just got tripped.
            -- This will go in the BODY variable
            set T = the number of words in item 2 to 6 of line L of field¬
            "areas"
            set T2 = line LL of field "data"
            set E = the number of words of line LL of field "data"
            set B = word (T+1) to E of T2
            set BODY = " "&B&" "&BODY
            set LL = LL - 1
            set FLAG = 1
            exit repeat
         else
            set BODY = line LL of field "data" &" "& BODY
            set LL = LL - 1
         end if
      end repeat
```

```
        -- We're out of the search loop. Did we
        -- find a match to our area?
        if FLAG = 1 then
          -- Now that we have a match, we find out
          -- what rule to follow for this match
          -- and apply it.

          set HEADER = item 2 to 6 of line L of field "areas"
          set BODY = BODY

          -- Update DATALINES so if we don't find a match, we start
          -- again at the DATALINES line of the data set.
          set DATALINES = LL
        else
          -- If we didn't find a match, let the user know it.
          put "Didn't find a Match for "&item 2 to 6 of line L of field¬
          'areas"

          set HEADER = item 2 to 6 of line L of field "areas"
          set BODY = "No report available."

          -- We need to backup where we're looking in the data field
          set LL = DATALINES
        end if
        -- We use a do command here because we want to execute the rule in¬
  the rules text field.
        do "put "&line (value(item 1 of line L of field "areas")) of field¬
        "rules"& " before field "&QUOTE&"output"&QUOTE
        set BODY = ""

    end repeat

    -- Now we top off the file with the header
    put field "file head" before field "output"

  end
```

The RUN_DATA handler examines the report text from the end of the text to the beginning. This is done for two reasons.

One reason is that the number of lines of text might alter during the parsing stage. By working from the end of the text to the beginning, this will not be a problem because an increase in line count only alters the position of lines occurring after the line currently being parsed.

The other reason is that by working from the end of the text to the beginning, bodies of text associated with a particular header can be collected into the "body" variable and then parsed in the appropriate manner.

To see how the REPORT.DIR movie works, load it into Director and follow these steps:

1. Run the REPORT.DIR movie. On the screen you see the text of the report and the rules that are used to parse the report.

2. Click on the "load report text" button. In the typical operation of this application, this enables you to load a document to be parsed. This feature has been disabled in this example and just takes you to the next screen.

    This screen shows the head and foot of the HTML document and enables you to make any changes necessary.

3. At this point, open the Director message window and then click on the "process" button on-stage. This runs the RUN_DATA handler and also prompts you to save the resulting text file.

    If, during the course of the parsing routine, it does not find a match to an area, it lists that area as not found in the Director message window. It then puts a "No report given" in the HTML document for that area.

4. Save the text file, and then open it in your favorite web browser. You should see that the Director movie has taken the report and used it to create an HTML document complete with embedded links to the different regions listed in the report.

FIGURE 10.3

*The HTML docu-
ment created by the
REPORT.DIR movie
as it appears in a
web browser.*

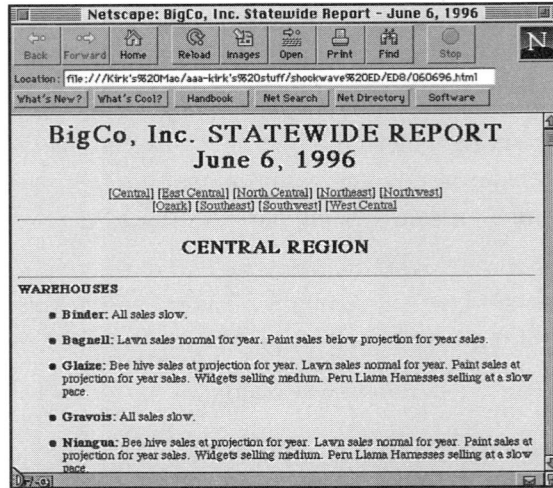

The REPORT.DIR movie is a simple example of how an HTML report generator
can be built using fields cast members. The most time-consuming part of using
this movie for a new type of document would be writing the rules and making
certain that the text in each report maintains a consistent format. The potential
time savings is significant. An HTML expert could probably mark up the report
in this example in about half an hour to an hour. With the REPORT.DIR movie,
the markup takes about one minute.

Moving Between Lingo Scripts and Field Cast Members

The do command demonstrates how field cast members can hold Lingo commands. You can, however, go even further in exchanging data between field
cast members and Lingo.

The scriptText function enables you to search Lingo scripts as well as move the
scripts to and from field cast members. One example of how this can be used is
demonstrated in the SCRIPTXT.DIR movie.

You should recognize the interface of the SCRIPTXT.DIR movie. It is a modified
version of the movie you looked at earlier dealing with salespeople. Because
you are using field cast members for data storage, the modification consisted of

new text and minor changes in the mousedown handler used when the user clicks on the "choices" field cast member. This is another example of how using field cast members enables you to rapidly retool an application.

Instead of data about salespeople, the field cast member at the top of the stage contains information about text stored in the "handler data" field cast member. The first item is the name of a handler. The second item is a description of the handler. The third and fourth items are the beginning and ending lines of the handler as it exists in the "handler data" field cast member.

The "handler data" field cast member contains the text you would typically find in handlers. It is important to realize, however, that it is ordinary text and not Lingo. It can be searched using the handlers looked at earlier in this chapter. It can also be saved and retrieved as a field cast member via Director's fileio function. The fred handler, for example, found at the bottom of this field cast member, will not execute because it is not really a Lingo handler. To demonstrate this, open the message window in Director and call the fred handler by typing:

```
fred
```

You should get an error indicating that the handler is not found.

The SCRIPTXT.DIR movie also contains a cast member called "handler library". This is a movie script cast member that contains no handlers when the movie is first opened. The SCRIPTXT.DIR movie enables you to select handlers from the "handler data" field cast member and turn them into real Lingo handlers that will be placed in the "handler library" cast member.

When you run this movie, you can either list handlers in the "handler info" field cast member by handler name or by description. When listed, you can select one of the handlers by clicking on it. Click on the fred handler in the "choices" field cast member. It appears that nothing happened. This is not the case, however.

Stop the movie and open the "handler library" cast member. Although this contained no handlers when first opened, the cast member now contains the fred handler.

Open the message window in Director again and type:

fred

This time you should get an alert sound from your computer. (If you didn't, select Recompile all scripts under the Control pull–down menu to recompile the script containing the newly added `fred` handler.) The text listing the `fred` handler in the `"handler data"` field cast member has been used to create a new handler.

The Lingo that converts the text to Lingo is found in the `mousedown` handler in the `"choices"` field cast member see listing 10.10.

Listing 10.10—The mousedown Handler for the SCRIPTXT.DIR Movie

```
on mousedown

  -- Find out if they clicked on the scrollbar
  if the mouseline = -1 then exit.

  -- Find out what line we're choosing
  put line (the mouseline) of field "choices" into field "search item."

  -- We're going to search for a line which contains a match to
  -- the data we chose in the "choices" field.
  -- Notice that we've set wordno and itemno to zero.
  GETLINE "handler info",0,0,(the text of field "search item")

  -- We put the line number returned from GETLINE into the
  -- list MATCHLINE.
  set MATCHLINE = []
  put the result into MATCHLINE

  -- Now that we know what line in the database we're dealing with
  -- We can work directly with that line and move the text from the¬
  handler data
  -- to the handler library.

  -- We clear out the temporary text field we're going to use.
  put "" into field "temptext"
```

```
-- We put the current lingo in the handler library into
-- the temporary text field.
put the scriptText of cast "handler library" into field "temptext"

-- We now put the handler data we just chose at the end of this¬
temptext field
set NEWLINE = the number of lines of field "temptext"
set NEWLINE = NEWLINE + 1

set FIRST = value(item 3 of line getAt(MATCHLINE,1) of field "handler¬
info")
set LAST = value(item 4 of line getAt(MATCHLINE,1) of field "handler¬
info")

repeat with a = FIRST to LAST
  put line a of field "handler data" into line NEWLINE of field¬
  "temptext"
  set NEWLINE = NEWLINE + 1
end repeat

-- Now that we're finished preparing the new addition
-- we put the entire thing back into the scripttext of
-- the handler library.
set the scripttext of cast "handler library" = the text of cast¬
"temptext"
end
```

The script is essentially the same as it was in the SALES.DIR movie. The real change is found in the second half of the handler.

The scriptText command is used to place handlers or comments that currently exist in the "handler library" into the "temptext" field cast member.

The third and fourth items in the "handler info" field cast member are used as values for lines to be extracted from the "handler data" field cast member. These lines of text are then placed in the "temptext" field cast member after whatever is already in the field.

The entire "temptext" field cast member then replaces the existing Lingo script in the "handler library" cast member. The end result is that a Lingo handler is added to the Lingo of the "handler library".

Changes made to a cast member's script are not visible until Director recompiles the script. This means that if you happen to have the "handler library" script window open, you probably won't see the new Lingo until you close the script window and then open it again, or until you select Recompile all scripts from the Control pull-down menu in Director.

Searching Lingo with the LIST_HANDLERS Handler

When Director recompiles the Lingo, it generates an error if it finds duplicate names of handlers. This means that if you run this movie and select the fred handler twice, you will get an error from the Director environment the second time. Avoiding this error is a matter of checking the names of existing handlers before adding one (avoiding duplication). Do this by searching the existing Lingo in the movie in much the same way as searching field cast members. Do this by using the LIST_HANDLERS handler.

Listing 10.11—The LIST_HANDLERS Handler

```
on LIST_HANDLERS outputfield
  put "" into field outputfield
  repeat with a = 1 to the number of Members
    -- Does the cast member have Lingo?
    if the scripttext of cast a > 0 then
      -- Search each line and see if a line
      -- starts a handler (i.e., it starts with "on ").
      repeat with b = 1 to the number of lines of the scripttext of¬
      cast a
        if word 1 of line b of the scripttext of cast a = "on" then
          put word 2 of line b of the scripttext of cast a & return¬
          after field outputfield
          end if
      end repeat
    end if
  end repeat
end
```

The LIST_HANDLER handler is actually pretty simple for what it does. You know that any handler will have to begin with the word "on". The handler name is the second word on that line.

With this in mind, the `LIST_HANDLER` handler first gets a number of the last member in the cast window. It then steps through each possible cast number to see if it has Lingo script. Because cast members such as bitmapped images can also have Lingo scripts associated with them, it checks to see if the cast member has any type of script associated with it. If it does, the handler then steps through each line of the Lingo script to see if the first word is `"on"`. If it is, it places the second word into a field cast member given as a parameter.

Give the handler a try. Open the message window in Director and type the following command:

```
LIST_HANDLER "list of handlers"
```

If you look at the `"list of handlers"` field cast member (displayed on the stage in frame 5 of the movie), you see that it has a list of every handler in this movie.

This handler could be called in the mousedown script of the `"choices"` field cast member. In this way, the script could check to see if a handler by a given name already exists before trying to create a new one.

Altering Fonts in Field Cast Members

Those who have worked with field cast members might have noticed that the field cast members in the REPORT.DIR movie have varying font sizes and colors. This is an undocumented feature of field cast members that can be of use as long as the developer is aware of its limitations.

The font, style, size, and color of a field cast member can be set with the `font of member`, `fontstyle of member`, `fontsize of member`, and `forecolor of member` Lingo commands. Although the backcolor can be set of the field cast member with the `backcolor of member` command, it can only be called with a reference to a member and not a reference to a field. These commands (with the exception of the `backcolor of member` command) can affect not only the entire field, but can also affect a line, word, or character of that field cast member. One can write Lingo code that, for example, changes the second word of the third line of field cast member `"fred"` to font size 12 by executing the following Lingo code:

```
set the fontsize of word 2 of line 3 of field "fred" = 12
```

This feature enables the developer to write Lingo code that can spice up an otherwise dull field cast member.

Because this is an undocumented feature of the field cast member commands, it is unclear whether it will continue to be supported in future releases of Director.

Conclusion

The handlers discussed in this chapter are generic enough that they can be used with little or no modification in existing projects you develop. Limitations to the use of field cast members for data storage, however do exist.

Field cast members are limited to 32 KB in size. This means that field cast members are not good for large databases. Also, the larger the field cast member in file size, the longer some search and retrieval handlers take to execute.

Another problem is that anti-aliasing and manipulation of some font properties are not available to field cast members. Thus, they are not cosmetically attractive in the way text cast members or bitmapped images can be. Furthermore, because the field cast members do not become bitmapped images in the final Director application, the fonts the members use must be installed in the host machine. This problem can be overcome somewhat by using fonts that are generic enough to be found on most host computers or by using the FONTMAP.TXT document for cross-platform mapping of fonts. This solution, however, further complicates the preparation of a cross-platform application using field cast members.

Note

Using the FONTMAP.TXT File for Cross-Platform Font Control

When you execute a Director application, the application looks for a font map in the same directory as the application. This font map is called FONTMAP.TXT. If no font map exists, then the application executes in a normal fashion.

The FONTMAP.TXT file can be used to map the usage of fonts on both Mac and Windows platforms. A Director application, for example, might be created on the Mac platform and use one particular font in a field cast member. When this application is run on Windows machine, the font map determines which Windows font should be used in place of the unavailable Mac font. In this example, the Mac font has been mapped for the Windows platform.

The FONTMAP.TXT file can contain information on mapping Mac fonts for the Windows platform and for mapping Windows fonts for the Mac.

A FONTMAP.TXT file can be found in the same directory as your Director authoring software. This file contains mappings for standard Mac and Windows fonts. Additional font mappings can be added to this font map file.

To preserve a similar look on both platforms, a general rule is to map Mac fonts to smaller size Window fonts. More information on font mapping as well as a sample file can be found on page 93 of your Director 5 manual, *Using Director*.

Despite these problems, field cast members can be useful tools that enable rapid prototyping and easy debugging of multimedia applications, use of small databases, application navigation, and quick manipulation of text. Some of the basic uses for field cast members reviewed in this chapter lay the foundation for multimedia tools discussed in Chapter 11, "Building Multimedia Tools in Director."

chapter 11

Kirk Keller

BUILDING MULTIMEDIA TOOLS IN DIRECTOR

Chapter 10, "Power-Using Text Fields," examined the REPORT.DIR movie. This application takes text files and parses them in HTML format for display on the World Wide Web. The unique aspect of this application is that the Director application is being used not as a final multimedia application, but as a development tool for another multimedia application—in this case, a Web browser.

One feature of Director often overlooked is the power of Director to create tools that ease the burden of creating multimedia applications. With features added in Director 5, this use of Director becomes even more powerful.

This chapter splits into the following sections:

- ✻ *Identifying the Need for Development Tools*
- ✻ *Determining How the Tool will be Used*
- ✻ *Building a Development Tool*
- ✻ *Examining Multimedia Development Tools*

Identifying the Need for Development Tools

All multimedia projects have three distinct phases of development. These phases are

- **Planning:** The project is planned and media is developed.

- **Programming:** Programming for the project is created.

- **Finishing:** The project is debugged and prepared for mastering.

Multimedia developers have always known that the right development tools in each of these phases can significantly reduce the workload involved in the typical production cycle. Although project planning and media development tools fill the marketplace, the Director developer is out of luck when it comes to finding tools to aid in the development of programming and debugging. This is unfortunate because this is where development tools are most needed.

In terms of simple debugging, Director 5's release helps to some extent. With the addition of the Debugger and Watcher tools, it is now easier to track variable values and program execution than it was in earlier Director environments. This only addresses half the problem, however.

It is not unusual for a Director multimedia application to be comprised of several independent movies. Each of these movies can contain several media cast members and links to even more. Each cast member may contain its own Lingo script or be referenced by Lingo in a movie handler. Either hundreds of frames of score or hundreds of lines of Lingo can exist in the entire application. The movies with their frames and scores control the presentation of 5 to 500 MB of media.

While this complex collection of multimedia is being developed, outside issues further complicate matters. Changes in media during the production phase require the relinking or importing of files. Several different programmers might work independently on movies that are then incorporated into a final project. Unforeseen problems in programming, time, or content may lead to major changes in programming or the way media is linked.

All these factors lead to a situation in which the developer begins to ask serious questions. Are all media elements linked or imported in a consistent manner? Do movies contain cast members that once served a purpose but now waste valuable space and load time? How much time did the summer intern spend creating this simple effect? How much time was wasted building Lingo handlers that could have been imported from previous applications had the programmer been aware of them?

All these issues point to the need for the serious multimedia developer using Director to spend time building a suite of development tools. Taking time to create development tools is not a luxury; it is a necessity. As the multimedia development market becomes more competitive, the ability to quickly create prototypes with solid programming and to shave hours or days off a change in production will begin to determine the success of a company.

What should these development tools do? Development tools for the programming and finishing phases of multimedia production should do one or more of the following:

❖ **Automate repetitive tasks:** Checking the `directToStage` property of a digital video cast member is a simple task in Director. Checking 20 digital video cast members in 20 different movies, although still a simple task, is something that no multimedia developer (with typical hourly pay) should be doing.

❖ **Perform complex reference or computational tasks:** Purging extraneous cast members, changing variables, or computing media size or play length is almost impossible for one individual to do in a highly complex multimovie project. Change employees in mid-project, and the task becomes almost impossible. By using solid development tools, you can cut the time involved in these tasks and at the same time ensure a higher level of insurance against a costly human error.

❖ **Coordinate individual efforts:** More than one programmer or a series of programmers on a project can cause serious delays unless some common development framework is applied. Development tools can aid here as well. Consider, for example, a tool that creates a standard series of handlers. During the programming phase of production, several instances of the same handler may be used in different movies. In the finishing phase of production, it is an easy task to shift from these multiple instances of a handler to one handler in a shared cast. Similarities in product look and feel can also be more easily preserved in this manner. More importantly, developments made by one individual for one project continue to be a resource for future projects.

Determining How the Tool Will Be Used

After the particular task for a development tool is identified, the developer should consider how the tool will be used. The way the tool uses global variables and shared cast members will be affected by the final form in which the tool is used.

Creating Stand-Alone Applications or Handlers

Development tools can be of use not only to developers, but to clients as well. It is not unusual in today's marketplace to sell a client a static multimedia application. The content and function of the application is fixed by the multimedia developer. Any change in function or content requires additional contract work on the part of the multimedia developer. As customers become more sophisticated in multimedia and more aware of the availability of developers, however, the sale of static applications becomes more difficult. As the general public becomes accustomed to the glitter of multimedia, serious questions will be raised concerning the cost effectiveness of paying top dollar for an application that cannot be easily updated/modified. Static multimedia applications will give way to applications that can be altered by the customer. A stand-alone development tool to parse text for display in a kiosk, for example, might easily be modified for use by the customer as a bonus piece of software they get in addition to the kiosk software developed for them. This bonus piece of software could be a modified version of a development tool used to create display text in the development of the kiosk application.

Creating MIAWs and Xtras

Most development tools, however, will be used by developers in the Director authoring environment. Before the release of Director 5, this meant either copying and pasting a handler into a current movie under construction or opening a Movie in a Window (or MIAW). Director 5 simplifies this task with the Xtra menu option.

Using the MIAW and Xtra

One of Director 5's most exciting new features is the Xtra Plug-in API. This API enables third-party developers to create applications that enhance the capabilities of applications developed in Director. Xtras have been developed that enable Director to make use of Photoshop Plug-ins or access database files.

MIAWs can also be used as Xtras. By placing a MIAW in the Xtra folder, the MIAW becomes an option in the Xtra pulldown window. This means that MIAWs developed in earlier versions of Director can now be used easily within the Director authoring environment. Director developers can now easily develop their own development tools for use in Director.

Communicating Between the Xtra or MIAW and Stage

Developing an Xtra within Director is a matter of creating a Director movie that will be used as a MIAW. Any MIAW to be used as a development tool will need to communicate with the stage movie being developed.

This communication is somewhat difficult. MIAWs and the Stage cannot pass values to each other unless these values are somehow made global. Handlers in a MIAW cannot be called directly by the Stage movie. Because of these two constraints, the traditional method for a MIAW and the Stage to communicate is to do the following:

* Tell the Stage exactly what to do with a `tell the stage to` command.

* Pass information between the MIAW and Stage via global variables, shared cast members, or the MacOS or Windows clipboard.

The disadvantage of this approach is that multiple `tell` commands are sometimes used where one handler would be more effective. Stage movies, however, cannot directly call handlers in a MIAW. Another problem with this approach is that it creates new global variables. If the global variables the MIAW uses have the same name as global variables in the stage movie, this overwrites the values of those original global variables. Copying and pasting from the clipboard can likewise overwrite important cast property information.

MIAWs as Xtras are most effective if they can communicate with the Stage without the use of global variables and without introducing new handlers to the cast of the Stage or through a shared cast. This can be done.

Handlers placed in a movie script of the MIAW can be called by the Stage movie by the MIAW telling the stage to do so. A MIAW has a handler Fred that consists of the following script:

```
on Fred
  beep
end
```

If this handler is called from the message window (that is, by the Stage movie) an error occurs because the Stage cannot see the handler. If the MIAW contains a movie script that tells the Stage to use this handler, however, the Stage can execute it. Thus, in this example, if the MIAW has the following startmovie handler

```
on startmovie
  tell the stage to Fred
end
```

the Stage executes the called handler and beeps.

For this method of calling handlers, both the handler and the tell command that refers to the handler must be in a movie script in the MIAW. This is, so far as the author is aware, an undocumented feature of Director up to version 5. As such, it may not remain in future upgrades.

Information can be passed from the Stage to the MIAW via the return and result commands. If the MIAW needs to find the number of lines in a particular text field in the Stage movie, this value can be passed back to the MIAW by the script in listing 11.1:

Listing 11.1—MIAW Lingo Telling the Stage to Execute a Handler in the MIAW

```
on startmovie
  tell the stage to CountLines
  put the result into LINES
end
on CountLines
  return the number of lines of field "text"
end
```

The `startmovie` handler tells the Stage to execute the `CountLines` handler. The Stage counts the number of lines of its cast member called `"text"` and returns this number. The `startmovie` handler in the MIAW puts this number into the `LINES` variable. The value is thus passed from the Stage to the MIAW.

Passing values from the MIAW to the Stage is a more difficult task. It's typically thought that to pass values from a MIAW to the Stage one must either use global variables or put the values into a field cast member that is in a cast shared by the stage and the MIAW. This is not entirely true, however. To pass values, one must use some type of "global" value container. An alternative to global variables, however, can be found in the `return` command.

The `return` command places a value into a pointer in memory and then exits the handler in which the `return` is encountered. Typically, the next line in a script that called this handler has a `result` command. This need not be the case, however. The next line in the script can call an entirely new handler, and this second handler can get the value stored by the `return` command.

An examination of the `Digital Video Property Checker` Xtra follows later in the section "Examining Multimedia Development Tools." The examination of this Xtra shows how the use of the `return` command enables us to pass values between the MIAW and the Stage without the use of global variables.

The methods just discussed are specifically designed for creating MIAWs as development tools. For more ideas on how to use MIAWs, look at Chapter 15, "Movies in a Window."

Building a Development Tool

After determining the need for a development tool, you find that the best method for using that tool is usually as an Xtra in the Director authoring environment. Using a few simple techniques ensures that the Xtra you create works to your best advantage.

To demonstrate these techniques, we'll create a small MIAW Xtra. Although this Xtra won't be particularly useful, it can serve as a template for creating your own Xtra with Director.

Remember that MIAWs as Xtras are most effective if they can communicate with the Stage without the use of global variables and without introducing new handlers to the cast of the Stage or through a shared cast. The Xtra we'll make should follow these rules of effectiveness.

The Xtra we'll create will display a list of names of the cast members of the Stage cast.

The first thing to do is create a new movie in Director. This will be our Xtra. We'll call it CASTNAME.DIR. Set the stage size of this movie to a fairly small size (about 200×200). This allows us to see the movie displayed underneath this Xtra when we finally use it.

Create a field cast member called "names". Place it anywhere on the Stage in the first frame of the movie (it does not matter what channel you place it in). Change the display type of the field cast member to a scrolling field (you do this by opening the cast member information window for the field cast member). This is the field that displays the names of the cast members. By having it as a scrolling field, we don't have to worry about there being too many names to see in the field.

When this Xtra runs we want it to continue to run in a loop. In the first frame of the movie add the following Lingo score script:

```
on exitframe
  go to the frame
end
```

Now we'll work on the Lingo script for the Xtra. Create a movie script cast member with the handlers in listing 11.2.

Listing 11.2—The Initial Movie Script for a MIAW Xtra to Name Cast Members

```
on startmovie
   --Initialize anything needing it in the Xtra
   put "" into field "NAMES"
   set MIAWTEMPLIST = []
   --Tell the stage to execute handlers in the Xtra's movie scripts
```

```
  tell the stage to NAMEALL
    --Values get passed from stage to MIAW via the return command
    put the result into MIAWTEMPLIST
    -- Now parse out the result into a display
  repeat with a = 1 to count(MIAWTEMPLIST)
    put getAt(MIAWTEMPLIST, a) into line a of field "NAMES"
  end repeat
end

-- The PASS_TO_STAGE, stopmovie, and closewindow handlers should appear
-- in every Xtra you develop.

on PASS_TO_STAGE thingtobepassed
  return thingtobepassed
end

on closeWindow
  stopmovie
end

on stopmovie
  -- do any housecleaning here (although if the Xtra is created
  -- correctly, you won't need to do anything other the next line).
  forget window "NAMECAST.DIR"
end


on NAMEALL
  -- Initialize any temporary lists or variables you might use for¬
storage
  set TEMPLIST = []
  repeat with a = 1 to the number of members
    if the name of member a <> "" then
      add TEMPLIST, the name of member a
    end if
  end repeat
  -- Pass this information back to the MIAW via the return command
  return TEMPLIST
end
```

These are the basic handlers that appear in every MIAW Xtra you develop. The startmovie handler initializes, and variables for the Xtra typically can gather any needed initial information from the Stage. This is done by telling the Stage to execute a handler in one of the Xtra's movie scripts. That handler then return a value that the Xtra uses.

In this example, the startmovie handler initializes a field cast member and a list variable. It then tells the Stage to execute the NAMEALL handler. This handler gathers the names of the cast members of the Stage (because the Stage is executing the handler). The NAMEALL handler uses the return command to pass this information to the MIAW.

Any passing of information about the Stage to the MIAW is done in this manner.

While we are building this Xtra, it is the Stage movie. If we run the movie, the "NAMES" field cast member lists the cast members in the NAMECAST.DIR movie.

Listing 11.2 contains three handlers that all your MIAW Xtras should have. They are the PASS_TO_STAGE, closewindow, and the stopmovie handlers.

The closewindow and stopmovie handlers clear all pointers to the MIAW Xtra when it is opened as a MIAW. Then you use the NAMECAST.DIR movie as an Xtra and when you are finished, click on the close box for the NAMECAST.DIR window. When this is done, the closewindow handler executes the stopmovie handler. This handler does any housecleaning that should be done for this Xtra. If you have created any global values you should clear them here. However, if you've created your Xtra correctly, you usually won't need to do this. The most important thing the stopmovie handler does is tell the Stage to forget all pointers to the NAMECAST.DIR window. This means that if the Xtra is called again, it starts as a fresh MIAW and executes its startmovie handler. If the forget window command is not used, the MIAW only executes its startmovie handler the first time it's opened during a Director authoring session.

We have an Xtra that can get information from the Stage. This is useful for getting a report on the status of the Stage movie. However, it cannot be used to change the Stage movie. For this to occur, we must have some way for the MIAW to send information back to the Stage.

Suppose we want our NAMECAST.DIR Xtra to enable us to delete a cast member of the stage movie simply by clicking on the name of the cast member in the "NAMES" field cast member. We'll first need to add a mouseDown script to the "NAMES" field cast member that will get the name we've clicked on. We'll add the following script to the "NAMES" cast member:

```
on mouseDown
   set temp = line (the mouseline) of field "NAMES"
   -- Call a movie handler for MIAW to Stage communication
   KILLCAST temp
end
```

This handler gets the name of the cast member we want to delete and takes us back to a movie handler so that we can communicate with the Stage.

The KILLCAST handler passes information about the cast name to the Stage via the PASS_TO_STAGE handler.

The PASS_TO_STAGE handler has only one function: to put any parameter it gets into a memory pointer with the return command. The Xtra stores a value via the PASS_TO_STAGE handler. The stage is then told to execute the STAGEKILL handler. When the stage executes the STAGEKILL handler, it uses the result command to put the cast member name that was stored in memory into a temporary variable (temp). It then uses this information to erase that cast member. In this way, values are sent from the MIAW to the stage without the use of global variables, shared cast members, or the clipboard.

The final listing of the CASTNAME.DIR movie script is shown in listing 11.3.

Listing 11.3—The Final Movie Script for a MIAW Xtra to Name Cast Members

```
on startmovie
   --Initialize anything needing it in the Xtra
   put "" into field "NAMES"
   set MIAWTEMPLIST = []
   --Tell the stage to execute handlers in the Xtra's movie scripts
  tell the stage to NAMEALL
   --Values get passed from stage to MIAW via the return command
   put the result into MIAWTEMPLIST
```

```
      -- Now parse out the result into a display
    repeat with a = 1 to count(MIAWTEMPLIST)
      put getAt(MIAWTEMPLIST, a) into line a of field "NAMES"
    end repeat
end

-- The PASS_TO_STAGE, stopmovie, and closewindow handlers should appear
-- in every Xtra you develop.

on PASS_TO_STAGE thingtobepassed
  return thingtobepassed
end

on closeWindow
  stopmovie
end

on stopmovie
  -- do any housecleaning here (although if the Xtra is created
  -- correctly, you won't need to do anything other the next line).
  forget window "NAMECAST.DIR"
end


on NAMEALL
  -- Initialize any temporary lists or variables you might use for
storage
  set TEMPLIST = []
  repeat with a = 1 to the number of members
    if the name of member a <> "" then
      add TEMPLIST, the name of member a
    end if
  end repeat
  -- Pass this information back to the MIAW via the return command
  return TEMPLIST
end


on KILLCAST casttokill
  -- we store the cast member name in the return holder
```

```
    PASS_TO_STAGE casttokill
    -- we tell the stage to execute the delete function
    tell the stage to STAGE_KILL
    -- With the cast member deleted, we update the list
    put "" into field "NAMES"
    tell the stage to NAMEALL
    put the result into MIAWTEMPLIST
    -- Now parse out the result into a display
    repeat with a = 1 to count(MIAWTEMPLIST)
      put getAt(MIAWTEMPLIST, a) into line a of field "NAMES"
    end repeat
  end

  on STAGE_KILL
    -- pass information from the MIAW to the stage via the results command
    put the result into temp
    erase member temp
  end
```

Let's briefly recap the techniques for building an effective Xtra that does not introduce new global values or rely on shared casts.

* Place all handlers the Stage will use into a movie script.

* Use the `tell` command to tell the Stage to execute these scripts. This can only be done in a movie script.

* Handlers that the Stage executes cannot refer to cast members in the Xtra. Handlers that the Xtra executes cannot refer to cast members in the Stage (although it can refer to global values created by the Stage).

* To get information from the Stage to the Xtra, store the values in a variable or list and have the handler the Stage is executing return this variable or list.

* To get information from the Xtra prepared so that the Stage can use it, use the `PASS_TO_STAGE` handler to store the information into memory. Then have the handler that the Stage is executing get that information with the `result` command.

By following these techniques, you can use the movie scripts of the CASTNAME.DIR movie as a template for creating new Xtras.

Examining Multimedia Development Tools

The rest of this chapter is devoted to examining examples of development tools for the programming and finishing phases of a multimedia production. These are meant not only to be used by the reader, but also to provide basic tools that the reader can customize for particular production environments.

Warning

The handlers and movies examined in the rest of this chapter make major modifications to cast members of movies. These tools are useful, but only when used with care. When using development tools of this sort, always follow these simple rules:

🎥 Read all documentation associated with the tool.

🎥 Take time to test the tool on a sample movie.

🎥 Read the scripting of the tool to understand it.

🎥 Never use a tool on a movie that has only one copy. Always make a backup copy.

🎥 Check a movie modified by a tool to make certain it did what you thought it did.

The author of this chapter and New Riders Publishing take no responsibility for loss of multimedia materials resulting from the use or misuse of these movies.

Final Import Media Handler

This handler was written by Miles Lightwood, Director developer and frequent contributor to Direct-L, a listserv dedicated to multimedia development in the Director environment. Miles was kind enough to grant permission for the use of the FinalImportAll handler in this book. The handler is a modification of a handler originally written by John Dowdell of Macromedia.

During the programming phase of a multimedia project, the media being used is often altered. It is a time-consuming task to import this altered media into a Director movie. Instead of doing this, many developers prefer to make external links to media during the programming phase. By doing this, changes to the media are reflected in the Director movie that has to import the changed media. The downside to this approach is that, to ensure good play and media security, developers usually want to import this media into the movie during the finishing phase. It's often easy to miss a cast member during this final series of imports.

The `FinalImportAll` handler examines the cast members of a movie and, if they are externally linked, imports them into the movie. As it is written here, the handler is placed in a movie handler of the movie to be finished and called from the Director Message window. Little work would be required, however, to develop this handler into a MIAW to be used as an Xtra.

The handler imports PICT, sound, and Director movies. The palette, purge priority, and script text of the linked files are preserved. It also specifies the file name and cast member of the imported file and writes this to a report file (although this last feature is still in need of some development). Developers wanting to handle other media types need to alter the appropriate section of this handler.

Because this handler makes major modifications to a Director movie, please test this handler on sample movies until you are satisfied with its performance. On large movies with several casts, the execution of this handler may take some time. Also, because of how this handler generates reports, its decision branches duplicate operations. If you do not care about the report, you can incorporate all the checks for type of cast member into one import command.

The script of the handler in listing 11.4 was written for Director prior to the version 5 release. It has been modified here to conform to the change of the `castType` property to the `type of member` property in Director 5.

The following has only been tested with Director 4.0.3 Macintosh. Results with other versions and platforms have not been determined. Use at your own risk.

Warning

Listing 11.4—Mile Lightwood's Modified FinalImportAll Handler

```
--*
--
on FinalImportAll
  -- Put this in a Movie Script. Call it from the message window.
  -- Depending upon how many cast you will be importing, this
  -- could take quite a while to execute. Be patient. You also might
  -- want to try this first on a sample movie to see how it works. This
  -- is a utility handler that can be used as the last stage in
  -- production, to bring all linked media into the Director movie
  -- itself.
  --*  This  "if" imports PICT cast.
  repeat with i = 1 to the number of castmembers
    if the fileName of cast i <> "" then
      if the type of member of cast i = #bitmap then
        set myName = the name of cast i
        set myScript = the scriptText of cast i
        set myRegPt = the regPoint of cast i
        set myPurgePriority = the purgePriority of cast i
        set myPalette = the palette of cast i
        importFileInto cast i, the fileName of cast i
        set the name of cast i = myName
        set the scriptText of cast i = myScript
        set the regPoint of cast i = myRegPt
        set the purgePriority of cast i = myPurgePriority
        set the palette of cast i = myPalette
        put "Imported PICT cast number " & i & "," && the name of cast¬
i & "," & " successfully."


        --* This "if" imports Sound cast.

      else if the type of member of cast i = #sound then
        set myName = the name of cast i
        set myScript = the scriptText of cast i
        set myPurgePriority = the purgePriority of cast i
        importFileInto cast i, the fileName of cast i
        set the name of cast i = myName
```

```
        set the scriptText of cast i = myScript
        set the purgePriority of cast i = myPurgePriority
        put "Imported Sound cast number " & i & "," &&  the name of cast
i & "," & " successfully."

    --* This "if" imports Director movie cast.

      else if the type of member of cast i = #movie then
        set myName = the name of cast i
        set myScript = the scriptText of cast i
        set myPurgePriority = the purgePriority of cast i
        importFileInto cast i, the fileName of cast i
        set the name of cast i = myName
        set the scriptText of cast i = myScript
        set the purgePriority of cast i = myPurgePriority
        put "Imported Director movie cast number " & i & "," &&  the
name of cast i & "," & " successfully."
      end if
    end if
  end repeat

put the short date into date
  put the short time into time
  put date & "," & time into dateTime
end
```

The function of this handler is actually quite simple to follow. It is composed of three main logical branches that determine whether a cast member is empty and then whether its cast type is a PICT, sound, or Director movie. If the cast member is one of these types, its name, Lingo script, registration point (if it has one), and purge priority are stored in variables. The cast member is then imported into the exiting cast member position with the `importFileInto` command. The variables are used to set the properties of the imported cast member. A `put` command reports on the progress of the imported files.

Additional file types specific to the IBM or Mac platform can be checked by creating logical branches to check for the appropriate `type of member`. In Director 5, these logical branches can also be incorporated into a single `case` command—although this is left as an exercise for the reader.

Commenting Out Put Commands Handler

Another utility written by Miles Lightwood is the putOut handler. During production and debugging, Director developers often use the put command to direct information to the Director Message window. Tracking down these extra commands and eliminating them in the finishing phase can be time-consuming. The putOut handler takes care of these put commands.

The handler examines a range of cast members and comments out all put commands directed to the Message window. It optionally saves backup copies of the modified scripts prior to commenting them out.

Miles wrote this handler and released it as freeware to the Direct-L community in November of 1995. Because this handler was developed prior to the release of Director 5, you may be able to employ modifications to enhance this handler.

The putOut handler script has been modified to incorporate the type of member property introduced in Director 5:

Listing 11.5 — Miles Lightwood's putOut Handler

```
-- == putOut() 13Nov95 19Nov95 v 0.7 =====================
-- This handler walks a range of castmembers commenting out all Message
-- window 'put' statements.  It also optionally saves backup copies of
-- scripts prior to commenting them out.
--
-- Example: putOut(1,          23,        FALSE)
-- Syntax:  putOut(^startCast, ^endCast, ^makeBackups)
on putOut startCast, endCast, makeBackups
  if voidP(startCast) then set startCast = 1
  if voidP(endCast) then set endCast = the number of castmembers
  if voidP(makeBackups) then set makeBackups = TRUE
  if makeBackups then
    set alertList = ["A backup of each script will be stored in '" &¬
the pathname & ,
  "' as individual files named 'scriptText <cast number>'"]
    alert getAt(alertList,1)
    put getAt(alertList,1)
  end if
  put "Started:" && the long date && the long time
  put "Working on:"
```

```
repeat with currCast = startCast to endCast
  if the type of member of cast currCast <> #empty then
    if the scriptText of cast currCast <> EMPTY then
      set currCastName = "'" & the name of cast currCast & "'"
      put "cast" && currCast && currCastName & "..."
      set currScriptText = the scriptText of cast currCast
      if makeBackups then
        set xWriteFile = FileIO(mNew, "write", the pathName &
"scriptText" && currCast)
        if xWriteFile = -43 then
          alert "xWriteFile instantiation failed. Error code: -43"
          return
        end if
        xWriteFile(mSetFinderInfo, "TEXT", "ttxt")
        xWriteFile(mWriteString, currScriptText)
      end if
      repeat with currLine = 1 to the number of lines in¬
currScriptText
        if word 1 of line currLine of currScriptText = "put" then
          if line currLine of currScriptText contains "after" then¬
next repeat
          if line currLine of currScriptText contains "before" then¬
next repeat
          if line currLine of currScriptText contains "into" then¬
next repeat
          put "-- " before line currLine of currScriptText
        end if
      end repeat
    end if
    set the scriptText of cast currCast = currScriptText
    put "finished."
  end if
end repeat
if objectP(xWriteFile) then xWriteFile(mDispose)
put "Finished:" && the long date && the long time
end putOut
```

This handler uses the following parameters:

❀ **startCast:** This is the beginning cast member number

❀ **endCast:** This is the ending cast member number

❀ **makeBackups:** This is a flag for making backups of the script (set to either TRUE or FALSE)

The handler uses the voidP command to detect whether these parameters have been passed and whether they are valid parameters. If the parameters fail, their default is to begin at the first cast member of the current movie, end as the last cast member of the current movie, and save a backup of the modified scripts. Backup scripts are saved in the path name of the movie. An error trapping routine alerts the user if this path name for saving the files is invalid.

The handler first determines whether the cast member is empty and, if not, whether it has a Lingo script. At this point, if backups of altered scripts are to be made, a copy of the unaltered script is saved.

The putOut handler then walks through each line of the script to determine whether the line begins with a put command. If it does, the handler determines whether the put command is putting an expression *before*, *after*, or *into* a variable or field. If not, the put command must be directing the output to the message window. The beginning of the line is altered from put ... to -- put ..., thus commenting out the line.

Handler Database

An immediate example of how to use existing MIAWs as Xtra development tools is the handler database discussed in the previous chapter. Figure 11.1 shows the handler database modified from a MIAW to an Xtra. With minor modifications to enable calls to the stage, this MIAW can become a useful tool for the quick installation of generic handlers into your Stage movie.

FIGURE 11.1

The handler database modified from a MIAW to an Xtra.

Digital Video Property Checker

It is not unusual for a multimedia project to be composed of several Director movies that, in turn, have several digital video cast members. During the finishing phase, it is sometimes difficult to ensure that all properties of the digital video cast members are correctly set. Checking all QuickTime movie cast members to ensure that the DirectToStage property is set, for example, requires highlighting each cast member and checking its properties with the Cast information button. The Digital Video Property Checker (DVPC) is an Xtra that automates this task.

The DVPC Xtra enables the developer to select a multiple number of movies to be checked. The developer can then step through each movie and be presented with a list of digital video cast members in that movie. Selecting each cast member presents the developer with a control panel of properties for that cast member. These properties can be changed and saved.

Version 1 of the DVPC also has a DirectToStage option. When this option is selected, the DVPC Xtra steps through each of the selected movies and checks the DirectToStage property of each digital video cast member. If this property is not set, the DVPC sets it and saves the movie. Future versions of this Xtra will enable additional properties to be automatically checked and set.

This Xtra does not create any new global variables nor does it depend on shared casts or the introduction of handlers into the Stage movie. The main movie scripts for the DVPC Xtra are as follows in listing 11.6.

Listing 11.6 — The Main Movie Script for the Digital Video Property Checker

```
-- Read filenames into a field
on filename destfield
    if the machinetype <> 256 then
        -- To read in Director 4.0 files for Macs
        -- change the type below to MV93
        put FileIO(mNew, "?read", "MV95") into gReadObject
    else
        put FileIO(mNew,"?read", "dir") into gReadObject
    end if
```

```
put gReadObject (mFilename) after field destfield
gReadObject(mDispose)
-- make sure the font is small enough
set the textsize of field "movies" = 9
-- add a RETURN for a new line
put RETURN after field destfield
end
```

The filename handler is used to call up a file dialog box through which the user can select Director movies to check. The file filter is set to recognize only Director 5 movies. As these movies are selected, their names are put into a text field named by the destfield variable. This text field displays the movies the Xtra will check. When the Xtra checks the movies, the first thing it must do is construct a list of digital video cast members in the Stage movie. This is done with the LIST_QT and FIND_QTs handlers as shown in listing 11.7.

Listing 11.7—Handlers for Loading a Movie and Listing Its Digital Videos

```
on FIND_QTs movienumber
  -- first load the movie we're going to check
  set a = line movienumber of field "movies"
  tell the stage to go to movie a

  -- Now we compile a list of digital video cast members
  -- We do this by having the stage movie execute the LIST_QT handler
  -- and then put the list of digital video cast members into a list
  -- called xjqt.  This list is then returned to the MIAW.

  set templist = []
  tell the stage to LIST_QT
  put the result into templist
  put '" into field "QTs"
  repeat with a = 1 to count(templist)
    put getAt(templist, a) into line a of field "QTs"
  end repeat

end
--
-- This handler lists digital video cast members
```

```
on LIST_QT
  set xjqt = []
  set xjg = the number of castMembers
  repeat with a = 1 to xjg
    -- Is the cast member digital video?
    if the type of member a = #digitalVideo then
      append xjqt, the name of cast a
    end if
  end repeat
  return xjqt
end
```

These two handlers are used to load a selected Director movie and list its digital video cast members. The return command is used to eliminate the need for global variables.

The FIND_QTs handler loads the movie being checked on to the stage. It then initializes a temporary list and tells the Stage to execute the LIST_QT handler. The LIST_QT handler initializes a temporary list and walks through all cast members to determine whether they are digital video. If they are digital video, the name of the cast is added to the temporary list. When the handler completes its task, it returns the temporary list.

The FIND_QT handler takes the list returned by the LIST_QTs handler and places it in its own temporary list. This is then placed in a text field that displays the digital video cast members of the Stage movie. In this way, values are passed from the stage to the MIAW without the use of global variables. This same method of passing values from the Stage movie to the MIAW is used to get the properties of a particular digital video cast member in the GET_PROP and CHECK_PROPERTIES handlers (see listing 11.8).

Listing 11.8—The Handler the Xtra Uses to Display Properties of Digital Video Cast Members

```
on GET_PROP
  set selqt = the text of member "selected QT"
  PASS_TO_STAGE selqt
  tell the stage to CHECK_PROPERTIES
  put the result into qtprop
```

```
  if getAt(qtprop, 1) = 1 then
    set the hilite of member "looped" = TRUE
  else
    set the hilite of member "looped" = FALSE
  end if
  if getAt(qtprop, 2) = 1 then
    set the hilite of member "pause" = TRUE
  else
    set the hilite of member "pause" = FALSE
  end if
  if getAt(qtprop, 3) = 1 then
    set the hilite of member "video" = TRUE
  else
    set the hilite of member "video" = FALSE
  end if
  if getAt(qtprop, 4) = 1 then
    set the hilite of member "sound" = TRUE
  else
    set the hilite of member "sound" = FALSE
  end if
  if getAt(qtprop, 5) = 1 then
    set the hilite of member "preload" = TRUE
  else
    set the hilite of member "preload" = FALSE
  end if
  if getAt(qtprop, 6) = 1 then
    set the hilite of member "controller" = TRUE
  else
    set the hilite of member "controller" = FALSE
  end if
  if getAt(qtprop, 7) = 1 then
    set the hilite of member "direct" = TRUE
  else
    set the hilite of member "direct" = FALSE
  end if
  updatestage
  return qtprop
end
```

The CHECK_PROPERTIES handler is executed by the Stage movie. It compiles a list of properties of a particular digital video cast member (see listing 11.9).

Listing 11.9—The Handler the Stage Uses to Get and Return Properties of Digital Video Cast Members to the Xtra

```
-- This handler checks the properties of
-- a digital video cast.
on CHECK_PROPERTIES
  put the result into digvid
  set qtprop = [0,0,0,0,0,0,0]
  if the loop of member digvid then
    setAt qtprop, 1, 1
  end if
  if the pausedAtStart of member digvid then
    setAt qtprop, 2, 1
  end if
  if the video of member digvid then
    setAt qtprop, 3, 1
  end if
  if the sound of member digvid then
    setAt qtprop, 4, 1
  end if
  if the preLoad of member digvid then
    setAt qtprop, 5, 1
  end if
  if the controller of member digvid then
    setAt qtprop, 6, 1
  end if
  if the directToStage of member digvid then
    setAt qtprop, 7, 1
  end if
  return qtprop
end
```

The CHECK_PROPERTIES handler creates a temporary list containing zeroes for each possible digital video property to be checked. It then checks these properties and returns this list to the GET_PROP handler. The GET_PROP handler highlights the appropriate radio buttons in the cast member property panel of the Xtra.

The GET_PROP handler indicates the properties a selected digital video cast member has.

For the Stage to execute the CHECK_PROPERTIES handler, it must know which digital video cast member to check. This value must be passed from the MIAW to the Stage (a more difficult task without the use of global variables).

The cast member name to be checked is passed from the MIAW to the Stage by using the return command method mentioned earlier in this chapter. The GET_PROP passes the name of the cast to be checked to the PASS_TO_STAGE handler.

```
on PASS_TO_STAGE value
   return value
end
```

The CHANGEPROP handler is used to change the properties of a digital video cast member. It checks the highlight of the property radio buttons in the DVPC Xtra and creates a property list. This list is placed into a memory pointer with the PASS_TO_STAGE handler. Because the MIAW must pass the name of the cast member as well as its properties to the Stage, an additional element (the cast name) is added to the end of the property list. The Stage is then told to execute the SET_PROPERTIES handler (see listing 11.10).

Listing 11.10 — The Handler the Xtra Uses to Tell the Stage to Change Digital Video Cast Member Properties

```
on CHANGEPROP
   set qtprop = [0,0,0,0,0,0,0]
   if the hilite of member "looped" then
      setAt qtprop, 1, 1
   end if
   if the hilite of member "pause" then
      setAt qtprop, 2, 1
   end if
```

```
   if the hilite of member "video" then
     setAt qtprop, 3, 1
   end if
   if the hilite of member "sound" then
     setAt qtprop, 4, 1
   end if
   if the hilite of member "Preload" then
     setAt qtprop, 5, 1
   end if
   if the hilite of member "controller" then
     setAt qtprop, 6, 1
   end if
   if the hilite of member "direct" then
     setAt qtprop, 7, 1
   end if
   setAt qtprop, 8, (the text of member "selected QT")
   PASS_TO_STAGE qtprop
   tell the stage to SET_PROPERTIES
 end
```

Listing 11.11 shows the handler the Stage uses to change its digital video cast members. The SET_PROPERTIES handler first pulls the digital video property cast list from the memory pointer by using the result command. It takes the last element of the list to be the cast member name. The remaining elements of the list are then used to set the properties of the cast member. When finished, the Stage saves the movie.

Listing 11.11—The Handler the Stage Uses to Change Its Digital Video Cast Members

```
on SET_PROPERTIES
  put the result into qtprop
  set selqt = getAt(qtprop,8)
  set the loop of member selqt = getAt(qtprop,1)
  set the pausedAtStart of member selqt = getAt(qtprop,2)
  set the video of member selqt = getAt(qtprop,3)
  set the sound of member selqt = getAt(qtprop,4)
  set the preLoad of member selqt = getAt(qtprop,5)
  set the controller of member selqt = getAt(qtprop,6)
  set the directToStage of member selqt = getAt(qtprop,7)

  saveMovie
end
```

In addition to viewing individual digital video cast members with their properties, the DVPC Xtra can also automate changes in the properties of digital video cast members in several movies. One example of this is the DIRECTTS_ALL handler shown in listing 11.12.

Listing 11.12 — A Handler to Automate Setting the Direct to Stage Property in Digital Video Cast Members in Several Movies

```
-- This handler changes all QTs to direct to stage
on DIRECTTS_ALL
  put the number of lines in field "movies" into word 5 of field¬
"status"
  repeat with b = 1 to (the number of lines in field "movies")
    put b into word 3 of field "status"
    -- find out what QTs are in the movie
    FIND_QTs value(word 3 of field "status")
    repeat with a = 1 to (the number of lines in field "QTs")
      -- get properties of the QT
      put line a of field "QTs" into field "selected QT"
      GET_PROP
      put the result into qtprop
      -- change the directToStage property to TRUE
      setAt qtprop,7,1
      setAt qtprop, 8, (line a of field "QTs")
      PASS_TO_STAGE qtprop
      tell the stage to SET_PROPERTIES
    end repeat
  end repeat
end
```

The DIRECTTS_ALL handler uses all the handlers previously mentioned in the DVPC Xtra. It automates the process and walks through the list of movies that have been selected. For each movie, it compiles a list of digital video cast members with the FIND_QTs handler. For each digital video member in this list the handler finds the cast member's properties with the GET_PROP handler. It then sets the directToStage property to TRUE and has the Stage set this property using the PASS_TO_STAGE and SET_PROPERTIES handlers.

With minor modifications, the DIRECTTS_ALL handler could be automated to modify any property of a digital video cast member. With further modifications, the entire Xtra could automate the modification properties for any type of cast member.

Cast Use Checker

The Slacker Xtra is designed to help eliminate extraneous cast members in a finished product. During the programming phase of a project, it is not uncommon to create cast members that are not used in the final product. Score scripts and graphic cast members might be replaced or duplicated. The Slacker Xtra walks through the Score of the Stage movie and determines which cast members are referenced by the Score. It then generates a report of which cast members are not referenced in the Score and displays this report in a scrolling screen.

It is important to realize that cast members might still be essential to a movie even if they are not directly referenced in the movie score. Movie scripts, for example, are not directly referenced in a Score. Image cast members not referenced in the Score might be used by puppetsprites. Thus, it would be unwise to automatically delete all cast members in the Slacker report. The report generated by this Xtra is designed to narrow the search for useless cast members.

At the heart of the Slacker Xtra are two handlers—the CheckScore and Look_for_Slackers handlers. These handlers use the return command discussed earlier in this chapter to provide communication between the Stage and MIAW without additional global variables. The script for the two handlers is as follows:

```
on CHECKSCORE
  tell the stage to LOOK_FOR_SLACKERS
  put the result into field "report"
end
```

The CHECKSCORE handler tells the Stage to execute the LOOK_FOR_SLACKERS handler that can be seen in listing 11.13. It puts the result of that handler into the "report" text field for the user to examine.

Listing 11.13—The LOOK FOR SLACKERS Handler for Finding Unused Cast Members

```
on LOOK_FOR_SLACKERS
  set CASTS = []
  set REPORT = ""
  set FRAMES = the lastframe
  set CASTMEMS = the number of castMembers

  repeat with a = 1 to CASTMEMS
    -- make a list of all cast numbers
    if the castType of cast a <> #empty then

      add CASTS, a
    end if
  end repeat

  -- now we go through each frame and see
  -- if the cast is used.  If it is then
  -- we kick it out. Only unused cast members
  -- will be left.
  repeat with a = 1 to FRAMES
    -- Step through the frames
    go to frame a

    -- check the transition track
    if the frametransition <> 0 then
      repeat with b = 1 to count(CASTS)
        if the frametransition = getAt(CASTS,b) then
          deleteAt CASTS, b
          exit repeat
        end if
      end repeat
    end if

    -- check the sound track
    if the frameSound1 <> 0 then
      repeat with b = 1 to count(CASTS)
        if the frameSound1 = getAt(CASTS, b) then
          deleteAt CASTS, b
          exit repeat
```

```
          end if
        end repeat
      end if
      if the frameSound2 <> 0 then
        repeat with b = 1 to count(CASTS)
          if the frameSound2 = getAt(CASTS, b) then
            deleteAt CASTS, b
            exit repeat
          end if
        end repeat
      end if

      -- check the frame script
      if the frameScript <> 0 then
        repeat with b = 1 to count(CASTS)
          if the frameScript = getAt(CASTS, b) then
            deleteAt CASTS, b
            exit repeat
          end if
        end repeat
      end if
      -- go through the channels
      repeat with c = 1 to 48
        -- check for every item on the list
        -- until we get a hit
        repeat with b = 1 to count(CASTS)
          if the castnum of sprite c = getAt(CASTS, b) then
            deleteAt CASTS, b
            exit repeat
          end if
        end repeat
      end repeat
    end repeat
  end repeat

  repeat with a = 1 to count(CASTS)
    put "member"&& getAt(CASTS, a)&":"&&the name of member¬
getAt(CASTS,a)&&"("&the type of member getAt(CASTS,a)&")"&RETURN after¬
report
  end repeat
  return report
end
```

The LOOK_FOR_SLACKERS handler compiles a list of all cast members (by cast number) in the Stage movie. It then tells the Stage to go to the first frame of the movie. The handler checks the transition, sound, frame script, and cast channels to see whether they are occupied. It they are, the name of the number of the cast member that occupies them is eliminated from the list of cast members. The handler steps through each frame of the movie in this manner until the last frame used is reached. At this point the original cast member list only contains cast members that did not appear in the Score. The handler goes though this list and generates a report of the remaining unused cast members by their number, name, and member type. This report is returned to the CHECKSCORE handler that then displays this report in a text field.

Conclusion

Time spent in creating development tools for multimedia is a necessary investment. Development tools enable increased productivity during the programming and finishing phases of a project. Development tools for clients enable the creation of dynamic multimedia projects that a more sophisticated market will demand in the coming years.

As Macromedia incorporates common scripting standards across its suite of tools, techniques learned here on creating development tools for Director may be useful in creating scripts for new features in Macromedia's other tools. In the next few years, Director developers may be able to create Director Xtras that will create macros for FreeHand, for example.

The Xtra option in Director 5 enables the typical developer to create his own suite of development tools. By using the techniques developed in this chapter, Xtras can be developed that do not introduce new global variables into the programming environment. The examples of development tools in this chapter can be the beginning of your development tool suite as well as give you ideas of some tools of your own to design.

chapter 12

Kirk Keller

BUILDING SHOCKWAVE APPLICATIONS

With the Shockwave suite of plug-ins, developers in Authorware, Director, SoundEdit, and FreeHand have an entirely new market for multimedia development. Just in case you are one of the few Director developers who has not already heard about Shockwave, Shockwave for Director enables movies created in Director to be played in HTML documents on the World Wide Web. To view these Shockwave documents, users must have the Shockwave plug-in and web browsers that support the Shockwave plug-in. The Shockwave plug-in is free.

The Shockwave movies have most of the interactivity of regular Director movies (there are some limitations to the media a Shockwave movie can play and how it can use functions such as fileio). They are created by using the Afterburner Xtra in Director 5. The Afterburner Xtra is also free.

With the release of Shockwave for Audio, sound files of incredible quality can be played across the Internet. Shockwave movies can now provide a rich visual, audio, and interactive resource for the web.

This chapter presumes a general familiarity with Shockwave and Director. If you are not familiar with either, you should obtain general information from the Macromedia web site (www.macromedia.com) or refer to *Shockwave for Director User's Guide* by Sasha Magee and Noel Rabinowitz from New Riders Publishing (ISBN 1-56205-595-X).

This chapter gives concrete examples of how to incorporate the new features of external casts and files for Shockwave movies and the newly released Shockwave Audio file format into HTML documents. It also touches on new developments in the Microsoft Internet Explorer OBJECT tag.

In keeping with the theme of the previous chapters, this chapter also discusses how generic Shockwave movies can be created that can save valuable time in multimedia and web development.

This chapter discusses the following:

- Web browser issues
- The basics of Shockwave
- External files in Shockwave movies
- Shockwave Audio
- Useful Shockwave examples

Creating Shockwave for Director Movies

One of the most important points to remember about Shockwave movies is that not all web browsers support the Shockwave plug-in. When working with clients, Shockwave developers should determine who will be accessing Shockwave movies and which web browsers will most likely be used.

Netscape and Microsoft Browsers

At this time, Netscape's Navigator is the major web browser in use with Microsoft's Internet Explorer coming in second. Both these web browsers support the Shockwave suite of plug-ins. Macromedia's web site documentation suggests that, for best results, use browsers compatible with Netscape 3 or later, or Internet Explorer 3.

At the time of this writing, web browsers that in some way support the Shockwave plug-in architecture are

- Netscape Navigator 2.x

- Netscape Navigator 3.x

- Attachmate's Emissary

- Netmanage's WebSurfer

- Microsoft's Internet Explorer 2.x (Macintosh and Windows 3.1)

- Microsoft's Internet Explorer 3.x (Windows 95 and Windows NT)

Shockwave for Director works as a plug-in for Netscape Navigator 2 and 3 and an ActiveX Control for Internet Explorer 3. With the Shockwave for Director plug-in in a Netscape browser, Shockwave movies are called from an HTML document through the use of an EMBED tag. With the Shockwave for Director ActiveX Control, Shockwave movies are called from an HTML document through the use of either an EMBED or OBJECT tag.

The advantage of using an EMBED tag is that both Netscape- and Microsoft-compliant browsers support it. The disadvantage is that users must download the Shockwave for Director plug-in to play the movies. Netscape's browsers make this somewhat easy by notifying the user that a plug-in is required and then jumping them to a plug-in support page.

The advantage of using the OBJECT tag is that this tag includes URL information needed to download the Shockwave for Director plug-in. When a user who does not have the Shockwave for Director plug-in hits a Shockwave movie, the Microsoft-compliant browser asks the user if he wants to download the plug-in. If so, then the browser downloads and installs the plug-in. The idea behind the OBJECT tag is that it is supposed to make getting and installing a plug-in easier. Once a user has the plug-in installed, however, there seems little advantage to the OBJECT tag over the EMBED tag.

The disadvantage to the OBJECT tag is that it is not supported by all Netscape- and Microsoft-compliant browsers. Also, writing the HTML code that will load a Shockwave movie and pass parameters is somewhat easier to do with the EMBED tag than the OBJECT tag. This chapter presumes that Shockwave is being developed for use with Netscape Navigator 2 or higher compliant browsers. Microsoft's Internet Explorer will be discussed where differences in the browser necessitate a brief discussion.

Covering the Basics

The next few pages examine the basic steps in creating Shockwave movies and incorporating them into HTML documents. They also look at some basic techniques to ensure that users who do not have Shockwave or Shockwave-compatible browsers will not be adversely affected by the introduction of Shockwave movies to your web site.

Calling a Shockwave Movie via the EMBED Tag

The basic HTML code for calling a Shockwave movie is the following:

```
<EMBED SRC="path/filename.ext" WIDTH=width HEIGHT=height>
```

Additional parameters can be used in the EMBED tag. These will be discussed in the section "Creating Additional Parameters" later in this chapter.

The SRC parameter refers to the location of the Shockwave movie. This can either be an absolute path name or one relative to the location of the HTML document. For browsers that do not have the Shockwave for Director plug-in, the NOEMBED tag can be used to load an alternative .GIF or .JPG image. The following two HTML tags are used to load the SWMOVIE.DCR Shockwave movie or the sorry.gif image (if the user does not have the Shockwave plug-in). Notice that both these commands use an absolute or relative path name.

```
<EMBED SRC="http://www.company.com/shockwave/swmovie.dcr">
<NOEMBED> <IMG SRC="./sorry.gif"> </NOEMBED>
```

Calling a Shockwave Movie via the OBJECT Tag

The use of the OBJECT tag is slightly more complex. The HTML code in listing 12.1 is an OBJECT tag that loads the SWMOVIE.DCR Shockwave movie.

Listing 12.1—The OBJECT Tag for Calling a Shockwave Movie

```
<OBJECT CLASSID="clsid:166B1BCA-3F9C-11CF-8075-444553540000"
CODEBASE="http://active.macromedia.com/director/cabs/¬
     sw.cab#version=5,0,1,61"
WIDTH="356" HEIGHT="128" NAME="Shockwave"
ID="swmovie1">
<PARAM NAME="SRC" VALUE="/shockwave/swmovie.dcr">
</OBJECT>
```

The OBJECT CLASSID and CODEBASE must not be altered. These parameters tell the ActiveX-compliant browser which type of plug-in is needed for the Shockwave movie and where to download this plug-in. They are the same for every Shockwave movie you want to call with the OBJECT tag.

The ID parameter can be used to uniquely identify an HTML document. This can be used with ActiveX to reference other HTML documents during a session.

The NAME parameter tells ActiveX-compliant browsers the type of ActiveX FORM being submitted. For Shockwave movies, the name should be Shockwave.

The WIDTH, HEIGHT, and SRC parameters function the same as in the EMBED tag.

Your HTML page can have both the OBJECT tag for Microsoft browsers and the EMBED tag for Netscape-compliant browsers if the EMBED tag is placed within the NOOBJECT tag.

Listing 12.2—The OBJECT and EMBED Tags Together for Calling a Shockwave Movie

```
<OBJECT CLASSID="clsid:166B1BCA-3F9C-11CF-8075-444553540000"
CODEBASE="http://active.macromedia.com/director/cabs¬
     sw.cab#version=5,0,1,61"
WIDTH="356" HEIGHT="128" NAME="Shockwave"
ID="swmovie1">
<PARAM NAME="SRC" VALUE="shockwave/swmovie.dcr"></OBJECT>
<NOOBJECT> <embed src=/shockwave/swmovie.dcr width=320 height=240>
</NOOBJECT>
```

Browsers that support the OBJECT tag execute this code as normal. Browsers that cannot read the OBJECT tag read the EMBED tag enclosed in the NOOBJECT tag.

Because the OBJECT and NOOBJECT tag are relatively new, the way EMBED and OBJECT tags interact with each other may change in new releases of browsers that are OBJECT or EMBED tag compliant. For the best results, you should experiment with these tags using browsers that you think will be accessing your site.

Hiding Broken Icons

If users have a browser that supports the Shockwave plug-in architecture, the EMBED tag solves most problems a user encounters when accessing a Shockwave site. If they have the Shockwave plug-in, they will see the movie. If they don't, the NOEMBED tag displays an alternate graphic to them.

Many browsers don't support the EMBED command, however. Netscape Navigator 1.1, for example, recognizes the EMBED tag as referring to an OLE link. When it comes across a Shockwave EMBED tag, it searches for the OLE link and, failing to find it, displays a broken icon.

One solution to this problem is to place the EMBED tag inside a JavaScript routine that is, itself, inside a comment tag. If a browser that does not support JavaScript (for example, versions of Netscape prior to 2) accesses this comment tag, it does nothing. If a browser that supports JavaScript (for example, Netscape 2 and later) accesses this comment tag, it also executes the JavaScript routine inside the comment and places the EMBED tag in the HTML document. It then accesses the Shockwave movie referred to in the EMBED tag (or the alternate image in the NOEMBED tag).

Note that this solution works only on the assumption that a browser that does not support JavaScript will not support the Shockwave plug-in, and that any browser that does support JavaScript will also support EMBED tags and the Shockwave plug-in.

Confused? Just remember that the HTML code in listing 12.3 stops those who are not using Netscape Navigator from seeing the EMBED tag that launches the Shockwave movie.

Listing 12.3—Using JavaScript to Hide the EMBED Tag from Browsers that Cannot Use It

```
<SCRIPT LANGUAGE="JavaScript">
<!-- Hide this script from non-Navigator 2.0 browsers. document.write(¬
    '<EMBED WIDTH=240 HEIGHT=320 SRC="swmovie.dcr">');
<!-- Done hiding from non-Navigator 2.0 browsers. -->
</SCRIPT>
<NOEMBED>
<IMG WIDTH=60 HEIGHT=60 SRC="sorry.jpg">
</NOEMBED>
```

The drawback to this approach is that people using Microsoft's Internet Explorer, Attachmate's Emissary, or Netmanage's WebSurfer will not be able to see your Shockwave movie either. A second way exists to avoid broken links and is more forgiving of Shockwave-ready browsers that don't belong to Netscape.

This method works on the assumption that a broken icon cannot appear to the user if the width and height of the SRC link are too small to display it. The Shockwave developer creates a Shockwave movie that is 1×1 pixel in size (like the Shockwave 1×1 player Macromedia has in its SWA example files). This movie immediately sends the user to another web page that contains the Shockwave movie the developer really wants the user to see.

If users do not have the Shockwave plug-in, they never get sent to the second Shockwave movie page. If their browser does not support the EMBED tag, they will never get sent to the second Shockwave page (because the EMBED tag won't work), and they have a broken icon measuring 1×1 pixel in size on-screen—rendering it essentially invisible.

Depending on your web audience and the nature of the Shockwave movie, either of these two methods can be used to eliminate broken icons resulting from lack of support for the EMBED tag.

Starting Network Communications (Asynchronous Operations)

Several Shockwave Lingo commands provide for asynchronous communication from within the Shockwave movie. These network communications differ from regular Lingo commands in that these network commands do not immediately execute. Instead, they begin network functions that take time to complete. To use network communication within a Shockwave movie, follow these three basic steps:

* Begin an asynchronous operation

* Check the state of the asynchronous operation

* Obtain the results of the asynchronous operation if completed

Appendix A, "Shockwave Lingo Commands," has the appropriate Lingo commands listed under each of these three types of operations.

A Shockwave movie can perform other tasks during an asynchronous operation. It can loop through a series of frames for an animation. At the end of each loop, it can check the status of the asynchronous operation with a netDone() command. Depending on the result of the netDone() command, it can display the result or abort the operation.

You can only have a certain number of asynchronous operations at the same time. This is not because of Shockwave, but because of how users have their browsers configured. Netscape's browser, for example, is typically set to limit the maximum number of simultaneous network connections allowed to four (see fig. 12.1).

FIGURE 12.1

Netscape's Network Preferences set for a maximum of four simultaneous connections.

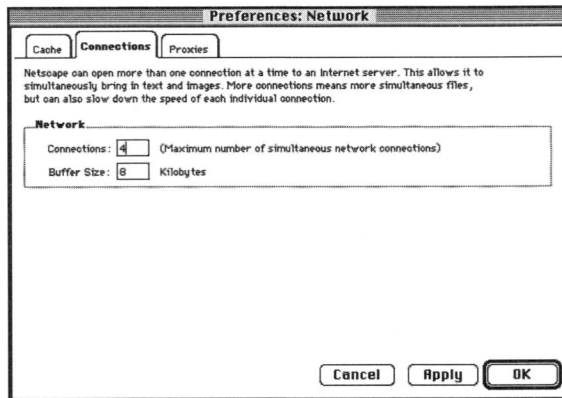

If you are developing for an intranet, you might have some control over this setting in a user's browser. If you are developing for the Internet, however, you don't have this luxury. Therefore, you should limit your simultaneous asynchronous operations to four.

Make certain that you do not execute asynchronous operations in a looping frame of a Shockwave movie. Otherwise, you immediately create the maximum number of operations the user's browser allows.

If you do use more than one asynchronous operation, be certain to use the `GetLatestNetID` function to obtain a unique identifier so that you can distinguish which operation is complete.

Using Internet Shockwave Resources

A number of excellent resources exist on the Internet for Shockwave development.

The Shockwave Frequently Asked Questions (FAQ) is compiled by Dorian Dowse. It covers the basic mechanics of creating Shockwave movies and integrating them into HTML documents. The Shockwave FAQ is located at

```
http://www.shocker.com/shocker/faq.html
```

The Shockwave (or ShockeR) listserv is home to Shockwave developers at all levels of skill. To subscribe to the Shockwave listserv, send e-mail with the following line in the body of the message:

```
SUBSCRIBE shockwave your name
```

The ShockeR listserv can be searched by keyword via a web form. Although the search is not as robust as the one available for the Direct-L listserv, it is useful. The search form for the ShockeR listserv is located at

```
http://www.shocker.com/shocker/digests/index.html.
```

The ShockeR listserv has a companion web site. This web site contains links to FAQs, lists of Shockwave sites, a search engine for the ShockeR listserv, and several other resources of interest to the Shockwave developer. The ShockeR web site is located at

```
http://www.shocker.com/shocker/digests/index.html.
```

Of course, the Director Internet resources listed in Chapter 9, "Building Generic Handlers in Director," are useful Shockwave resources as well.

Using External Files and Xtras

Shockwave for Director 5 supports external files as well as Xtras that are located on the client's machine.

These cast libraries and Xtras must be downloaded by the user to be used. These items must be placed in the Director Plug-in support directory of the user's web browser. If the user prefers, however, aliases (Macintosh) or short-cuts (Windows) to these files can be placed in the plug-in directory instead. By using this last method, a user could have a reference to cast libraries on a CD-ROM that is only in the browser machine when a particular Shockwave site is accessed.

In external cast libraries, cast members can be linked externally as well. This enables for the first time digital videos such as QuickTime movies to be played within Shockwave movies. To use linked media in Shockwave for Director 5, import the media as a linked cast member. Then save and create the Shockwave movie as usual.

Xtras are a new type of application extension in Director 5 created using Macromedia Open Architecture (MOA). Shockwave for Director 5 supports all three types of Xtras that can be used during play of a Shockwave movie:

* **Castmember Xtras:** Xtras that enable special insertion of media into the cast (3D models, for example)

* **Lingo Xtras:** Xtras that enable the addition of custom functionality to Director

* **Transition Xtras:** Xtras that enable custom transitions

Using External Casts

External casts can also be accessed by Shockwave movies. This enables users to download large media files to the plug-in support folder and then view Shockwave movies that refer to this media. The Shockwave movies use little bandwidth because their media has already been downloaded to the plug-in support folder.

To use external casts in a Shockwave movie do the following:

1. Open the movie in Director. Under the File menu, choose New and Cast. This opens a dialog box for a new cast window.

2. Choose the External option to create an external cast window. Assuming that no Lingo script refers to cast members by number, move some or all of your existing cast members from the internal cast window to this external cast window.

3. Save your movie and then use the Afterburner Xtra to create your Shockwave movie (external casts will not work with .DIR movies used as Shockwave movies).

Your Shockwave movie is now ready to be used. Users have to download the external cast before they use this Shockwave movie. After they download the cast, they must place it in the Shockwave plug-in support folder. Alternatively, they can make an alias or shortcut to the cast library and place this alias or shortcut in the Shockwave for Director Plug-in support folder.

On Windows 3.1 computers, the standard support directory is "NP16DSW." The default directory for Netscape Navigator is C:\NETSCAPE\PLUGINS.

On Windows 95 computers, the standard support directory is "NP32DSW." The default directory for Netscape Navigator is C:\Program Files\Netscape\ Navigator\Program\Plugins.

On 68 KB Macintosh computers, the standard support folder is "NP-Mac68K-Dir-Shockwave Folder." This folder is placed in the "Plug-Ins Folder" along with the Shockwave for Director Plug-In executable. The path is Hard Disk:Applications:Navigator 3.0:Plug-ins.

On Power Macintosh computers, this folder is placed in the "Plug-Ins Folder" along with the Shockwave for Director Plug-In executable. The path is the same as shown above for 68 KB Macintosh computers.

The external file must be located in the Shockwave standard support folder or directory because that's where Shockwave looks for external files.

When the user accesses the Shockwave movie on the web page, Shockwave for Director locates the file automatically and loads it correctly at the appropriate time. If your movies use an external file, it's a good idea to include Lingo in your movie that will display an alert message at the beginning of the movie if the user does not have the external file or if it's in the incorrect folder.

Passing Parameters to Shockwave Movies

Parameters can be passed to a Shockwave movie in two ways. These are related to how the Shockwave movie is being called from a web document. A Shockwave movie can be called from an EMBED tag or an ActiveX OBJECT tag.

The basic difference between the EMBED and OBJECT tag concern how the parameters, in addition to the SRC width and height parameters, are written. For an EMBED tag, the general code is as follows:

```
<EMBED SRC="path/filename.ext" WIDTH=width HEIGHT=height
    paramName=paramValue>
```

For OBJECT tags, the general code is as follows:

```
<OBJECT CLASSID="clsid:166B1BCA-3F9C-11CF-8075-444553540000"
CODEBASE="http://active.macromedia.com/director/cabs/
sw.cab#version=5,0,1,61"
WIDTH="356" HEIGHT="128" NAME="Shockwave"
ID="uniqueIdentifier">
<PARAM NAME="SRC" VALUE="\path\swmovie.dcr">
<PARAM NAME="parmName" VALUE="parmValue">
</OBJECT>
```

The basic difference between how the two types of tags pass parameters is that the EMBED tag passes a parameter using the form

parametername=parametervalue

whereas the OBJECT tag uses the form

<PARAM NAME= "*parametername*" VALUE = "*parametervalue*">

Several parameters can be passed in one EMBED tag. Each parameter passed in the OBJECT tag must appear in its own line enclosed by tag brackets. When the EMBED or OBJECT tag is used in the HTML document to call a Shockwave movie, three parameters are being passed to the Shockwave plug-in: the location of the movie, the width, and the height of the movie about to be played. In addition to these three basic parameters, Shockwave also has two additional special parameters that can be used: the `palette` parameter and the `bgcolor` parameter.

Using the palette Parameter

The use of either of these parameters enables a Shockwave movie to affect the browser palette. By setting the `palette` parameter to `foreground`, the Shockwave movie takes control of the browser palette. By setting the `palette` parameter to `background`, the web browser retains control of the browser palette.

When setting the foreground color, remember that this palette setting can have undesirable results if a user browsing the Shockwave site has a monitor set to eight bits or less. If your Shockwave application uses palettes with many subtle shades of brown, for example, your Netscape application and other images on-screen also turn shades of brown—and maybe not so subtle. This should be a familiar problem to most Director developers. It's a problem of working with eight bit displays.

With this mind, you might ask why anyone would want to control the palette. The reason is that by controlling the palette, eight bit pictures can be produced with a high quality due to their customized palette.

To enable a Shockwave movie to take control of the web browser's palette, use the following HTML code to call the Shockwave movie:

```
<embed src="swmovie.dcr" height=240 width=320 palette=foreground>
```

Using the bgcolor Parameter

This parameter sets the stage color of the Shockwave movie. This is useful because it enables a Shockwave movie to blend into the background color of the existing web page. By using this parameter to set the stage color instead of the stage color being set in the Shockwave movie, Shockwave developers can tailor the stage color to the color of the particular web page the Shockwave movie is on.

The `bgcolor` parameter sets the stage color in the same manner that the BGCOLOR HTML command sets a web page background color. The parameter uses hexadecimal numbers to set red, green, and blue values to produce the needed color. To set the stage color of a Shockwave movie to white, use the following HTML code to call the Shockwave movie:

```
<embed src="swmovie.dcr" width=200 height=300 bgcolor=#000000>
```

Creating Additional Parameters

In addition to the two preceding parameters, Shockwave developers can create their own parameters to pass to a Shockwave movie. To pass the title of a current web page on which the Shockwave movie is being displayed, use the following HTML code to call the Shockwave movie:

```
<embed src="Movies/movie.dcr" width=300 height=300 title="The Shockwave¬
    Page">
```

The Shockwave movie then reads this parameter through use of the external parameter commands in Lingo.

Using External Parameter Commands

The external parameter commands for Shockwave are similar to the parameter commands for Director.

externalParamCount()

This function returns the number of external parameters passed to the Shockwave movie from an HTML-embedded tag. The following startmovie handler places the number of parameters passed to the Shockwave movie to a variable named parcount:

```
on startmovie
  put externalParamCount() into parcount
end
```

externalParamName(number)

This function returns a string containing the names or arguments being passed to a Shockwave movie from a particular parameter in an HTML-embedded tag.

The externalParamName retrieves external parameters either by string or by number. If the function is given a number, it retrieves the corresponding external parameter. Remember in counting parameters that the width and height parameters are also external parameters.

If the function is given a string, it retrieves the first external parameter with a name matching that string. If no match is made, the function returns a void value. To display the web page name in the earlier example, the Shockwave movie uses the following Lingo script:

```
put externalParamName("title") into field "web title"
```

or (because the title is the third external parameter in the tag)

```
put externalParamName(3) into field "web title"
```

Creating Shockwave Audio Files

Shockwave audio boasts compression rates of up to 176:1, thus providing the delivery of quality audio at low baud rates found in 14.4 and 28.8 modem connections to the Internet. Because Shockwave Audio uses standard servers and TCP connections, streaming audio files can be placed on almost any web server without the purchase of specialized web server software. This makes it easy for the Director developer to implement streaming audio applications on existing web environments.

Internal and External Shockwave Audio Files

Shockwave Audio comes in two basic varieties: audio internal to a Shockwave movie and streamable audio (SWA) files. Internal Shockwave Audio files are embedded in a Director Shockwave movie and are compressed using the SWA Compression Xtra in Director 5. External streamable audio (SWA) files are audio files compressed with the SWA export Xtra for SoundEdit 16 (version 2). These SWA files can then be referenced by Director Shockwave movies.

Whether the Director developer uses audio internal to a Director Shockwave movie or external as a streamable file depends on the particular web application the developer has in mind. As a rule of thumb, short audio files for use with Director Shockwave movies should be compressed with the Director Compression Xtra. Large audio files (such as sound tracks or lengthy instructions) should be compressed as streamable audio files with the SoundEdit 16 Export Xtra.

Creating Compressed Audio Embedded Files

By using the Compression Xtra in Director, developers can set compression options for audio embedded within a Director Shockwave movie. Developers can set the bit rate and channels of audio used in the Shockwave movie to affect the file transfer time and quality of the audio. A low bit rate setting produces a compressed audio cast member that will quickly download but may suffer in quality.

After setting the audio compression options, choose the Afterburner Xtra to compress the entire Director movie. Afterburner uses the audio compression settings specified in the Compression Xtra.

Creating Streamable Audio (SWA) Files

By using the SWA export Xtra in SoundEdit 16, you can export a streamable audio file for web use. This streamable Shockwave Audio file (SWA) features a new compression format that reduces download time.

Using the SWA Xtra requires two steps. The developer customizes the properties of exported SWA files by accessing "Shockwave for Audio Settings" in the Xtras pulldown menu in SoundEdit 16 (shown in figure 12.2).

FIGURE 12.2

The Export Xtra being set for 24 Kbps.

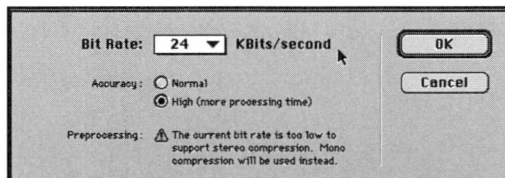

The SWA export Xtra enables SoundEdit 16 version 2 users to customize audio to suit their particular web needs. Bit rate and number of channels can be set to affect the time for file transfer and audio quality of the streamable audio. A SWA saved with a lower bit rate or at mono can stream at lower baud rates, but may also have a reduced quality compared to a stereo SWA file with a higher bit rate.

When setting the bit rate of an embedded audio or SWA file, Director developers should consider both the resources of the users who will be accessing these files and the resources of the web site hosting the SWA files. High bit rate files, for example, can create a set of SWA files or Shockwave movies that users with slow baud rate connections will be unwilling to download. Depending on the type of Internet provider servicing the Shockwave site, larger files might also cause access problems for the entire web site should hard file transfer limits be exceeded.

A general rule of thumb is that for Internet solutions where the range of user resources is broad and file transfer limits may exist for a server, use low bit rate mono embedded audio and SWA files. In intranets where the range of user resources is more controlled and where few or no file transfer limits are placed on the server, use higher bit rates and stereo for better quality embedded audio and SWA files.

Both the embedded audio Compression Xtra and SWA Export Xtra automatically set files with a bit rate of less than 32 Kbps to monophonic.

For more specific bit rates, Macromedia suggests the following bit rates for various connections. This table provides only a general idea of what bit rates to expect on various network connections. Many factors can affect the real-world network bit rate for a user.

TABLE 12.1

SUGGESTED SWA SETTINGS FOR VARIOUS NETWORK CONNECTIONS	
Use This Bit Rate	*For a Target Audience Using*
64 Kbps–128 Kbps	T1 delivery
32 Kbps–56 Kbps	ISDN lines
16 Kbps	28.8 modem connections
8 Kbps	14.4 modem connections

Although Macromedia suggests using a 16 Kbps rate for SWA files being accessed via a 28.8 modem, you can get dramatic results by using a 24 Kbps rate and setting a slightly higher than normal buffer rate on the Shockwave movie playing the SWA file. To give some idea of the numbers involved in this type of file, a sound file 1 minute and 25 seconds in length compressed to a SWA file for a 24 Kbps play rate creates a file size of about 265 KB. Setting a buffer rate at 5 seconds typically enables the play rate to keep up with the transfer rate when the SWA file is being accessed via a 28.8 modem connection. The buffer rate can have a dramatic effect on playback. Setting the buffer rate up by a couple of seconds can eliminate audio breakup during playback.

For best results in creating high quality Shockwave Audio files, follow these general rules:

* Work with 22 KHz 16 bit audio files. Upsample lower bit or sample rate audio files to this sample and bit rate.

* When possible, filter low to low-mid range audio (for example, 4–8 KHz in a 22 KHz sample) to reduce distortion during compression.

* To avoid undesirable compression effects, do not use stereo channels in an audio sample that are too dissimilar.

* Close SoundEdit 16's Levels control palette when using the Export Xtra.

* Avoid cutting a sound clip too close at the end. Add a little dead space so the user can hear the end of the audio.

Note

SWA and FPUs

To hear SWA files, your computer must have a floating point unit (FPU). Some Macintosh computers and PCs do not have FPUs and, thus, will not be able to stream SWA files.

PowerMacs without an FPU (like the 7100) can simulate an FPU with a $10 shareware extension called *Software FPU*, distributed by John Neil & Associates, P.O. Box 2156, Cupertino, CA 95015. This enables them to stream SWA with no problems.

This FPU requirement does not affect the play of Audio embedded in Shockwave movies.

Referencing External SWA Files in a Shockwave Movie

To refer to a SWA file from within a Shockwave movie, you must first create the SWA file in SoundEdit 16 and save it to the web server you will be using. Typically, you will want to save the SWA file in the same directory as the Shockwave movie to avoid path name resolution problems. In Director, use the Insert/ Other menu option to create a cast member that refers to a SWA Streaming Audio file. Now create or modify the STARTMOVIE movie script for this movie so that it includes information similar to that shown in Listing 12.4.

Listing 12.4—Sample Movie Handler for Calling SWA Files from a Shockwave Movie

```
on startMovie
    set the URL of member "shockaudio" ="http://www.company.com/shockwave/¬
        song.swa"
    set the preLoadTime of member "shockaudio" = 5
end
```

This handler sets the URL of the SWA file being referenced by the Shockwave movie. It also sets the number of seconds of audio to be downloaded before audio playback begins. Developers need to play with this number to achieve the best results for their environment. Higher bit rate files require longer preload times to avoid the audio choking.

When you close the cast script window, Director compiles the script and gives you an error stating that there is a Lingo error in the script. This results because the script uses commands understood only by Afterburner. Ignore the warning. Complete any additional programming of the Director movie and convert it to a Shockwave movie with the Shockwave Xtra as normal.

A later part of this chapter, "Macromedia's Generic "player.dcr", "examines how to use external parameters to create a more generic Shockwave movie SWA file player.

Using Lingo Commands on SWA Files

Director 5 and the corresponding Afterburner Xtra contain additional Lingo commands by which developers can control the playback of SWA files. These commands affect the location, playback, and buffering of SWA files. For a complete set of these new commands, refer to Appendix A in this book.

Looking at Useful Shockwave Examples

Taking the time to build generic handlers can save valuable time in production. This point is especially true when it comes to building Shockwave movies. In fact, valuable production time can be saved by not only building generic handlers, but by building generic Shockwave movies. In the same way that generic handlers can be customized on the fly by passing parameters, generic

Shockwave movies can be customized by passing external parameters through the EMBED or OBJECT tag calling the Shockwave movie.

The process of creating a functional Shockwave HTML page requires editing a Director movie, "burning" it with the Afterburner Xtra, writing an EMBED tag in an HTML document, and uploading the movie, associated SWA files, and the HTML document to the web server. If a change is made to the web page, the entire process is repeated.

Using generic Shockwave movies can reduce this process to one of only changing and uploading a changed SWA and HTML file, or possibly even changing and uploading an HTML file. By editing and loading an HTML file locally, debugging can even be done locally in some cases.

The best example to demonstrate how generic Shockwave movies can save production time is provided by Macromedia itself.

With the release of Shockwave for Audio Xtras, Macromedia included two types of sample players for SWA files. These files are included in the Afterburner Xtra package available at www.macromedia.com. When the Afterburner Xtra is installed or updated, these files are automatically placed in either the SWA examples (Macintosh) or SWAexamp (Windows) directory in the Director 5 directory.

One Shockwave movie is designed to play an SWA file automatically without a visible Shockwave movie on the page. This is the 1×1 movie. The other movie (the one focused on here) provides the user with some type of interface by which to control the play of the SWA file. This is the player movie.

In the example of playing an SWA file through a Shockwave movie listed earlier in this chapter, the call to the URL of the SWA file was hardcoded into the startmovie handler of the Shockwave movie. This approach has a major drawback. While developing the SWA file for play, a developer may have several versions of the SWA—each with different compression settings. Playing each of these SWA files via a Shockwave movie requires building and burning several Shockwave movies—each having a hardcoded URL location to a different SWA file.

The template Shockwave movie Macromedia created, however, does not have the URL location of SWA files hardcoded in the Shockwave movie. Instead, the URL is passed to the Shockwave movie by an external parameter in the EMBED tag of the HTML document. This means that by changing the HTML document EMBED tag, an entirely different SWA file can be loaded and played.

The template player files included by Macromedia are the perfect example of how building generic Shockwave movies that use external parameters can cut production time.

Macromedia's Generic "player.dcr"

The HTML code included by Macromedia to play its template player movie follows in listing 12.5.

Listing 12.5—HTML Document that Calls and Passes Parameters to the PLAYER.DCR Shockwave Movie

```
<HTML>
<HEAD>
<TITLE>the SWA Player</TITLE>
</HEAD>
<BODY BGCOLOR="#666666">
<!-- Shockwave Audio Player HTML
     by Buzz Kettles, buzz@macromedia.com
-->
<center>
<script language="LiveScript">
<!-- hide this script tag's contents from old browsers
     document.write('<embed  width=416 height=32 SRC="http://
     poppy.macromedia.com/~beta/elmo/b1r3/swa/player.dcr" sw1=off
     swURL="http://poppy.macromedia.com/~beta/elmo/b1r3/swa/classic.swa"
     swTEXT="Audio Streaming Over the Internet" swPreLoadTime=3 sw2=0
     sw3=1>');
<!-- sw1= debugger mode, sw2= Autoplay, sw3= LogoMode -->
<!-- done hiding from old browsers -->
</script>
<noembed>
</noembed>
</center>
</BODY>
</HT
HTML>
```

The bulk of this HTML code includes LiveScript that will hide the EMBED tag from old browsers that cannot support it. The essential HTML code is found in the EMBED tag:

```
<embed  width=416 height=32 SRC="http://poppy.macromedia.com/~beta/elmo/¬
    b1r3/swa/player.dcr"

sw1=offswURL="http://poppy.macromedia.com/~beta/elmo/b1r3/swa/¬
    classic.swa" swTEXT="Audio

Streaming Over the Internet" swPreLoadTime=3 sw2=0 sw3=1>
```

The SRC parameter calls the Shockwave movie called PLAYER.DCR. The rest of the parameters are user-defined. The sw1 parameter toggles a debugging mode. When this is set to on, debugging messages are displayed in the Shockwave movie. The swURL parameter gives the URL of the SWA file to be played. The swTEXT parameter is the default text displayed in the Shockwave movie. The swPreLoadTime parameter sets the buffer time of the SWA file. The sw2 parameter toggles an autoplay feature. If this parameter is set to 1, the SWA file begins playing immediately. If it is set to 0, the user must press the play button to begin the play of the SWA file.

The sw3 parameter is an ingenious parameter that sets the look of the Shockwave movie. If the parameter is set to 1, the player displays volume controls, song name display, and start and stop buttons. If the parameter is set to 2, the player does not display volume controls. If the parameter is set to 3, the player only shows the start and stop buttons. If the parameter is set to 4, the Shockwave logo only is displayed. When the logo is clicked on, this toggles play of the SWA file.

Here we have an example of a generic Shockwave movie that can have its functionality, SWA file, and even look changed through the use of external parameters in the EMBED tag of an HTML document.

Alex Zavatone's Faux-MIAW Shockwave Movies

Shockwave does not currently support movies in a window (MIAW). Developers who want intermovie communication in Shockwave must rely on some alternative method. Alex Zavatone of Macromedia has developed the following two movies that act in a similar manner to MIAWs.

In Zavatone's example shown in figure 12.3, one Shockwave movie generates a math problem when the user selects the Generate Problem button. When the user selects the Calculate Result button, the answer to the problem displays in the second movie.

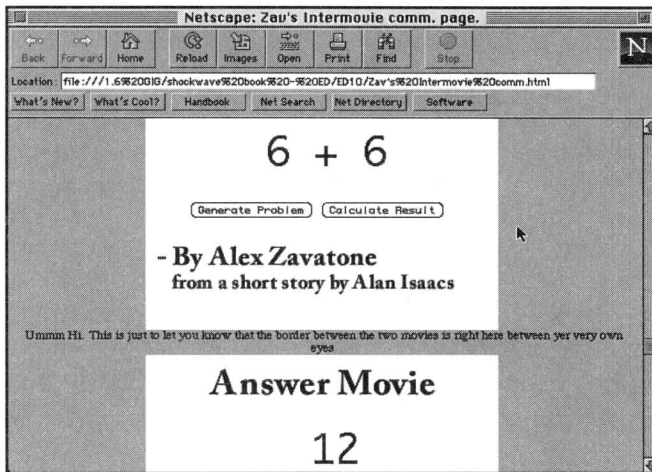

FIGURE 12.3

Alex Zavatone's simulation of a MIAW in Shockwave.

The communication between the two Shockwave movies takes place via a text file in the Prefs directory within the Shockwave for Director Plug-in directory.

The main movie contains two movie handlers as shown in listing 12.6.

Listing 12.6—The Two Handlers in the Main MIAW Simulation Shockwave Movie

```
on calculate
  set c1 = random(10)
  set c2 = random(10)
  put c1 & " + " & c2 into member "EvalField"
end
on WriteResults
  set myField = "ZavData"
  setpref "ZavData", the text of member "EvalField"
end
```

The calculate handler randomly generates a math problem and saves the solution in the "EvalField" text field. This handler is executed when the user clicks on the Generate Problem button.

When the user clicks on the Calculate Result button, the WriteResults handler uses the setPref command to write the solution into a text file named "ZavData".

As you can see in listing 12.7, the second movie loops in one frame and calls the GetFileData handler each time it exits the frame.

Listing 12.7—The Handler in the Second MIAW Simulation Shockwave Movie

```
on GetFileData
  if getPref("ZavData") <> empty then
    set myEvalStr = getpref("ZavData")
    set myResult = value(myEvalStr)
    put myResult into member "Answer"
  end if
end
```

As soon as the data is written from the first movie to the "ZavData" text file, the GetFileData handler reads that file by using the getPref command. The text data is then converted into a value and placed into the "Answer" text field.

With Zavatone's example is a basic use of the getPref and setPref commands to enable intermovie communication. This intermovie communication need not occur just between Shockwave movies, however. Pref files can be used to communicate information between Shockwave movies and other Director movies. One example of this is the Handler Database Xtra Xchange.

The Handler Database Xtra Xchange

The Handler Database Xtra discussed in Chapter 11, "Building Multimedia Tools in Director," enables a Director developer to catalog generic handlers that can then be imported into a Director movie under development. What if a developer could browse a web site for additional handlers and add them to a handler database? This is the idea behind the Handler Database Xtra Xchange (see fig. 12.4).

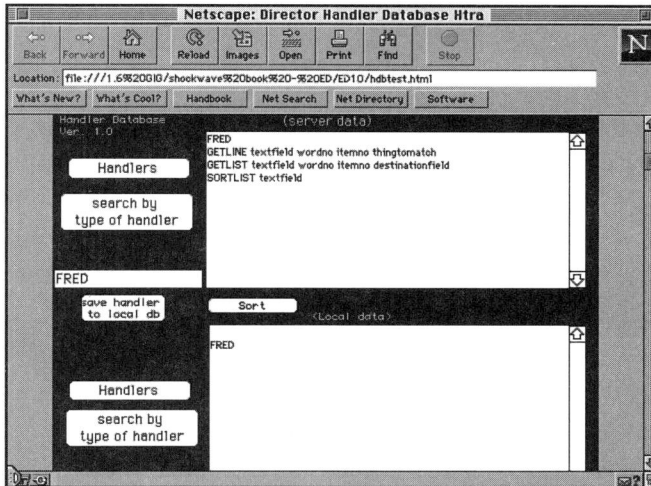

FIGURE 12.4

Copying the "fred" handler from the server handler database to the handler database on the user's machine.

One modification to the Handler Database Xtra needs to be made for this to work. Although alias or shortcuts can be used by Shockwave movies to refer to external casts or Xtras, they cannot be used to refer to text files in the "prefs" directory. The actual text files must be located in the "prefs" folder.

Because of this, the Handler Database developed in Chapter 11 must have a "save database" option added. In addition, this database that is saved must be in a text format that is, in turn, saved in the "prefs" folder of the Shockwave for Director Plug-in directory.

When these two criteria are met, it is fairly simple to use a combination of the `getNetText`, `getPref`, and `setPref` commands to create a Shockwave movie that can view the current handler database of a user and import new handlers from a server file to that database.

A current working version of the Handler Database (HDB) Xtra as well as the HDB Xtra Xchange is available at `http://www.thoughtport.com/~kirk/hbd.html`

Conclusion

It is clear that Shockwave applications will play an important role in web-based multimedia. Recent agreements between Macromedia and both America Online and Netscape ensure that a large web viewing audience will have browsers that make use of the Shockwave plug-in.

Shockwave for Director opens a new market for the Director developer. Clients are not restricted, however, to developers who are geographically near. The ability to rapidly create rich graphics, audio, and interactive content will go far to ensure a Shockwave developer's success. The key to this rapid Shockwave development is in creating generic Shockwave movies that make extensive use of external parameters. By using this approach, one richly developed Shockwave movie can perform a multitude of tasks.

To what extent and in what useful ways Shockwave movies can interact with JavaScript, Java, CGI scripts, and HTML documents is still being explored by Director developers. To keep abreast of these developments, serious Shockwave developers should join the Shockwave discussion list.

It is still unclear how much of a market will develop around the use of external casts in Shockwave. The ability, for example, to design a CD-ROM game with rich media elements that is driven by a storyline delivered via a Shockwave movie is now present. To what extent this will affect the increasing amount of hard drive space the typical user devotes to web-related software remains to be seen.

To what extent Shockwave developers will cooperate on the use of external casts and files also remains to be seen. The creation of a generic set of handlers would be easy enough to accomplish. The savings on Shockwave download times, however, would most likely be minimal. The creation of a generic set of graphics would be most helpful on shortening download times. Aesthetic considerations, however, would make this an almost impossible task.

chapter 13

Tab Julius

AUTOMATING DEMONSTRATIONS

In any program other than a simple slide show, it becomes necessary to provide the user with some sort of instruction on how to use the program. The amount of instruction varies—it could be nothing more than printed documentation, a help item on the menu bar, or even a help button. If the developers were particularly lax, there might not be any help at all. (Of course, we all know no one releases programs like that…) An alternative to the options listed previously exists, an automated demo. An automated demo is one in which a voiceover describes how to do something while the program automates it before your very eyes. A checkbook program, for example, could have an automated help. The automated help might enable you to press a button marked Show Me that would then take you through the steps of writing the check or any other function of the program.

In such a case, when it came time to balance the checkbook, you could stare at the program, scratch your head, rifle through your check register, turn to ask your wife (but not find her), and then finally spot the Show Me button cleverly placed in a prominent position. Clicking on it, you stare in amazement as a voiceover begins, "To balance your checkbook...," and goes on to describe how to use the program.

When the voice mentions a particular feature ("...to sort the entries by check number, click on the Date button"), the button highlights automatically. In fact, if it were sophisticated enough, you would watch the mouse travel over to the button, hear the clicking sound, and the button would highlight—just as if you were watching someone else demonstrate the program for you. In addition to having a Show Me button, it might be appropriate to do a demo the first time in a particular area. This is, in fact, the approach often used in better children's games.

When developing a children's game (this author's specialty, actually) a good idea is to have the program demonstrate itself the first time the user enters a section. This demonstration helps because often the children are preliterate (depending on the target age group), and cannot read the instructions, understand or even distinguish the words "Show Me". Mom and Dad, meanwhile, would really like to sit the child in front of the computer and keep little Joey occupied while they make dinner (or do whatever else Mom and Dad do without Joey).

Joey, when seeing a game that requires interaction from him, benefits greatly from having the game describe itself: "This is a game about matching patterns! I'll show you a tail...," (an animal's tail reveals itself), "and you have to figure out which animal goes with it!" (Program reveals different animals hidden under cards.) "When you've found the animal it goes with, ring the bell!" (Mouse moves to the bell, simulates a click, and the bell rings back and forth.) "If you're right, you'll win a prize!" (Sample prize appears.)

This sort of demo is invaluable for children's games, and also useful in other regards, such as the Show Me button described previously. You are probably wondering how to do this in Lingo. You could, of course, write a score sequence to do this. If you've got a Lingo-based movie, however, it might not necessarily be an easily available option. As shown here, one way you can accomplish this is to write a Demo Manager.

Creating a Demo Manager

The concept of the Demo Manager is simple. First, it assumes you have a voiceover (a wavefile recording to talk the user through the process).
If not, you must tweak the code somewhat. The assumption is that the voice will talk, and while the voice is talking different actions will happen on-screen. Because the actions you want to happen are tied to the voiceover, it becomes imperative to figure out their timing in advance.

Take our example of Joey. If you were going to program such a demo, you first need to determine when each action is going to occur, so that you could "schedule" it. You would need, therefore, a timeline that looked like this:

> 00:00—Voice starts: "This is a game about..."
>
> 00:07—"I'll show you a tail..."
>
> [Reveal tail in demo box]
>
> 00:13—"which animal goes with it?"
>
> [Reveal different animals at random]
>
> 00:21—"...ring the bell!"
>
> [Animate bell ringing]

With that in hand, you have a fair idea of what needs to be done.

From this example you know that at the :13 second point you need to begin showing different animals at random on the screen. At the :21 second point you need to start the ringing-the-bell animation.

With the timeline established, you still need to make the demo "happen". There are two components to this. The first is the actual code to do whatever the demonstrated action is. For instance, if the demo is supposed to ring the bell at :21 seconds, then you need code somewhere to ring the bell. The other component is that you need some sort a Demo Manager to invoke that code at the appropriate time. This next section teaches you how to build a demo manager.

The Demo Manager Interface

The best way to approach the internals of the Automated Demo Manager is by first looking at the externals, the interface to the Demo Manager itself. Ask yourself how you will make use of the Demo Manager.

```
startNewDemo("SHOWME.AIF")
```

Next, you need to schedule each of the actions you want to occur:

```
scheduleDemoAction(seconds(7),     "pickNewPattern()")
scheduleDemoAction(seconds(13),    "showRandomFaces()")
scheduleDemoAction(seconds(21),    "ringBell()")
```

Finally, set it running by calling `runDemo()`:

```
runDemo()
```

Not too taxing, is it? Well, it's not supposed to be, at least on the interface end. The internals are a little more involved, but still fairly straightforward.

Demo Manager Internals

As you can see from the call to `scheduleDemoAction()`, you supply both a time and an action. This, in fact, is basically all that is required in a demo: knowing what to do and when to do it. Give the time in ticks (although this example is converted from seconds [see Note]), and the action specified as a Lingo command to be executed, given as a string.

Note

Because Director measures time in ticks (at 60 ticks to a second), any time references should also be given in ticks. It is a real pain to figure out how many ticks one minute and 14.2 seconds consists of, however. So, I have a handy-dandy little seconds-to-ticks converter that I like to use. Usually it is in a movie script, and you can keep it with the Demo Manager. It looks like this:

```
on seconds  howMany
        return(howMany * 60)
    end
```

Basically, the function returns 60 times whatever number you supply. You will find it much easier to say `seconds(48)` rather than 2880. Some people use `48 * 60` in the middle of their code, which is an acceptable alternative, but I like my seconds handler because it is abstracted a little bit from the 60 ticks per second value, and it is instantly clear what `seconds(48)` means (as opposed to, say 48 * 60). You can also provide partial seconds to this if you need to, like `seconds(2.5)`. As far as the Demo is concerned, however, it is highly unlikely that you will need such split-second timing.

The time value given is the point in the voiceover when you want to perform the action. A helpful hint is to schedule the action to occur after the voiceover has described it. If the voiceover says, "...to return to the kitchen, click on the big purple arrow," for example, you should have the arrow highlight or flash after the sentence has completed. Not for any technical reason, it is purely psychological. You hear the voiceover suggest clicking on the big purple arrow, and instantly start scanning the screen, looking for the arrow. If it then highlights, you can register its exact location and know its use. On the other hand, if it started flashing or highlighting when the voice said, "...to return," and was done by the time the sentence finished, you might see the flashing, but have trouble putting it into context. In demos, it is always better to have the action follow the description. The code for `scheduleDemoAction()` adds the action and the time point into an internal list of all the things that need to be done and when. You should start with `startNewDemo()`, however, and work from there.

1. First, the Demo Manager code goes in a movie script because it will conceivably be accessed from elsewhere in the program. The Demo Manager is generic, in that a number of different sections can schedule demos and run them. If you did need to schedule a bunch of demos in advance and then run them as needed, you could rework this script into an object (a fine learning experiment). For our purposes, however, a movie script does just fine.

2. Stick the following declarations at the top of the script, before any handlers:

```
global demoSequenceList
global demoAudioFile
global timerThreshold
global scheduledAction
global numDemoSequenceItems
global nextDemoSequence
global moreDemoLeft
global demoRunning
global demoStartTime
```

A further description of these declarations will be offered as they appear later in this chapter.

The Demo Manager Functions

Let's look at `startNewDemo`:

```
on startNewDemo whichAudioFile
  set demoAudiofile =whichAudioFile
  set demoSequenceList =[]
end
```

In calling `startNewDemo()`, you pass in the name of the audio file you want to use. The first global variable comes in here: set `demoAudioFile` as the name of the audio file to be used later.

Note that this Demo Manager is written assuming an audio file on disk. The reason being that demos can go on for a minute or more, typically too long for a puppetSound. Of course, you can change it to handle whatever kind of sound you want. You can also use linked cast members, however, or whatever else. Just make certain that you pass in the appropriate information (cast member name, number, for example), and handle it appropriately in the area that plays the sound.

The next thing required is to reset the sequence list. The sequence list keeps track of what needs to be done and when. Setting it to empty brackets initializes it to be an empty list. This is the second global variable. (I won't bother to point them out to you any more—I'm sure you can noodle it out.)

Starting a new demo does not require much—just clearing out or initializing the lists. The scheduling, though, takes place in the next function. It is `scheduleDemoAction()`:

```
on scheduleDemoAction numTicks, whichAction
  set thisEntry =[:]
  addProp(thisEntry, #triggerTime, numTicks)
  addProp(thisEntry, #action, whichAction)
  add(DemoSequenceList, thisEntry)
end
```

Although it looks pretty innocuous, it is doing a little mind-bending work here. This shows each entry, or scheduled action, and carries with it two pieces of information: the trigger time (the time at which you want the action to occur) and the action itself. These are put into a property list, and then that list is added to the demo sequence list.

The net effect is that demoSequenceList is a list of other lists. Those other lists have only two entries each—a trigger time and an action, but demoSequenceList becomes a convenient way to carry all this information all around in one basket.

In this handler, use the symbol called #triggerTime as the property for the associated time, and a symbol called #action as the property for the associated action (the string you provided when you called scheduleDemoAction()). Later, you will pull this tiny list out and retrieve each of the individual entries. If you need to expand the number of associated items, the property list becomes a convenient way to do so (which is why I chose to do things this way).

An alternative method would be to have two parallel lists, one representing all the trigger times, and another representing all the actions. The choice is up to you—there's no particular benefit to one or the other, just whatever you find easiest.

As you can tell from the initial example, you call scheduleDemoAction() over and over as you add items. Each time you do so, it adds another entry into the demoSequenceList. Finally, it becomes time to run the demo, introducing the next handler, runDemo():

```
on runDemo
  set demoRunning =TRUE
  set numDemoSequences =count(demoSequenceList)
  set nextDemoSequence =1
  sound stop 1
  puppetSound 1, 0
  sound playfile 1, demoAudioFile
  set demoStartTime =the ticks
  prepareNextDemoSequence()
  repeat while soundBusy(1)
    updateDemo
  end repeat
  set demoRunning =FALSE
end
```

RunDemo begins by setting a global flag demoRunning to TRUE. Although the Demo Manager itself does not need this flag, it becomes very helpful for the rest of your program—it provides an easy way for a function to check if it was invoked during the demo or not. The fictional RingBell() handler, for example, would probably be used by the program any time the bell needed to be rung. It would probably do the animation and play a bell-ringing sound.

During a demo with a voiceover, however, the bell-ringing sound might not be desirable to have. The demoRunning variable comes in handy here. The handler might end up looking something like this:

```
on ringBell
  global demoRunning
  .. start animation ..
  if not demoRunning then
    puppetSound "bell ringing"
  end if
end
```

Of course, you can accomplish this in other ways, but I have found in general that a global variable acting as a flag is sometimes the easiest way.

Back to runDemo(). RunDemo() next gets a count of how many sequences are in the demoSequenceList and stores this away in numDemoSequenceItems. This is used later to see if you have run out of items. It also sets the variable nextDemoSequence to be 1, because you start with the first action scheduled.

In theory, this does not need to be in a variable—you could just get a count of the list each time you need to check it. Because the list is not going to change, however, getting a count would be a little silly because the number will stay the same. An alternative might be to delete the items from the list as you go along, but it really does not matter one way or the other. This method should be fine.

Continue by stopping any existing sound in channel 1, by using both sound stop and puppetSound to be safe. I suspect it is redundant to use both, but it does not hurt anything. This way you will know for sure that the audio is stopped.

When the sound is stopped, start playing the sound file and then immediately register the current tick value. This value is important, because it represents what time it was when the sound began, and all the sequence items have a time relative to the beginning of the voiceover.

Then prepare the next demo sequence and begin looping around updating the demo. At this point, you need to look at how the demo sequences are prepared and how the update works, but first you will notice that the loop continues until you run out of sound (the voiceover, and therefore the demo, is over). You can also modify this so that the demo stops if the user interrupts it. That's a good project if you want to experiment a bit more with this code.

Code to Prepare the Demo Sequence

To prepare the demo sequence, you have a handler aptly named prepareNextDemoSequence()! This handler is called at runtime, while the demo is going on. It retrieves the next demo sequence, if any, to use.

First, it checks to see if the sequence you are on (nextDemoSequence) exceeds the count in the list. If so, then you have exceeded the list and there's nothing more to do, except to wait for the voiceover to finish.

```
on prepareNextDemoSequence
  set moreDemoLeft =(nextDemoSequence <= numDemoSequenceItems)
  if not moreDemoLeft then
    exit
  end if
  set scheduledAction =getAt(demoSequenceList, nextDemoSequence)
  set timerThreshold =getaProp(scheduledAction, #triggerTime)
  set timerThreshold =timerThreshold + demoStartTime
  set nextDemoSequence =nextDemoSequence + 1
end
```

prepareNextDemoSequence sets a flag, moreDemoLeft, to indicate whether the count exceeded the list. If there are no more left, we just exit the handler.

If demo remains, then we need to retrieve the necessary information for the next item in the demo sequence. First, retrieve the item record from the demoSequenceList. (You'll recall that this is a list of lists, each sublist being the actual information scheduled.) Save this as scheduledAction. ScheduledAction is really a property list consisting of two items: the trigger time and the action to perform.

Next, extract the timer threshold from scheduleAction, and save into a variable, timerThreshold. (I don't bother extracting the action item itself, because it's not needed yet, although I guess it couldn't hurt).

After you have the `timerThreshold`, you must add in the `demoStartTime`. Remember that the threshold is just a time offset into the time it takes to play the voiceover. You will later continually check the current tick count against the threshold time to know when to execute the demo action. Instead of performing the same math over and over, it is easier to just do it here.

Finally, increment `nextDemoSequence` because you are all done with this demo entry and want to be ready to work with the next one in line later on.

Now the fun begins. You are in a loop in `runDemo()` that calls `updateDemo()` continually as long as a sound plays. Look at `updateDemo()`:

```
on updateDemo
  if the ticks > timerThreshold then
    -- Perform the action
    set whichAction =getaProp(scheduledAction, #action)
    do whichAction
    -- And get the next one ready
    if moreDemoLeft then
      prepareNextDemoSequence
    else
      set the timerThreshold =the maxInteger
    end if
  end if
end
```

First it sees if the current tick count is higher than the threshold of the upcoming sequence item. If it isn't, skip to the end of the `if` statement and effectively out of the handler. `RunDemo()` continues to loop around with little impact from `updateDemo()` until it hits a threshold.

Upon reaching a threshold, perform the action requested. First, get the action to be performed out of the property list, `scheduledAction`, and then `do` it.

The `do` statement is the core of the Demo Manager. `Do`—you can look it up in your trusty *Lingo Dictionary*—executes any Lingo string you give it. So, if you give the instructions

```
scheduleDemoAction(seconds(2), "set the forecolor of sprite¬
backgroundChannel to 4")
scheduleDemoAction(seconds(2), "updateStage")
```

then the `do` command, when invoked in `updateDemo()`, executes each of those action items (e.g., "updateStage") in turn.

The main drawback of the do command is in referencing global variables within it. I've not found an easy way to do this. If I need to reference a global variable in a demo, therefore, I actually give the command to run a handler that sits in a movie script, and that handler is the one to execute the command. For example:

```
on highlightMenuIcon whichIcon
  global menuIcons
  highlight(menuIcons, whichIcon, TRUE)
end
```

This handler (taken from another program that uses the demo) references the variable menuIcons. Because it's a multiline statement (a global declaration, followed by the actual command), you cannot do it directly from a do. Instead, you must do it from a handler (all puns intentional). This remains true of any multiline statement. If you need to run a loop, for example, you have to put the loop in a handler and call that handler.

That's all that there is to actually invoking the action. Next in the demo update routine, you need to prepare the next sequence if more demo remains. If not, you need to ensure that you don't get called again.

Stopping Any Further Updates

To make certain that your demo code doesn't get called again, set the timerThreshold so high that you know that you will never hit it. As an alternative, you could set some flag that RunDemo() could test to see if it should call updateDemo(). Just because you have run out of items, however, you don't necessarily want to stop the demo because it is entirely possible (and probable) that the voice will go on beyond the last action performed. That is why you don't want to cut off the voice, just stop the updating upon running out of items.

The maxInteger provides a cheap way to pull this off. The maxInteger is a Lingo property equal to the largest number that can be represented in 32 bits. Even at 60 ticks per second, you'd never come close to exceeding the maxInteger during the time that your program is running; so it's a pretty safe way to set a high threshold.

Enhancing Your Demo

When the demo is all over—when the sound has stopped playing—`runDemo()` sets the global `demoRunning` to `FALSE`. In practice, however, you might want to add a few enhancements.

First, you might want to have the program ignore mouse events while the demo is running. You can do this via `set the mouseDownScript` as described in your manuals. You would then want to make certain that you reinstate them when you have finished.

You might want to rework the Demo Manager to enable interruptions—via keyboard or mouse click or something else. You might also want to combine the two by passing in a parameter to `runDemo()` that indicates whether interruptions are allowed and then you can run the demo both ways.

The calling side (where you scheduled the actions and called `runDemo()`) might want to perform some cleanup—refreshing the screen and turning off highlighted icons at the conclusion of the demo, for example. This is particularly important if the demo is interruptible, as this would mean that the demo could be left in an indeterminate state.

You might want to consider automating your cursor so that the user can watch it move to a particular section of the screen. This can be a very effective demonstration device, because it shows the user what to do with the mouse itself. To automate the cursor, turn off the mouse cursor and instead move a sprite that looks like the mouse cursor to the positions you want. This has the added advantage of being impervious to the user moving the cursor and disrupting your demo.

Finally, make certain that the rest of your program does not react in undesirable ways while a demo is running. A natural tendency is to try to perform the action being demonstrated, for example. You want to handle such situations appropriately. As an example, a voiceover might say, "Click on this," the icon highlights, and then the user immediately wants to click on that icon, forgetting for a moment that he or she is just watching the demo. To begin with, you probably want to make your `mouseDown` handlers demo-aware (if you haven't overridden them with `the mouseDownScript`), as well as any other handlers that might be affected. You should also consider hiding the mouse during the demo so as to remove the temptation.

Remember also that in a demo you have to perform all the actions you would normally perform in a program. That is, you might have to remember to update the stage by scheduling a demo action to do so. You can schedule more than one demo action for the same time point; they will just get executed one after another. The only important thing to remember is to schedule them in the order in which you want them to appear. Even if you time them in the order in which you want them to appear, it is still important to actually schedule them in that same order. The same order is necessary because (you'll recall) you go through the list one item at a time, not going on to the next one until the previous one has completed. If the list is not in order, you will never go through it properly.

Conclusion

All in all a demo scheduler is a handy little piece of code. If you have difficulty getting the actions you need performed *to be* performed, you might first want to look up, and experiment with, the do command. Also, just before you have the instruction to do whichAction, you might want to use either PUT or ALERT to write out whichAction so that you can see what it's about to execute before it actually does it. With a little creative thought, you can come up with some interesting uses for the Demo Manager. Enjoy!

chapter 14

Raúl Silva

THE POWER OF LISTS

Lists enable you to organize a group of values simply and efficiently. With Director 5.0, you can define an indefinite set of values using a single variable (Director 4 was limited to 10,920 elements in a linear list on Windows 3.1). Lists resemble arrays in Basic. The best way to visualize lists is as a consecutive row of mailboxes. These mailboxes can contain any kind of data or even a pointer to the data on another mailbox or set of mailboxes. These mailboxes can be referred to by their position, or you can label them and refer to them by name. You can add or remove mailboxes at any time. You can even sort the contents of the labeled boxes themselves. Lists prove immensely powerful and add a lot of flexibility to Director. A list can even contain other lists.

Types of Lists

The two types of lists are linear lists and property lists. Understanding their differences is essential to their proper implementation.

Linear Lists

Linear lists are like a row of unlabeled mailboxes. Linear lists are made of single values in sequence. You may want to have a list of consecutive temperature readings, for example, or record the position of the pointer over time. Linear lists can be sorted by the value of their contents.

Property lists

Property lists differ from linear lists in that each value has a property attached to it. Properties can be seen as labels for the mailboxes. You may want to keep track of the score of four different players, for example. On a property list, you assign the specific values to a property list on which each property is the name of a player. The labels can be strings or symbols. Property lists in which each property is a symbol (for example, #foo) provide the greatest performance when accessing values in the list.

Both types of lists can contain any data type in Director, but you cannot mix and match list types on a single list. That is, if you have a property list, every value has to have a property; on a linear list, no value can have a property.

Creating Lists

Lists have to be assigned to a variable to be of any use. You can either assign the list to a global variable so that you can access it from anywhere on your movie or pass it as an argument.

A linear list is defined by using two corresponding brackets or using the `list()` function:

```
set gMyList to []
set gMyList to list()
```

These two examples create empty linear lists that you can manipulate. You can also assign values as part of the declaration by enclosing them between the brackets or parentheses. To separate the values, use a comma as a delimiter:

```
set gMyList to [5,3,2,6]
set gMyList to list(5,3,2,6)
```

Lists can contain any kind of value, and you can mix and match types of values within the same list:

```
set gMyList to ["Hawaii",5,#0]
```

The preceding example defines a linear list that contains three different types of data: a string ("Hawaii"), an integer (5), and a symbol (#0).

Property lists are defined by two corresponding brackets ([]) with each property set separated by a colon (:). The colon has to be present even if no initial properties are defined when you declare the property list. This tells Director that you are declaring a property list, even if it is empty. The list() function has no equivalent for property lists. Almost no one uses the list() function anyway. Here is an example of a property list declaration:

```
set gMyPropertyList to [:]
```

You can also define properties and their values when you create the list:

```
set gMyPropertyList to [#property1:0,#property2:1]
```

The preceding example created a property list with two properties: #property1 and #property2 with corresponding values of 0 and 2.

Note that the properties start with a pound (#) sign. This defines them as symbols. Symbols are a data type in Director. Symbols are not variables because you cannot change their values. The advantage to symbols is that they take up less memory and are retrieved from memory much faster than any other data type. You can use any other data type for a property, but in most cases, symbols are the best way to go.

More About Lists

It is useful to understand how lists work. When you create a list and assign values to it, those values get stored in a position in memory. From that point on, any reference to an item affects only the contents of that location in memory. This can become confusing when you make a copy of a list. If you type this on the message window

```
set listA to [1,5,6]
set listB to listA
```

and then type

```
put "listA= " listA & "', listB= " & listB
```

you get

```
-- listA= [1,5,6], listB= [1,5,6]
```

What happens if you change item 2 on listB?

```
setAt(listB,2,1)
```

Look at listA and listB and you will find what may be an unexpected result.

```
put "listA= " listA & ", listB= " & listB
-- listA= [1,2,6], listB= [1,2,6]
```

Changing the value of item 2 of listB also changed the value of item 2 of listA. The reason for this is that item 2 of listB (or listA for that matter) is not really a constant but rather a pointer to a position in memory that holds the actual value. Change the value in that position, and anything that points to it reflects the changes.

Note that this only happens if you change the items on the list itself. If you assign a new value to a variable that points to a list, that variable gets a pointer to a new location. The list it used to point to will not be modified; therefore, any other variables that point to the original list will be unaffected.

```
set a to [1,2,3}
set b to a
set a to [9,10,11]
put b
-- [1,2,3]
```

To make the mailbox analogy a bit more accurate, think of the mailboxes as containing keys to a P.O. box. You can make as many copies of the key as you like, but when you open that P.O. box with any of those keys, you always get the same contents.

As mentioned earlier, a list can contain references to other lists. Think of that reference as a key to a P.O. box that has another key inside. It doesn't matter how many layers of keys you have. They lead to only one P.O. box.

This can be useful. Imagine you have all sorts of calculations that depend on the same tax rate, and suddenly the IRS decides to change that rate. You need to change that rate only once, and all calculations update.

This can also be a problem. There may be situations where you want to make a copy of a list and modify that copy without modifying the original. Many different approaches can solve this problem. One elegant one comes from fellow Director expert Gretchen Macdowall:

```
set newList to value(string(oldList))
```

This takes list `oldList` and converts it to the string equivalent, and then turns that string back into a value. The reason this works is that when you convert the contents of a list to a string, Lingo creates a new entity that no longer refers to the original memory locations. You must turn it back into a value to use it as a list and not a string.

> **Note**
> Director 5 includes a new command to duplicate lists. Appropriately enough, it's called `duplicate()`. Here is the syntax:
> ```
> set listB to duplicate(listA)
> ```

The power of lists lies in the many ways you can access and modify the information they contain. Lingo has several commands and functions that serve this goal. Although these commands and functions are explained in the *Lingo Dictionary*, most would benefit from further explanation.

add(list,value)

This command adds the specified value to a linear list. If the list is sorted, the value is placed in the proper position. If the list is not sorted, it is placed at the end.

> **Note**
> Lists that are sorted perform faster according to JT, the creator of Lingo.

```
set gMyList to [1,5,9]
add(gMyList,3)
put gMyList
--[1,5,9,3]
set gMyList to [1,5,9]
sort(gMyList)
```

```
add(gMyList,3)
put gMyList
--[1,3,5,9]
```

addAt(list,position,value)

This command adds the specified value at the specified position of the list.
This command should perhaps be called insertAt because that's what it does.

```
set gMyList to [1,2,3,5,6,7,8]
addAt(gMyList,4,4)
put gMyList
--[1,2,3,4,5,6,7,8]
```

If you use addAt with a position beyond the range of the list, Lingo fills in the in-
between spaces with zeros.

```
set gMyList =[]
addAt (gMyList,4,4)
put gMyList
--[0,0,0,4]
```

addProp(list,property,value)

The addProp() command adds the specified property with the specified value to
the specified property list. If the list is sorted, the value gets added on the
corresponding position. If the list is not sorted, it is placed at the end.

```
set gMyList to [#peter:3,#paul:8]
addProp (gMyList,#mary,5)
put gMyList
--[#peter:3,#paul:8,#mary:5]
set gMyList to [#peter:3,#paul:8]
sort(gMyList)
addProp (gMyList,#mary,5)
put gMyList
--[#peter:3,#mary:5,#paul:8]
```

If an instance of the property is already there, Director creates a duplicate
entry. Avoid this by using the setaProp() command.

append(list,value)

This command adds the specified value at the end of the specified list, even if
the list is sorted.

```
set gMyList to [1,4,6,8]
  sort gMyList
append(gMyList,2)
put gMyList
-- [1,4,6,8,2]
```

After you execute an `append()` command, a sorted list loses its sorted attributes. Any values that you add afterward will not be sorted.

You can re-sort the list including the value added with `append()` by issuing another `sort()` command.

count(list)

The `count()` command returns the number of items on the specified list.

```
set gMyList to [1,4,66,77,12,127]
put count(gMyList)
--6
```

`count()` is a useful function. You will see it quite often on the real-world examples.

deleteAt(list,position)

This command deletes the item at the specified position of the specified list.

```
set gMyList to [5,6,7]
deleteAt(gMyList,2)
put gMyList
-- [5,7]
```

deleteOne(list,value)

This command deletes an item of the specified value from a list. On a property list, the item with the specified property value gets deleted. If the value is present, `deleteOne()` returns a value of 1. If the value is not present, `deleteOne()` returns a value of 0.

```
set gMyList to [5,6,7]
deleteOne(gMyList,6)
put gMyList
-- [5,7]
```

deleteProp(list,property)

The `deleteProp()` command deletes the item with the specified property from the specified list. If more than one instance of the property exists, only the first one is deleted.

```
set gMyList to [#peter:5,#paul:6,#mary:7]
deleteProp(gMyList,#paul)
put gMyList
-- [#peter:5,#mary:7]
```

If you try to delete a property that does not exist, `deleteProp` returns a value of 0. Otherwise, it returns a value of 1. Return values like this are more useful than they appear at first glance. If you have people on your list, for example, and you have a function to delete them, you can use the returned value to implement a feedback routine that tells the user whether the name was deleted or whether there was nothing to delete.

findPos(list,property)

This function returns the position of the specified property on the specified list. If the property cannot be found, `findPos()` returns a <VOID> value.

```
set gMyList to [#peter:1,#paul:1,#mary:1]
put findPos(gMyList,#paul)
-- 2
```

findPosNear(list,property)

The `findPosNear()` command attempts to find the position of the specified property on the specified list. If an exact match isn't there, `findPos` then finds the closest position available on the list.

```
set gMyList to [#peter:1,#paul:1,#mary:1]
put findPosNear(gMyList,#mark)
-- #mary
```

For this function to be of any use, you must use it on a sorted property list. Otherwise, if no exact match for the specified property exists, you get the last position of the unsorted list.

getaProp(list,value)

The getaProp() command returns the value of the specified property on a list. This is a sister function to getProp(). They are used the same way. If you try to look up a property that does not exist, getaProp returns a <VOID> value. If you attempt to do this with getProp(), you get an error message and your movie will stop.

You can use the returned value to check for an instance of a property. Here is a sample script:

```
on startMovie
    global gMyList
    set gMyList to [#property1:5,#property2:20,#property3:3]
end
on amIaMember myName
    global gMyList
    set areYouThere to getaProp(gMylist,myName)
    if not voidP(areYouThere) then
        put "I am a member of the list!"
    else
        put "I am not a member of the list!"
    end if
end
```

You can then execute the handler from the message window:

```
amIaMember(#property1)
--I am a member of the list!
amIaMember(#barney5)
--I am not a member of the list::
```

getAt(list, position)

This function returns the value on the *list* located at the position indicated by *value*. For example:

```
set gMyList to [2,5,6,7]
put getAt(myList,2)
--5
```

The returned value is 5 because it occupies the second position on the list. If you try to fetch a value at a position that does not exist, you get an error message. You can use the count() function to avoid this type of error.

```
on startMovie
    global gMyList
    set gMyList to [3,67,3,45,12,5,98]
end
on lookUpPosition whichPosition
    global gMyList
    if whichPosition > count (gMyList) then
        put "Oops! you asked for position " & whichPosition &¬
        " but there are only " & count(gMyList) & " positions! Try ¬
        again."
    Else
        put "The value at position " & whichPosition & " is " &
        getAt(gMyList,whichPosition)
    end if
end
```

The following is the result when you try it out on the message window:

```
lookupposition(2)
-- "The value at position 2 is 67"
lookupposition(9)
-- "Oops! you asked for position 9 but there are only
7 positions! Try again."
```

getLast(list)

This function returns the last value on a list.

```
set gMyList to [1,6,7,4,3,7]
put getLast(myList)
-- 7
```

getOne(list,value)

When used on a linear list, this function returns the position of the given value on the list. If the value is not present on the list, it returns a 0. If there is more than one instance of the value, it returns the position of the first instance of the value.

```
set gMyList to [3,67,3,45,12,5,98]
put getOne(gMyList,45)
-- 4
put getOne(gMyList,100)
```

```
-- 0
put getOne(gMyList,3)
-- 1
```

Note that on the last put statement, the result was 1 when looking for value 3. Even though value 3 was also a position 3, Lingo found it first on position 1 and returned that result.

If you use getOne on a property list, the result is the property at that position (not the position of the value). For example:

```
set gMyList to [#property1:5,#property2:20,#property3:3]
put getOne(gMylist,20)
--#property2
```

To obtain the position of the value on a property list, use the getPos() function.

getPos(list,value)

When used on a linear list, getPos() performs the same function as getOne. When used with a property list, getPos() returns the position of the value within the list.

```
set gMyList to [#property1:5,#property2:20,#property3:3]
put getPos(gMylist,20)
--2
```

When the specified value is not part of the list, getPos() returns a 0. When a value has more than one instance, getPos() returns the position of the first instance on the list.

getProp(list,property)

The getProp() command returns the value of the specified property on a list.

```
set gMyList to [#property1:5,#property2:20,#property3:3]
put getProp(gMylist,#property2)
--20
```

getProp has a sister function called getaProp(). They perform the same function. The difference is that with getProp(), you produce an error message if you try to look up a property that does not exist. getaProp does not produce an error message.

getPropAt(list,position)

This function returns the property name at the specified position.

```
set gMyList to [#property1:5,#property2:20,#property3:3]
put getPropAt(gMyList,2)
--#property2
```

If the specified position is higher than the amount of items, Lingo generates an error message.

max(list)

The max() command returns the highest value on a list.

```
set gMyList to [9,1,4,6,25,7]
put max(gMyList)
--25
```

min(list)

The min() command is the opposite of max(). It returns the lowest value on a list.

```
set gMyList to [9,1,4,6,25,7]
put min(gMyList)
--1
```

repeat with variable in list

Although repeat is not a list-specific command, this version is. The difference lies with the in word. When issued, this command steps through every value on a list and assigns that value to the specified variable.

```
on beatleThing
    set gMyList to ["John","Paul","George","Ringo"]
    repeat with beatle in gMyList
            put beatle & " was a Beatle"
    end repeat
end
```

Here is the output if we call the beatleThing handler from the message window:

```
beatleThing
-- "John was a Beatle
```

```
-- "Paul was a Beatle
-- "George was a Beatle"
-- "Ringo was a Beatle"
```

This is far more elegant than creating an extra variable to use as an incremental pointer, but it has a drawback: If you delete an item from the list while it is executing, you get an error message.

setaProp(list,property,value)

This command replaces the value of the specified property on the specified list with the new specified value. If the property does not exist, Lingo creates a new instance and assigns it the specified value.

```
set gMyList to [#property1:5,#property2:20,#property3:3]
put gMyList
-- [#property1:5,#property2:20,#property3:3]
setaProp(gMylist,#property2,89)
put gMyList
-- [#property1:5,#property2:89,#property3:3]
```

In the preceding example, Lingo changes the value of property #property2 from 20 to 89.

```
set gMyList to [#property1:5,#property2:20]
put gMyList
-- [#property1:5,#property2:20]
setaProp(gMylist,#property3,3)
put gMyList
-- [#property1:5,#property2:20,#property3:3]
```

In the preceding example, Lingo did not find an entry for property #property3, so it created a new instance of it.

setAt(list,postition,value)

This command replaces the value at the specified position with the new specified value. If you exceed the number of items on a linear list, Lingo extends the list to the indicated position and fills in the extra positions with zeroes. On a property list, exceeding the number of items produces an error message.

```
set gMyList to [4,77,3,5]
setAt gMylist(a,2,-50)
put gMyList
```

```
-- [4,-50,3,5]
setAt gMylist(a,8,5)
put gMyList
-- [4,-50,3,5,0,0,0,5]
```

Note that in the last command, Lingo filled in the new spaces with zeros.

setProp(list,property,value)

The setProp() command replaces the value of the specified property on the specified list with the specified value.

> **Note**
> setProp() is identical to setaProp() except setProp() produces an error message if the property does not exist. setaProp returns a value of 0 if the property does not exist; otherwise, it returns a value of 1.

This may be useful for debugging. If your program has to set the specified property to work correctly, you may want to be alerted by Director if that property could not be set.

sort(list)

This command sorts a list in ascending order. Linear lists get sorted by value, and property lists get sorted alphabetically by property.

```
set gMyList to [5,4,1,3,2]
sort(gMyList)
put gMyList
-- [1,2,3,4,5]
set gMyList to [#charles:4,#brian:4,#ann:4,#david:4]
sort gMyList
put gMyList
-- [#ann:4,#brian:4,#charles:4,#david:4]
```

After a list is sorted, it remains that way even after you add items to it. The only exception is if you use the append() command.

the property of propertyList

The the keyword is an alternative way to fetch and set property values on a property list. It makes for more readable code.

```
set moe to [#mood:"angry",#stoogeClass:"leader",#haircut:"goofy"]
put the mood of moe
-- "angry"
put the stoogeClass of moe
-- "leader"
put the haircut of moe
--" goofy"
```

You can also set values:

```
set moe to [#mood:"angry",#stoogeClass:"leader",#haircut:"goofy"]
set the mood of moe to "happy"
put moe
-- [#mood:"happy",#stoogeClass:"leader",#haircut:"goofy"]
```

To use the the function, your list has to be declared as global.

Real-World Examples of Lists

The following examples show lists in action. Feel free to experiment with the sample code after you are finished with the chapter.

Using a List to Animate a Sprite

A simple use for a linear list is to step animate a sprite. You can create a list that has all the cast numbers for a step animation. You can then implement a pointer that fetches each value in order and assigns it to your sprite.

Open the movie BABY.DIR found on the web site.

The sample movie BABY.DIR animates a baby taking three steps. The cast members can reside anywhere as long as they are called "step1", "step2", and "step3" respectively.

The movie script follows:

```
on initVariables
    global gMyListPointer, gBabySteps
    set gMyListPointer to 1
    set gBabySteps to [the number of cast "step1", the number of cast ¬
    "step2", the number of cast "step3")
end
```

```
on animateBaby
    global myListPointer
    set targetCast to getAt(gBabySteps,gMyListPointer)
    set the castnum of sprite 1 to targetCast
    updateStage
    set gMyListPointer to gMyListPointer + 1
    if myListPointer > count(gBabySteps) then set myListPointer to 1
end
```

Figure 14.1

BABY.DIR uses a list to control the animation of the baby.

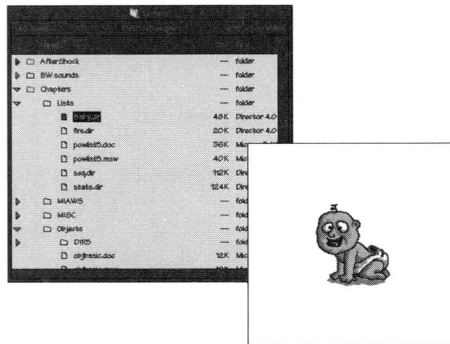

The `initVariables` handler initializes two global variables: `gMylistPointer` and `gBabySteps`.

```
set gMyListPointer to 1
set gBabySteps to [the number of cast "step1", the number of cast
"step2", the number of cast "step3")
```

The `gMyListPointer` numeric variable is increased every time you move a step ahead on the animation, and it points at one of the values in `gBabySteps`. The `gBabySteps` variable contains the cast numbers of all the frames of the animation. Note that when you defined `gBabySteps`, you did not enter the actual numbers but instead had Director look them up by name. The advantage to this approach is that you can rearrange the cast members and Director can still find them. Looking up cast members by name is much slower than looking them up by number, but in this case, you get their number at the start of the movie. From that point on, they are actually stored as numbers on the list. With this approach, you have both the convenience of name lookups and the speed of number lookups.

The next handler, `animateBaby`, is where the actual work gets done.

1. First, fetch the value that equates to the current value of `gMyListPointer` from `gBabySteps`, and assign it to the local variable `targetCast`.

   ```
   set targetCast to getAt(gBabySteps,gMyListPointer)
   ```

2. Assign that cast member to the baby sprite, and update the stage.

   ```
   set the castnum of sprite 1 to targetCast

   updateStage
   ```

3. Next, increment the pointer so that next time around it points to the corresponding cast member.

   ```
   set gMyListPointer to gMyListPointer + 1
   ```

4. After incrementing, check that the pointer has not exceeded the number of items on `gBabySteps`. If it has, reset it to 1 so that the cycle can begin again.

   ```
   if myListPointer > count(gBabySteps) then set myListPointer to 1
   ```

If the pointer exceeds the number of items on `gBabySteps`, an error message appears when you try to retrieve item 5 from a list that has only four items. A hidden advantage to this method is that it enables more flexibility. You finish your animation, for example, and decide you need to add more frames to the animation to make it look smoother. All you need to do is add those extra cast numbers to the declaration of `gBabySteps`. Everything else adapts accordingly.

If you decide to have different moods for the baby, you can make a series of lists for the animation sequence of each mood. When you want to change the mood, just replace the values of `gBabySteps` with the ones on those lists.

A simple repeat loop used to accomplish this is not so simple. The biggest problem with a repeat loop is that it eats up the processing time, and the computer cannot do anything while it executes. If you want to have anything else animate at the same time, it must wait for the animation cycle to complete before proceeding. With this approach, you can call `animateBaby` anytime you want (possibly from the `on idle` handler) and it animates exactly one frame when called up, thereby enabling the computer to move on to other things.

Using a List to Record a Sequence of Events

Sometimes it is necessary to record a sequence of events for playback or just to keep a record of usage. You might want to record all the screens a user navigates so that he can trace his way back, for example, or you might want to record how many times each button is clicked. These are perfect uses for lists.

Follow the example of recording the navigated screens to enable the user to backtrack his progress. An easy way to implement this is by creating a "Stack." This stack holds the number of each new frame the user goes to and accumulates each number on top of each other. If the user wants to step back a frame, just look up the number at the top of the stack, go there, and delete it from the stack. Instead of a stack, you could also choose not to delete that number and use a pointer instead; that way the user can also go back to the turning point. You could also have a stack for each new user and keep a record of how people use the program. The program could save the results to a text file, and this data could later be used for statistics.

Open the movie RECFRAME.DIR found on the web site.

FIGURE 14.2

RECFRAME.DIR in action.

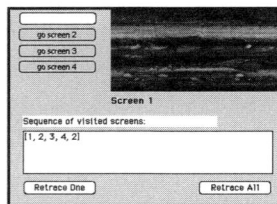

Try going to several frames and then retracing by one frame using the RetraceAll button.

Did you ever imagine you would have so much fun with this book?

Here is the movie script with the comments removed:

```
on startMovie
    global gFrameSequence
    set gFrameSequence to []
    put gFrameSequence into field "sequence"
end
on recordFrame
    global gFrameSequence
    add(gFrameSequence, the frame)
```

```
        put gFrameSequence into field "sequence"
    end
    on retraceOne
        global gFrameSequence
        if count(gFrameSequence) then
            go getLast(gFramesequence)
            deleteAt(gFrameSequence,count(gFrameSequence))
            put gFrameSequence into field "sequence"
        end if
    end
    on retraceAll
        global gFrameSequence
        if count(gFrameSequence) then
            set howMany to count(gFrameSequence)
            repeat with loop=1 to howMany
                retraceOne
            end repeat
        end if
    end
```

The startMovie handler sets up an empty list variable and updates the screen.

The recordFrame handler is called up by each button when a legal mouseUp is present (the cursor was over the button when the button was released). It adds the present frame to the stack and updates the screen.

retraceOne is called when there is a legal mouseUp on the Retrace One button or by the retraceAll handler. First, it checks if any numbers are on the stack to retrace. If none, it does nothing. If a number is there (or numbers), it makes the playback head jump to that frame. Next, it deletes that number. To do this, first find out the count of items and then use the result with deleteAt to delete that item from the list. You cannot use deleteOne() because it is possible to have more than one entry for a frame. deleteOne would delete the first instance of a value and that would mess up the stack. Finally, the screen is updated.

retraceAll is called when a legal mouseUp is on the retraceOne button. First, it checks if any numbers are on the stack to retrace. If none, it does nothing. If a number (or numbers) is there, it sets a local variable to the total of items and then calls up retraceOne that number of times. The result is the same as if the user clicked on the retraceOne button repeatedly. It is comparable to having a robot perform a boring repetitive task.

This simple example can be modified to do all sorts of neat things with lists. You can set up a property list with a property for each frame that would record how long a user stays on a frame. It could also keep a property list that records how many times the user went to a frame. The possibilities are endless.

Using a List to Detect Collisions

You might want to write a space game where you have to shoot at some aliens. At some point, you must figure out if a collision has occurred between the aliens and the missile. The hard way of doing this is to define an if-then statement for each alien. Something like the following may work:

```
if sprite myMissile intersects sprite 5 then doBoom
if sprite myMissile intersects sprite 7 doBoom
if sprite myMissile intersects sprite 9 then doBoom
if sprite myMissile intersects sprite 23 then doBoom
if sprite myMissile intersects sprite 56 then doBoom
```

To do it more easily, use a list.

The first step is to define the alien sprites list that holds the sprite number for each alien:

```
set myAlienSpritesList to [5,7,9,23,56]
```

After the list is defined, you can use a simple repeat loop to check for a collision:

```
repeat with value in AlienSpritesList
if sprite myMissile intersects value then doBoom
End repeat
```

This approach has more than one advantage over the multiple if-then method. If you decide to add more aliens to your game now, all you need to do is add the extra sprite number to the list. It is automatically checked for a collision. If you decide to change the position of one or more of the alien sprites, all you need to do is change the number entry on the list one time.

Open the movie FIRE.DIR found on the web site.

The movie FIRE.DIR shows a sample of this technique. You are more than welcome to look at and experiment with the extra Lingo found here, but it is the Lingo in cast member 1 that pertains to this discussion.

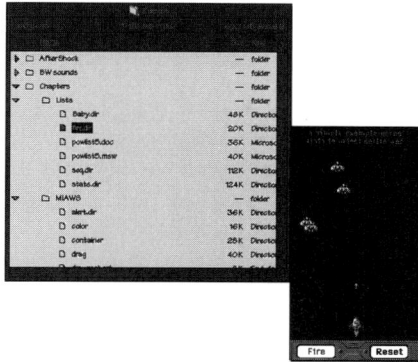

FIGURE 14.3

*FIRE.DIR in
action.*

```
on setInvaderList
    global gCollisionList
    set gCollisionList to [4,5,6,7]
end
on idle
    animateSprites
    checkHit
    updateStage
end
on checkHit
    global gCollisionList
    if count(gCollisionList) then
        repeat with value in gCollisionList
            if sprite 20 intersects value then killInvader(value)
        end repeat
    end if
end
```

Break it down:

```
set gCollisionList to [4,5,6,7]
```

The `setInvaderList` handler is called by the `startMovie` handler. It declares a
global variable and assigns a list of sprites that are checked for a collision.
(You can add more numbers to this list as long as you don't go higher than
nineteen. Try it out!)

```
animateSprites
checkHit
updateStage
```

The idle handler calls a handler called animateSprites that resides elsewhere in the movie. Next, it calls the checkHit handler and updates the Stage.

```
if count(gCollisionList) then
    repeat with value in gCollisionList
        if sprite 20 intersects value then killInvader(value)
    end repeat
end if
```

The checkHit handler first checks to see if any items are on the collisionList. If there are, the checkHit handler does a loop one time for every item on the list. The loop checks if sprite 20 (the missile) is colliding with any of the sprites on the list. If a collision exists, the loop kills the sprite by calling the killInvader handler (that resides elsewhere in the movie).

Conclusion

Lists are an efficient way to store and process a group of values. You have learned that there are two types of lists: linear and property. You have also learned the syntax necessary to create, access, and modify scripts. After having gone through the examples in this chapter, you should have a very good grasp on how to implement this powerful tool into your Director projects.

chapter 15

Raúl Silva

MOVIES IN A WINDOW

At their simplest, movies in a window (affectionately known as MIAWs) enable you to play a movie within a separate window (hence the name) while your main movie in the stage is still playing. If you have made several Director movies, for example, and you want to make an interactive portfolio, you can make a portfolio movie that plays all your movies within a frame. Movies in a window perform the same way as regular movies.

More creative uses exist for MIAWs. You can make a MIAW to control the playback of a QuickTime movie. A MIAW can be used as a control panel to control system settings such as volume and color depth. Other possible uses include dialog boxes, status displays, and note pads.

This chapter shows you all the necessary steps to implement MIAWs on your own presentations as well as the syntax for working with them.

How Do I Use MIAWs?

Like most anything else in Director, planning ahead on how and when to use MIAWs on your project helps a lot toward a timely and successful implementation. First, ask yourself what it is that you want to display in that MIAW. Do you want to enable the user to move the window around the screen? Will you enable the user to dismiss the MIAW at will? Do you want your MIAW to blend with the other elements on your movie?

After you have decided the exact behavior and function of your MIAW, you can sit down and actually code it.

A MIAW can be opened with a command as simple as `open window "myFile.dir"`. This approach, at times, may be all you need. Director has predefined defaults that apply to the window automatically.

In most cases, it is better to define most aspects of your window before you actually open it. Lingo has many window properties to do this, and the next section of this chapter covers most of them. If you are not familiar with them, go there now. If you are familiar with them, go there anyway. You may find something that you did not know.

Okay! You're back.

MIAWs are not really objects in the strict sense but they can be treated as objects in several cases. Objects can store data and so can MIAWs. When a variable is used to hold a reference to the information the MIAW contains, the variable becomes the object that refers to the real data stored within the MIAW. For ease of use, storing a MIAW within a global is encouraged. Otherwise, they can be hard to find when you want to dispose of them and gain back some memory.

Here is a sample window declaration:

```
on openMyWindow gMyWindow
    set gMyWindow to window "myFile"
    set the title of gMyWindow to "This is my window"
    set the windowType of gMyWindow to 5
    open gMyWindow
end
```

You may have noticed that after assigning the window object to a global variable you no longer use the window keyword when addressing any of the window's properties. You can still use the window keyword, but you need to refer to the window by name and not by object.

```
set gMyWindow to window "myFile.dir"
set the windowType of a to 5
set the windowType of window "myFile" to 5
```

In the preceding example, both calls to the windowType property are legal. If you try to access a window property by object and use the window keyword, you get an error message. If you try to access a window property by name and do not use the window keyword, you also get an error message. You can, at any point, look up the names of all the active windows by using the windowList property.

```
put the windowList
--(window "myFile.dir", window "yourFile.dir")
```

MIAW Syntax

Following is a description of the syntax to work with MIAWs. Some of these commands have changed in Director 5. When a change has occurred it will be indicated. The old syntax was used because it works with both Director 4 and 5.

close window windowID

The close window command closes the specified window ID. The ID can be a given name or the window's number.

```
close window "myFile.dir"
```

When you use the close window command, it is the same as setting the visible property of a window to zero. The window remains active and responds to events. It's just not visible.

the drawRect of window windowID

the drawRect property determines the rectangular coordinates of a MIAW. The coordinates are specified using a Rect data type (top, left, right, bottom).

```
set the drawRect of window "myFile.dir" to rect(0,0,160,120)
```

Think of the drawRect as a rectangular porthole that defines the area where objects can be drawn in your window. It is usually the same as the rect of the window or less if you only want to draw to a small area of your window. Depending on the size of the cutout and the size of the photo, you may be able to see only portions or the entire photograph through the cutout on the screen.

FIGURE 15.1

You can picture the drawRect of a window as a cutout on the screen.

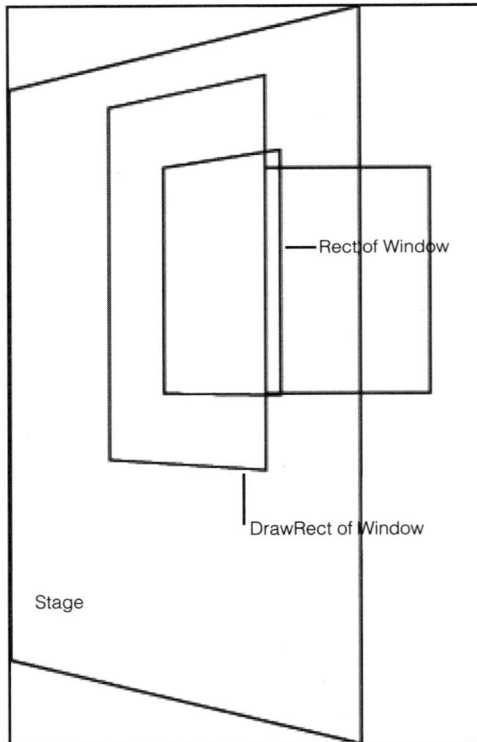

Rect of Window

DrawRect of Window

Stage

This property is useful if you want to make a portfolio movie with other full screen Director movies you made as MIAWs. This property enables you to scale your movies to fit within a full screen portfolio movie. Another use is to have a scrolling map in a MIAW.

When you do not specify the drawRect of a MIAW, Director makes it the same size as the stage size of the file you are opening and flushes it to the top left corner of the window.

the fileName of window windowID

the filename of window property determines the file name of the Director movie assigned to the specified window. Director looks for the file in the same folder as the main movie. If Director cannot find the file, the user sees the prompt "Where is file". To avoid this, you can define the exact path name for the file. Usually you will want to use the path name function to define your path.

```
set the filename of window gMyWindow to the pathname & "myFile.dir"
```

Director also prompts the user if it cannot find a file with the exact specified name. Keep this in mind, especially if you are authoring on a Mac and plan to have your title run on a PC.

Director names your window the same as the indicated file name.

forget window windowID

This command closes and deletes the window from memory. This command differs from close in that it not only hides the widow, but also disposes of it and frees the memory taken up by the window.

```
forget window "myFile.dir"
```

the modal of window windowID

This property determines whether this window, when active, will enable Lingo to process events that happen outside the window (the stage or any other window). This property can be either TRUE or FALSE. A value of TRUE means that only that window responds to events. A value of FALSE means that any other windows also process events.

```
set the modal of window "myAlert.dir" to 1
```

The best use for this property is to create custom dialog boxes on which the user is required to enter some information before proceeding. A good example of a modal dialog box is the Movie Info window in Director.

moveToBack window windowID

The moveToBack command places the specified window behind all other windows.

```
moveToBack window "myFile.dir"
```

moveToFront window windowID

The moveToFront command places the specified window in front of all other windows.

```
moveToFront window "MyFile.dir"
```

openWindow windowID

This command opens a MIAW. You should first define the file name of the window using the fileName of window property. You can, however, just specify the exact file name as the window ID. As long as the file is in the current directory, the window opens just fine. If the movie is not in the current directory, you receive a prompt with a dialog box to look for it.

```
open window "myFile.dir"
set the filename of gMyWindow to "myFile.dir"
open gMyWindow
```

The openWindow command can also be used to show a window that has been hidden with either the close window command or the visible of window property.

the rect of window windowID

This property determines the coordinates of the MIAW on-screen. Note that these coordinates are based on the screen, not the stage. If your stage is smaller than your screen (or the Director task window on Windows), you may get unexpected results. You need to do some math based on the rect of the stage if you want to position your window based on the stage coordinates. The most common way to do this is to find out the top and left coordinates of the stage, and then add those amounts to the position you would like to occupy on the stage.

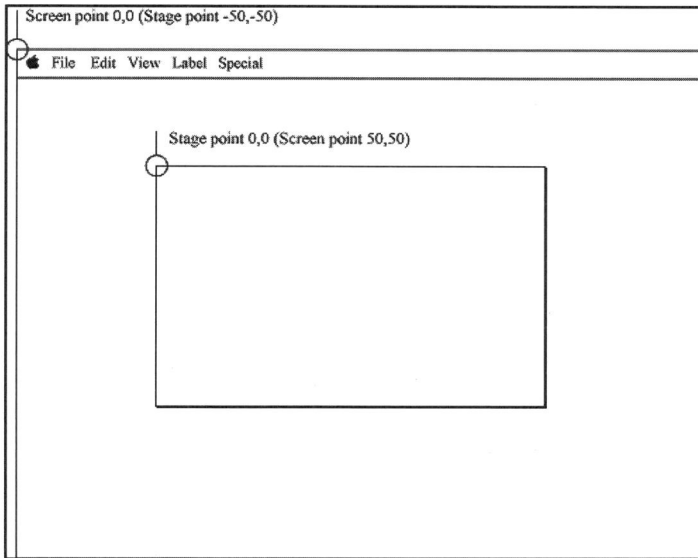

FIGURE 15.2

Stage coordinates and screen coordinates are different. In this case stage point 0,0 corresponds to screen point 50,50.

When you specify the rect of a MIAW, you are specifying the dimensions and location of the container. To change the contents, you need to use the drawRect of window property.

```
tell window windowID to statement
tell window windowID
     statement(s)
end tell
```

The tell command sends the specified statement or statements to the specified window. Not only is this command useful, but it also makes for readable and clear code.

```
tell window "myFile.dir" to beep 2
tell the stage to doMyHandler
```

In the second line of the preceding example, the system property the stage is used to send a message from a window to the stage. This two-way communication is essential to functional MIAWs.

If you look at the syntax, you see two ways to compose a `tell` command. You can either send a single command or many (as long as you enclose them between the `tell` and `end tell` commands).

the title of window windowID

This property specifies the title of the specified window.

```
set the title of window "myFile.dir" to "This is my window"
```

Please note that the title of a window is independent from the name of a window. The title is visible only on those window types that have a title bar.

the titleVisible of window windowID

This property determines whether there is a visible title bar on the window.

```
set the titleVisible of window "myFile.dir" to 1
```

the visible of window windowID

This property determines whether a window is visible or not.

```
set the visible of window "myFile.dir" to 0
```

Setting this property to 0 is the same as using the `close window` command. The window remains active and responds to events but is not visible.

the windowList

This property holds a list of all the active movie windows.

```
put the windowList
--(window "myFile.dir", window "yourFile.dir")
```

the windowType of window windowID

This `window` property determines the style of the window. Eight basic `windowTypes` exist plus one floating palette (49).

```
set the windowType of window "myFile.dir" to 1
```

Refer to your *Lingo Dictionary* for a full list of available styles.

Other undocumented types exist, but these only seem to work on the Mac and may not work in future versions of Director. Try them at your own risk!

More About MIAWs

MIAWs are self-contained movies running in a child window of the stage and remain active even when you go to another movie. They will be automatically disposed of when the main window, the stage, is disposed of. This happens on a quit.

If you create a Tool window to be used during authoring, you should remember to set the exitLock property to TRUE on your MIAW file. If you don't, the movie will stop executing if you or another user types command-period. If you notice that your tool MIAWs mysteriously stop playing, check this first.

Global variables are shared by the Stage and all windows. This can be a great thing, or it can be a disaster if you are not careful. A possible disaster scenario is where you build a great tool MIAW that gives you all sorts of information about your movies (such as keeping track of all your scripts and sprites). What happens if the movie you are working on issues a clearGlobals command? You guessed it. Suddenly your tool MIAW is left in a state of limbo. Another potential disaster is giving your MIAW global variables that the user is likely to use during authoring, something like gActiveSprites. Different approaches have been used to try to solve this kind of problem. You could, for example, use very unusual global variable names for your MIAWs, or you can store values on text cast members.

Whenever you need to have a MIAW talk to another MIAW, the best approach is to use the stage as a mediator. In other words, tell the stage to tell something to the other MIAW.

Problems with MIAWs

As handy as they are, MIAWs do have some problems. Trying to play simultaneous sounds on different windows is asking for trouble. If you must, play each sound in a different sound channel. If you program a MIAW to control some elements of your main movie, be careful on how you code it. You don't want your MIAW taking up too many resources and slowing down your main movie.

Version 4 of Director did not enable you to play protected movies as MIAWs. This deterred many people from releasing some very good tool MIAWs for fear of having their code completely available to anyone who may have wanted to unfairly appropriate it. Director 5 fixes this problem.

Shockwave does not support MIAWs. According to Macromedia, this is because of limitations of Microsoft Windows and not Director. Macromedia hopes to implement MIAWS for Shockwave in the future.

Real-World MIAW

Following are a few examples of Director movies that use MIAWs. After finishing the chapter feel free to experiment with them.

Making a Portfolio-Style Container Movie

What if you have a few Director movies that you would like to compile within a portfolio with a common interface? MIAWs are just what you need.

Take a moment to look at the movie CONTAINER.DIR on the web site.

This is a simple example of a container movie. You can select from three movies to play in the small window on the side. All three choices are actually 640×480 movies that have been resized to fit into that small square.

You should be able to use most of this code on your own projects. The following code is the complete movie script (comments have been removed).

```
on bringUpMyWindow file
    placeMovie (the pathname & file,199,40,160,120)
end

on placeMovie¬
myFilename,myHorizontalLocation,myVerticalLocation,myWidth,myHeight
    global gMyMiaw
    if objectP(gMyMiaw) then
        forget gMyMiaw
    end if
    set gMyMiaw to window myFilename
    set movieRect to rect(0,0,myWidth,myHeight)
    set the drawRect of window myFilename to movieRect
    set the rect of window myFilename to
    movieLocation(myHorizontalLocation,myVerticalLocation,movieRect)
```

```
        set the windowType of window myFilename to 2
        open window myFilename
end

on movieLocation hposition, vposition, movieRect
        set hlocation to the stageleft + hposition
        set vlocation to the stageTop + vposition
        return rect(hlocation,vlocation,hlocation,vlocation) + movieRect
end

on killMyWindow
        global gMyMiaw
        if objectP(gMyMiaw) then
                forget gMyMiaw
        end if
end

on stopMovie
        killMyWindow
end
```

The first handler bringUpMyWindow is called each time you click on one of the
movie buttons. Here is the score script for one of the buttons:

```
on mouseUp
        bringUpMyWindow ("threed.dir")
end
```

bringUpMyWindow takes only one parameter, the MIAW file name.

```
on bringUpMyWindow file
        placeMovie (the pathname & file,199,40,160,120)
end
```

bringUpMyWindow has only one line of code, a call to the placeMovie handler.
This handler, however, takes five parameters: the file name (passed by
bringUpMyWindow), the draw width of the MIAW, the draw height of the MIAW,
the horizontal location (relative to the stage) of the MIAW, and the vertical
location (relative to the stage) of the MIAW. It is useful to have this handler
here because it provides a clear and convenient place to change the size and
location of the MIAW. If you prefer, you could even call placeMovie directly as
long as you provide all the required parameters.

The `placeMovie` handler is considerably more complex.

```
on placeMovie¬
myFilename,myHorizontalLocation,myVerticalLocation,myWidth,myHeight
```

1. First, declare a global to house the pointer to the MIAW

```
global gMyMiaw.
```

2. Next, check if an instance of the `gMyMiaw` already exists. If it does, dispose of it.

```
if objectP(gMyMiaw) then
    forget gMyMiaw
end if
```

3. Next, assign a window object to the global variable. From this point on, you can refer to the MIAW by its global variable.

```
set gMyMiaw to window myFilename
```

4. Now, declare a global variable that puts the width and height values into a rect data type so that you can use it with the `DrawRect of window` property.

```
set movieRect to rect(0,0,myWidth,myHeight)
```

5. Then, assign that value to the drawRect of window property.

```
set the drawRect of window myFilename to movieRect
```

6. This line calls another handler called `movieLocation` and sets the rect of the MIAW to the result. (Please read the description of the `movieLocation` handler.)

```
set the rect of window myFilename to
movieLocation(myHorizontalLocation,myVerticalLocation,movieRect)
```

7. Set the window to be a borderless window.

```
set the windowType of window myFilename to 2
```

8. Finally, open the window.

```
open window myFilename
end
```

The `movieLocation` handler takes three parameters: the horizontal position of the MIAW, the vertical position of the MIAW, and the dimensions of the MIAW in a Rect format. This handler then uses the top and left coordinates of the stage to translate the MIAW coordinates to work as stage coordinates rather than screen coordinates. It does this by adding the horizontal position to the left coordinate of the stage and by adding the top position to the top coordinate of the stage. Finally, it adds the `movieRect` to include the size in the final result. The final result in the form of a Rect data type is returned.

```
on movieLocation hposition, vposition, movieRect
    set hlocation to the stageleft + hposition
    set vlocation to the stageTop + vposition
    return rect(hlocation,vlocation,hlocation,vlocation) + movieRect
end
```

`killMyWindow` is called when you want to dispose the MIAW. In this movie, it is called by the no movie button and by the `stopMovie` script.

```
on killMyWindow
    global gMyMiaw
    if objectP(gMyMiaw) then
        forget gMyMiaw
    end if
end
```

Whenever the movie stops, dispose the MIAW.

```
on stopMovie
    killMyWindow
end
```

Building a Simple Tool with a MIAW

Wouldn't it be nice if Director had an on-screen display of the mouse coordinates? (I used to type `put the mouseh` and `put the mousev` on the message window again and again.) Fortunately, MIAWs lend themselves perfectly to developing this kind of tool.

1. Open Director and make a new document. Now open your message window and type: **open window "mloc.dir"**.

2. You will probably be asked to locate the file MLOC.DIR. It is located on the web site. When you find it, click on OK.

3. Now move your mouse around the screen. Nifty!

The movie script for MLOC.DIR follows.

```
on startMovie
    set the exitLock to true
end

on exitFrame
    tell the stage
        set h to the mouseh
        set v to the mousev
    end tell
    put h into field 1
    put v into field 2
end
```

The `startMovie` handler sets the `exitLock` movie property to TRUE. If you don't set the `exitLock` to TRUE, the mouse locator stops working if you press Command+. (period) while it is in the foreground.

```
on startMovie
    set the exitLock to true
end
```

The `exitFrame` script tells the stage to set the local variables h and v to the `mouseh` and `mousev` respectively. Then, put these values into the two corresponding text fields.

That's it! A very simple but practical MIAW tool. Think of the possibilities. Lingo is a powerful language. Now with MIAWs, you can create all sorts of useful and clever utilities that take full advantage of Lingo.

Using MIAW for Custom Dialog Boxes

You probably know that Director enables you to bring up a very simple alert box by using the `alert` command. Unfortunately, the alert box is plain and limited. With MIAWs, you can make any dialog box that your heart desires.

Open the movie MODDEMO.DIR found on the web site.

The sample movie MODDEMO.DIR has a button that, when clicked, opens the ALERT.DIR MIAW that acts as a custom dialog box. It only has one button just like the one Director produces when you use the alert command, but this one is customized with a 3D look. You can modify this movie to show an about box or an alert screen, or you can add all the buttons and switches you want.

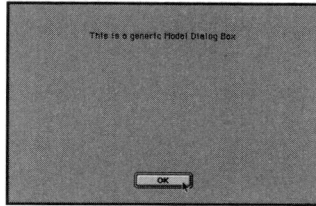

FIGURE 15.3

A simple Modal dialog box.

Because this is an alert box, you want to be certain that you set some necessary properties before you open the window. These are set by the MODDEMO.DIR movie. Here is the movie script.

```
on displayModalDialogBox
      set myDialogBox to window "alert"
      set the modal of myDialogBox to true
      set the windowType of myDialogBox to 2
      open myDialogBox
end
```

The displayModalDialogBox handler is called from the mouseDown score script of the Display Modal Dialog Box button. It first assigns the window object to the local variable myDialogBox. This is an exception to the rule about window objects being stored on globals. The reason this window is not put on a global is because it is a modal dialog box that will discard itself. Next, set a few properties like the modal to TRUE and the window type to 2 (a plain window). Finally, open the window.

Open the movie ALERT.DIR found on the web site.

The movie script for ALERT.DIR (the actual MIAW file) follows.

```
on okButtonDown
animateButton
      if rollOver (the clickon) then
            killMe
      end if
end
```

```
on animateButton
     set myCastNumber to the castnum of sprite the clickon
     repeat while the mouseDown
          if rollover( the clickon ) then
               set the castnum of sprite the clickon to myCastNumber + 1
          else
               set the castnum of sprite the clickon to myCastNumber
          end if
          updateStage
     end repeat
     set the castnum of sprite the clickon to myCastNumber
     updateStage
end

on keyDown
     if the key = RETURN then killMe
     if the key = ENTER then killMe
end

on killMe
     forget window "alert"
end
```

The okButtonDown handler is called by the mouseDown score script of the OK
button. The animate button handler is a standard button animation handler.
After the mouse is released, Lingo returns to the okButtonDown handler and
checks if the pointer is still over the button. If the pointer is indeed over the
button, it executes the killMe handler that, as you may have guessed, disposes
of the window. The keyDown handler serves as an alternative input method for
the user. The user can press either the Return on Enter key to dismiss the
dialog box.

Conclusion

This chapter taught you what you need to know to work with movies in a
window (MIAWs). MIAWs are great for modularizing large Director projects
and for providing custom tools, both for authoring and for final projects. You
learned that MIAWs can communicate with each other and with the stage and
stay active even between different movies.

This chapter explored possible uses for MIAWs as well as the procedure and
syntax to implement them. You learned about problems and limitations of MIAWs
and had the chance to look at sample code that implements them.

chapter 16

Raúl Silva

PARENT SCRIPTS AND CHILD OBJECTS

Objects are independent entities on Director. They can hold their own values and handlers. Objects get their own allocated position in memory and stay active as long as there is a reference to them, even between movies. Director enables you to define your own objects. Objects you define yourself are called code objects. For convenience, this chapter refers to code objects simply as objects from this point on.

Although custom objects are similar to other Director objects, custom objects have no initial properties or practical use. You have to explicitly define all aspects of your object. You can, for instance, change the name property of a MIAW because Director automatically defines the name property as a property for that window object. If you send a close command to the window object, it will automatically know what to do when it receives it. For your objects to have similar functionality, you must declare that your object will have a name property and what its initial value may be. You also must declare if it will respond to a close message, and exactly what it will do with it after it's received.

Why Objects?

Objects enable you to simplify your code. After you define an object, you can use it as many times as you want. If you want to change a small aspect of your project and that aspect is controlled by an object, you need to change only that object's script. Values within an object can be made to be specific to that object a concept known as *scoping*. Other objects can access these values by retrieving the specific property of the other object. This scoping further helps in the creation of objects that perform specific tasks because each object is basically a standalone entity.

Your kitchen, for example, is full of objects. If one day you decide to replace your single slice toaster with a deluxe model, all you need to do is plug in the new one. Everything else in your kitchen continues to work as usual because the toaster is an independent object. Now imagine a kitchen where all the appliances and the counter are made of just one piece. If one of the appliances breaks, or if you want to upgrade it, you will need to remove the whole kitchen counter along with all the appliances attached to it. It is clear that the object-based approach in kitchens is a desirable one. This concept applies to object-oriented programming. Your final program ends up being a collection of self-contained objects. They are easy to manage, replace, and modify.

Parent Scripts

Parent scripts are the blueprint for an object. Just like a real parent's genetic code describes the physical attributes and instincts of a child, a parent script describes the properties and behavior of an object. The parent script, however, is not an object; it is only used to define objects. The object is created from the script that defines it.

Parent scripts can be seen as recipes. They determine which ingredients will go into your dish and how to prepare it. After you have a recipe, you can make as many servings of the dish as you want.

Properties

Everything in life has properties. A child can be tall, intelligent, and have dark hair. Objects in Director also have properties, but, in your object scripts, you define what those properties will be. Although a real-life object may have millions of properties, objects in Director only have the properties necessary to do what you want them to do.

Properties can be seen as the ingredients for a recipe. A recipe can have as many ingredients as you want. Changing the quantity of each ingredient in the recipe affects how the final dish comes out. You can make two different dishes from the same recipe by changing the quantity of one or more ingredients. A soup can be salty or salt-free for those guests who are on a low sodium diet. You can eliminate the meat to please vegetarians. Your recipe can also include directions on how to proceed if you don't have a particular ingredient.

Properties in Lingo work in a very similar fashion. Every parent script has a list of properties and a group of instructions. You can set the values of your properties and have the outcome of an action be affected by those values. Properties cannot do anything but hold values; ingredients will do nothing but sit on the counter until you indicate what to do with them.

Handlers

Human genes not only determine physical properties but also determine certain instincts. Instincts are basic instructions for survival. A baby will instinctively cry when it is hungry and will instinctively try to suckle on anything that comes near its mouth. Objects in Director can also have instincts. In Director, these instincts or instructions are called *handlers*. Handlers determine how an object reacts to a message and what messages it reacts to.

Handlers are instructions that tell an object what to do when it receives a message. It is possible to have an object without handlers, but you need handlers if you want your object to do more than simply hold some values.

Messages

A human being is equipped with senses to receive a wide variety of messages. Humans can also send messages in a variety of ways. Likewise, objects can receive messages, as long as you describe which messages they can receive. Objects can also send messages to other objects, handlers, or to Director itself.

Messages make everything happen in Director. Without messages, everything would stand still. Messages are being sent in Director constantly. Every time you move the mouse or touch the keyboard a message is sent. Director sends many messages automatically. Most ready-made objects in Director know by default what messages they will respond to. Think of Director as a movie director (where did you think the name come from?) that is always with megaphone in hand yelling out messages. These messages travel from object to object waiting for someone to react to them. When an object has been instructed to respond to a message, it does what it is instructed to do. If an object has not been instructed to respond, it just passes the message along to the next object. This metaphor is key to understanding Director, and you will run into it time and time again.

Ancestry

A parent's genes are the combination of the grandparents' genes. Parent scripts in Director can have ancestors. Any properties and handlers that these ancestors have will automatically be available to any child of the parent script. This permits creating different objects that share common properties and common handlers. A parent script can also override an ancestor's properties or handlers. This way you can inherit only the properties and handlers you want in your object from its ancestor and customize the ones you want to be different.

Think of an ancestor script as a recipe within a recipe. An eggs benedict recipe, for example, tells you to make one cup of the hollandaise sauce recipe that resides somewhere else in the cookbook. The hollandaise sauce has its own ingredients and instructions. The eggs benedict recipe can also override some of the directions for the hollandaise sauce by instructing you to use, for example, two lemons instead of one in the hollandaise sauce.

How to Create a Parent Script

Parent scripts are usually defined in a separate movie script. Parent scripts need to be named because you will use the cast name when you want to create an object from them. It is a good idea to adopt a naming convention for your parent scripts. A common convention is to give them a single word name, separating the elements with capitalization. An example would be BirdBirthScript.

> This naming convention is known as *camel notation*. It is frequently used by programmers because it enables you to string a sequence of words into one. For some reason, this flowed over to many names of commercial products, mostly for the Mac platform. MacWrite, PowerPC, and PowerBook are all examples of camel notation.
>
> *Note*

Following is a sample parent script:

```
property pBirdType,  pColor
on birth me, birdType, color
     set pBirdTypeto birdType
     set pColor to color
     put "a bird of type: " & pBirdType & " and of: " & pColor & " color¬
is born!"
     return me
end
```

> Starting with Director 5 the keyword `birth` has been changed to `new`. We decided to use the `birth` keyword in this book because it works with both Director 4 and 5.
>
> *Note*

To make a parent script, you first need to define what properties it will have. To do this, just type the keyword **property** and a space, and then start typing your properties. If you have more than one, you need to separate them with commas (the same way you declare globals). It is a good idea to adopt a naming convention for properties so that you can tell them apart from other variables. A common convention is to start the name of any property with a lowercase *p*.

```
property pBirdType, pColor
```

The parent script then needs, at the very least, a specialized handler called `birth`. The `birth` handler needs, at the very least, the me parameter variable. You can append any other parameter variables you want. Separate any additional parameter variables with commas.

```
on birth me, birdType, color
```

In the body of the handler, you assign initial values to your properties. Do anything else you want to do when you create the object, and return the me variable, which holds a pointer to the newly birthed object. The me parameter is used to hold a pointer to an object whenever a handler within this script is called. This is how each handler is able to access the data associated with it.

```
set pBirdTypeto birdType
set pColor to color
put "a bird of type: " & pBirdType & " and of: " & pColor & " color is¬
born!"
return me
end
```

If you do not return the me variable and assign its value to a global variable, the object will cease to exist. Remember that objects exist as long as there is a reference to them. The only way you can refer to an object is with the pointer returned as the value of the me variable. This is important to understand if you want to master the fundamentals of object-oriented Lingo programming. If the returned me was not stored in another variable (usually a global), the object would be created, the variable would be assigned, and then it would disappear. Sometimes objects are created to do just that but if you want your object to stay around, the returned me variable must be placed in a global.

How to Create an Object

Now that the parent script is defined, you can create objects.

```
set bird1 to birth(script "birdBirthScript","robin","red")
put the pBirdType of bird1
-- "robin"
put the pColor of bird1
-- "red"
```

To create the object, declare a variable (usually a global) and use the birth() function to get its value. The birth() function will place the instructions and declared properties from the parent script into the me variable. The "return me " returns that information so whoever called it can store it. This is similar to creating a birdhouse from a blueprint and holding it in your hand. Your hand is what contains the object and the birdhouse is the object. This variable that ends up storing the "instance" of the object actually points to the place it exists in memory; thus, it is called a *pointer*.

> A pointer is a variable that points to a memory location. Remember that objects
> get their own position in memory. The only way to refer to an object is by using
> this pointer variable. The pointer is similar to a key to a P.O. Box. In less friendly
> programming languages, you have to take care of freeing up memory after you
> no longer need an object. Fortunately, Director is very good at freeing up memory
> automatically. As soon as Director sees that no keys exist to open a P.O. Box, it
> disposes of the P.O. Box and its contents.
>
> *Note*

To create more objects, declare any other variable by using the `birth()` function.

```
set bird2 to birth(script "birdBirthScript","jay","blue")
put the pBirdType of bird2
-- "jay"
put the pColor of bird2
-- "blue"
put the ppBirdType of bird1
-- "robin"
put the pColor of bird1
-- "red"
```

You can see the object on `bird1` is not affected by any other objects you create
from the same script.

That's all there is to it! These are bona fide, true, honest-to-God objects.

Looking Up and Changing Properties

You may have noticed from the previous examples that you can look up an
object's properties by using the combination of the `the` and `of` keywords.

```
put the pColor of bird1
```

Use the same combination to change a property.

```
set the pColor of bird1 to "pink"
```

Confirm the change.

```
put the pColor of bird1
-- "pink"
```

Defining Object Handlers

Objects can have their own handlers. This is where most of their power is situated. To define an object handler, include it in the same cast script.

```
property pBirdType,  pColor

on birth me, birdType, color
    set pBirdTypeto birdType
    set pColor to color
    put "a bird of type: " & pBirdType & " and of: " & pColor & " color¬
is born!"
    return me
end

on displayInfo me
    put "I am a " & pBirdColor & " " & pBirdType
end
```

When you make a new `birdBirthScript` object and call its `displayInfo` handler, you see the following code:

```
set bird4 to birth(script "birdBirthScript","flamingo","pink")
displayInfo(bird4)
-- I am a pink flamingo
```

Notice that the handler definition also uses the `me` parameter variable. This is important to remember. Using the `me` variable tells the handler to execute only if the message was sent to this object.

This is a simple handler, but handlers can be as complex as you need them to be. They can control any aspect of your movie (including puppet sprites and sounds).

Using ancestry

Parent scripts provide a more efficient way to code. `ancestry` takes this efficiency one step further. No requirement exists to use `ancestry`, and in fact, many Director projects have no need for it. But if you need `ancestry`, it is ready to be used.

To use an `ancestor` script, you need to declare a special property. This special property, as expected, is called `ancestor`.

```
property ancestor, anotherProperty, yetAnotherProperty
```

You also need to assign a parent script to your `ancestor` property.

```
on birth me
  set ancestor to birth (script "myAncestorScript")
  return(me)
end
```

From this point on, your object will be able to use any of the handlers or properties of its `ancestor` script.

Syntax

Following is a description of the syntax to work with objects. Some of these commmands have changed in Director 5. When there is a change it will be indicated. I chose to use the old syntax because it works with both Director 4 and 5.

☀ **actorList:** This property holds a list of objects that receive a `stepFrame` message when the playback head advances.

```
add the actorList myObject
```

You can clear the `actorList` by setting it to an empty list. ([])

You add an object to the `actorList` using the `add` command. For example:

```
add the actorList, myObject
```

You can add your object to the `actorList` if you want your object to do something every time the playback head enters a new frame. Keep in mind that if you use the `actorList`, the frequency on which your object will receive a `stepFrame` message will depend on the frame rate of your movie.

☀ **ancestor:** The `ancestor` property declares another parent script as an ancestor. A parent script with an ancestor can use any of the properties and handlers of its ancestor.

```
property ancestor
```

```
on birth me
```

```
set ancestor to birth(script "someBirthScript")
```

```
end
```

When a message is sent to an object, Lingo first tries to locate its handler using its parent script. If Lingo cannot find it in the parent script, it proceeds to look for it on the ancestor script. This behavior enables you to override an ancestor's properties or handlers by defining them on the parent script.

Note that even though an object has access to an ancestor's properties, these properties are not contained within the object itself. For this reason, you have to use the the and of me keywords to access ancestor properties within an object.

```
on displayAncestorProperty me

put the someAncestorProperty of me

end
```

✤ **birth(*script parentScriptName, parameter1, parameter2, ...*)**: The birth function is used to create an object from a parent script. To be of any use, it has to be assigned to a variable (and usually a global variable).

Director 5 uses the new keyword instead of birth. If you want to follow Director 5 syntax just substitute the word birth with the word new.

```
set myObject to birth(script "aParentScript")
```

This statement looks for a cast script called aParentScript. It then executes the birth handler within that script. The birth handler on the parent script has to take the keyword me as a parameter and return me, which holds a pointer to the object.

```
on birth me

return me

end
```

✤ **property *property1, property2, ...***: The property keyword declares the specified properties as object properties. The property keyword is used at the beginning of the parent script.

```
property name, age, gender
```

Objects Miscellaneous

If you create an object, assign it to a variable, and tell Lingo to put the value of that variable, you get what looks like a very cryptic message. For example:

```
put bird1
-- <offspring "birdBirthScript" 2 1ee6e78>
```

The first two items, `offspring "birdBirthScript"`, indicate that this object is a child of the `"birdBirthScript"` parent script.

The third item indicates the number of references to the object. This one has two. One is the object itself and the other is the `bird1` variable. If you were to refer to this object from any other variable, the reference number would increase accordingly. If you want to dispose of this object, its references have to be brought down to zero.

The fourth item is the memory address of the object. This is interesting if you are fond of hexadecimal numbers.

Real World Example: A Widget Factory

The hardest part about objects is figuring out the best way to use them. Following is an example called Widget Factory. It is a simple movie that enables you to create standing and flying Widgets on-the-fly.

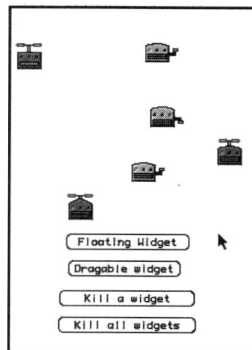

FIGURE 16.1

Widget Factory in action.

Open the movie WIDGET.DIR and play with it a bit.

Following is the movie script (minus comments):

```
global gWidgetList, gFreeChannels
```

```
on startMovie
    set gFreeChannels to¬
[1,2,3,4,5,6,7,8,9,10,11,12,13,14,15,16,17,18,19]
    repeat with loop = 1 to count(gFreeChannels)
        set the puppet of sprite getAt(gFreeChannels,loop) to 1
        set the visible of sprite getAt(gFreeChannels,loop) to 0
    end repeat
    set gWidgetList to []
end

on idle
    repeat with loop=1 to count(gWidgetList)
        myTurn(getAt(gWidgetList,loop))
    end repeat
    updateStage
end

on addWidget
    set freeChannel to findFreeChannel()
    if freeChannel then
        addgWidgetList,birth(script"WidgetBirthScript",19,22,freeChannel)
    end if
end
on addFloatingWidget
    set freeChannel to findFreeChannel()
    if freeChannel then
        add gWidgetList, birth(script¬
    "flyingWidgetBirthScript",28,31,freeChannel)
    end if
end

on findFreeChannel
    if count(gFreeChannels) then
        set freeChannel to getAt(gFreeChannels,1)
        deleteAt(gFreeChannels,1)
        return freeChannel
    else
        return 0
    end if
end

on killAwidget
    if count(gWidgetList) then
        set dommedWidget to getAt(gWidgetList,1)
```

```
            set the visible of sprite the pMySprite of dommedWidget to 0
            add(gFreeChannels, the pMySprite of dommedWidget)
            deleteAt(gWidgetList,1)
        end if
    end

    on killAllWidgets
        set howMany to count(gWidgetList)
        repeat with loop=1 to howMany
            killAwidget
        end repeat
    end
```

This is quite a bit of code, and the two parent scripts are still to come. First break down the movie script.

Start the movie script by defining your global variables. You may have noticed that the global variables have been defined outside of a handler. This is actually allowed in Director. When you define a global outside a handler, you are declaring it for all handlers on that script. This can be useful and save you a lot of typing.

> Use this feature at your own risk. It is not documented and may cease to work on future releases of Director. Macromedia itself uses this feature all the time.
>
> *Note*

```
    global gWidgetList, gFreeChannels
```

The first global gWidgetList holds a list of all the widget objects you make. The gFreeChannels global holds a list of possible channels where the sprites for our widgets can reside.

```
    on startMovie
        set gFreeChannels to¬
[1,2,3,4,5,6,7,8,9,10,11,12,13,14,15,16,17,18,19]
        repeat with nChannel in gFreeChannels
            set the puppet of sprite nChannel to 1
            set the visible of sprite nChannel to 0
        end repeat
        set gWidgetList to []
    end
```

The startMovie handler first sets the list of possible channels for your sprites. In this movie, you can have up to 19 widgets; they will use up channels 1–19.

The `repeat` loop goes through all the values of the `gFreeChannels` list puppets and makes them invisible. Finally, declare your `gWidgetList` global as an empty linear list.

```
on idle
    repeat with objCurrent in gWidgetList
        myTurn(objCurrent)
    end repeat
    updateStage
end
```

The `idle` handler is where most of the work gets done. First, set up a loop with the total amount of objects on `gWidgetList`. If no widget objects exist, the loop repeats 0 times (nothing will happen). If objects are on `gWidgetList`, the loop sends a `myTurn` message to each of them. Finally, after every object has been sent the `myTurn` message, update the stage to reflect any changes.

```
on addWidget
    set freeChannel to findFreeChannel()
    if freeChannel then
        add gWidgetList, birth(script
"WidgetBirthScript",19,22,freeChannel)
    end if
end
```

The `addWidget` handler is called by the draggable widget button. First, use the `findFreeChannel()` handler to find a free channel to display the widget. If a free channel is around, add a widget object to the `gWidgetList` (actually a pointer to the object). To add the object, use the `birth()` function by using the "WidgetBirthScript" and passing three parameters. The first parameter is the cast number of the first step of the animated widget. The second is the last cast member. The third parameter is the free channel the object can use to display the widget.

```
on addFloatingWidget
    set freeChannel to findFreeChannel()
    if freeChannel then
        add gWidgetList, birth(script¬
"flyingWidgetBirthScript",28,31,freeChannel)
    end if
end
```

The `addFloatingWidget` handler works almost the same way as `addWidget`, but creates a different type of object, a flying widget. To make a flying widget, use the `birth()` handler in the `"flyingWidgetBirthScript"`. The floating widget uses different cast members, so send those as parameters.

```
on findFreeChannel
    if count(gFreeChannels) then
        set freeChannel to getAt(gFreeChannels,1)
        deleteAt(gFreeChannels,1)
        return freeChannel
    else
        return 0
    end if
end
```

The `findFreeChannel` handler goes throughout the `gFreeChannels` list looking for an available channel. If it finds one, it deletes it from the list and returns its number. If no free channels exist, it returns a 0.

```
on killAwidget
    if count(gWidgetList) then
        set dommedWidget to getAt(gWidgetList,1)
        set the visible of sprite the pMySprite of dommedWidget to 0
        add(gFreeChannels, the pMySprite of dommedWidget)
        deleteAt(gWidgetList,1)
    end if
end
```

The `killAwidget` handler is called by the Kill a Widget button. It first checks if there is anything to kill. If there is, it makes the channel for that widget invisible, adds the channel to the pool of free channels, and finally removes it from the `gWidgetList`. Because this was the only reference to the object, Director disposes of it and makes that memory available.

```
on killAllWidgets
    set howMany to count(gWidgetList)
    repeat with loop=1 to howMany
        killAwidget
    end repeat
end
```

The `killAllWidgets` handler has the same effect as the user repeatedly clicking on the Kill a Widget button. It first checks how many widget objects exist, and then calls the `killAwidget` handler that amount of times.

So far you have not seen any parent scripts, only birth functions. Here is the WidgetBirthScript.

```
property pAnimationList, pMySprite
on birth me, firstMember, lastMember, spriteNumber
    set pMySprite to spriteNumber
    set the visible of sprite pMySprite to 1
    set pAnimationList to []
    repeat with loop=firstMember to lastMember
        add pAnimationList, loop
    end repeat
    return me
end

on myTurn me
    animate me
end

on animate me
    set nextMember to (the castNum of sprite pMySprite)+1
    if getLast(pAnimationList) < nextMember then
        set nextMember to getAt(pAnimationList,1)
    end if
    set the castNum of sprite pMySprite to nextMember
end
```

Here is a breakdown:

```
property pAnimationList, pMySprite
```

The widget object has two properties. The pAnimationList property holds the cast member numbers to animate the widget. The pMySprite handler holds the channel the widget uses.

```
on birth me, firstMember, lastMember, spriteNumber
    set pMySprite to spriteNumber
    set the visible of sprite pMySprite to 1
    set pAnimationList to []
    repeat with loop=firstMember to lastMember
        add pAnimationList, loop
    end repeat
    return me
end
```

This is the all-important birth handler. The birth handler takes four parameters. The first is the important me parameter. The firstMember parameter is the first cast member number for the animation. The lastMember parameter is the last cast member number for the animation. The cast members for the animation of the widgets are located in sequence, which is why only the first and last casts are provided. Use these numbers to fill the in-between values. The last parameter is the sprite channel where the widget will reside.

The first instruction sets the pMySprite property to the value of the spriteNumber parameter. Next set the visibility of that channel to TRUE. The pAnimationList property is declared as an empty linear list. Next use a loop to fill the pAnimationList with the cast members for the animation. Finally, return me. If you forget to return me, your object will cease to exist as soon as you are finished creating it.

```
on myTurn me
    animate me
end
```

The myTurn handler is called by the idle handler. All myTurn does is call another handler, animate. Why not make that handler part of my turn? The reason you shouldn't is that widgetBirthScript is used as an ancestor by flyingWidgetBirthScript, and you want to be able to override myTurn while still having access to the animate handler.

```
on animate me
    set nextMember to (the castNum of sprite pMySprite)+1
    if getLast(pAnimationList) < nextMember then
        set nextMember to getAt(pAnimationList,1)
    end if
    set the castNum of sprite pMySprite to nextMember
end
```

animate takes care of animating the sprite. It cycles to the cast member values of pAnimationList and assigns them to the sprite.

That takes care of a straightforward parent script. Now the flyingWidgetBirthScript that uses ancestry will be explored.

```
property ancestor, pHdir, pVdir

on birth me, firstMember, lastMember, spriteNumber
    set ancestor to birth(script "WidgetBirthScript", firstMember,¬
lastMember, spriteNumber)
```

```
            set pHdir to random(2)
            set pVdir to random(2)
            return me
      end


      on myTurn me
            fly (me)
            animate (me)
      end
      on fly me
            set myHloc to the locH of sprite the pMySprite of me
            set myVloc to the locV of sprite the pMySprite of me
            if myHLoc > 200 or myHLoc < 20 then set pHdir to - pHdir
            if myVLoc > 200 or myVLoc < 20 then set pVdir to - pVdir
            set the locH of sprite the pMySprite of me to myHLoc + pHdir
            set the locV of sprite the pMySprite of me to myVLoc + pVdir
      end
```

Break it down.

```
property ancestor, pHdir, pVdir
```

The flyingWidgetBirthScript has three properties. The first is the special
property ancestor. The other two properties, pHdir and pVdir, hold values for
how far and in which direction the sprite will move.

```
on birth me, firstMember, lastMember, spriteNumber
      set ancestor to birth(script "WidgetBirthScript", firstMember,¬
lastMember, spriteNumber)
      set pHdir to random(2)
      set pVdir to random(2)
      return me
end
```

The birth handler takes four parameters. The first one is the now familiar me.
The next three parameters are the first and last cast members of the animation
and the channel for the object. Although the flying widget object itself will not
use any of these three parameters, they will be used by the ancestor (widget
object). Pass these parameters to the ancestor object.

Next set up the pHdir and pVdir properties to random numbers between 1 and
2. These numbers determine how many pixels the flying widgets will move with
each turn. Because the number is random for each object, each flying widget
you make will fly in a different pattern. Finally, return me. Notice that when

changing the properties that are inherited from the ancestor script, you must use the "the pProperty of myObject" syntax. Normally, when changing the properties of your object you simply change the property. Because the properties of the ancestor are contained in the me parameter, they have to be referred to in this fashion.

```
on myTurn me
     fly (me)
     animate (me)
end
```

The myTurn handler on flying widget overrides the myTurn handler of its ancestor (widget object). Director first looks on the object itself for a handler. Only if it doesn't find it does it go looking for it on the ancestor object. The myTurn for flying widget first calls the fly handler to move the sprite, and then calls the animate handler to animate it. Notice that the flyingWidgetBirthScript does not have an animate handler defined. It executes the animate handler of the ancestor object.

```
on fly me
     set myHloc to the locH of sprite the pMySprite of me
     set myVloc to the locV of sprite the pMySprite of me
     if myHLoc > 200 or myHLoc < 20 then set pHdir to - pHdir
     if myVLoc > 200 or myVLoc < 20 then set pVdir to - pVdir
     set the locH of sprite the pMySprite of me to myHLoc + pHdir
     set the locV of sprite the pMySprite of me to myVLoc + pVdir
end
```

The flyMe handler takes care of moving the floating sprite around the screen. It is made up of pretty straightforward Lingo.

Take some time to experiment and change things around. Try adding more frames to the animation or making your own objects with different behaviors—maybe bouncing widgets or projectile widgets.

Conclusion

In this chapter you learned what objects, properties, ancestors and messages are and how to use them. You learned the syntax for objects and now know that objects are made from parent scripts that provide a blueprint for the object. You learned that objects can inherit handlers and properties from other objects. Finally, you saw a real-world example of a movie that uses objects.

Mark Castle

Using External and Multiple Casts

This chapter covers the use of the new external casts available in Director 5.

They are a new and flexible way to design software for easy upgrading and

modularity.

This chapter covers the following:

* *Description of external cast*

* *Comparison between animations using internal and external casts*

* *Designing and implementing an image browser by using the external*
  cast modularity for clip art books

Multiple and external casts are improvements to the single cast per movie available in previous versions of Director. It is now possible to have more than one cast associated with each movie created. The cast file can be contained within the Director movie file, or stored on disk externally, and accessed by more than just a single movie.

This new functionality replaces and enhances the old SHARED.DIR file that enabled movies within the same directory to share assets. Now a movie can use a cast file in another directory entirely. The cast file may contain any valid cast member types, including scripts.

This chapter is primarily concerned with external casts that contain data for the central or main movie to manipulate. The three examples within the chapter illustrate progressive techniques for taking advantage of the new capabilities of external cast files.

Example one is a "normal" animation using the internal cast; example two moves the cast information to an external cast and switches between the two cast files; example three shows an extension of the external casts by using them as repositories for data to be displayed in a clip art browser.

Example One: A Simple Animation

This example is a simple animation with three sprites animating across the Stage. The logo drops from the top of the stage, and the two bullet points come in from either side, with a frame part way through the sequence (see fig. 17.1).

The motion and screen layout are not complex. This familiarizes you with how external casts can be used in place of internal ones.

This example file has a total of four cast members: one bitmap logo, two Rich Text members, and one script. In version 5 of Director, the assets in a movie file are no longer referred to as "castmember(s)", but as "member(s)". This enables a specific member within a particular cast file to be referenced. The actual cast files are referred to as "libraries" or "castLibs".

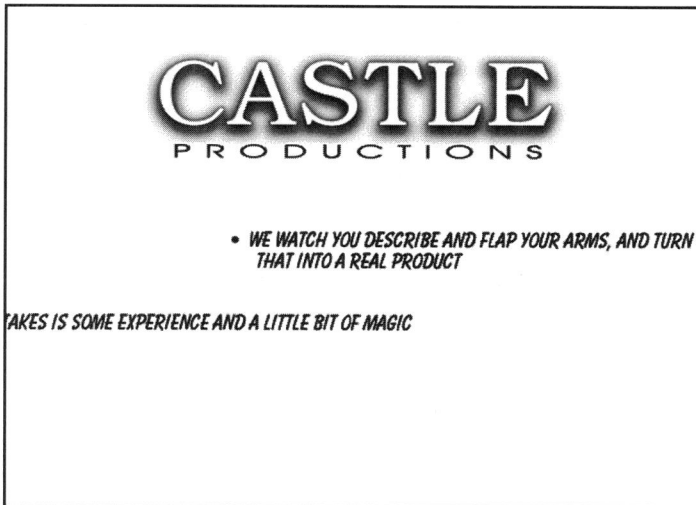

FIGURE 17.1

The first example file with bullets animating onto the Stage.

Older Lingo code that uses the now outdated "castNum" term is assumed to be referring to the internal cast library. Therefore, the common use of

```
set the castNum of sprite cast 1 = the castNum of sprite 2
```

is replaced with

```
set the memberNum of sprite 3 = the number of member 2 of castLib 3
```

In both of these examples, the actual numbers of members and libraries are arbitrary. They merely illustrate how a reference is made to a specific member. As in previous versions of Director, the use of "the number of" can be inserted in lieu of the numeric value.

Example Two: An Alternate Animation

This example seems to be the same animation, but in fact uses a cast file external to the movie. The cast members are arranged exactly as they were when they referred to the internal cast, so the movie plays the same.

You can alter the entire cast being used and retain the original functionality by telling Director to use a castLib other than the initial one. You can do so by rewinding the movie and typing the command

```
set the fileName of castLib "Data" = "NewData"
```

into the message window. The actual reference to each cast member is the same, but the cast library being used is switched. Now playing back the movie yields the same motion and type of animation, but the particular elements differ (see fig. 17.2).

FIGURE 17.2

The altered animation, before completion, displaying the new castLib.

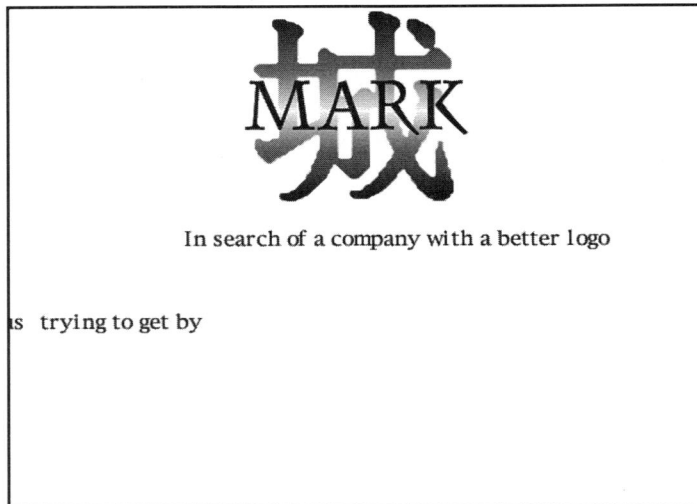

With that single line of Lingo it is possible to alter the entire look of a movie. This opens up the possibility of easily creating alternate versions of a movie. Perhaps you need a version of the standard corporate presentation with raucous rock music for a tradeshow demo, or customized art displaying a client's logo, or maybe even localized information for overseas markets; all these become easy to maintain and update by using external castLibs.

It's possible to reference multiple cast libraries with a single Director movie; you're not limited to a single file. This also allows very flexible work environments for teams working simultaneously on the same project. You can alter all the elements in your cast library without worrying about conflicting with anything in anyone else's file. When done, you can merely replace the old file with your updated one, and everyone playing the movie will have your changes.

Another benefit is pure organization above and beyond team member responsibility. You might want to place all your scripts in one cast library, all the sounds in another, all the bitmaps in a third. The Director movie simply references the file on disk with the proper name, so updating is just a drag-copy away. (This can be a bad thing too, but let's not get into that right now.)

Example Three: Nits and Grits

With those points covered, let's move on to a scenario in which the external casts enable a Director developer to do something in version 5 that would have been impossible to do in earlier versions.

The premise is a clip art database with modules of various types of art that can be dropped into a particular folder and becomes available to the browsing Director application. The engine, or Director file that enables the clips to be viewed, is just under 100 KB, but it browses external casts that are megabytes in size.

The opening screen is shown in figure 17.3. While this screen is shown, quite a lot goes on out of the user's sight.

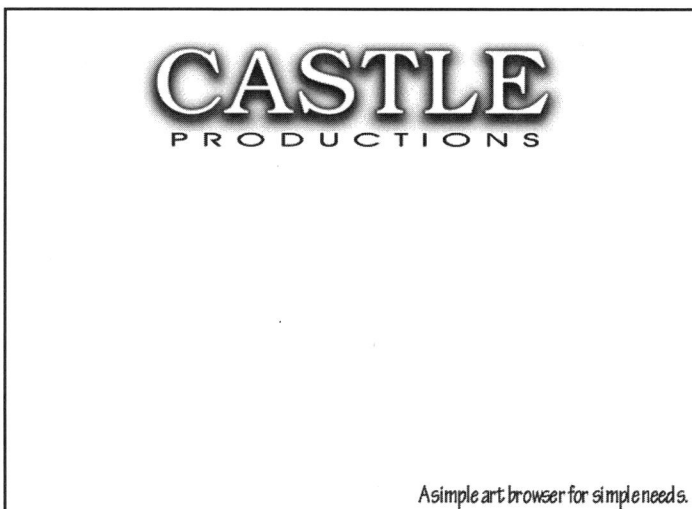

CASTLE

PRODUCTIONS

A simple art browser for simple needs.

FIGURE 17.3

The main screen for the clip art browser appears while the real work is done behind the scenes.

While the user gets to look at the logo, Lingo scripts are initializing global variables, finding out what files are in the subfolder called Books and creating a list of the found books.

After this is done, the second and final screen is displayed, as shown in figure 17.4.

FIGURE 17.4

The final screen for browsing the clip art appears after the available books are found.

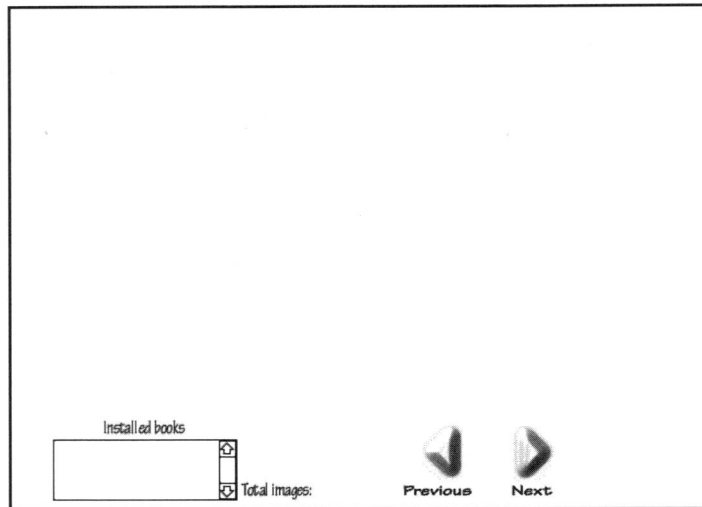

This screen is filled in with all the clip art books in the Books folder. When one is selected from the scrolling list, the number of images in that book is placed in the field indicated for that value, and the first image from the book is put on the screen.

At that point, the user can click through the images in order by using the Previous and Next buttons.

The entire application is not exceptionally complicated; it is the use of external casts that is unique. At any point, the user can acquire a new clip art book and drop the file in the Books folder. The next time the viewer is launched, the new book appears in the list and its contents are viewable.

This gives great potential for updating existing titles and games that might use modules of some kind. Imagine supplying your users with an update of a single file rather than another entire executable. It also has tremendous application for reselling to the same user again and again. What if you actually produced clip art? You could continue to sell packages or suites to people long after the initial purchase.

The Not-So-Secret Code Behind It All

For extremely reusable capability, you might expect skads of code to be necessary. Not so. The Lingo command previously mentioned for setting the actual path to a cast library is the key to managing the technique.

The code that the viewer movie actually executes is straightforward when looked at closely. At the top of the movie script (there's only one in the movie) is a list of global variable descriptions and their declarations. This is a technique that enables you to avoid having to continually declare your globals at the beginning of each handler in which you want to use them. Declare them at the top of any script in which you intend to use them, and that's it.

```
-- Global declarations
-- gBookFolder: This is the path to the folder containing the books of
art for viewing
global gBookFolder
-- gBookFileList: This is a property list containing the name of the
book as the property and the actual file it's contained in as the
associated value
global gBookFileList
-- gArtworkSprite: This is the channel that the actual artwork is
displayed in
global gArtworkSprite
```

When reviewing the following walk through of the code itself, you should be aware of several things:

* Handler names all begin with a capital letter and use inter-caps within the word. This immediately distinguishes them from other variables and Lingo terms.

* Local variables begin with a small letter and use inter-caps within the word.

* Global variables begin with a small letter "g" (for global) and use inter-caps within the word.

* Global variables are used as constants for easy updating.

The StartMovie handler resets the built-in Director timer. The InitGlobals handler sets the global variables used to their initial values. The FillBookList handler does several things that result in a list of the books available being placed in a global variable. Lastly, the field for showing how many images are in the currently open book is set to none.

```
on StartMovie
  startTimer
  InitGlobals
  FillBookList
  set the text of member "Book count" = "00"
end
```

The internal Director timer is used later in the exitFrame handler of the first frame. The exitFrame handler checks to see that at least two seconds have passed since the movie started. This keeps the first frame visible even on a fast machine that might quickly run through the StartMovie handler. (Normally I don't like this type of forced-wait behavior, but the first screen should be readable, and anything less than two seconds seems like it flashes too quickly.) On very slow machines, the StartMovie handler could conceivably take longer than the two seconds to complete, and the exitFrame script would never hold back the playback head.

InitGlobals is the next handler, and it checks the platform in which the movie is being run and sets a local variable for the path name delimiter to the proper character. This delimiter is then concatenated to the Books folder so that the files in that folder can be found later. The entire path is stored in a global variable named gBookFolder.

The InitGlobals handler then stores the channel number of the sprite that will be used to display any of the pictures from the clip art books. Using the global for this means that if for some reason you need to move the channel, all you need is to update this one line and the new channel is referred to correctly throughout the movie.

Finally, the IntiGlobals handler declares and initializes the gBookFileList global to an empty property list. This will be used later, but is initialized here in the handler, which is meant to do all the intializations of globals.

```
-- This handler is called when the movie begins playing
-- It initializes all the globals to their proper starting value
on InitGlobals
```

```
  -- Check the machine to see if Windows is running or not
  if the machineType = 256 then
    -- If it's Windows OS, use the backslash as the path delimiter
    set theDelimiter = "\"
  else
    -- Otherwise, use the colon as the path delimiter
    set theDelimiter = ":"
  end if
  set gBookFolder = string( the pathName&"BOOKS"&theDelimiter )
  set gArtworkSprite = 8
  set gBookFileList = [:]
end
```

The StartMovie handler continues and next calls the FillBookList handler. This handler sets a variable named theBooks to the value returned by the GetAllBooksAvailable() handler. It sets the variable named bookTitles to the result of GetBookTitles(), by using the previously retrieved value in theBooks. Finally, it uses both the returned values as arguments to a third handler named MakeBookFileList(). Lastly, it fills in the field showing the installed books available with the bookTitles variable.

```
on FillBookList
  set theBooks = GetAllBooksAvailable()
  set bookTitles = GetBookTitles( theBooks )
  MakeBookFileList( bookTitles, theBooks )
  set the text of member "Installed Books" = bookTitles
end
```

Looking in more detail at each of these lines, the GetAllBooksAvailable() handler returns a string containing each of the files in the Books folder. The string has each file on a separate line.

You can see that the handler initializes a variable to an empty string, starts iterating through all the files in the Books folder by using the getNthFileNameInFolder() function, and then returns the string that is built.

```
  -- This handler is called when the movie begins playing
  -- It looks in the folder/directory at the same level as the Viewer
  movie for a folder called "BOOKS"
  -- Inside the Books folder each file is added to the list of available
  books for display
  -- This handler actually returns a string that has each book name on a
  line
on GetAllBooksAvailable
```

```
  set bookString = ""
  set currentBookNum = 1
  repeat while TRUE
    set theCurrentBook = getNthFileNameInFolder( gBookFolder,¬
currentBookNum )
    if theCurrentBook = EMPTY then exit repeat
    put theCurrentBook&RETURN after bookString
    set currentBookNum = ( currentBookNum + 1 )
  end repeat
  delete line currentBookNum of bookString
  return bookString
end
```

The next line in FillBookList calls the GetBookTitles() handler. This uses the return-delimited string that was returned by the previous line and looks at each of the listed files in turn. By looking at them, it switches the default cast named Data to the new file. Now, it has access to the members within the castLib. In member 1 of each book castLib, there is a text cast member containing information about that book. The first line is the name of the theme or type of artwork contained in the castLib. You can also think of it as the long name for the book itself.m

The name was placed within the member because of the limitations imposed by DOS file name conventions. There is no way to have a book named *Sunsets Around the World* in eight characters or less. The ugly version used to actually name the file is only used on disk. The longer human-readable form is stored in the first member, named Book Info.

This same technique could be extended to accommodate multiple data types in a single castLib. You might have both bitmap and digital video and store some information regarding them in the Book Info field. Possibly you want to distinguish between artists or periods of art style. With some changes to the Book Info field and the scripts that access it, the prospects for extending the available information opens up.

To accommodate the largest number of people on the lower-end machines, these types of solutions become necessary.

```
-- This handler is called when the movie begins playing
-- It looks in the folder/directory at the same level as the Viewer
movie for a folder called "BOOKS"
-- Inside the Books folder each cast file is examined to see what the
title for the book is
```

```
-- The title is stored in member 1, which is named "Book Info"
-- This handler actually returns a string that has each book title on a
line
on GetBookTitles bookNamesString
  set titlesString = ""
  set totalBooks = the number of lines in bookNamesString
  repeat with currentBookNum = 1 to totalBooks
    set the fileName of castLib "Data" = gBookFolder&( line 1 of¬
bookNamesString )
    set newInfo = the text of member "Book Info" of castLib "Data"
    put line 1 of newInfo&RETURN after titlesString
    delete line 1 of bookNamesString
  end repeat
  delete line currentBookNum of titlesString
  return titlesString
end
```

Next on the hit parade is MakeBookFileList(). Because you now have a string
containing the names of the files and another containing the long name of the
book, these two strings are passed to this handler, which creates a property
list of the long book titles matched with the file names.

You might wonder why this is necessary. Strictly speaking, you have a listing of
each of them separately and could place them in globals and use them. For just
a small number of books, this might be a workable solution. Whenever you
work with more than a few books, working with strings becomes very slow.
Making the global property list and referring to it instead is much faster and
saves more work in the long run. This is actually a perfect application for the
use of a property list.

Begin by determining how many lines to iterate through in the string holding
the book titles. This number will also be the same for the file names because
they were created almost simultaneously. The repeat structure then adds to
the global property list gBookFileList the human-readable title as the property,
and the file name containing that clip art as the value. The deletion of the first
line of the string is a handy technique to speed up string operations that loop
like this. It is much faster for Lingo to always read the first line of any string
variable than to count down successive lines.

```
-- This handler is called from FillBookList
-- It takes the two strings containing the names of the books and the
names of the files they reside in
```

```
-- A property list is created that contains both the items associated
for future reference
on MakeBookFileList titles, fileNames
  set totalLines = the number of lines in titles
  repeat with currentLine = 1 to totalLines
    addProp( gBookFileList, line 1 of titles, line 1 of fileNames )
    delete line 1 of titles
    delete line 1 of fileNames
  end repeat
end
```

When this handler finishes, you have a property list that looks something like `["Backgrounds": "bgds.cst", "Hand Tools": "Tools.cst"]`. You can see each of the paired bits of information stored in the list.

This is used later to open and display any one of the clip art books.

Showing the Images

The process by which one of the books is accessed and the contents displayed is very straightforward. The scrolling field on the second screen that shows the installed books enables the user to click on the name of the book and have the first image from it appear. Figure 17.5 shows the first image from the Backgrounds book displayed.

FIGURE 17.5

The first image in the Backgrounds book is displayed when the book title is clicked on in the scrolling list.

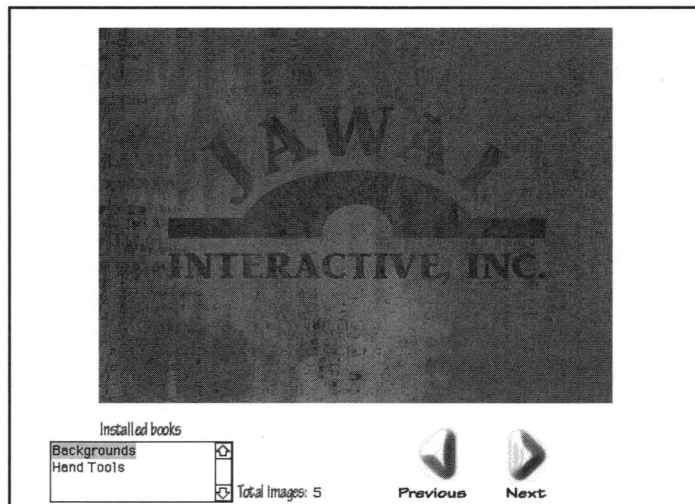

This image was brought up on-screen by clicking on the first line in the scrolling field with Backgrounds in it. Clicking on the line below it shows the first image in the Tools book.

The field directly to the right of the scrolling field displays the number of images in the currently open book. There are five background images.

Farther to the right are the arrows that page back and forth to each image in the open book. If no book is open, they do nothing.

This section examines the script that opens and displays the books. There is a sprite script attached to the scrolling field. This script is triggered by the mouseUp event, and determines if a valid line was clicked on. Clicking on the gutter area of a text field yields an invalid line number, so the first two lines are common when dealing with user selection in a field. If the user has not clicked on a valid line in the field, the execution exits the handler.

Assuming that the user clicks on a valid line, the line is highlighted, and the text from the highlighted line is placed in a variable named bookChosen. The final step in the process is to call the handler that opens the book, displays the contents, and updates the field showing total images. This handler is named OpenBook(), and it takes the string of the long name for the book.

```
on mouseUp
  set lineClicked = the mouseLine
  if ( lineClicked < 1 ) then exit
  hilite line lineClicked of member "Installed Books"
  set bookChosen = line lineClicked of the text of member "Installed¬
Books"
  OpenBook( bookChosen )
end
```

The OpenBook() handler is also found in the movie script. This is the meat of the entire engine. This single handler switches the castLib to display the new clip art book.

The first line of the handler takes the human-readable name of the book passed in as a string and extracts from the global list of book names and file names the correct file name for the selected book name. If Backgrounds had been selected, the book name would have that string in it. This first line would use the built-in getAprop() function that enables you to name the list and property to find, and return the associated value. In the case of Backgrounds, the associated value is the file name `bgds.cst`. The variable `theNewFilename` now contains that file name.

The next line is checking to make certain that you do not have an error. There should never be a case where a book name does not have an associated file name, but this line assures the handler will go no further if no file name was returned.

The visibility of the sprite channel containing the artwork is temporarily turned off. This off state avoids any flashing or distracting updates that might occur while the book is being opened and the new image is being displayed.

The file name of the castLib Data is changed to the new file name just retrieved from the global list. This changing of file names is similar to having linked media like QuickTime movies in a castLib. It's possible to set the file that the QuickTime movie references during runtime. For this to work, you must first have a QuickTime movie imported. You cannot reset the path if you don't have a QuickTime movie. The same logic applies to castLib files. You need to have an initial file linked to the Director movie to reset its path. You can link a file using the Modify menu. Select the `"Movie"` menuItem and the `"Casts"` submenu item. The Data castLib is an empty castLib used only for resetting the fileName to the new books being opened.

The placement of the Data castLib is arbitrary. It could just as easily go in the Books folder, or another folder entirely if the project had other ones. As long as the movie is linked to the viewer movie, the technique of resetting the file name is valid.

Note

An important note regarding any linked castLibs is that Director builds some type of internal identifier for the cast library. If you replace a linked castLib with another of the same name, you will be presented with a dialog box telling you that the contents of the library have changed. Although this is fine and good during development, it is not something for an end user to see. Be certain to avoid this behavior by only replacing libraries that get set on the fly, and are not linked directly to the playback movie.

The next two lines of the handler make certain to set the sprite pointing to the right castLib. In previous versions of Director, it was possible to switch the cast member in a sprite, but now with the capability to switch the castLib too, it's necessary to set the castLib as shown here. With the castLib of the sprite set, the memberNum of the sprite can be updated.

The next line again checks the information stored in the first member of the castLib. You should recall that the member is a text field with the first line containing the human-readable form of the title of the book. The second line of the field contains the number of images found in the book. This number can be generated on the fly by examining the Cast, but if there are several hundred images, there is an annoying delay whenever a book of that size was opened. As it is, manually counting the images is easy. Look at the last member in the castLib and subtract one because the first member is the information field. If necessary, a handler to determine the number can be written. The string (it looks like a number, but it's actually a number character, making it a string) is then placed in the field showing the number of images.

An updateStage command is necessary to make certain that Director redraws the stage with the new member in the sprite.

Lastly, the visibility of the sprite channel is turned back on to reveal the new image on stage.

```
-- This handler is called when the user clicks on the name of a book in
the scrolling field
-- It takes the name of the book as the parameter
-- The cast containing that book is switched into the linked cast and
the first of the members is shown on stage
on OpenBook theBookName
  set theNewFilename = getAProp( gBookFileList, theBookName )
  if voidP( theNewFilename ) then exit
  set the visible of sprite gArtworkSprite = FALSE
  set the fileName of castLib "Data" = gBookFolder&theNewFileName
  set the castLibNum of sprite gArtworkSprite = the number of castLib¬
  "Data"
  set the memberNum of sprite gArtworkSprite = member 2 of castLib¬
  "Data"
  set totalImages = line 2 of the text of member "Book Info"
  set the text of member "Book count" = totalImages
  updateStage
  set the visible of sprite gArtworkSprite = TRUE
end
```

The Previous and Next Buttons

The interface elements remaining undiscussed are the Previous and Next buttons that increment and decrement through the images in the open book. Both buttons call the same handler, but slightly different values in the arguments are passed in. You can see in figure 17.6 that the Previous button's sprite script is

```
on mouseDown
   if ButtonClicked( ) then GetPicture( -1, "Streak 2" )
end
```

The Next button's sprite script is

```
on mouseDown
   if ButtonClicked( ) then GetPicture( 1, "Streak 1" )
end
```

FIGURE 17.6

The sprite script attached to the Previous button.

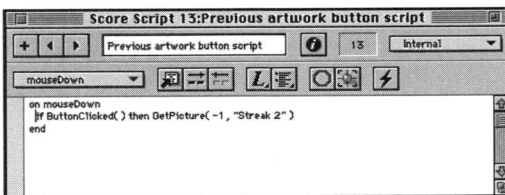

Both occur during a mouseDown rather than the traditional mouseUp, thus making the button pushing effect work correctly. The ButtonClicked() handler sees if there was a valid click on the button, and if so, calls the GetPicture() handler with the direction to move in the castLib and the sound to play when the image is displayed.

This chapter does not go into details on the ButtonClicked() handler because it is basically gratuitous. (It comes from a standard set of routines I always keep on hand.) It handles the mouse clicking on a sprite, showing the down state, updating properly if the cursor rolls off the sprite, and returns a TRUE if the mouse actions were both down and up while over the sprite. If the actions weren't, a FALSE is returned. The same functionality can be achieved without button effects (but I like offering the feedback to the user).

The GetPicture() handler also resides in the movie script, and checks to see what the current member of the artwork sprite is. The value passed in first is then used to move one member slot forward or backward in the open castLib. If that slot is not occupied by a cast member of type #bitmap, you cannot move any further through the book in that direction, so the handler exits. This works for the beginning of the castLib because member one's type is #field. It also works for the unoccupied slots after the last members are type #empty.

If the slot has a bitmap in it, the next line of the handler sets the memberNum of the artwork sprite to that new member. A puppetSound command follows that uses the second parameter passed in to name the sound played back. The updateStage serves two purposes: It forces the stage to be redrawn and reveal the new image, and it forces the puppetSound to begin playing. Sounds play only when a new frame is drawn or an updateStage command is issued.

```
-- This handler is used by the two buttons paging through the pictures
in the currently open book
-- The first parameter is either 1 or -1, for the direction of the
movement through the castLib
-- The second is the name of the sound to play when displaying the image
on GetPicture direction, soundName
   set currentMember = the memberNum of sprite gArtworkSprite
   if not (the type of member ( currentMember + direction ) of castLib¬
"Data" = #bitmap ) then exit
   set the memberNum of sprite gArtworkSprite = member  ( currentMember¬
   + direction ) of castLib "Data"
   puppetSound soundName
   updateStage
end
```

The only thing left to do is to clean up when the movie is finished playing. The StopMovie handler does this. For playback with a projector, this is not actually needed because the fields get cleared and the castLib automatically resets when the applications quits. For development purposes, it is important to make certain that the linked castLib is set back to the original. This enables the clip art books to be worked on or updated without affecting the viewer movie.

```
on StopMovie
   set the fileName of castLib "Data" = the pathName&"Data"
   set the text of member "Installed Books" = " "
   set the text of member "Book count" = " "
end
```

With the exception of the ButtonClicked() handler and a couple of frame scripts, this chapter sums up all the code in the viewer movie. Using Director 5's new capability to access external casts gives a lot of added functionality with very little effort. The entire project uses ten handlers and three global variables. The real power comes when new castLibs are created and dropped into the folder.

Creating new cast libraries is a matter of selecting the New Cast Menu item from the pop-up menu in the Cast window, as seen in figure 17.7. You'll be prompted for a name and where to save the castLib, either internally or as an external file. Make it an external file, and you can populate it and save it into the Books folder to add another clip art book to your collection. Do not forget to supply the information in the first member.

You can also protect these files by selecting Update Movies menuItem from the Xtras menu. This protecting procedure locks out the capability to open or edit the file from Director. You can only access it through your provided browser. This means users will not be able to get the contents of the file directly as they would from a non-protected castLib. Doing this does not change the functionality of the movie, and no code changes are necessary.

FIGURE 17.7

Creating a new castlib by selecting "New Cast" from the pop-up menu in the Cast window.

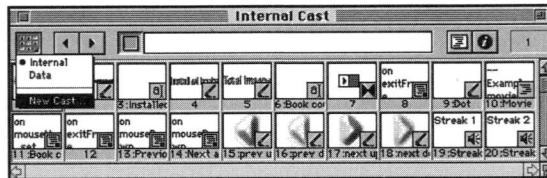

You also need to keep a couple of other points in mind when dealing with external casts. The first is that there is a limit on the number of open files you may have in Windows 3.1. Typically, this means that when you simultaneously open somewhere around 12 external castLibs, you will begin to have problems with the System. This isn't a problem within Director per se, but rather is a System limitation that Director allows you to abuse. If you experience problematic behavior on a large project, you may want to count open files. You can do this with the aid of the number of castLibs function in Lingo. It will return the number of castLibs being used by the current movie, both internal and external.

One last thing is the use of castNums and memberNums. Earlier in the chapter it was mentioned that the old syntax of "set the castNum of sprite n" refers to the internal castLib. This is actually a simplification to make sure that the waters are not muddied too soon. What is in fact going on is the "castNum of sprite" and "number of member x of castLib y" return a unique identifier for the cast member. The numeric identifier can then be used to refer to that cast member if you so wish.

If you try this, you are likely to get an outlandish-looking value such as 327702 for a member. This number is derived by taking the castLib number and multiplying it by 65,536 and then adding the number of the member for that particular castLib. For example, if you have a cast member named "Morris" in position 25 of the second castLib, you will get the number 131,097. That is the number of the castLib multiplied by 65,536 plus 25—that is, (2×65536) + 25.

This may appear useless at first, but it can be handy when applied to actual problems. If you tell Director to get the castNum of a sprite and get back the unique ID, you can then avoid referring by name and castLib because it's all wrapped up in the one number. Along with the flexibility of the new multiple casts comes the burden of referring to them by both member and castLib; this unique identifier enables you to avoid that and use one value to identify any cast member in any library.

You can also take a member and castLib reference and figure out the unique ID for that member if you so wish. The scripts for converting between the two are below and also are available along with the other example files on the web site.

```
-- This utility will convert from a member and castLib name or number to
the unique numeric ID for the member
on ConvertToUniqueID theMember, theCastLib
  if stringP( theCastLib ) then set theCastLib = the number of castLib¬
  theCastLib
  if stringP( theMember ) then  set theMember = the memberNum of member¬
  theMember of castLib theCastLib
  if theCastLib > 1 then
    set libOffset = theCastLib * 65536
  end if
  return libOffset + theMember
end


-- This utility will convert from a unique member number to a compound
member and castLib
```

```
on ConvertFromUniqueID theIDNumber
   set theNewCastNumber = (theIDNumber mod 65536 )
   set theCastLib = ( theIDNumber / 65536 )
   set theCastNumber = member theNewCastNumber of castLib theCastLib
   return theCastNumber
end
```

Conclusion

With the techniques described in this chapter, you should now be able to create and use multiple or external castLibs in any future projects that might require this type of functionality or even in those that may benefit from using the organization or localization aspects.

appendix

Kirk Keller

SHOCKWAVE LINGO COMMANDS

The manuals that come with Macromedia's Director do not yet list all of the Lingo commands available for use in Shockwave movies. This is likely due in large part to the recent developments in Shockwave movies and Shockwave audio.

This document is created as a resource to the Shockwave developer. It lists parameters and Lingo commands particular to Shockwave movies. For easy reference, Lingo commands are listed alphabetically and also by general function.

Reserved Parameters

Shockwave movies can have properties set by parameters passed from the HTML documents that call them. Some parameters that can be passed are reserved for setting particular properties of the Shockwave movie. These reserved parameters control the palette and background of the Shockwave movie.

Palette

This parameter sets the control of the web Browser palette. By setting the palette parameter to `foreground`, the Shockwave movie takes control of the browser palette. By setting the palette parameter to `background`, the web browser retains control of the browser palette.

To call a Shockwave movie to take control of the web browser's palette, use the following HTML code:

```
<embed src="swmovie.dcr" height=240 width=320 palette=foreground>
```

bgcolor

This parameter sets the Stage color of the Shockwave movie. This is useful because it allows a Shockwave movie to blend into the background color of the existing web page.

The `bgcolor` parameter sets the Stage color in the same manner that the `BGCOLOR` HTML command sets a web page background color. The parameter uses hexadecimal numbers to set red, green, and blue values to produce the needed color. To set the Stage color of a Shockwave movie to white, use the following HTML code to call the Shockwave movie:

```
<embed src="swmovie.dcr" width=200 height=300 bgcolor=#000000>
```

User-Defined Parameters

Shockwave developers can create their own parameters to pass to a Shockwave movie. To pass the title of a current web page on which the Shockwave movie is being displayed, use the following HTML code to call the Shockwave movie:

```
<embed src="Movies/movie.dcr" width=300 height=300 title="The Shockwave¬
    Page">
```

This parameter is then read by the Shockwave movie through use of the `externalparam` commands in Lingo.

Lingo Commands and Functions

In addition to regular Lingo commands, Shockwave movies have Lingo commands for the networking operations of Shockwave movies.

the bitRate of member member

This cast member property returns the bit rate of the SWA file referenced by a cast member. For this property to return a useful value, the SWA must be preloaded using the `PreLoad` command.

```
put the bitRate of member "soundSWA" into field "bitrate text"
```

the duration of member member

This cast member property is much like the digital video cast member duration property. This property determines the duration in seconds of the SWA file referenced by a cast member. Because the SWA files are streaming, this property will be 0 until streaming has begun. The SWA file must be preloaded using the `PreLoad` command for this property to return a useful value. This property can be tested but not set.

```
put the duration of member "soundSWA" into field "duration text"
```

externalParamCount()

This function returns the number of external parameters passed to the Shockwave movie from an HTML-embedded tag. The following `startmovie` handler places the number of parameters passed to the Shockwave movie to a variable named `parcount`:

```
on startmovie
  put externalParamCount() into parcount
end
```

externalParamName(number)

This function returns a string containing the names or arguments being passed to a Shockwave movie from a particular parameter in an HTML-embedded tag.

The `externalParamName` can retrieve external parameters either by string or by number. If the function is given a number, it retrieves the corresponding external parameter. Remember in counting parameters that the width and height parameters are also external parameters.

If the function is given a string, it retrieves the first external parameter with a name matching that string. If no match is made, the function returns a void value. To display the web page name in the earlier example, the Shockwave movie uses the following Lingo script:

```
put externalParamName("title") into field "web title"
or (since the title is the third external parameter in the tag)
put externalParamName(3) into field "web title"
```

getError (member member), getErrorString (member member)

These two functions can be used to return specific information about an SWA-related error.

```
if getError (member "soundSWA")<> 0 then
    put getErrorString (member "soundSWA") into field "error text"
end if
```

The error code and related error string are as follows:

0	OK
1	memory
2	network
3	playback device
99	other

getErrorString (member member)

See `getError`.

getLatestNetID()

This function returns a unique identifier for the last asynchronous operation started.

```
if netDone() = TRUE then
    put getLatestNetID() into field "http operation"
end if
```

The getLatestNetID() function is typically used in conjunction with the getNetText, preloadNetThing, gotoNetMovie, or gotoNetPage commands.

getNetText URL

This command is used to retrieve an HTTP item from a particular URL to be read by the Shockwave movie as text.

```
getNetText "http://www.company.com/textfile.txt"
```

Use this command in conjunction with the netDone command to find out when this operation is completed by the Shockwave movie.

getPref(filename)

This command returns the contents of a file on the user's disk. The file must exist in the Plug-in Support folder.

```
set temp = getPref("readme.txt")
put temp into field "directions"
```

gotoNetMovie URL

This command is used to retrieve a Shockwave movie from a particular URL. It functions in much the same way that the Director goto movie command works.

```
gotoNetMovie "http://www.company.com/newmovie.dcr"
```

gotoNetPage URL,target

This command opens a particular URL that can be either a Shockwave movie or some other MIME type.

```
gotoNetPage "anotherpage.html","topframe"
```

The target command is optional. It can specify a new window or frame (for browsers that support frames). If it is omitted, the new MIME item loads into

the current browser window. In this example, the command loads
`"anotherpage.html"` into a current window or frame named `"topframe"` or (if no
such window or frame is present) creates a new browser window named
`"topframe"`.

The target command can also make use of Netscape's magic target commands.
For example

```
gotoNetPage "newdoc.html", "_blank"
```

creates a new browser window containing `"newdoc.html"`.

netAbort

This command cancels a network operation without waiting for a result of the
operation.

```
netAbort
```

netDone()

This function determines whether a command to retrieve an HTTP item has
been completed. The function defaults to TRUE. After an asynchronous network
operation has begun, the `netDone` command returns a FALSE value until the
operation is complete.

```
if netDone() = TRUE then
   -- go to a frame to display what we just downloaded
   go to frame "show"
end if
```

The `netDone()` command is typically used in conjunction with the `getNetText`,
`preloadNetThing`, `gotoNetMovie`, or `gotoNetPage` commands.

netError()

This function returns an empty string until the most recently started asynchronous network operation is finished. Examples of possible strings are the
following:

"ok"operation finished with no problem

"none"no operation has been started

```
put netError() into field "network operation"
```

The `netError()` command is typically used in conjunction with the `getNetText`, `preloadNetThing`, `gotoNetMovie`, or `gotoNetPage` commands.

netLastModDate()

This function returns the date last modified string from an HTTP item that has been retrieved.

```
if netDone() = TRUE then
    put netLastModDate() into field "date last modified"
end if
```

This function is typically used with the `getNetText` or `preloadNetThing` commands.

netMIME()

This function returns the MIME type of an HTTP item that has been retrieved.

```
if netDone() = TRUE then
    put netMIME() into field "mime type"
end if
```

This function is typically used with the `preloadNetThing` command.

netStatus msg string

This command inserts a message in the status area of a browser window (usually at the bottom of the browser window).

```
netStatus ".......welcome to the shockwave page...."
```

This command has no effect on some browsers.

netTextResult()

This function returns the text result of a network retrieval operation.

```
if netDone() = TRUE then
    put netTextResult() into field "text we got"
end if
```

Pause

This command pauses the play of an SWA file.

```
Pause (member "soundSWA")
```

the percentPlayed of member member

This cast member property returns the percent of an SWA file referenced by a cast member that has been played from the server.

```
put the percentPlayed of member "soundSWA" into field "played text"
```

the percentStreamed of member member

This cast member property returns the percent of an SWA file referenced by a cast member that has been streamed from the server.

```
put the percentStreamed of member "soundSWA" into field "streamed text"
```

Play

This command begins play of an SWA file.

```
Play (member "soundSWA")
```

PreLoadBuffer (member member)

This command preloads an SWA file into memory. The amount of the SWA file loaded into memory is determined by the PreLoadTime property of the linked SWA cast member.

```
PreLoadBuffer (member "soundSWA")
```

preloadNetThing URL

This command preloads an HTTP item from a particular URL into the browser's cache so that it can be used without a download delay. The HTTP item can be any media type (a Director movie, graphic, text, and so on).

Use this command in conjunction with the netDone command to find out when this operation is completed by the Shockwave movie.

```
preloadNetThing "http://www.company.com/movie.dcr"
```

Remember when preloading an HTML document that a separate preloadNetThing command must be issued for every graphic and text element in an HTML document.

Use the netMIME() function to determine the MIME type of a downloaded item.

the PreLoadTime of member member

This cast member property sets the number of seconds of an SWA file to be downloaded before it begins playing.

```
on mousedown
    set the PreLoadTime of member "soundSWA" = 5
end
```

setPref filename, string

This command writes out a string to a file on the user's disk. The file must exist in the Plug-in Support folder.

```
setPref "storage.txt", the text of field "report"
```

the state of member member

This cast member property determines the current state of an SWA referenced by that cast member. This property can be tested but not set.

```
put the state of member "soundSWA" into field "state text"
```

The possible states of an SWA are the following:

0	Stopped
1	PreLoading
2	PreLoadDone
3	Playing
4	Paused
5	Done
6	error

Stop

This command stops the play of an SWA file.

```
Stop (member "soundSWA")
```

the URL of member member

This cast member property sets the URL of the resource referenced by that cast member (that is, the location of the file the cast member plays).

```
on mousedown
    set the URL of member "soundSWA" = "http://www.company.com/shockwave/¬
song.swa"
end
```

Shockwave Lingo Commands by Function

For quick reference, Lingo commands particular to Shockwave movies are listed below. They are grouped by their general function.

Asynchronous Operations (Network Operations)

```
gotoNetMovie

gotoNetPage

getNetText

netAbort

preloadNetThing
```

Results of Asynchronous Operations

```
getLatestNetID()

netTextResult()

netLastModDate()

netMIME()
```

State of Asynchronous Operations

```
netDone()

netError()
```

Client-Side File Operations

```
setPref
```

Browser Interface Commands

```
netStatus
```

Shockwave Audio Commands

```
the bitrate of member

the duration of member

getError

getErrorString

Pause

the percentStreamed of member

the percentPlayed of member

Play

PreLoadTime of member

PreLoadBuffer

the state of member

Stop

URL of member
```

Conclusion

Future developments in Shockwave and Shockwave for Audio will most likely result in additional Lingo commands for Shockwave movies. Shockwave developers should routinely check for news of such developments at Macromedia's web site (`http://www.macromedia.com/`) or on the Director developer listserv (direct-L).

index

Symbols

Xtras for Director by Zeus Productions

http://users.aol.com/ZeusProd   800-797-2968

I'm Bruce Epstein, Principal of Zeus Productions. I hope you enjoyed my chapters regarding digital video and saving the user's game state. Zeus Productions offers a wide variety of Xtras and add-ons and we are always coming out with new products. Please visit our web site (where you'll find lots of Director tips and tricks as well) or give us a call. Here are just some of the products that we offer:

Blast-Off with zLaunch: zLaunch seamlessly launches other applications from Director. zLaunch is perfect for software samplers, ReadMe files, Acrobat documents, and much more! Need to launch other applications without modification? Tired of the flashing desktop? Running low on memory using Lingo's Open command? Then zLaunch is for you!

Zeus Cross-platform Toolkit: Whether you develop on Mac, Windows, or both, this toolkit contains great utilities, tips, and tricks regarding projectors, files, fonts, palettes, QuickTime, sound, performance, and memory usage! A must-have for creating cross-platform CD-ROM titles.

zScript: Access the power of AppleScript! Control AppleScriptable applications from Director and vice-versa! (Mac only.) Free sample on Director 5.0 CD!

zCast and zScore: Versatile utilities to manage your Cast and Score. Prevent problems by analyzing your Movie for suspicious items! These tools are a must!

zAnimator: Automatically animates sprites along a path in the Score or via Lingo. Animate a bouncing ball in seconds! Very cool.

Zingo: Indispensable Lingo library gives you all the power of the pros! Button handlers and much more!

zCrypt: Encrypt external text files to keep your data secure.

zWinUtils and zMacUtils: Copy, rename, and delete files and folders and much more!

At Zeus Productions, we pride ourselves on providing cost-effective cross-platform solutions to your Director needs. Our products feature excellent documentation and examples, and we offer world-class support. Your feedback and suggestions are always welcome. We accept Visa, MasterCard, and American Express.

Good luck in all your multimedia pursuits.

Lingo™ User's Journal™

The Journal of Professional Lingo Developers

Special Offer!

Offer valid to new subscribers only, thanks

To readers of this book—get **sixteen issues** *for the price of twelve* by sending in this order form with your payment!

1. Fill it out - Please print clearly and include all information
2. Fax it out - *For fastest service*, fax to 1-800-PW-FAXNUm (+1 603-968-3341 intl.)
3. *Or*, Send it out - *Mail to:* Lingo User's Journal • PO Box 531 • Holderness, NH • 03245-0531

I'll take 16 issues for the price of 12! Payment by Visa, MasterCard, American Express, Check, or Money Order (U.S. funds only). **Special Rate**: $42 for 16 issues to US/Canada/Mexico, $64 for 16 issues for all other addresses when this form is returned with your payment.

International check/money orders note: Payment must be in U.S. funds *and* drawn on a U.S. bank (your bank can help you with this). If you cannot draw on a U.S. bank, include an additional U.S. $25 to cover international banking fees.

Name _____

Company _____

Address _____

_____

City, State, Zip, etc. _____

E-mail address _____

credit card number _____

___/___ expires on

signature _____

telephone _____

___Mac ___PC ___Web___   Beginner ___Intermediate ___Advanced